Job asked, 'How then can ma[...] [...]ow
we react to and answer this [...] [...]ling
of who God is, who we are, v[...] [...]one
about it. In light of these la[...] [...]kles
some difficult and nuanced questions over law and gospel, merit and
mercy, and nature and grace. Showing that God designed Adam to be
both righteous by nature and absolutely dependent on his Creator, he
showcases the superlative grace of God in Christ by comparison and
contrast. Particularly, his painstaking attention to nuances in medieval
views on righteousness and merit, with their lasting implications,
represents ground rarely covered by Reformed Protestants. Though the
subject matter treated here is not easy, Perkins shows clearly why it
matters, and he presents his matter clearly.

RYAN M. McGRAW
Professor, Systematic Theology, Greenville Presbyterian Theological
Seminary, Greenville, South Carolina; author, *A Divine Tapestry*

Harrison Perkins has produced an exemplary and much-needed work of
constructive retrieval on the relationship between nature and grace. He
probes behind the use of similar terms and 'signs,' that has caused much
confusion in this discussion, to the substance and reality of the main
issues at hand. He argues, persuasively in my judgment, that original
humanity was created in a positive orientation toward God and that
grace addresses sin, and not nature as such.

N. GRAY SUTANTO
Assistant Professor, Systematic Theology,
Reformed Theological Seminary, Washington, D.C.

Our supernatural destiny is woven into our very nature, argues Harrison
Perkins. Offering a sustained argument against the notion of pure nature,
he carefully situates Reformed covenant theology within the history of
medieval, Reformed, and recent Roman Catholic theology. *Righteous
by Design* offers a powerful argument that the covenant of nature was
properly meritorious of eternal life. Perkins's study is a stellar orientation
point for the ongoing discussion on the nature-supernatural relationship.

HANS BOERSMA
Professor of Ascetical Theology, Nashotah House Theological Seminary,
Nashotah, Wisconsin

The first thing Scripture tells us about ourselves is that God made us in his own image, and the rest of the biblical story hinges on this fact. But what exactly the image of God entails and how it relates to so many other crucial doctrines has challenged Christian theology, including the Reformed tradition, for a very long time. Harrison Perkins has written a marvelous book explaining these old theological debates and proposing compelling systematic resolutions. Perkins' volume showcases God's wisdom, goodness, and grace in his works of creation and redemption, as well as our high human calling – from the beginning and finally realized in Christ. This book will enrich and bless its readers.

DAVID VANDRUNEN
Professor of Systematic Theology and Christian Ethics,
Westminster Seminary California,
Escondido, California

This is a deep and detailed study of God's covenantal relationship and promise to Adam, rich in exegetical, historical, and doctrinal insights and pastoral reflections. Fruitful reading for anyone interested in this fascinating topic!

LEE GATISS
Lecturer in Church History, Union School of Theology, Wales

The value of righteous deeds, or merit, is a key concept in Western Christian doctrines of sin and salvation, protology and eschatology, as well as faith and obedience. The value of this book is found in its close engagement with primary and secondary sources arguing in favor of and alongside the Reformed confessional heritage since the sixteenth century on such topics as the covenant of works and the covenant of grace as that heritage is in conversation with medieval authors. It is worth our time as pastors, theologians, and students to engage with this book and its concepts.

TODD M. RESTER
Associate Professor of Church History,
Westminster Theological Seminary, Philadelphia, Pennsylvania

R.E.D.S.

REFORMED, EXEGETICAL AND DOCTRINAL STUDIES

RIGHTEOUS BY DESIGN

COVENANTAL MERIT AND ADAM'S ORIGINAL INTEGRITY

HARRISON PERKINS

SERIES EDITORS J.V. FESKO & MATTHEW BARRETT

MENTOR
Encouraging Christians to Think

Copyright © Harrison Perkins 2024

Paperback ISBN 978-1-5271-1157-8
Ebook ISBN 978-1-5271-1232-2

10 9 8 7 6 5 4 3 2 1

Published in 2024
in the
Mentor Imprint
by
Christian Focus Publications Ltd,
Geanies House, Fearn, Ross-shire,
IV20 1TW, Great Britain.

www.christianfocus.com

Cover design
by Pete Barnsley

Printed by
Bell & Bain, Glasgow

CONTENTS

Series Preface 7

Foreword 9

Preface and Acknowledgments 13

CHAPTER ONE
Introduction: Getting Oriented toward 17
Nature and Grace

CHAPTER TWO
Covenantal Merit in the Reformed Tradition 51

CHAPTER THREE
Medieval Discussions about Adam's 83
Original Righteousness

CHAPTER FOUR
The Road to (Modern) Rome 137

CHAPTER FIVE
An Ongoing Reformed Conversation 183

CHAPTER SIX
Covenant, God's Image, and the Nature/ 233
Grace Question

CHAPTER SEVEN
Merit in the Covenant of Works 281

CONCLUSION
Pastoral Reflections on Covenant Theology 325
for Communion with God

Bibliography 341

Subject Index 365

Scripture Index 381

For Bryan Estelle and Dave VanDrunen.
Brothers committed to creation, covenant,
and, most of all, Christ.

Series Preface

Reformed, Exegetical and Doctrinal Studies (R.E.D.S.) presents new studies informed by rigorous exegetical attention to the biblical text, and engagement with the history of doctrine, with a goal of refined dogmatic formulation.

R.E.D.S. covers a spectrum of doctrinal topics, addresses contemporary challenges in theological studies, and is driven by the Word of God, seeking to draw theological conclusions based upon the authority and teaching of Scripture itself.

Each volume also explores pastoral implications so that they contribute to the Church's theological and practical understanding of God's Word. One of the virtues that sets R.E.D.S. apart is its ability to apply dogmatics to the Christian life. In doing so, these volumes are characterized by the rare combination of theological weightiness and warm, pastoral application, much in the tradition of John Calvin's *Institutes of the Christian Religion.*

These volumes do not merely repeat material accessible in other books but retrieve and remind the Church of forgotten truths to enrich contemporary discussion.

Matthew Barrett

J. V. Fesko

Foreword

Reformed theologians have always confessed that God saves sinners by his grace alone through faith alone in Christ alone. The apostle Paul summarizes the need for the absolute necessity of God's grace in salvation when he writes: 'For by grace you have been saved through faith. And this is not your own doing; it is the gift of God, not a result of works, so that no one may boast' (Eph. 2:8-9). The Westminster Confession of Faith therefore describes the state of fallen humans in no uncertain terms: 'Man, by his fall into a state of sin, hath wholly lost all ability of will to any spiritual good accompanying salvation: so as, a natural man, being altogether averse from that good, and dead in sin, is not able, by his own strength, to convert himself, or to prepare himself thereunto' (IX.iii). Given humanity's fallen nature, 'When God converts a sinner, and translates him into the state of grace, he freeth him from his natural bondage under sin; and, by his grace alone, enables him freely to will and to do that which is spiritually good' (IX.iv). There is no debate among Reformed theologians on the necessity of God's grace in salvation. But things become more complex when we turn to unfallen humanity. That is, did Adam require God's grace prior to the fall, prior to the entrance of sin into the world?

Some answer this question confidently in the negative. Adam did not require God's grace before the fall. They stake their claim on the notion that there is a stark difference between Roman Catholic and Reformed understandings of protology, or first things: Rome promotes the doctrine of the *donum superadditum* ('the super added gift') whereas Reformed theologians have rejected this notion as being unbiblical. According to Rome, God gave to Adam the *donum superadditum* because he was incapable of attaining the blessings of eternal life in a purely natural state. Reformed theologians opposed this idea and instead argued that God created Adam righteous and holy, and thus even in his natural state he had the ability to attain eternal life. Some have characterized this supposed stark antithesis between Rome and Geneva as the 'deeper Protestant conception.' Namely, that the Protestant reformers had a more deeply biblical understanding of pre-fall humanity. At the historical level, the issues in this supposed Roman vs. Genevan antithesis are more complicated and not easily disentangled. While Reformed theologians commonly rejected the idea of the *donum superadditum*, this does not mean that they entirely scuttled the idea of Adam needing pre-fall grace. John Calvin (1509–64), for example, argued that Adam's chief failing in the garden was his refusal to rely upon God's grace in Christ (Calvin, *Commentary on Genesis*, Gen. 2:19), and like Augustine (354–430) and some medievals such as Peter Lombard (1100–60), Calvin divided Adam's gifts into natural and supernatural categories (*Institutes*, II.ii.12). Calvin codified these ideas when he co-wrote the French Confession (1559) with Theodore Beza (1519–1605) and Pierre Viret (1511–71), which states: 'We believe that man was created pure and perfect in the image of God, and that by his own guilt he fell from the grace which he received' (IX). In fact, speaking of pre-fall grace was quite common among early modern Reformed theologians. What is the difference, then, between the *donum superadditum* and the Reformed idea of pre-fall grace and do these theologians fall short of the so-called 'deeper Protestant conception' of Adam's pre-fall nature?

Other Reformed theologians, however, began to speak of Adam's relationship to God in terms other than grace. Rather than grace, the likes of Scottish theologian Robert Rollock (1555–99) characterized Adam's pre-fall nature as one that was holy, good, and upright, which meant that Adam had no need of grace prior to the fall. Rollock's understanding of both Adam's nature and his potential ability to merit eternal life was based not in pre-fall grace but rather in terms of God's covenant. In other words, there was a shift to the concept of *ex pacto* merit – God sets the terms of the covenant and creates Adam with the ability to merit eternal life. In the words of the Westminster Confession, 'Man, in his state of innocency, had freedom, and power to will and to do that which was good and well pleasing to God; but yet, mutably, so that he might fall from it' (IX.ii). And rather than speak of pre-fall grace as in Calvin's 1559 French Confession, the Westminster Confession instead uses the more elastic and deliberately ambiguous phrase 'voluntary condescension' to describe the relationship between the infinite creator and the finite pre-fall Adam: 'The distance between God and the creature is so great, that although reasonable creatures do owe obedience unto him as their Creator, yet they could never have any fruition of him as their blessedness and reward, but by some voluntary condescension on God's part, which he hath been pleased to express by way of covenant' (VII.i). This understanding of *ex pacto* merit arguably has precedent in the earlier medieval Scotist nominalist view of sacramental efficacy. These two different streams within the Reformed tradition defies the overly reductionistic compartmentalization between Rome and the so-called 'deeper Protestant conception,' as if the differences between the two trajectories could be reduced to two different principles. Both the pre-fall grace and *ex pacto* merit understandings of Adam's pre-fall state and are Reformed confessional positions, and both have roots in the theology of the early church and Middle Ages, albeit from different fonts within the catholic tradition.

Given the complexity of the question regarding Adam's pre-fall state, Harrison Perkins's *Righteous by Design* cuts through shallow analysis and pushes past superficial juxtapositions of Rome versus Geneva and gets to the heart of the theological and historical issues. Mind you, there are significant differences between a Roman Catholic and Reformed soteriology. If we contrast Rome with Geneva on humanity's post-fall state, there are big differences. The Reformed position of *sola gratia* (salvation by 'grace alone') stands out. But if we look at the question of Adam's pre-fall state, understanding the issues requires a scalpel rather than a chainsaw, and Perkins brings a steady hand and a sharp scalpel to cut carefully through the exegetical, theological, and historical layers to make a compelling case that God designed Adam righteous and thus he did not require pre-fall grace. Moreover, God located Adam's obedience within the framework of the covenant of works, which does not require grace to boost the value of Adam's work to make it worthy of meriting eternal life. Perkins does not linger on the shores of a few scattered common Reformed theological texts but takes a deep dive into the Middle Ages and mines many previously untranslated Latin texts to unearth relevant discussions. This deep research illuminates the Reformed discussion so that readers can see the genealogy of the two chief conceptions. Readers will not be disappointed with this work, and they will read a convincing case for why Adam neither required the *donum superadditum* nor pre-fall grace because he was created righteous by design.

J. V. FESKO
Harriet Barbour Professor of Systematic and Historical Theology,
Reformed Theological Seminary,
Jackson, Mississippi

Preface and Acknowledgments

A literary lifecycle can be a funny thing. This book began its life as a footnote in another work, growing from a few references to three hundred words, to three thousand words, into a forty-five-page appendix, which was then cut from that project for space. To my surprise, that deletion became a happy providence because it gave me the opportunity to expand that material into this fuller treatment.

In many ways, this book is the capstone in an accidental trilogy about Reformed covenant theology, attempting to think the biblical, historical, and theological issues as far to the bottom as I am able. That wider project began with the historical argument that James Ussher (1581–1656), one of the stronger lights of divinity in the mid-seventeenth century, built his doctrine of the covenant of works in conversation with the catholic tradition, codifying his view by packaging several strands of highly traditional teaching into one synthesized formulation.[1] The next installment was a systematic exploration of Reformed covenant theology, attempting to do what I previously argued Ussher did: build a coherent presentation of the covenants of redemption, works, and grace from exegetical foundations and in conversation with the broader catholic tradition.[2] That second work

1. Harrison Perkins, *Catholicity and the Covenant of Works: James Ussher and the Reformed Tradition* (Oxford Studies in Historical Theology; New York, NY: Oxford University Press, 2020).

2. Harrison Perkins, *Reformed Covenant Theology: A Systematic Introduction* (Bellingham, WA: Lexham Press, 2024).

provided enough remit to think thoroughly through – at least to my own satisfaction – how to state our covenant theology in relation to issues of classical theism, Christological hermeneutics, and the necessity of life in the church. Nevertheless, the restrictions of space and the accessibility level which I was trying to achieve prevented me from including some of the goals I'd hoped to achieve. Specifically, I was not able to engage as much with some major contours of the medieval tradition or get to the historical and theological bottom of the issue of nature and grace, especially regarding the medieval and Roman doctrine of the *donum superadditum*. That issue has felt like a dangling thread left untied since even that first book publication.

This book represents my effort to situate the Reformed doctrine of the covenant of works in relation to that set of issues. Given the scope of the ideas involved, this project could encompass at least a thousand more avenues of exploration. I have, therefore, carefully limited my investigation and argumentation to how these issues directly apply to the best way to formulate the covenant of works. The relationships among the medieval doctors, the Reformers, and the Reformed Orthodox are complicated, with the Reformed making highly eclectic use with widely varying points and degrees of criticisms for their medieval forebears. The ways that this book documents areas of Reformed continuity and disagreement with specific medieval theologians will not necessarily hold true concerning other doctrinal areas. There is a sense in which this trilogy has thought through Reformed covenant theology under the lens of differing historical periods: the first engaging the Reformation and post-Reformation era directly, the second coordinating Reformed covenant theology to patristic trajectories, and this one formulating a contemporary statement of the covenant of works in conversation with medieval themes.

The impetus for this volume is the conviction that the way we relate grace to creation affects how we formulate the differences between the covenant of works and the covenant of grace. This book argues for the integrity of Adam's created nature as righteous by design, therefore able to fulfill the terms of the covenant of works by nature, with a view to protecting the integrity of the gospel in the covenant of grace.[3] In other

---

3. Ligon Duncan, 'Foreword,' in Guy Prentiss Waters, J. Nicholas Reid, and John R. Muether (eds.), *Covenant Theology: Biblical, Theological, and Historical Perspectives* (Wheaton, IL: Crossway, 2020), 29.

words, the goal is to defend the law-gospel distinction from the vantage of the *imago Dei.*

As far as I know myself, this book fulfills my (present) capacity to think through the theoretical foundations of Reformed covenant theology. Much work needs to be done to make these principles accessible and to apply them. Maybe the Lord will be kind to let me do some of that work in future projects. Regardless, I am thankful for the ways that he has enabled me to do what I have already done. I pray that he will bless these efforts for the sake of his people.

This sort of work is never achieved alone, and I am grateful to the many who have made it possible. First thanks must go to J. V. Fesko and Matthew Barrett for kindly accepting this work into their R.E.D.S. series. I am glad to stand alongside their other fine authors in this series and especially under their editorial guidance. Next, I cannot express adequately enough my thanks to Oakland Hills Community Church (OPC), where I get to be their pastor, for their encouragement with time and prayer to work on various writing projects. No pastor is more blessed than I by the congregation that I get to serve. Unending thanks must go to my wife Sarah for her constant grace and understanding as I sink myself into writing endeavors. Especially in the moments when this work had particularly stressful seasons at the conceptual and efficiency levels, she has been incessantly supportive. She and my son, Scott, are the greatest worldly joys I have, making it all the harder to get entrenched in disputing medieval theology when I would rather be with them.

Thanks, of course, to the R.E.D.S. editors J. V. Fesko and Matthew Barrett for their helpful feedback in shaping this volume into its final product. Thanks also to Gray Sutanto in a special way for his encouragement and help in improving this volume, Carlton Wynne for his detailed eye for precise phrasing, R. Scott Clark for helpful discussions surrounding the Reformed interaction with these ideas (especially as he developed his commentary on the Heidelberg Catechism), David VanDrunen for his keen sense of clarity, Ryan McGraw for his helpful insight on where to clarify and qualify my claims, Keith Mathison especially for his advice about composing the survey chart at the end of chapter four, Lane Tipton for some encouraging discussions and some probing feedback about the relation of natural and special revelation concerning Adam's covenant, and Adam Ostella for fielding this topic on a number of occasions. Thanks to Todd Rester for help pressing through some dicey bits of Latin in the early printing of Ockham's works, and to Scott Clark for helping me with some hard-to-access sources.

Special thanks to John Fesko for writing the foreword to this book. John is a true gift to the church and has a most profound effect upon me both as a scholar and a pastor. To have one of my great mentors and good friends positively endorse this particular work, which has felt like an Everest-scale effort at times, especially by contributing a full-length foreword, is a significant honor.

I've dedicated this book to Dave VanDrunen and Bryan Estelle because both have forced me to think hard about these issues pertaining to the image of God. I am grateful for how they taught me during my seminary studies and for all the support that they have given me in years since. They set a trajectory of developing these ideas in a faithful way for application to our most cherished Reformed concerns. Undoubtedly, this book bears marks from the shape of the theological training I received from them, which I make no effort to hide. I hope this effort honors their investments to explain creation, covenant and, above all, Christ.

CHAPTER ONE

Introduction: Getting Oriented toward Nature and Grace

God made humanity for fellowship with himself in this life and the next. Westminster Shorter Catechism 1 reminds us of a profound truth: 'Man's chief end is to glorify God, and to enjoy him forever.'[1] *Forever* waits before us all, beckoning us to desire the best experience of everlasting life. That best prospect is living in God's glorious presence as those *welcomed* to enjoy him. We are meant to be near to God in blessed communion: 'Whom have I in heaven but you? And there is nothing on earth that I desire besides you .... But for me it is good to be near God; I have made the Lord God my refuge, that I may tell of all your works' (Ps. 73:25, 28). Nonetheless, only those who have received Christ are given 'the right to become the children of God' (John 1:12). Thus, a fate without the familial *enjoyment* of God's glory rests before sinners who have not trusted Jesus for salvation. Life's overwhelming question for every human being then ought to be: How can I reach the everlasting, highest enjoyment of God?

This book is about how God fashioned us for fellowship with himself from our very creation. God wove our very being together in such a way that we are intrinsically related to him, specifically as those who bear his own image (Gen. 1:27). We are fundamentally religious creatures who cannot escape a relationship with God. Moreover, God also crafted our

---

1. Philip Schaff (ed.), *The Creeds of Christendom*, 3 vol. (New York, NY: Harper and Brothers, 1877), 3:676.

nature with the inbuilt potential to advance to higher, deeper fellowship with him in the everlasting state. He built eschatology into creation itself, meaning that despite how good and wonderful creation was at the outset, God had even more blessedness in store for us in the new heavens and new earth. In this vein, Geerhardus Vos has famously summarized the biblical-theological shape of these dogmatic categories, writing, 'the eschatological appears as predeterminative [for] both the substance and form of the soteriological.'[2] As we hope for the everlasting blessed enjoyment of God because of our salvation, God fixed that blessed end into our nature as he created us and before we sinned and needed saving.

Creation's relation to eschatology does bear fruit in our soteriology. Although Adam sinned and plunged us all into death and misery, Jesus Christ restores that hope of blessed enjoyment of God's presence to us as we take hold of him by faith. Westminster Larger Catechism 39 affirms that our mediator for salvation had to be man, among other reasons, 'that he might advance our nature.'[3] That advance occurred as Christ rose from the grave in glorified life (1 Cor. 15:20-23, 35-49). Since Jesus advanced our nature in himself at his resurrection, we will personally experience that advance when he raises us to join him in glorified life (Rom. 8:16-21, 29-30). The true, full sense of the advancing or elevating of human nature applies to our glorification at the resurrection. In salvation, Christ secures for us that eschatological advancement to which we already were oriented by creation.

What is the connection between creation and eschatology? What is the relationship among our created, fallen, and consummate states? How can we reach that new creation condition? Do the principles by which we reach that consummate state differ in any way from those by which God offered consummate life to Adam before the fall? This book probes these questions, seeking to establish what we ought to believe about how God made Adam in original righteousness, offered him – acting

---

2. Geerhardus Vos, *The Pauline Eschatology* (Princeton, NJ: Princeton University Press, 1930; repr. Phillipsburg, NJ: P&R, 1994), 60; Geerhardus Vos, *Biblical Theology: Old and New Testaments* (Grand Rapids, MI: Eerdmans, 1948; repr. East Peoria, IL: The Banner of Truth Trust, 2020), 140.

3. John R. Bower, *The Larger Catechism: A Critical Text and Introduction* (Principal Documents of the Westminster Assembly; Grand Rapids, MI: Reformation Heritage Books, 2010), 73. Thanks to Ryan McGraw for his comments that made obvious my need to spell out this point more fully.

on behalf of us all – the prospect of highest blessedness in even greater communion, and used a covenant to connect original righteousness to the hope of eschatological fellowship in the new creation. Since God 'has put eternity into man's heart,' showing how he fashioned us by our very creation to desire and to obtain consummate communion with him (Eccles. 3:11), how do we attain that end?

This book argues that God forged the covenant to our nature thereby connecting our eschatological destiny to the means to reach it. The covenant conjoins our natural orientation toward eschatological communion with God and our capacity as his image bearers for loving and reflecting him by obeying him with the way to realize that desire by acting upon that very design. Respectively, we recognize the distinction of how God *oriented* and *ordered* us toward an eschatological end. On the one hand, God *oriented* us by creation toward eschatological communion with him by tailoring our nature so that we have our ultimate resting point in consummate, glorified fellowship with God in the new creation. On the other hand, God *ordered* us toward that eschatological end by covenant, meaning that the covenant bound our nature's native principles to terms that enabled us to attain the end for which we are made.[4] Thus, God's work of special creation naturally oriented us to that prospect of eschatological reward while his simultaneous judicial act of special providence to covenant with Adam ordered us to that end.[5] God's covenant with Adam then encompassed our natural propensity for God in order to provide terms for obtaining it.

This connection then bears direct fruit upon how we construe protology in relation to soteriology with a specific connection to the law-gospel distinction.[6] More precisely, Adam's original righteousness, which was natural to him by creation, came with the demand for perfect

---

4. Concerning technical considerations for the category of 'order,' see Bernard Wuellner, SJ, *Dictionary of Scholastic Philosophy* (Milwaukee, MN: The Bruce Publishing Company, 1956), 85.

5. As argued and applied more fully in chapter six, the terminological distinction between the *work* of creation and the *act* of special providence reflects the language of Westminster Shorter Catechism 9–12; Schaff, *Creeds of Christendom*, 3:677-78.

6. 'Protology' refers to the study of first things, making it the other end of the redemptive historical spectrum from eschatology. It includes distinct consideration of the constitution, function, and purposes of creation as God made it before sin entered the picture.

obedience. By the covenant, God's offer of the reward of eschatological life accompanied that demand. As further argued, this structure was a situation of *covenantal merit*, helping Reformed theology uphold the integrity of humanity's original creation, truly differentiate our created and fallen conditions, defend the freeness of grace in justification by Christ's work alone, and make room for a robust doctrine of sanctification as our present experience of exclusively grace-based salvation.

This argument reflects upon what it means to bear God's image. We will reckon with how bearing the divine likeness entails a natural righteousness. Furthermore, God built an eschatological potential into our very nature as he made us, focusing our existence upon a higher state of fellowship with him, everlastingly confirmed in true righteousness. God's covenant with Adam, which should not be radically separated or disjointed from our created nature, was how he met us in the way that he made us as his image-bearing creatures. In this manner, he provided the method for how a creature, who intrinsically (*realiter*) could never place God in his debt, can obtain that eschatological blessedness.[7] In this manner, our argument is a defense of the law-gospel distinction, covenantally understood, from the vantage of the *imago Dei*.

From the outset, we should mark how these truths display God's rich love for his creatures. Humanity is blessed to bear God's image, thus being uniquely fit for special relationship with God. Amidst God's true care for all his earthly creatures, he forged humanity alone for a destiny

---

7. This study distinguishes 'inherence' and 'intrinsic' precisely to keep in view the issue of contingency related to the notion of *realiter*. If something has *realiter* status, it cannot be otherwise in an absolute sense – which is why older theologians denied that we have a 'real' relation to God, since we are contingent beings rather than beings related *realiter* to the divine essence. Respectively, *inherence* means 'existence in another being as in a subject of being or as modification of another being.' Particularly the last aspect of this definition shows how something can inhere in a subject without being *sine qua non* part of it. On the other hand, especially as we consider these issues, *intrinsic* means 'pertaining to the nature of a thing or person; constitutive.' In other words, intrinsic involves a *sine qua non* aspect and contributes essentially to the nature of a particular thing; Wuellner, *Dictionary of Scholastic Philosophy*, 61, 64. Regarding the issue above, the point of *intrinsic* is that human beings do not have the right before God to deserve a reward that constitutes what it means to be human – or even more what it means to be God – as such. The covenant of works as related to our natural capacities for supernatural realities can be said to have given Adam an inherent right, although it could in fact be modified, namely by sin in breaking the covenant of works. Some versions of Roman pure nature theology confuse this issue so that merit remains possible for sinners, meaning that this view casts the standing to deserve reward as intrinsic.

of everlasting enjoyment of his beauty. As God's creatures, our obedience to him was by nature always the way that we needed to express our love to our Maker. In his infinite love, God wove the prospect of even higher reward into our natural obligation to show us that he made us to know his kindness, care, love, and tenderness, displaying his generosity in that even as he made us as most blessed among his creatures, our abounding God is inexhaustible in how much blessing he can pour upon his people so that it seems that he could always outgive what he has already given. By this book's end, we will see how God's covenant with Adam manifests the Lord's deep love for humanity both in the nature of that covenant itself and in how it informs our understanding of how God saves sinners in the gospel covenant he made after Adam's fall.[8]

Charting the Course: The Aim and Outline

Retrieval dominates the landscape of theological discourse in contemporary discussions. Rightly so, since much of the late-nineteenth and early-twentieth centuries saw Christian theology lose its moorings concerning even some of our most important doctrines, such as the Trinity.[9] Doctrinal formulation always needs a strong dose of historical theology, a reminder of our theological grammar from ages past, and a reconnection to the nourishing roots of our confessional heritage.[10] True retrieval, however, must be far richer than finding quotes from the past that support our present position. Lifting a particular phrasing, even if recurring, from some early-modern sources does not count as retrieval but amounts to superficial proof-texting. In this regard, true retrieval involves understanding doctrines not simply in sound-bite quotes but within the context of doctrinal development across the centuries.

This book aims at systematic-theological construction through the lens of historical retrieval, focusing on precisely formulating the doctrine of the covenant of works. Westminster Confession 7.2 outlines this doctrine: 'The first Covenant made with Man, was a Covenant of Works,

---

8. Wilhelmus à Brakel, *The Christian's Reasonable Service*, trans. Bartel Elshout, ed. Joel R. Beeke, 4 vol. (Grand Rapids: Reformation Heritage Books, 1992), 1:355.

9. Matthew Barrett, *Simply Trinity: The Unmanipulated Father, Son, and Spirit* (Grand Rapids, MI: Baker, 2021), 17-94.

10. J. V. Fesko, *The Need for Creeds Today: Confessional Faith in a Faithless Age* (Grand Rapids, MI: Baker Academic, 2020).

wherein Life was promised to Adam, and in him to his Posterity, upon condition of perfect and personal obedience.'[11] Given that we had no claim to demand anything from God in our position as simple creatures, God's covenant with Adam joined the prospect of blessed reward to our obligation to obey our Maker. The condition of this covenant was the law's demand for perfect obedience. Although some Reformed theologians have thought otherwise, the best way to understand Adam's potential reward is as the prospect of heavenly, eschatological, glorified life.[12] The covenant of works was then our original condition before God, prior to sin, wherein we were naturally oriented to supernatural, that is eschatological, communion with God and ordered to obtain that end by virtue of our covenant relationship with him.

Adam's breach of the covenant of works did not make it irrelevant. It has tremendous categorical significance within the full system of Reformed theology. In the early-modern period, Reformed theologians introduced the distinction between the covenant of works and the covenant of grace to express categorically *and* redemptive-historically their view of the law-gospel distinction, the unity of salvation across the Testaments, and Christ's centrality in God's plan of redemption.[13] Despite the characteristically Reformed terminology, the contents of the doctrine were highly traditional, packaging together concerns about Adam and original sin, the natural law, the role of works in relation to our right standing before God, and the basis on which we might relate to God for blessings.[14] God's covenant with Adam was, therefore, based on

---

11. John R. Bower, *The Confession of Faith: A Critical Text and Introduction* (Principal Documents of the Westminster Assembly; Grand Rapids, MI: Reformation Heritage Books, 2020), 204.

12. For the historical issues, see Mark A. Herzer, 'Adam's Reward: Heaven or Earth,' in Michael A.G. Haykin and Mark Jones (eds.), *Drawn into Controversie: Reformed Theological Diversity and Debates within Seventeenth-Century British Puritanism* (Göttingen: Vandenhoeck & Ruprecht, 2011), 162-82. For exegetical and theological defense of this position, see Harrison Perkins, *Reformed Covenant Theology: A Systematic Introduction* (Lexham Press, 2024), 56-75.

13. Concerning the historical development and decline of this doctrine, see J. V. Fesko, *The Covenant of Works: The Origins, Development, and Reception of the Doctrine* (Oxford Studies in Historical Theology; New York, NY: Oxford University Press, 2020). For exegetical and theological considerations, see J. V. Fesko, *Adam and the Covenant of Works* (Fearn: Mentor, 2021).

14. For the argument that Reformed theology depended on ecumenical ideas in building the doctrine of the covenant of works, see Harrison Perkins, *Catholicity and the*

the law and on Adam's obedience in order to obtain reward, helping the Reformed to express how they differentiated Adam's ability before the fall from sinners' ability after the fall to obtain salvation by contributing works. In the former, Adam could earn blessings; in the latter, our works cannot contribute to our right standing with God in the slightest.

This book focuses on how to formulate our understanding of Adam's original righteousness, specifically his ability to keep God's law before the fall in relation to our explanation of how the covenant of works offered a reward to Adam. This focus clarifies our perception of how God made us as fundamentally religious creatures, fashioned for fellowship with him. The integrity of our original state and its connection to the covenant shows how God formed us in an inescapable relationship with him but also loved us enough to offer even greater experience of his blessed presence.

The connection between a doctrine of covenantal merit to the wider issue of our fundamental relationship to God may not be immediately obvious. As one historian of medieval theology contended, our understanding of merit helps measure our central theological and anthropological convictions, the severity of sin, and grace's role in how we relate to God.[15] The relationship between our natural capacities as humans, especially before the fall and distinguished from our abilities as sinners, informs how we understand our very constitution.[16] In other words, a proper understanding of our capacities in original righteousness, namely that ability to obtain eschatological life with God without any supplementing of our created nature, shows that our original nature was ordered to, and meant for, supernatural communion with God in eschatological life.

The underlying problem in this discussion is the issue of finding an adequate principle to explain why the Creator should recompense his creature, who *de facto* owes obedience to his Maker, with a reward of heavenly value. The question revolves around how no (even hypothetical) situation exists wherein a creature made in God's image is not obliged

---

Covenant of Works: James Ussher and the Reformed Tradition (Oxford Studies in Historical Theology; New York, NY: Oxford University Press, 2020).

15. Joseph P. Wawrykow, *God's Grace and Human Action: 'Merit' in the Theology of Thomas Aquinas* (Notre Dame, IN: University of Notre Dame Press, 1995), vi.

16. Wawrykow, *God's Grace and Human Action*, 64-65n12, 66n13.

by nature to render perfect righteousness, thus reflecting the character of God whose likeness he was made to reflect. Why then should God reward his creature for his obedience with a reward of infinite value that seemingly surpasses the worth of what the creature could achieve?

This challenge is not new since theologians have long wrestled with the problem of proportionality. Accordingly, proportionality applies to several issues in theology, always concerning some sort of comparative relation.[17] On one hand, proportionality according to the *analogia proportionalitatis* addressed the discussion of the Creator-creature distinction in terms of relating how creatures, namely humanity, have attributes corresponding to God's attributes. This use of proportionality was one way that the Reformed rejected univocal understandings of the Creator-creature distinction in favor of our *analogical* participation in God's attributes.[18] Although coming to bear occasionally, this variation in the problem of proportionality is not our main focus in this book.

On the other hand, the problem of proportionality has applied to the comparative relation about the principle of reward. Bernard Wuellner has explained 'moral proportion' as 'the comparative measure of equality or inequality between two moral factors, such as that between good and evil in an act or its consequences, between deed and merit, between law and penalty [or especially for our purposes, reward], between right and obligation, etc.'[19] In this respect, the issue of proportionality involves the apparent discrepancy between the value of the obedience a creature could render (most specifically for our discussion, of Adam before the fall) and the value of a divine, heavenly reward. Given the *analogia proportionalitatis* concerning, in principle, the Creator-creature distinction, which indicates God's superiority over us, we cannot posit an *intrinsic* value to our creaturely works that as such obligates God to remunerate us with the specific recompense of eschatological life. The issue of proportionality pertaining most directly throughout this book concerns this comparative relation of creaturely works to heavenly

---

17. Wuellner, *Dictionary of Scholastic Philosophy*, 99.

18. Richard A. Muller, *Dictionary of Latin and Greek Theological Terms: Principally Drawn from Protestant Scholastic Theology*, 2nd ed. (Grand Rapids, MI: Baker Academic, 2017), 24-25, 383. Concerning how *proportio* was often used in connection with *analogia*, see Muller, *Dictionary*, 295.

19. Wuellner, *Dictionary of Scholastic Philosophy*, 99.

reward. How do we explain that relation of creaturely obedience, to which we are naturally obligated, as ordered to our eschatological end?

This subject matter takes us right to the heart of the longstanding discussion about the distinction between nature and grace. This book addresses our existing deficient understanding of this whole category set. One goal for the whole of this book is to provide a clearer picture of nature, grace, and their relationship, especially given the varying ways that theologians have employed these terms in church history. We must enter exploration of the long development of these issues to come to a more precise formulation by the end.

This lack of clear understanding is why this book about systematic theology focuses so much on historical theology. J. Gresham Machen remarked, 'A man cannot be original in his treatment of a subject unless he knows what the subject is; true originality is preceded by patient attention to the facts ...'[20] Historical theology, as J. V. Fesko notes, 'is important not only so that the investigator can stand on the shoulders of giants and learn from great theological minds, but also so he can trace the development of the doctrine.'[21] We often make the greatest fools of ourselves when we insert ourselves into others' conversation after they are halfway through it, presuming to speak up with expertise even though we have no awareness of the ground already covered. On snowy winter days, when white covered the whole surface of the road, my father often advised me: 'Just make sure to keep the car between the ditches.' This book's historical exploration intends 1) to clear the road so that we can see the lane on which we are driving and 2) to get us somewhat up to speed in the conversation so that we can contribute without making fools of ourselves by overcorrecting from one ditch into the other.

This book's structure presses toward a prescriptive theological statement by the end. The shortage of exegetical argumentation for several chapters will be felt in a book on systematic theology. The more historical focus in chapters two through five functions to give us our bearings about the issue of the nature-grace distinction so that we can more precisely conclude with a more rounded, exegetically informed, systematic conclusion. Although Scripture is our sole final authority

---

20. J. Gresham Machen, *What is Faith?* (Edinburgh: Banner of Truth, 1991), 19.

21. J. V. Fesko, *Word, Water, Spirit: A Reformed Perspective on Baptism* (Grand Rapids, MI: Reformation Heritage Books, 2010), 16.

for theological *answers*, the rationale for detailed historical-theological analysis is that history often provides and clarifies the *questions*. Even with the eagerness for exegetical footing, this book's particular systematic aim demands lots of reasoning through concepts to clarify and refine how we implement them. Such is the nature of a ground-clearing endeavor.

Signs and Realities: Performing Theological Discourse

Theology is about God and our relationship to him.[22] Summarizing the stance of Thomas Aquinas (1225–74) that *everything* in sacred study concerns God, either about God himself or the effects he causes, a medieval maxim captures the essence of God-entranced doctrine: theology is taught by God, teaches about God, and leads to God.[23] Inasmuch as our contemplation concerns our Maker and how we relate to him, theology is both theoretical and practical. Our reflection upon how to formulate principles to talk about God in the best ways and our meditation upon divine truth should carry us into our highest end of enjoying the God who made and saves us.[24] Paul wrote to Titus, 'for the sake of the faith of God's elect and their knowledge of the truth, *which accords with godliness*,' marking how our understanding of right doctrine ought to swell our souls with nourishment enough to affect how we walk with the Lord (Titus 1:1).

Theological orthodoxy should bear fruit for the life of the soul and our practice of our faith.[25] Bearing this truth in mind re-energizes the

---

22. John Webster, '*Omnia ... Pertractantur in Sacra Doctrina sub Ratione Dei*. On the Matter of Christian Theology,' in *God without Measure: Working Papers in Christian Theology Volume I: God and the Works of God* (London: T&T Clark, 2016), 3-10; John Webster, 'Theological Theology,' in *Confessing God: Essays in Christian Dogmatics II* (London: T&T Clark, 2016), 11-31.

23. St. Thomas Aquinas, *Summa Theologica*, trans. by Fathers of the English Dominican Province, 5 vol. (New York, NY: Benziger Bros., 1948; repr. Notre Dame, IN: Christian Classics, 1981), 1.1.7.

24. Petrus van Mastricht, *Theoretical-Practical Theology*, 7 vol., trans. Todd M. Rester, ed. Joel R. Beeke (Grand Rapids, MI: Reformation Heritage Books, 2018–), 1.1.1.20; Franciscus Turrettinus, *Institutio Theologiae Elencticae*, 3 vol. (Geneva, 1679–85), 1.7.1-14.

25. Ronni Kurtz, *Fruitful Theology: How the Life of the Mind Leads to the Life of the Soul* (Nashville, TN: B&H, 2022).

theological task even for the most complicated topics that need new, careful, and precise explanation. The practice of diligence, attentiveness, and synthesis teaches the theologian *patience* in reading and listening vigilantly, *kindness* and *gentleness* in taking seriously what other professing believers have written, and *peace* in trying to incorporate and harmonize what voices from our theological past have said as much as possible into and with our own dogmatic construction today. The continuation and reciprocation of that theological stance fosters humility for us all when we set aside the prospect of having our 'silver bullet' theologian who got everything right. The sort of antagonism that is committed to one or a few voices neglects faithfulness, since laziness likely drives our desires not to need to read more nor think hard, and kills rather than fosters joy (Gal. 5:22-23).

Doing theology requires us to consider difficult subjects, using nuanced language and at times parsing out what we mean in a very fine way. The difficulty is in part because many of the realities of which we speak in theology transcend the expected limits of our normal capacity, since they are divinely revealed mysteries. To be clear, the biblical sense of 'mystery' does not mean that it is too vague or ethereal for our minds to comprehend at all nor that we are trying to compile clues into a solution – at least not in the Hercule Poirot manner. Rather, the biblical sense of mystery refers to something that we could not have known had not God revealed it in special revelation.

Mystery must then factor into how we think about the theological task. In Romans 16:25-26, Paul wrote,

> Now to him who is able to strengthen you according to my gospel and the preaching of Jesus Christ, *according to the revelation of the mystery* that was kept secret for long ages but has now been disclosed and through the prophetic writings has been made known to all nations, according to the command of the eternal God, to bring about the obedience of faith.

In Christian theology, mysteries are not simply what we cannot understand but realities that God has disclosed to us so that we will understand them. Wrapping our minds around these truths takes deep reflection, patience against speaking too quickly, working together toward understanding in the community of faith, and humility in recognizing that we speak beyond ourselves. In this regard, Thomas wrote, 'it was necessary for man's salvation that there should be a knowledge revealed by God besides philosophical science built up by human reason.'[26] We are dependent upon God to disclose these realities to us.

Biblical mystery has layers. Some mystery needs to be disclosed through special revelation because it is not part of the book of general revelation.[27] The gospel itself belongs in this category because it addresses our need as *sinners* rather than as creatures as such, meaning God never made the gospel known in nature. That is, the gospel concerning redemption is not part of general revelation. Alternatively, even though the event of creation belongs to nature, since we were not there to see it and therefore have no way to investigate it, creation *ex nihilo* is always a matter of divine mystery. It was disclosed to us to be believed by virtue of God's special revelation. On the one hand, philosophers have long debated the ideas of eternal matter and the world's beginnings. On the other hand, Christians believe 'on account of faith,' as Thomas argued, that God made the universe from nothing, so giving it a concrete beginning.[28] We depend entirely upon what God has said in special revelation concerning those things which we cannot know otherwise.

This discussion about mystery highlights how complicated theological discourse can be because we are speaking of divine mysteries. In this respect, we know that inscripturated, special revelation speaks of these mysteries, pointing beyond itself to the triune God who works all things according to his will. Scripture's words are then our entryway into divine mysteries.

The church has a long history of seeing theology as reckoning with mystery. In the church's early centuries, Augustine (354–430) articulated a robust theory of signs and what they signified. Concerning how we use language to teach about God, he wrote, 'For a sign is a thing

---

26. Thomas, *Summa Theologica*, 1.1.1.

27. J. V. Fesko, *Reforming Apologetics: Retrieving the Classic Reformed Approach to Defending the Faith* (Grand Rapids, MI: Baker Academic, 2019), 11-26.

28. Thomas Aquinas, *Commentum in Libero II Sententiarum*, dist. 1. q. 1. art. 2, in Stanislai Eduardi Fretté and Pauli Maré (eds.), *Opera Omnia*, 34 vol. (Paris, 1871–80), 8:10 (Si autem accipiamus tertium oportere ad rationem creationis, ut scilicet etiam duratione res creata prius non esse quam esse habeat, ut dicatur esse ex nihilo, quia est tempore post nihil, sic creatio demonstrari non potest, nec a philosophis conceditur, sed per fidem supponitur).

which, over and above the impression it makes on the senses, causes some thing else to come into the mind as a consequence of itself.'[29] He explained how words are signs of other realities, arguing that 'among men words have obtained far and away the chief place as a means of indicating the thoughts of the mind.'[30] Augustine also explained how we must interpret Scripture to show how its words reveal God and his specially revealed works to us because 'the signs of divine realities are visible but the invisible realities themselves are granted in them.'[31] In the medieval period, Peter Lombard (1100–60) drew on Augustine's teaching, opening his magnum opus *The Sentences* by stating, '*All teaching concerns things [i.e. realities] or signs.*'[32] Thus, in theology we deal with divine realities made known to us in the signs of God's revelation. For Augustine, the holy Trinity is the true and ultimate reality sought and received through the signs. Doctrine is then not for its own sake but for the sake of knowing the true God and walking before him.

God has fit that revelation for us to know him. John Calvin (1509–64) helps us understand two important corollaries from divine mystery for doing theology. First, God's revelation of divine realities is *accommodated* to us in signs fit to our capacity. Refuting heretics who insisted upon an over-literalized interpretation of Scripture, he responded that 'as nurses commonly do with infants, God is wont in a measure to "lisp" in speaking to us.' So, 'such forms of speaking do not so much express clearly what God is like as accommodate the knowledge of him to our slight capacity. To do this he must descend far beneath his loftiness.'[33] Our response to God's wonderful condescension in making himself known to us should be radical humility. In other words, as Calvin's second corollary, a proper sense of what we are doing in the

---

29. Augustine, *On Christian Doctrine*, 2.1, in Philip Schaff (ed.), *Nicene and Post-Nicene Fathers, Series 1*, 14 vol. (New York, NY: Christian Literature Company, 1887), 2:535.

30. Augustine, *On Christian Doctrine*, 2.3, in *Nicene and Post-Nicene Fathers 1*, 2:536.

31. Augustine, *On Catechizing the Uninstructed*, 50.26, in Jacques Paul Migne (ed.), *Patrologia Cursus Completus: Series Latina*, 221 vol. (Paris, 1844–64), 40:344 (signacula quidem rerum divinarum esse visibilia, sed res ipsas invisibiles in eis honorari).

32. Peter Lombard, *The Sentences: Book 1: The Mystery of the Trinity*, trans. Giulio Silano (Toronto: Pontifical Institute of Medieval Studies, 2007), 1.1.1 (emphasis added).

33. John Calvin, *Institutes of the Christian Religion*, trans. Ford Lewis Battles, ed. John T. McNeill, 2 vol. (The Library of Christian Classics; Louisville, KY: Westminster John Knox, 1960), 1.13.1.

theological task, namely reckoning with divine mysteries, should prompt us to greater piety. As Calvin wrote:

> Now, the knowledge of God, as I understand it, is that by which we not only conceive that there is a God but also grasp what befits us and is proper to his glory, in fine, what is to our advantage to know of him. Indeed, we shall not say that, properly speaking, God is known where there is no religion or piety.[34]

Where theology is done rightly, God is known more fully. Where God is known more fully, holiness should deepen. The intersection of contemplating God and furthering sanctification is then more like merged lanes on a freeway than a crossroads with a traffic light.

How does this discussion of mysteries and piety pertain to our topic of Adam's original righteousness? Although a work of academic theology, this book still recognizes that theology is for the church, therefore, this book itself is for the church. Even in tangling with complicated, nuanced, and intricate issues, its purpose is ultimately not to stroke the intellect but to serve God's people. This book likely meets its purpose more through pastors and teachers digesting this material into their instruction rather than by reaching a popular audience. Nonetheless, we must consider this material as the community of faith striving for understanding.

There are then two applications for this study. First, as a contribution to the *Reformed* Exegetical and Doctrinal Studies series, the audience is primarily readers broadly associated in some way with the Reformed tradition. To be direct, Reformed theology often has a reputation for being internally argumentative and overly aggressive. The modern cultural climate that perceives any disagreement as a personal insult exacerbates this accusation. Regardless, the criticism has some validity.

The fault in view concerns that issue of signs and realities. Too frequently, Reformed theologians insist upon saying things a certain way without recognizing a shared concern. In other words, a proclivity prevails to focus on the signs being a certain way without conceding that differing signs may express likeminded realities. Sometimes, this talking past one another is a failure to understand meaning, which can still be a moral fault. We should be slow to criticize until we understand well. Other times, we outright neglect the concern being addressed

---

34. Calvin, *Institutes*, 1.2.1.

because it does not fit the form of words that we have come to prefer. The accusation of antagonism lands when we focus on the signs *to the expense of the realities* to which those signs refer. As Hans Küng has noted, 'The fight about words can be quite a spectacle if all we want is to have the last word.'[35] Within ecclesiastical politics, we can slip to insist that others keep a party line on the way our most treasured theologians have said things, thereby neglecting deeper reflection upon doctrinal matters.

This book's arguments address debated issues on two fronts. Historically, medieval scholars remain divided about whether the Franciscan and Thomist traditions articulated the nature-grace distinction along the same lines. This book argues from the primary sources that these traditions do build different trajectories. The Franciscan trajectory implemented the nature-grace distinction to divorce our natural and supernatural ends more thoroughly. This differing use of the signs expresses two differing understandings of the realities. Most who contend that these traditions are united on the points discussed have dogmatic stakes in the debate, since most of these scholars stand in the Roman Catholic tradition.[36] In this regard, the Franciscan trajectory became the prevailing view in Roman Catholicism.

To keep these issues clearer, this book distinguishes 'medieval views' from the 'Roman view.' The diverse medieval views predate the Reformation and so are not strictly speaking, at least for our purposes, considered 'Roman Catholic.' Throughout this study then, 'the Roman view' refers to a theological trajectory that has prevailed since it fomented in the early modern period and began standardizing in the Counter-Reformation efforts around the Council of Trent (1545–63). The medieval views predate this increasingly codified Roman view and stand in various needing-to-be-determined relations to later Protestant theology. The polemical point in this categorization is to contest the assumption that all medieval theology belongs most naturally to Roman Catholic tradition. As we will see, the Roman view most thoroughly appropriated the distinct Franciscan trajectory concerning the issues

---

35. Hans Küng, *Justification: The Doctrine of Karl Barth and a Catholic Reflection*, 40th Anniversary ed. (Louisville, KY: Westminster John Knox, 2004), 273.

36. As highlighted within Roman Catholic scholarship itself; Wawrykow, *God's Grace and Human Action*, 16-19.

of nature and grace. *Later* Roman thought embodied the pure nature tradition – a category we need to explain below – as we know it.

Theologically, Reformed theologians – whether in print, on denominational committees, or off the record – have disputed about the felicity of applying the notion of grace to Adam's prelapsarian condition in the covenant of works. Most Reformed uses of grace in reference to the pre-fall context differentiate pre- and postlapsarian forms of grace. This arguable equivocation explains some of the sweeping historical claims about how the Reformed recast grace to address sin rather than nature.[37] It also raises the question if we would not be better served by a clearer distinction of divine benevolence before the fall and grace as God's merciful response to sin. This issue of potential equivocation, wherein the words might express agreeable or problematic substance, marks why we have raised the whole notion of signs and realities. This book argues against the felicity of applying the term 'grace' to God's relationship to humanity before the fall and makes a major effort in ground-clearing for this discussion. This argument for the most felicitous use of language targets problems of substance while accepting that not all who share the same concerns about realities will agree with the arguments about the signs we use. This argument's ground-clearing aspect entails two more points about this study's method in reference to a contribution to church theology.

First, the realities behind the formulations (signs) are concerns for creation's goodness, for our formation as creatures made for communion with God, for the true freeness of God's grace to sinners, and for the integrity of our understanding of justification and sanctification as connected to Christology. Every theologian within the Reformed orbit ought to sympathize with these concerns. Insofar as these issues are universal interests for Reformed churches, this book's arguments should resonate with all who hold confessional commitments. Recognizing the realities undergirding the signs requires reckoning with the argument's structural payoff.

---

37. Andrew A. Woolsey, *Unity and Continuity in Covenantal Thought: A Study in the Reformed Tradition to the Westminster Assembly* (Grand Rapids, MI: Reformation Heritage Books, 2012), 75-76; Michael Horton, *Justification*, 2 vol. (Grand Rapids: Zondervan, 2018), 1:221-310; Herman Bavinck, *Reformed Dogmatics*, ed. John Bolt, trans. John Vriend, 4 vol. (Grand Rapids, MI: Baker Academic, 2003–2008), 3:573-79.

Second, the signs-and-realities issue demands that historical theology does more than quote an historical statement without contextualizing the issue within the wider scope of our doctrinal tradition. Although *homoousios* is the orthodox way to express biblical trinitarianism, controversy surrounded even that language because of its potential misuse. Orthodox trinitarians feared that Sabellians might abuse the affirmation that Father, Son, and Spirit are the same in substance to support their modalist theology. Despite these worries, preference shifted toward terminology that formerly may have been suspect as Arianism grew in dominance and needed theological response. Understanding the value of these terms requires an awareness of all these concerns working together.

Regarding this book's topic, the whole tradition – inasmuch as we are able to grapple with its long scope – must affect how we formulate our construction of the covenant of works today. Protestants committed themselves to the Augustinian priority of grace in response to the late-medieval developments that had diluted grace's true primacy. Still, the Reformation was not the end of the story for maintaining grace's priority. A proper understanding of grace's priority today must account for the shifting theological landscape left from Karl Barth's resounding call for the priority of grace, since it did not fully cohere with some basic Protestant concerns. Because of modern theology's shifting ground, it is no longer adequate simply to quote an early modern author's words without accounting for the reality defended in those signs. Although the argument's complexities and difficulties from even within the Reformed tradition are addressed, proper implementation of historical theology for the sake of theological retrieval must account for the full shape of doctrinal development and the contemporary concerns to be addressed, rather than just mere sound-bite quotes from early modern phrasing. Further, carefully calibrated historical investigation for the sake of application to contemporary theological construction helps prevent the effort at retrieval from becoming mere reversion.

This study attempts to reckon with the changing use and application of signs for Adam's original righteousness, grace before the fall, and merit. One purpose is to clear the fog that blocks discussion of these issues and the terminology involved today. In respect to theological retrieval, this work's extensive historical investigation aims to sharpen the reasons why we should use the categories argued here.

Clarifying Nature and Grace

Modern thought often has a preoccupying fear of 'dualisms.'[38] The nature-grace distinction has been a serious part of that fear for Protestant thinkers wanting to circumvent Roman Catholic theological structures. To slip momentarily into the personal voice, I frequently fail to understand what the criticisms have exactly *meant* in referring to a nature-grace dualism. Sometimes, the *reality* of the discussion gets clouded by vague use of *signs*, such as 'dualism.' The concepts of nature and grace are not clearly delineated when some sort of terminological slipperiness occurs.[39] Some appear to assume that true distinctions, especially when concerning principles with antithetical applications, are necessarily incongruous and need resolution. In truth, only upon Hegelian premises does every antithesis need synthesis. In other words, not every distinction is a dualism. Respecting our topic, the primary fear seems to be about making our spiritual life in reference to supernatural realities of everlasting life too distinct from our responsibilities in this age, possibly undermining our diligence within sub-eschatological endeavors.[40] The language of 'nature-grace dualism' is, therefore, not the best or clearest way forward for the development of categories in systematic theology. This section provides a working notion of how we want to understand and use these terms to get us off the ground for everything else in this book.

---

38. e.g. Karl Barth, *Church Dogmatics*, ed. G. W. Bromiley and T. F. Torrance, trans. G. W. Bromiley, 14 vol. (Peabody, MA: Hendrickson, 1936-77), IV.1:55-66; G. C. Berkouwer, *Sin* (Studies in Dogmatics; Grand Rapids, MI: Eerdmans, 1971), 67-98; Bishop André-Mutien Léonard, 'The Theological Necessity of the Pure Nature Concept,' in Serge-Thomas Bonino, OP, *Surnaturel: A Controversy at the Heart of Twentieth-Century Thomistic Thought*, trans. Robert Williams (Faith and Reason: Studies in Catholic Theology and Philosophy; Ave Maria, FL: Sapientia Press, 2009), 329-30.

39. e.g. the equating of 'nature' with 'first creation' and 'grace' with 'new creation' in Andrew Dean Swafford, *Nature and Grace: A New Approach to Thomistic Ressourcement* (Eugene, OR: Pickwick, 2014), 5. Although the link of nature and first creation works, the elision of grace and new creation merges our eschatological destiny, which is supernatural from the perspective of advancing our nature beyond our protological or fallen conditions, with the whole notion of supernatural operations to the effect of excluding what the specific operations of grace are. The first creation-new creation distinction is more clearly implemented in David VanDrunen, *Divine Covenants and Moral Order: A Biblical Theology of Natural Law* (Grand Rapids, MI: Eerdmans, 2014), 33-34.

40. Fesko, *Reforming Apologetics*, 161-92; Léonard, 'Theological Necessity of the Pure Nature Concept,' 326-27.

The language of 'dualism' distorts our discussion because it lacks exact clarity. Does it imply a mere distinction? Well, nature in the sense of original creation is distinct from grace as the free mercy of God to sinners. Does it intend an antithetical relationship? In that case, grace is antithetical to *sin* not nature, since (as this book argues) grace renews and consummates nature as it stands after the fall rather than completes nature as such. This point would then be partially well-taken. Does it imply a bifurcation between humanity's natural and supernatural capacities? This issue requires careful parsing; hence it is our historical investigation's main focus. Nevertheless, the notion of a sharp, separable, or antithetical divide between humanity's natural and supernatural ends does not properly account for the eschatological nature of our human constitution or of God's first covenant with us.

In arguing for covenantal merit, this book aims to overturn the concept of 'pure nature,' which posits that God must ontologically elevate our nature and our natural capacities as such in order to orient us toward eschatological existence. As Lawrence Feingold stated, 'One of the pillars of Catholic theology is the distinction of the natural and supernatural orders.'[41] The natural and supernatural orders are two parallel tracks of sorts running alongside one another on its own course toward its own distinct and appropriate fulfillment. Thus, the notion of pure nature entails that human *nature* lacks 'any consideration of grace or of a supernatural end' and is not naturally – intrinsically and as such – oriented toward a supernatural end of eschatological enjoyment of God.[42] Even Roman theologians have noted that the doctrine of pure nature entails that Adam could fulfill his natural duties and attain 'to a natural end *with no relationship to God*.'[43] The Roman distinction of natural and supernatural orders then entails

41. Lawrence Feingold, *The Natural Desire to See God According to St. Thomas Aquinas and His Interpreters*, 2nd ed. (Faith and Reason: Studies in Catholic Theology and Philosophy; Naples, FL: Sapientia Press, 2010), 1; C. C. Martindale, S.J, 'Man and His Destiny,' in George D. Smith (ed.), *The Teaching of the Catholic Church: A Summary of Catholic Doctrine*, 2 vol. (Waterloo, Canada: Arouca Press, 2021), 1:303-19.

42. Hans Boersma, *Nouvelle Théologie and Sacramental Ontology: A Return to Mystery* (Oxford: Oxford University Press, 2009), 91-92.

43. *Nouvelles Ecclésiastiques* (Aug 1, 1780); quoted in Henri de Lubac, *Augustinianism and Modern Theology*, trans. Lancelot Sheppard (Milestones in Catholic Theology; New York, NY: Crossroad Publishing, 2000), 270 (emphasis added).

that God did not tailor our nature as such to be oriented toward eschatological consummation.

Traditionally, this distinction of orders mainly concerns the issue of *proportionality*, addressing whether human nature is intrinsically fit for and ordered to supernatural life in obtaining the beatific vision. Alternatively stated, in the Roman paradigm, grace is elevating, *'elevans*, "bridging" the gap between the natural and supernatural and raising the person to a transcendent order of existence.'[44] The question at stake is if ordering human nature naturally to eschatological existence is like trying to pour a massive jug of orange juice into an eight-ounce glass or like asking a mouse to leap from earth's surface to the moon. Is there even capacity for this goal? The suggestion is that the glory of consummate life with God is beyond the *natural* proportions of human capacity to have and ability to achieve. Feingold explains:

> However, by faith we know that God has destined man for an end exceeding the proportionality of human nature or any nature which has been or could be created, and which is proportionate only to God Himself. In order for man to achieve this end, it is not enough for God simply to give man the means requisite for attaining it .... A new proportionality needs to be given to man's nature, by which he will be proportioned to the end of eternal life .... The new proportionality is given by sanctifying grace, the new inclination by the theological virtue of charity, and the acquisition or meriting of the end is given by means of the other infused virtues which are directed by charity.[45]

Everyone must reckon with the proportionality problem concerning what any creature could achieve and the glory that God offers in eschatological life. We address it from multiple angles by the end of this book. Mainstream Roman Catholic thought does so through a particular implementation of distinguishing the orders of nature and grace.

The more specific issue with which this book tangles is *how* Roman theology distinguishes the natural and supernatural orders as it posits *grace* as the necessary bridge between these disproportioned spheres. In other words, for Rome, grace elevates nature as such so to reproportion it to the supernatural order. This reproportioning is, then, essentially an

---

44. Wawrykow, *God's Grace and Human Action*, 66n13.

45. Feingold, *Natural Desire*, 87-88.

issue of ontological change. In the Roman view, grace raises nature so that it is inherently suitable for and able to merit supernatural life. In that paradigm, grace is necessary because our nature itself lacks what we need to obtain new creation life.[46] On that view, we are not ordered toward new creation life at all unless we are reoriented toward that higher end, which was not imbedded in us in our condition of 'pure nature.' In the Roman system, grace addresses nature as such, not *sin* as a corruption of nature. God had to supplement human nature (*donum superadditum*) to fit us with capacity for the supernatural.

This book uses covenant theology, specifically covenantal merit, to explain how we are oriented *by nature* toward supernatural communion with God and equipped to obtain it. Admitting that proportionality is a conceptual obstacle to overcome in explaining how creatures might fittingly acquire heavenly life, Reformed theology contains resources to formulate an alternative conclusion to ontological elevation. Westminster Confession of Faith 7.1 says,

> The distance between God and the Creature is so great, that although reasonable Creatures do owe obedience unto him as their Creator, yet they could never have any fruition of him as their Blessednesse and Reward, but by some voluntary condescension on God's part, which he hath been pleased to express by way of Covenant.[47]

Although later chapters substantiate the argument, this statement contains our basic thesis. On the one hand, Rome claims that God by grace elevates human nature to proportion it to supernatural reward. On the other, Reformed theology recognizes that God *condescends* to us to meet us in our natural capacities and thereby provides the means to reach him as our blessedness and reward.[48]

---

46. Even in modern, revisionist Roman theology, the same position still finds recognition: 'Catholic theology tends to define grace in response to the finitude of human nature and death, although it does not neglect the problem of sin.' Roger Haight, 'Sin and Grace,' in Francis Schüssler Fiorenza and John P. Galvin (eds.), *Systematic Theology: Roman Catholic Perspectives*, 2nd ed. (Minneapolis, MN: Fortress Press, 2011), 402n47.

47. John R. Bower, *The Confession of Faith: A Critical Text and Introduction* (Principal Documents of the Westminster Assembly; Grand Rapids, MI: Reformation Heritage Books, 2020), 204.

48. We will think about how this covenantal principle relates distinctly to the covenant of works and the covenant of grace more in chapter six.

On this exact issue, we can readily accept the premise, common in Roman thought, that a given nature such as ours contains its own principles to work toward its given ends. Our Reformed demurring from their paradigm of the natural and supernatural orders is that God designed human nature with the eschatological end of glorified life and adapted his covenantal economy at creation to our concreated nature. If we *need* to use the same terms that Rome has used, we can still express the problem differently: the covenant of works is a *judicial* rather than an ontological re-proportioning. The preferable way of getting at the issue, however, is to say that the covenant of works defined the proportion of works in relation to Adam's potential reward, taking account of human nature in original righteousness. God adapted the covenant to our nature so ordering the principles of our nature as having concreated original righteousness, without any alteration or elevation by grace, to that eschatological end.[49]

Although both acknowledge the problem of proportionality, Roman and Reformed theologies pose solutions that run in opposite directions. The solutions may well run in opposite directions because the problem itself is conceived differently along alternative planes. Rome says that God brings man up to be inherently proportioned to that eschatological reward so that we can condignly merit it. Reformed theology says that God stoops down to our capacities and accommodates himself to us. Accordingly, *covenant* bridges the infinite gap between, on the one hand, what a creature could intrinsically obtain and deserve by nature and, on the other hand, the infinitely glorious reward that God offers to us in the beatific vision.

One specification is needed concerning the contrast of the Roman and Reformed views as ontological versus covenantal paradigms: the Reformed view argued here is emphatically *not* anti-ontological when the matters are properly understood. Quite the contrary. The particular issue in contrast is the method of resolving the problem of proportionality. *In this regard*, the Roman paradigm is ontological in posing the solution of the *donum superadditum* as an elevation of nature. In this view, the proper basis for merit is added to human nature as an *ontological* supplement. The ontological aspect of the Roman view is its contention for the *elevation* of our nature.

---

49. Swafford, *Nature and Grace*, 8-10.

To specify the point that the Reformed view is not anti-ontological when the matters are properly understood, there is a sense in which the Reformed covenantal method of resolving the problem of proportionality is *more* ontological than the Roman doctrine of the superadded gift. This book defends the Reformed view of original righteousness as a *donum concreatum* – a concreated gift built intrinsically into Adam's nature as such.[50] Our view is then more ontological, at least in one sense, than Rome's because original righteousness, as the strength by which a person can perform the works that prove meritorious, was ontologically natural to Adam. The Reformed covenantal view then has a stronger ontological basis for human anthropology and the real standard of righteousness. Our resolution to the proportionality problem also then has a stronger ontological premise in that the basis of merit has real grounding in how God made us in his image *without needing supplemental elevation*. The covenant is a judicial solution because the Reformed ontology needs no shoring up.[51]

Several considerations grow out of this basic argument that covenant is the proper and Reformed way to address the disproportionality between the created and eschatological orders. First, this book does not tackle the specific nature of the beatific vision but assumes that some version of it pertains to our glorified life in the new creation. The Westminster Larger Catechism 86 articulates how the communion with Christ in glory, which we have immediately after death, includes that our 'souls are then made perfect in holinesse, and received into the highest heavens, where they *behold the face of God in light and glory*.'[52] Reformed people confess that we will have the beatific vision in some capacity. Westminster Larger 90 adds that after the resurrection, we are 'made perfectly holy *and happy* both in body and soul ... especially in the *immediate vision and fruition* of God the Father, of our Lord Jesus Christ, and of the holy Spirit.'[53] To behold the Trinity is the *beatific*

---

50. Muller, *Dictionary*, 97-98.

51. Thanks to Matthew Barrett for raising this point and helping me clarify the contrast intended in the labels 'ontological view' versus 'covenantal view.'

52. John R. Bower, *The Larger Catechism: A Critical Text and Introduction* (Principal Documents of the Westminster Assembly; Grand Rapids, MI: Reformation Heritage Books, 2010), 82 (emphasis added).

53. Bower, *Larger Catechism*, 83.

aspect bringing perfect happiness to us in everlasting life. Any attempt to delineate the more precise nature of this beatific vision would add many more layers of historical and theological complexity to this book's already dense discussion. Setting aside the nature of the beatific vision while presuming its reality facilitates this study's compatibility with differing conclusions on this issue, allowing that debate to be explored elsewhere.[54] Regardless how you might explain it, we look forward to meeting our blessed triune God face-to-face and enjoying his presence as the fruition of all the joy we might imagine.

Second, this book suggests that Reformed theology must recognize that Roman thought loads too much into the category of the supernatural order. For them, God himself, all God's actions, redemptive grace, and eschatology all fall within the scope of the supernatural order. That breadth easily causes vagueness or confusion. For our purposes, we need to use at least three clearly distinguished categories: nature, supernature, and grace. We also need further clarification to avoid loading too many ideas into the category of supernatural, as happens in Roman thought.

Reformed theology might best be served by distinguishing the created order, the eschatological order, and the redemptive order, all which have relation to supernatural realities.[55] This ordering helps us talk more clearly about the Creator-creature distinction and humanity's orientation to everlasting destiny. Discarding 'nature' and 'supernature' as our only basic categories sets aside the mire of ontological connotations wherein supernature encompasses grace and eschatology. We need a clear place for some ontological aspects of this discussion because God is ontologically distinct from the creature, full stop, meaning that the distinction between nature and supernature as it refers to God himself can *never* be overcome.[56] God himself, divine realities, and divine action

---

54. For a thought-provoking historical survey of varying explanations of the beatific vision, see Hans Boersma, *Seeing God: The Beatific Vision in Christian Tradition* (Grand Rapids, MI: Eerdmans, 2018).

55. We might just as easily label this same distinction of orders as protology, eschatology, and grace.

56. If not obvious, this argument concerns how God's condescension addresses the way that God provides a way to recompense creatures, whose obedience can never intrinsically merit supernatural blessings, with himself as their blessedness and reward. This point concerns an aspect *within* the Creator-creature relationship, not the relationship itself holistically. It is about eschatology and the beatific vision, not revelation and God's

belong to supernature and are clearly supernatural in an ontological sense by being necessarily above and beyond created nature. When it comes to the human *telos*, however, we need a primarily *eschatological*, rather than ontological, understanding of our 'supernatural' destiny. Within this eschatological sphere, glorification – the full perfecting or advancing of our bodies from perishable to incorruptible (1 Cor. 15:35-49) – definitely entails certain ontological dimensions to our reward in everlasting life. In this way, again, our Reformed view is not anti-ontological when the matters are properly defined. If the suggestion is that glorification, rightly understood, is the ontological elevation needed to enjoy the everlasting supernatural order, then it is fully compatible with Reformed theology and this book's arguments.[57] That said, this book's articulation of the supernatural order emphasizes what is before us more than what is above us. It focuses on supernatural life as eschatologically conceived in resurrection glory more than on ontological attainment. Our advancement to supernatural life was always about addressing God's design for us to reach a consummate (eschatological) state rather than an ontological deficiency. In other words, the ontological aspects pertaining to glorification as the advancement of our nature have nothing to do with transcending our creatureliness by ascending the ladder of being. Thus, the categorization of the created, eschatological, and redemptive orders better facilitates our discussion by allowing us to speak more efficiently about how by creation, in the new creation, and according to saving grace, we always have, in each estate, relation to supernatural realities, namely God himself and his working toward us.

Third, and related, we must emphasize this book's narrow focus as it considers the issues of the natural and supernatural. The contention that the created, eschatological, and redemptive orders

knowability as Creator (although that is an important issue in its own right). God's covenantal condescension, therefore, does not address God's role as Creator, as if he assumed new attributes to his essence in order to create and relate to his creatures. For an example of that alternative view, which is *not* argued here, see K. Scott Oliphint, *God with Us: Divine Condescension and the Attributes of God* (Wheaton, IL: Crossway, 2012), 12-19, 109-12. Thanks to Carlton Wynne especially for helping me clarify this point.

57. Harrison Perkins, 'What Is Required to See God? The Beatific Vision and the Ordo Salutis,' *Credo Magazine* 12, no. 3; December 5, 2022; accessed on May 29, 2024 at https://credomag.com/article/what-is-required-to-see-god/; cf. E. Towers, 'Sanctifying Grace,' in George D. Smith (ed.), *The Teaching of the Catholic Church: A Summary of Catholic Doctrine*, 2 vol. (Waterloo, Canada: Arouca Press, 2021), 1:558-60.

all relate to the supernatural highlights how one problem that has run throughout related discussions is the porous boundaries among several interconnected topics. The distinction of the natural and supernatural orders could easily prompt consideration of the nature of God's revelation to creatures, further raising the relation of reason and faith.[58] It needs no argument that traditional theology has recognized the necessity of special revelation for informing us about truths that surpass our ability to perceive and discover through the natural world.[59] Even though general revelation declares God's 'invisible attributes, namely, his eternal power and divine nature,' we could not reason to God's specific triune identity apart from special revelation (Rom. 1:20). We cannot know everything from nature, which presumably will remain true in the new creation, entailing that some supernatural action and input into the natural order is necessary. *Some* use of the distinction between natural and supernatural orders is inescapable, even though its proper use will be carefully defined by competing traditions, because it can arguably connect to or encompass nearly every theological loci.[60]

Respectively, we might obtain greater clarity by parsing these related issues into more specific theological categories. On the ontological side, the Creator-creature distinction, wherein God always remains supernatural to the creature even though we have our being via analogous participation in him, maintains what we need in terms of the ongoing divide of natural (created) and supernatural (divine) realities.[61] On the communicative side, our doctrine of general and special revelation maintains the theological categories that we need to explain how we know some truths by what creation contains and know other truths by God's specific action to make known what creation itself does not convey. Thus, we can set aside the very broad natural and supernatural orders in favor of more specific doctrinal categories.

Nevertheless, this book's focus is finely fixed upon the issues of nature in relation to our eschatological destiny. For the sake of a manageable

---

58. Bavinck, *Reformed Dogmatics*, 1:303-12, 321-22.

59. Bavinck, *Reformed Dogmatics*, 1:312-14, 340-51.

60. Bavinck, *Reformed Dogmatics*, 1:355-67.

61. Andrew Davison, *Participation in God: A Study in Christian Doctrine and Metaphysics* (Cambridge: Cambridge University Press, 2019), 1-197.

scope, this book cannot delve into this application of natural and supernatural orders to reason and faith, the wider issues of general and special revelation, or many other potential avenues of inquiry any further than the specific topic at hand absolutely necessitates. Other studies need to consider the important issue of nature, supernature, and grace in connection to reason and faith.[62] In light of our argued implementation of the doctrine of the covenant, the issue of epistemological grounds concerning supernatural truths – however extensive the scope for that category may be – is a different issue than the relation of created and eschatological blessedness. This study's remit is the connection between human nature as created, our eschatological (supernatural if you wish) destiny, and the grounds of our ability to obtain that end. Regarding *this issue*, the argument is that God created us oriented and ordered toward our eschatological/supernatural end, so that he did not have to superimpose a new telos onto a more basic 'pure' nature by superadding the order of grace.

Fourth, also following from the second point, our argued paradigm suggests that grace's antithesis is with *sin* not nature. As later chapters reveal, in medieval discussions, 'grace' was an all-encompassing category for everything that oriented humanity toward God, especially to enable us to do that which is beyond our nature for achieving a supernatural end, making grace synonymous with God's overall action at least as he works above our given nature.[63] In this respect, the rationale behind why some Reformed theologians in the early modern period applied

---

62. Arvin Vos, *Aquinas, Calvin, and Contemporary Protestant Thought: A Critique of Protestant Views on the Thought of Thomas Aquinas* (Washington, DC: Christian University Press, 1985), 123-60.

63. Philip McCosker, 'Grace,' in Philip McCosker and Denys Turner (eds.), *The Cambridge Companion to the Summa Theologiae* (Cambridge: Cambridge University Press, 2016), 206-21. This scope holds true, if not expands, even in modern, revisionist Roman theology: 'Grace, then, quite simply refers to God. But God is understood here as God at work outside of God's self, so to speak, and immanently present within human subjects as an offer of personal encounter.' In this paradigm, grace expands to include all that God does in creation, since all his action concerning creatures is free. Haight, 'Sin and Grace,' 407-9. Haight's position on grace, particularly in claiming 'no separation between the spheres of creation and redemption, or natural and grace,' seemingly contradicts Rome's own binding dogmatic requirements, specifically in Pius XII's encyclical *Humani generis*, esp. §26 (*The Holy See*, August 12, 1950; accessed at https://www.vatican.va/content/pius-xii/en/encyclicals/documents/hf_p-xii_enc_12081950_humani-generis.html on 8 March, 2023).

grace to the covenant of works in various ways, notably concerning the offer of reward for Adam's works, is easy to comprehend. Certainly, God was good to offer a supernatural (eschatological) reward to creaturely obedience. If grace is interchangeable with goodness, it easily refers to the covenant of works.

Clarity increases if we use 'grace' more specifically. Regarding eschatology, the categories of *nature* and *supernature*, or, better, the created and eschatological orders, provide more precision than just nature and grace. This book contends theologically that 'nature' refers to our original created state or specifically to the inbuilt structure of the human condition before sin. *This* distinction between nature and supernature simply acknowledges that creation, as God made it, was not consummated. Nature, specifically humanity in our original nature, had not reached its eschatological destiny. 'Supernature,' in this capacity, then refers to even Adam's potential *eschatological* communion with God, maintaining the distinction between humanity's original state and our glorified existence in the new creation. Supernature is above nature in the sense that it is beyond our original condition but, in another sense, is not above nature if meaning that God had to supplement human nature ontologically to orient us toward our eschatological destiny. Still, using 'supernature' rather than 'grace' in this regard maintains distance from medieval errors and avoids the trajectory of modern Roman Catholic thought which uses 'nature' and 'grace' as essentially synonymous with 'natural' and 'supernatural,' often still conceiving of the supernatural in merely ontological rather than also eschatological terms.[64]

This distinction between nature and supernature, between the created and eschatological orders, leaves a precise application for grace. By creation, God used covenant, rather than grace, as the means to offer an eschatological/supernatural reward to Adam. When Adam sinned, he lost the ability to obtain that reward of the new creation by those terms of the covenant of works. Grace is then specifically God's free gift through Christ and his work of bringing sinners, who have damaged our nature, to the supernatural end to which we were ordered

---

64. This seems to be the case for Vatican II documents; Henri de Lubac, *A Brief Catechesis on Nature and Grace*, trans. Richard Arnandez (San Francisco, CA: Ignatius Press, 1984), 177-90.

in the covenant of works.[65] Grace then opposes sin rather than nature.[66] This paradigm maintains the integrity of each element in Reformed theology's pattern of creation-fall-redemption, especially if expanded to include creation-fall-redemption-consummation. While the nature-supernature distinction maintains God's eschatological purposes for creation, the sin-grace distinction maintains the redemptive-historical difference between creation and fall. God has always been abundantly good and kind to sinners, and his grace is a subset of his goodness, namely as his demerited favor toward rebellious sinners.[67]

Covenantal merit helps clarify *how* nature fundamentally orients toward supernature and why we sinners desperately need grace. Accordingly, the law-gospel distinction is a pivotal implication of this whole investigation. As the historical investigation demonstrates, the Roman nature-grace paradigm has basic consensus that grace enables merit unto eschatological reward. The difference between creation and fall is that fallen human nature might require simply more grace to achieve that merit. Even the instances where a theologian proposes that we can merit from 'pure nature' – notably sometimes even after the fall in fundamentally Pelagian fashion – *that* merit obtains merely the first grace by which further merit of everlasting life is enabled. By contrast, the Reformed use of covenantal merit (*meritum ex pacto*) weaves together the condition of merit and our created state. Adam's original righteousness according to his natural constitution, apart from any ontological elevation, was all that Adam needed to render the sort of obedience that would fulfill the covenant and obtain eschatological reward. Thus, when sin damaged Adam's nature and corrupted his original righteousness, human nature is no longer such that any of us can render the sort of obedience that would be meritorious according to the covenant of works. Respectively, sin requires the covenant of grace wherein Christ renders that meritorious sort of obedience for us, and

---

65. N. Gray Sutanto, 'Consummation Anyway: A Reformed Proposal,' *Journal of Analytic Philosophy* 9 (Summer 2021): 223-37.

66. Bavinck, *Reformed Dogmatics*, 3:516-17, 573-79; Allison, *Roman Catholic Theology*, 48-50; de Lubac, *Nature and Grace*, 117-66; Brian G. Mattson, *Restored to Our Destiny: Eschatology and the Image of God in Herman Bavinck's Reformed Dogmatics* (Studies in Reformed Theology; Leiden: Brill, 2012).

67. Carl R. Trueman, *Grace Alone: Salvation as a Gift of God* (The Five Solas Series; Grand Rapids, MI: Zondervan, 2017), 98-102.

we rest upon him as our Savior and covenantal representative by faith. Covenantal merit, then, undergirds the law-gospel distinction from the perspective of protology in the *imago Dei* and eschatology in the avenues available to reach consummate new creation life.

The Felicity of Merit

With the focus on our purpose for the enjoyment of God's blessed presence and the nature-grace discussion, how does the issue of covenantal merit factor into this work more broadly than informing the law-gospel distinction from the perspective of the *imago Dei*? 'Merit' comes from a Latin word group relating to what is deserved.[68] In theological parlance, as Richard Muller describes, it concerns 'the value or worth of a good or obedient act or the act itself; by extension, the just desert of the person performing the act.'[69] In Roman Catholic thought, human obedience before and after sin can be truly meritorious before God, albeit in varying ways both according to differing paradigms but also within the same paradigm. In contrast, 'the Protestant scholastics, both Lutheran and Reformed, hold that no human acts, whether before or after grace, have merit.'[70] The Reformed impulse is that creatures as such have no intrinsic standing to deserve reward from God.

The notion of covenantal merit aims to resolve the problem concerning proportion between our creaturely works and God's amazing reward of eschatological life by establishing the firm basis for the law-gospel distinction without undermining the Creator-creature distinction. That compromise seems to be an outcome of placing God *intrinsically* in our debt for our obedience. First, the Reformed doctrine of covenantal merit applies to Adam in the covenant of works and not to sinners after the fall. Sinners can in no way merit something from God. Second, covenantal merit maintains the strict demand for *perfect* obedience, contrasting with some medieval views that provide a way for our imperfect works to earn God's blessings. Finally, covenantal merit clarifies that our creaturely obedience *per se* does not earn God's blessings, since God can never be in a creature's debt. Rather, by way of covenant, God ordered the offer of

---

68. Leo F. Stelten, *Dictionary of Ecclesiastical Latin* (Peabody, MA: Hendrickson Publishers, 1995), 161.

69. Muller, *Dictionary*, 215.

70. Muller, *Dictionary*, 216.

a reward to the obedience that Adam *de facto* owed to God as a creature. God's *covenant* established the condition, worth, and desert of Adam's works in the covenant of works. Covenantal merit contrasts with the idea of elevating our natural capacities with supernatural virtues that can inherently merit supernatural reward. Rather, it expresses God's accommodation to recompense the right use of our *natural* capacities with supernatural reward. Accordingly, we see how this Reformed articulation has a stronger ontological premise than the Roman paradigm and our judicial/covenantal solution to the problem of proportionality makes sense against a non-fluid anthropological constitution.

In these ways, the covenant of works helps us address the nature-grace distinction by establishing the nature-supernature relationship. Covenantal merit in the covenant of works emphasizes perfect obedience to the law according to the strength of our original nature. It locates our eschatological potential in God's promise, not in superadded ontological elevation. We were naturally oriented toward supernatural communion with God by virtue of being made in God's image and equipped to realize our natural orientation toward the supernatural by virtue of the covenant which God forged upon our fitting constitution.

The covenant of works, namely as Adam broke it, also establishes the distinction between nature and grace. *Sinners* need God's grace as his free but demerited favor to reconcile us to him. A proper understanding of this covenant then helps preclude 'pure nature,' relates our created state to our supernatural destination in eschatological life, and maintains the structures that secure justification by faith alone while also enabling us to rejoice in a life of new obedience that does not reimpose the law as a condition for life with God in the new creation. In this sense, we are reckoning with the proper formulation and application of the law-gospel distinction through the lens of our constitution as God's image bearers.

The last factor begs for further explanation. As chapter five documents, a modern trend exists among Reformed authors to adopt the pattern of ordering grace before law, inverting the law-gospel relationship, and at times veering (or in some cases careening) toward Roman structures of soteriology wherein grace-enabled faithfulness obtains everlasting life. The doctrine of covenantal merit, as articulated in historic Reformed theology, emphasizes that God's covenant links our natural obligation – the full measure of what we are required to do as God's image bearers

– to the prospect of eschatological reward in the covenant between God and Adam. In other words, only the perfect fulfillment of that natural obligation would satisfy the terms of the covenant. This construction then protects the law-gospel distinction in that only that obedience which we were able to perform *before the fall* could in any circumstance get the label of merit. Sin precludes a new arrangement of covenantal merit because we can never measure up even to our natural obligations as sinners. We would never meet the terms. Further, the gospel then does not bring us back into another grace-enabled situation of earning our way to the beatific vision. The gospel awards us with eschatological life only because Jesus Christ has fulfilled all the covenant's demands for us as our representative. Merit attached specifically to the covenant of works as bound to our nature as God's image bearers then undergirds the law-gospel distinction and helps us more clearly relate the place of our works to the Christian life without giving them any role of contributing to our standing with God for everlasting life.

Statement of the Argument

This book attempts to hold several complicated ideas together to argue for a formulation of the covenant of works that clarifies, supports, and defends several Reformed concerns. The need for this argument comes from the increasing use of the covenant of works in systematic theology, particularly as theologians realize its holistic value and significance for informing anthropology, Christology, soteriology, and other doctrines as well. With the main contours of our discussion outlined, this section succinctly states the full scope of this book's argument. The overarching conclusion, elaborated in the following premises, is that the righteousness required to merit eschatological reward was that which was natural to bearing God's image (which was damaged in the fall):

1) God created Adam with original righteousness hardwired into human nature.

2) This original righteousness, intrinsic to our constitution as bearers of God's image and likeness, entailed both a creational orientation to God and the natural strength to keep God's law, since the moral law reflects the character of the eternal God whose image we bear.

48

3) God wove the covenant of works innately into our natural obligation to keep the moral law, attaching an eschatological destiny as its reward and thereby ordering our natural strength toward supernatural communion with him in the new creation.

4) The standard for fulfilling the condition of the covenant of works was our natural obligation to render *perfect* obedience to God's law.

5) The relationship between our natural obligation to keep God's law and the reward God joined to it is covenantal, making Adam's ability to earn a reward in the covenant of works covenantal merit.

6) The category of covenantal merit, which both demands perfect obedience and supports the integrity of human nature at creation, supports the law-gospel distinction, magnifies Christ's work as the second Adam, upholds the Reformed doctrine of justification by faith alone, and makes space for a joyful and robust doctrine of sanctification.

Conclusion

With much work before us, this book's main objectives are clear. We want to see the dynamics of being made as a fundamentally religious creature, destined for eschatological life with God. The historical inquiry across several chapters is a ground-clearing exercise, providing much needed categorical clarification about many issues attached to our understanding of the covenant of works. As we see the need to avoid various pitfalls about the relations among nature, works, and everlasting life, we come to a clearer picture about how to formulate the covenant of works, and why that clarity will bless our souls with insight into Christ's work and the benefits of the Christian life.

CHAPTER TWO

Covenantal Merit in the Reformed Tradition[1]

The Christian tradition contains a long history of debate about the notion of merit and its proper place amidst the various theological categories. The reoccurring issue of dispute regards the role of works in humanity's relationship with God. Even in the early centuries of church history, Augustine wrote against Pelagius, when discussing Romans 14:23:

> For that reason, moreover, he [Paul] often says, righteousness is counted to us not by works, but by faith, seeing that rather faith works through love, not in that way as I should suppose that I come to that faith by the merit of works, since that faith is the first principle from whence good works begin, as it was said, that which does not come from that faith is sin.[2]

Augustine's doctrine of justification is not our focus, but his comments indicate that the notion of merit has been debated in Christian theology concerning issues of salvation since our early centuries.[3] Augustine's

---

1. This chapter is revised from Harrison Perkins, 'Meritum ex Pacto in the Reformed Tradition: Covenantal Merit in Theological Polemics,' *Mid-America Journal of Theology* 31 (2020): 57-87. Used with permission.

2. S. Aurelii Augustini, *De Gestis Pelagii*, §34, in Jacques Paul Migne (ed.), *Patrologia cursus Completus, series Latina*, 221 vol. (Paris, 1844–64), 44:341 (Ideo vero saepe dicit, non ex operibus, sed ex fide, nobis justitiam deputari, cum potius fides per dilectionem operatur, ne qui: quam existimet ad ipsam fidem meritis operum perveniri, cum ipsa sit initium, unde bona opera incipient; quoniam, ut dictum est, quod ex ipsa non est, peccatum est). English versions number sections in this work differently than the original Latin.

3. For varying discussion on Augustine and justification, see Michael Horton, *Justification*, 2 vol. (Grand Rapids: Zondervan, 2018), 1:84-91; Alistair E. McGrath,

clear statement that righteousness is not counted because of works and that we do not come to faith by merit did not prevent fierce debate in later periods even about how Augustine and other early church fathers should be understood on the topic of merit. The Reformation period produced furious arguments over the doctrine of merit both historically and theologically, which extended well into the post-Reformation era. For example, Archbishop James Ussher (1581–1656) produced historical research on the topic of merit, showing how early modern Roman Catholics tried to enlist patristic and medieval sources in support of their doctrine of merit, but Protestants aggressively responded with their alternative readings of the ancient sources.[4] As the period of Protestant orthodoxy continued, Reformed theologians offered increasingly nuanced accounts of their doctrine of merit as a polemic against Roman Catholic soteriology.

This chapter explores how theologians in the Reformed tradition used and interacted with the concept of *meritum ex pacto* – merit by the covenant. The argument is simply that *meritum ex pacto* was an operating concept that Reformed theologians implemented in various ways to connect several doctrines and to refute Roman Catholic notions of merit. This thesis is not necessarily that it was a predominating category of early modern Reformed theology. This investigation into various instances of *meritum ex pacto* in the Reformed tradition reveals that Reformed writers developed this category to explain Adam's obedience in the covenant of works, to clarify Christ's obedience as the mediator for the elect, and to formulate a polemical category against Roman doctrines of condign and congruent merit.

This argument makes a few contributions to our overall case about formulating the covenant of works properly concerning nature, grace, and merit. First, from an historical perspective, it shows how Reformed theology has long targeted Roman Catholicism's system of condign and congruent merit. In this system, Rome argues that 'a supernatural merit' aims at 'a supernatural reward, consisting ultimately in eternal

---

Iustitia Dei: A History of the Christian Doctrine of Justification, 4th ed. (Cambridge: Cambridge University Press, 2020), 42-58.

4. James Ussher, *An Answer to a Challenge Made by a Jesuite in Ireland* (Dublin, 1624), 492-527.

life, which is the beatific vision in heaven.'[5] Their system then focuses on obtaining eschatological blessing, namely by works both before *and after* the fall. The two types of merit differ in that condign merit is 'the strict sense' which 'supposes an equality between service and return; it is measured by commutative justice (*justitia commutative*), and thus gives a real claim to a reward.' On the other hand, congruent merit is 'quasi-merit (*meritum inadæquatum sive de congruo*)' which 'owing to its inadequacy and the lack of intrinsic proportion between the service and the recompense, claims a reward only on the ground of equity.'[6] In sum, a work of condign merit is truly, intrinsically, and proportionately worthy of its reward. On the other hand, a work of congruent merit obtains reward only because God concedes to accept it as fitting.[7]

As the Reformed see it, the problem with condign merit, which even this entry in the *Catholic Encyclopedia* admits, is that man can never *de facto* make a claim on God for reward. The reason is that our creaturely works are never intrinsically proportionate to the reward of supernatural, eschatological life with God in the new creation. Then, as the Reformed see it, the problem with congruent merit, *especially* as applied to our situation as sinners after the fall, is that it posits that God counts at least less than perfect, if not sin-stained, works as acceptable for earning grace and supernatural rewards.[8] This chapter shows how the Reformed found Rome's whole system of merit wanting. Its historical contribution establishes real precedent in the Reformed tradition for using covenantal merit as our way to address issue of the true disproportion between creaturely works and eschatological reward, contra Rome's condign-congruent distinction.

Second, its theological contribution establishes a precedent for addressing the issue of disproportionality between human works and heavenly reward through covenantal structures. As the previous chapter

---

5. J. Pohle, 'Merit,' in Charles G. Herbermann, Edward A. Pace, Condé B Pallen, Thomas J. Shahan, John J. Wynne (eds.), *The Catholic Encyclopedia*, special ed., 15 vol. (New York, NY: The Encyclopedia Press, 1913), 10:202.

6. Pohle, 'Merit,' 202.

7. Alister E. McGrath, *Iustitia Dei: A History of the Christian Doctrine of Justification*, 4th ed. (Cambridge: Cambridge University Press, 2020), 158-60.

8. Richard A. Muller, *Dictionary of Latin and Greek Theological Terms: Drawn Principally from Protestant Scholastic Theology*, 2nd ed. (Grand Rapids, MI: Baker Academic, 2017), 216-18.

outlined, the major challenge in the whole nature-supernature/grace discussion, which comes critically to bear on the covenant of works, is the issue of proportionality between human works and heavenly reward. As chapters three and four detail, Rome, to overcome this challenge, posited the ontological solution that grace elevates human nature. As this chapter argues, Reformed theology contained the impulse to address this issue through the biblical category of covenant.

This chapter's thesis demonstrates how Reformed theologians saw the issue of merit as a covenantal issue. This Reformed approach stands in stark relief to Rome's view of merit as related to a perceived ontological problem resolved through their use of nature and grace. This Reformed solution to the problem of proportionality implicitly shows again, as the previous chapter noted, that the Reformed have a stronger ontological starting point. Given the premise that Adam's original righteousness was a concreated rather than a superadded gift built into our nature, the Reformed view of original righteousness is more ontological than Rome's in the sense that the issue of proportionality did not involve an ontological *problem* with our nature concerning the sort of works that Adam could perform. That our solution to the issue of proportionality was covenantal and judicial confirms that Reformed theologians did not recognize the disproportion as being a *problem* with our nature as such. We should not see the *problem* to address in the proportionality issue as involving any attempt to overcome our analogous position in the Creator-creature distinction as if merit should rest on a true ontological proportion between us and God.

The theological payoff from this chapter's argument provides a bulwark against the idea of an ontological solution for the disproportion between Adam's creaturely works and his prospective eschatological reward. We need to think through what connects the condition of perfect obedience, as with Adam in the covenant of works, to the prospect of obtaining supernatural, glorified life in the new creation. The competing solutions to the issue of proportionality force a choice between an ontological model or some alternative. The Reformed tradition contains tools for retrieval that allow us to tackle this challenge with appeal to our own architectonic principle of covenant without blurring into certain Roman patterns about ontology. Covenantal merit is the ideal category to avoid the substructure of Roman Catholic understandings of merit, namely that rest on the notion of pure nature in the sense that man was created without natural orientation toward a supernatural end. This discussion about how Reformed theologians pressed against Rome's view of merit shows why the historical investigations of Roman views about merit via the ontological elevation of nature through *donum superadditum* are important.

Two motifs appear in the following historical analysis. First, many implemented *meritum ex pacto* to explain Christ's saving work. They used covenantal merit to establish why God the Son, whose life was of infinite value, would merit specific rewards for his incarnate obedience. This motif contributes to the development of the doctrine of the covenant of redemption, which posits a covenantal relationship among the persons of the Trinity. Although some of the cited writers predate this terminology, the description of the Son's merit being established on a covenantal principle with his Father requires the assumption of a covenant between them. Even the best and most helpful discussion of the historical development of the covenant of redemption have not incorporated consideration of Reformed use of *meritum ex pacto*.[9]

The second motif is the category's use to explain or integrate the doctrine of the covenant of works. Throughout the sixteenth to early-eighteenth centuries, the Reformed used this doctrine to place the contrasting issues of works and grace in a covenantal paradigm. In this paradigm, they used the covenant of works as an historical and principial foil for the covenant of grace wherein God promised the same everlasting life he had offered to Adam, but now on the condition of faith in Jesus Christ.[10] Some authors began incorporating the notion

---

9. J. V. Fesko, *The Covenant of Redemption: Origins, Development, and Reception* (Göttingen: Vandenhoeck & Ruprecht, 2016); Richard A. Muller, 'Toward the Pactum Salutis: Locating the Origins of a Concept,' *Mid-America Journal of Theology* 18 (2007): 11-65.

10. J. V. Fesko, *The Covenant of Works: The Origins, Development, and Reception of the Doctrine* (Oxford Studies in Historical Theology; New York, NY: Oxford University Press, 2020); Willem J. van Asselt, 'Christ, Predestination, and Covenant in Post-Reformation Reformed Theology,' in Ulrich L. Lehner, Richard A. Muller, and A.G. Goeber (eds.), *The Oxford Handbook of Early Modern Theology, 1600–1800* (Oxford: Oxford University Press, 2016), 221-25; Andrew A. Woolsey, *Unity and Continuity in Covenantal Thought: A Study in the Reformed Tradition to the Westminster Assembly* (Grand Rapids: Reformation Heritage Books, 2012), 399-539; R. Scott Clark, 'Christ and Covenant: Federal Theology in Orthodoxy,' in Herman J. Selderhuis (ed.), *A Companion to Reformed Orthodoxy*

of *meritum ex pacto* into this burgeoning covenant theology to explain how God promised to reward Adam on the basis of his works.

These two motifs help clarify why covenantal merit remains a useful category today. On the one hand, its appearance in connection to the covenant of redemption precludes any resemblance, in Reformed constructions, to congruent merit. Christ's obedience was absolutely perfect and fully, totally, and intrinsically fitting of highest reward since a divine person rendered it. Covenantal merit is then not God's concession to impute higher value to intrinsically deficient works, as is the case in congruent merit. Thus, covenantal merit upholds the Law's demand for perfect obedience. On the other hand, covenantal merit establishes the relationship between obedience and its *specific* reward. After all, a divine person's obedience is of infinite value, and so has no limit upon what it *could* merit. Nonetheless, Christ merited everlasting, eschatological life specifically for only the elect whom the Father gave him in the covenant of redemption.[11] In connection to the covenant of works, covenantal merit excludes the notion that a creature can intrinsically have claim upon God while also explaining why the condition of fulfilling the law was tied to the prospect of eschatological reward. By nature, Adam was obliged to keep God's law and ordered to the possibility of and desire for eschatological life. God's covenant with Adam explains how God enabled him to reach that potential end and provides it for us today in Christ.

Tension in the Reformed Tradition Regarding Covenantal Merit

The Reformed tradition's use of *meritum ex pacto* contains complexity and disagreement. For example, William Perkins (1558–1602), lecturer of Christ's College, Cambridge, took specific issue with the Roman notion that 'workes (as they teach) are meritorious in two waies: first*: by covenant*, because God hath made a promise of reward unto them:

(Leiden: Brill, 2013), 403-28; Harrison Perkins, 'Reconsidering the Development of the Covenant of Works: A Study in Doctrinal Trajectory,' *Calvin Theological Journal* 53, no. 2 (2018): 289-317.

11. For wider considerations concerning the proper squaring of the covenant of redemption with classical trinitarian theology and the connection between the Son's incarnate obedience on behalf of his people, see Harrison Perkins, *Reformed Covenant Theology: A Systematic Introduction* (Bellingham, WA: Lexham Press, 2024), 101-23, 171-83.

secondly, by their own dignitie, for Christ hath merited that our workes might merit.'[12] Instead he affirmed that 'we [the Reformed] renounce all merit of works, that is, all merit of any worke done by any meere man whatsoever. And the true merit whereby we looke to attaine the favour of God, & life everlasting, is to be found in the person of Christ alone: who is the storehouse of all our merits.'[13] Perkins clearly held that Christ was the only person who had real merit, therefore explicitly rejected merit even by the covenant (*ex pacto*). Just over fifty years later, however, Richard Baxter (1615–1691), the controversial English theologian, claimed that 'our own Divines generally approve of them that hold only Meritum ex pacto, as to the thing, denying only the fitness of the name, and that this is any proper Merit.'[14] Whereas Perkins eschewed the category of covenantal merit, Baxter propounded that most Reformed divines affirmed it. Disagreement existed among the Reformed about this category of *meritum ex pacto*.

This tension between Perkins' and Baxter's stances toward covenantal merit has historical reasons and contextual explanation. The major issue involved shifting terminology for various categories of merit in the transitions from the medieval to the post-Reformation eras. For example, Perkins rejected an understanding of covenantal merit that was synonymous with congruent merit.[15] As David Steinmetz argued, in this medieval covenant theology that was congruent merit, which is most associated with Gabriel Biel (*c.* 1420–95), 'God has agreed on the basis of His ordained power (*de potentia ordinata*) and according to the terms of His covenant (*ex pacto dei*) to justify every sinner who' acts in accord with their natural abilities to love God.[16] Heiko Oberman (1930–2001) and Richard Muller also linked Biel's notion of merit to the Franciscan doctrine of God's ordained power.[17] In that view,

---

12. William Perkins, *A Reformed Catholike* (Cambridge, 1598), 104 (emphasis added).

13. Perkins, *Reformed Catholike*, 104.

14. Richard Baxter, *Richard Baxter's Admonition to William Eyre of Salisbury concerning his Miscarriages in a Booke lately Written for the Justification of Infidels* (London, 1654), 10.

15. Muller, *Dictionary*, 215-16.

16. David Steinmetz, 'Medieval Nominalism and the Clerk's Tale,' *The Chaucer Review* 12, no. 1 (1977): 44.

17. Heiko A. Oberman, *The Harvest of Medieval Theology: Gabriel Biel and Late Medieval Nominalism*, 3rd ed. (Grand Rapids: Eerdmans, 2000), 131-45, 170-72; Muller, *Dictionary*, 215-16.

God appointed a covenant to accept humanity's deficient best efforts as meritorious. Medieval theologians did have a covenant theology, but it differed greatly from later Reformed covenant theology.

That medieval background is an important factor for understanding any Reformed use of merit in connection to covenant theology, especially the tension highlighted between Perkins' and Baxter's approaches to *meritum ex pacto*. Berndt Hamm has shown that the terminology of *meritum ex pacto* was used during the medieval period to refer to that system of congruent merit, creating a contextual factor that we must consider in analyzing Reformed discussions of *meritum ex pacto*.[18] Marking a concern about proportionality that would remain a live issue even in the formulation of Reformed covenant theology, Hamm noted how later medieval theologians discussed *meritum ex pacto* aimed at this issue of disproportion:

> By granting only a *meritum de condigno* in the form of a meritum ex pacto with regard to eternal life, he can accept the sentence 'grace and glory are not proportionate.' Even though *meritum ex pacto* is like *meritum ex condigno absolute* in being characterized by the debt of rewarding on account of the liable debt, it does not result from the value of the performance, but is anchored in the free will of the contracting party.[19]

In other words, covenantal merit resolves the tension between an infinitely valuable reward and a finitely valuable work. Steinmetz and Alistair McGrath have indicated that Reformation theology's problem with this formulation pertains to applying this meritorious construction to how fallen sinners can gain salvation.[20] Stephen Ozment has also noted how Martin Luther understood this medieval

---

18. Berndt Hamm, *Promissio, Pactum, Ordinatio* (Tübingen: J.C.B. Mohr (Paul Siebeck), 1977), 202-5; Stephen Strehle, *The Catholic Roots of the Protestant Gospel: Encounter between the Middle Ages and the Reformation* (Leiden: Brill, 1995), 21-25.

19. Hamm, *Promissio, Pactum, Ordinatio*, 204 (Indem er auch hinsichtlich der vita aeterna nur ein *meritum de condigno* in Gestlt eines *meritum ex pacto* einräumt, kann er den Satz 'Non sunt proportionalia gratia et gloria' akzeptieren. Zwar ist das *meritum ex pacto* wie das *meritum ex condigno absolute* durch die Schuldnerschaft des Belohnenden gekennzeichnet, dur ch eine Schuldnerschaft aber, die nicht aus dem Wert der Leistung resultiert, sondern in der freien Willensverfügung des Vertragspartners verankert ist).

20. Steinmetz, 'Medieval Nominalism and the Clerk's Tale,' 44; Alistair E. McGrath, 'Homo Assumptus? A Study in the Christology of the Via Moderna with Particular Reference to William of Ockham,' *Ephemerides Theologicae Lovanienses* 60 (1984): 283-97; McGrath, *Iustitia Dei*, 87, 114-15, 286.

use of covenant theology to have a direct relationship to the doctrine of congruent merit that undermined justification by faith alone, in some ways explaining Lutheranism's hesitancy to develop the Protestant law-gospel distinction in covenantal categories.[21] The salient point at this juncture is that some early-Reformation theologians perceived *meritum ex pacto* as a concept linked with medieval categories that undermined justification by faith alone.

Reformed theologians such as Perkins would obviously deny a premise that had enabled the development of the late-medieval soteriology, which was one cause of the Reformation. When Perkins refuted works that were meritorious 'by covenant,' he was rejecting that Roman doctrine of congruent merit, which is not the same thing that other Reformed writers meant when they positively implemented the category of *meritum ex pacto*. Whereas Perkins listed only two types of merit, condign and covenantal (by which he referred to congruent), other Reformed writers implemented *meritum ex pacto* specifically as a third type of merit, formulated precisely as a polemic to undermine Roman categories of condign and congruent merit.

That point becomes clear if we pay attention to the full context of Baxter's claim that most Reformed theologians approved of *meritum ex pacto*: he affirmed that this category was a tool used to argue against Catholic doctrine. He conceded that 'the Papists hold' – although there are 'several parties among themselves differing about this Point' by which we see that Baxter saw the differences between differing trajectories of Roman Catholic thought – 'the fitness of the word Merit: most assert both Merit of Congruity before Regeneration, and Merit of Condignity after; and *Scotus* and a few more that reduce all to the right by promise are rejected by the rest, who affirm a Merit of value or proportion.'[22] Baxter then parsed the Roman view as congruent merit pertaining to unregenerate sinners meriting first grace, which, as the next chapter shows, was characteristic of Franciscans. John Duns Scotus (1265–1308)

---

21. Stephen E. Ozment, *Homo Spiritualis: A Comparative Study of the Anthropology of Johannes Tauler, Jean Gerson and Martin Luther – 1509–1516 – In the Context of Their Theological Thought* (Leiden: Brill, 1963), 174-76; cf. Dino Bellucci, S.J., *Fede e Giustificazione in Lutero: Un Esame Teologico Dei 'Dictata Super Psalterium' e Del Commentario Sull' Epistola Al Romani (1513–1516)* (Rome: Libreria Editrice Dell Universita Gregoriana, 1963), 126-28.

22. Baxter, *Admonition*, 10.

and the later nominalist tradition categorized all merit under God's appointment since inherent meaning was at odds with their (to varying degrees) voluntarist premises.[23]

In contrast, Baxter noted that 'our own Divines generally approve of them that hold only *Meritum ex pacto*, as to the thing, denying only the fitness of the name, and that this is any proper Merit.' Thus, he acknowledged that a creature can never properly merit before God. He also recognized that Reformed theology has a place for this category as we 'read the Papists writings and ours against them.'[24] Reformed writers were, therefore, concerned to refute Roman Catholic understandings of merit. They used the concept of *meritum ex pacto* to support their understanding of the doctrine of justification as a definitive and purely forensic act that declared a person righteous before God, and used it to connect justification to their covenant theology. These connections did not occur all at once, but, throughout the sixteenth to early-eighteenth centuries, the Reformed increasingly knit these doctrines together.

The Development of *Meritum ex Pacto*

This section surveys sources in chronological order, showing an increasing Reformed integration of the doctrine of *meritum ex pacto* alongside other developing categories in covenant theology. It also notes the varying geographical locations in which these theologians labored, revealing the physically widespread use of this doctrine. The tags noting where the following theologians studied and ministered then serve the argument, rather than merely functioning biographically. This widespread factor demonstrates how the idea was not isolated to one group of theologians responding to an idiosyncratic problem or developing an equally idiosyncratic solution for it.

Daniel Chamier (1565–1621) was a French Reformed minister, who studied in Geneva under Theodore Beza (1519–1605). He was involved in shaping the Edict of Nantes (1598), which temporarily granted greater

---

23. Voluntarism is a philosophical school that prioritizes the will over the intellect. More specifically, reality is produced by God's choice without the governing factor of his nature as the reason for his choice. Nominalism is a philosophical school, derived from but not equivalent to voluntarism, that denies the reality of universals. In other words, only names, which we assign, bind various particulars into larger categories.

24. Baxter, *Richard Baxter's Admonition*, 10.

freedom to Protestants in France, and helped establish the academy at Montpellier, where he became a professor.[25] His writings tended to be published in Geneva, some being published after his death. *Panstratia Catholicae*, likely his magnum opus, was a polemical work against Roman Catholicism, uniquely significant as it was produced from within the French context.

Under his section 'concerning Christ's merits by the agreement,' Chamier raised the issue of *meritum ex pacto*. He argued: 'Customarily in fact, merit should be used in a twofold notion, as one is absolute merit, and the other is merit by the covenant.' He said that absolute merit was a good work that created obligation by its fulfillment of the law.[26] Then, 'In merit by covenant, however, the work is that to which whereas nothing on account of itself would be strong enough to obligate, nevertheless, by the voluntary communion, or agreement, obligation occurs, therefore, so that a reward of such great excellence is owed.'[27] Chamier argued then that Christ merited eternal salvation by the covenant, at least according to his human nature, and was able to restore those who are guilty to God because of that covenant.[28] In this sense, aimed at that issue of proportionality of human work and reward, Chamier used *meritum ex pacto* to define the value of Christ's saving work. His point to specify its value in reference to Christ's human nature distinguished what Christ would merit as a divine person, and what he merits according to the given economy of redemption in his saving work as the mediator for humanity. Chamier clarified: 'Therefore, Christ's blood purges by God's covenant and institution, not simpliciter and because of itself, that is, apart from any meaning.'[29] His point was that God's covenant assigned the reward for Christ's suffering merit. If God's Son had become incarnate and died, it did not necessarily have to be intended to forgive sinners. God's

---

25. Samuel MacAuley Jackson (ed.), *The New Schaff-Herzog Encyclopedia of Religious Knowledge*, 13 vol. (New York, NY: Funk and Wagnalls Co., 1908–14), 3:1.

26. Daniel Chamier, *Panstratiae Catholicae*, 4 vol. (Geneva, 1626), 3:241 (Meritum enim solitum usurpari duplice notione, ut sit unum absolute Meritum, aliud Meritum ex pacto).

27. Chamier, *Panstratiae Catholicae*, 3:241 (Meritum verò ex pacto, opus est, cui cùm per se nulla sit vis obligandi, tamen ex voluntate communi, sive compacto fit obligatorium, ita ut debeatur merces talis, tantque).

28. Chamier, *Panstratiae Catholicae*, 3:242.

29. Chamier, *Panstratiae Catholicae*, 3:242 (Ergo sanguis Christi purgat ex pacto & instituto Dei, non simpliciter & per se, id est, absque ulla acceptione).

covenant with Christ gave his death *that* value. Even though Chamier did not list *meritum ex pacto* as an explicit third category in contrast with condign (absolute) and congruent merit, his use was not interchangeable with congruent merit. He was propounding categories of merit that he thought were real, of which congruent merit was not one.

Chamier discussed *meritum ex pacto* elsewhere, again under the topic of Christ's merits. He described *meritum ex pacto*, distinguishing between absolute merit and merit by the covenant: 'merit by the covenant, whereas it does not have the strength to obligate on its own account, nevertheless, it does have it from the arrangement, so that either a full or greater reward for the work is owed to it.' So, the covenant establishes what reward a work must receive: 'That is by the promise it has strength to merit so far as by its arrangement by which reward is expected … indeed merit of such value is by the arrangement, but furthermore the method of the arrangement pays from only the will of the one who arranges.'[30] In each instance of Chamier's repeated use, his purpose in each case was to explain Christ's work in terms of its merit.

Chamier's appeal to covenantal merit was far from a voluntarist construct since he has Christ's merits in view. Christ's merits are undeniably real (*realiter*), not some prescript of nominalism. Hence, even covenantal merit as it establishes the link between *this* work and *this* reward has a kind of realist ground. Chamier's view of merit links to his training in Geneva and, although studying with Beza, he cited John Calvin. Calvin summarized the medieval scholastics as saying 'works have no intrinsic dignity but are meritorious by the covenant.'[31] According to Calvin, the scholastics 'did not see that works are always stained with sin,' but still 'nevertheless this principle is true: the reward

---

30. Daniel Chamier, *Corpus Theologicum Seu Loci Communes Theologici* (Geneva, 1653), 220 (At meritum ex pacto, etsi per se vim obligandi non habet, tamen ex instituto habet: ut ei operi merces, vel tota vel tanta debeatur. Hoc rursus geminum, alias ex promissione vim merendi habet, alias ex pacto; quod est ex promissione, vim merendi habet duntaxat ex eius instituto a quo merces expectatur: ut cum ludicris certaminibus proponuntur praemia sive a Rege, sive a populo: tunc enim non tantum meritum est ex instituto, sed etiam instituti ratio pendet a sola voluntate eius qui instituit).

31. Joannis Calvini, *Commentarius in Epistolam Pauli ad Romanos*, Rom. 3:20, in *Opera Quae Supersunt Omnia*, ed. Edouard Cunitz, Johann-Wilhem Baum, and Eduard Wilhem Eugen Reuss, 59 vol. (Corpus Reformatorum; Brunswich, 1863–1900), 49:56 (opera non intrinsica dignitate, sed ex pacto meritoria esse).

for works hangs from the voluntary promise of the law.'[32] Calvin's expression might gesture toward a more voluntarist underpinning than Chamier's, perhaps unsurprising in itself given Calvin's other doctrinal constructs.[33] That potential variance between Calvin and Chamier marks the Reformed tradition's eclecticism even as theologians formulated the same doctrines. Whatever we make of that philosophical issue, Calvin nonetheless saw God as the agent connecting *perfect* performance of the law – after all, he rejected any nominalist construct of *ex pacto* wherein works stained with sin could measure up to this works principle – to its reward.

Calvin's contribution links to covenant theology more at the redemptive historical level than to an overt categorical substantiation of the law-gospel distinction. It still, however, connects to it in the broader points of his system. Matthew Tuininga has demonstrated that these quoted passages, along with other similar ones, show Calvin's implementation of some understanding of *meritum ex pacto*. He explained that Calvin believed in two different types of covenants so that the Mosaic covenant, in contrast to God's covenant with Abraham, expressed a legal principle akin to that which was formulated in the later development of the covenant of works.[34] Although the elements of the covenant of works as later Reformed theology construed it are present in Calvin's writings, Tuininga's case presented Calvin's view as emphasizing the legal covenant more as something that ran within the Mosaic covenant parallel with, and hypothetical to, the free promise of the gospel. William Perkins also seemed to articulate the distinction between the covenants of works and grace in the same way.[35] Calvin and Perkins aimed to undermine the Roman doctrine of congruent merit, arguing that God cannot accept imperfect works

---

32. Calvini, *Commentarius in Epistolam Priorem ad Corinthios*, 1 Cor. 1:17, in *Opera*, 49:320 (non vident vitiis semper inquinta esse opera … verum tamen est illud principium, ex voluntaria legis promissione pendere operum mercedem).

33. Richard A. Muller, '*Fides* and *Cognitio* in Relation to the Problem of the Intellect and Will in the Theology of John Calvin,' *The Unaccommodated Calvin: Studies in the Foundation of a Theological Tradition* (Oxford Studies in Historical Theology; New York, NY: Oxford University Press, 2000), 159-173.

34. Matthew J. Tuininga, *Calvin's Political Theology and the Public Engagement of the Church: Christ's Two Kingdoms* (Cambridge: Cambridge University Press, 2017), 271-74.

35. Perkins, 'Reconsidering the Development of the Covenant of Works,' 302-9.

as sufficient for justification. As above, Calvin contended that since merit requires perfect works, and since a person cannot render perfect works, justification must be by faith.[36] Calvin, therefore, used *meritum ex pacto* to uphold the Protestant view of justification. Unsurprisingly then, Chamier also implemented *meritum ex pacto* in his discussion of Christ's work to explain how Christ perfectly earned salvation for his people. None of these thinkers yet linked *meritum ex pacto* with the structure of the covenant of works between God and Adam. Still, significant Reformed theologians in differing geographical and political contexts all interacted with the notion of covenantal merit, all three defending thorough Protestantism, and two of the three employing *meritum ex pacto* to do so.

Richard Crakanthorpe (bap. 1568, d. 1624) was a Reformed Episcopal and religious controversialist in England, well appreciated by those typically called puritans, especially for his preaching. Appreciating theology's catholic spirit, he argued that the English Reformation purified rather than departed from the medieval tradition. He polemicized against the archbishop of Spalato to defend that England's significant connections to foreign Protestant churches negated that the Roman communion was the mother of all churches.[37] Crakanthorpe at times, like Perkins, interacted with *meritum ex pacto* by treating it as synonymous with congruent merit.[38] Still, Crakanthorpe conceded that in 'positing the covenant of God with Adam, eternal life would have been delivered as the merit of justice, if people had continued in righteousness without the whole fall, and because they did not continue [in righteousness], therefore now eternal life is not given by merit and the dignity of works, but only by grace and because of grace.'[39] This instance first exemplifies a direct connection of the covenant between

---

36. Calvini, *ad Romanos*, Rom. 3:20, in *Opera*, 49:56.

37. A. P. Cambers, 'Richard Crakanthorpe (bap. 1583, d. 1624),' *ODNB*; *Mutandis mutatis* the same argument rightly abides for the Reformation generally; Matthew Barrett, *The Reformation as Renewal: Retrieving the One, Holy, Catholic, and Apostolic Church* (Grand Rapids, MI: Zondervan, 2023), 35-368.

38. Richard Crakanthorpe, *Defensio Ecclesiae Anglicanae* (London, 1625), 361.

39. Crakanthorpe, *Defensio Ecclesiae Anglicanae*, 324-25 ((posito Dei pacto cum Adamo) aeterna vita, ut meritum iustitiae (si in iustitia sine omni lapsu homines permansisset) refferetur: & quia non permanserunt, ideo iam non ex merito, & operum dignitate, sed solummodo ex gratia, & propter gratiam donator).

God and Adam with merit. Crakanthorpe's point was that it was possible to merit eternal life, namely because of the covenant with Adam, except for the entrance of sin, necessitating the reception of eternal life by grace. Crakanthorpe set this notion of covenantal merit, which accorded to some sort of justice, in sharp contrast to grace. He thereby connected covenantal merit to the law-gospel distinction that undergirds Reformed bi-covenantal thought. His point was that no category of merit is viable after Adam's fall. After the fall, grace, rather than covenanted justice, becomes the necessary method of relating to God.

Thomas Adams (1583–1652) was another Reformed Episcopalian, who was concerned to rid the Church of England of what he perceived to be lingering hints of Roman Catholic theology. Although Adams was a popular and well-known preacher, he never attained a high position in the church. The reason for his lack of advancement was likely twofold. On the one hand, his anti-Catholicism ran afoul both of James I's suggestion to wed his son to a Spanish princess and of William Laud's ecclesiastical approach. On the other hand, his staunch royalism then put him in ill graces with Oliver Cromwell.[40] In his lengthy explanation of issues surrounding *meritum ex pacto*, he again raised the issue of proportionality, arguing that '*Wages* is understood to be an equall retribution, a reward proportionable to the worke: and is either *ex pacto*, what is covenanted; *Didst thou not agree with me for a peny?* or *ex merito*, what is earned, *The labourer is worthy of hire.*' So, he underscored that 'Equality of recompence defines wages: if it be too much, and above desert, it is munificence: if too little, and short of desert, it is injustice.'[41] In distinguishing *ex pacto* from *ex merito*, Adams contended that God set certain terms as the mode by which he would grant reward. The argument moves in such a way to show that God never properly owed humanity anything and especially owes them nothing after the fall. All the same, if God agreed to certain conditions, he would honor them by his covenant. This move again was a way to circumvent Roman Catholic understandings of merit for the sake of salvation by grace alone.

---

40. J. Sears McGee, 'Thomas Adams (1583–1652),' *ODNB*; Joel R. Beeke and Randall J. Pederson, *Meet the Puritans: with a Guide to Modern Reprints* (Grand Rapids: Reformation Heritage Books, 2006), 11-14.

41. Thomas Adams, *A commentary or, exposition vpon the diuine second epistle generall, written by the blessed apostle St. Peter* (London, 1633), 851 (italics original).

Johannes Cocceius (1603–1669), a Dutch theologian who taught as professor of philology and Hebrew at Bremen, Franeker, and Leiden, made several contributions in the development of covenant theology. Some of those contributions were (and remain) controversial, particularly his teaching that the development of redemptive history entailed stages of abrogation for the covenant of works.[42] Despite the usual focus on Cocceius' doctrinal treatise, his Genesis commentary contained theological emphases in the development of covenant theology in connection to *meritum ex pacto.*

Cocceius argued that the covenant of works was immutable and fused to human nature because Adam's creation in God's image demanded continuation in perfect obedience. This contention marks a notable occasion wherein a Reformed theologian overtly addressed the issue of nature and grace, using the covenant to press against Rome's construction: 'Man, therefore, by the very fact that he was made according to God's image, has been constituted as in a covenant with God.' Hence, Cocceius tied our image bearing condition to our covenantal status. This *natural* covenant oriented Adam toward God, specifically toward loving him, culminating in eschatological enjoyment of the Lord: 'God bound Adam by oath unto loving and seeking him as his God, that is being examined also in an ardent attachment to God together with obedience throughout the examination period, performed to God's eternal glory in him who will be revealed in beatific life.' Even though God promised to reward Adam's perfect obedience, it was not condign merit since God owed nothing to creatures as such for their obedience. Although 'the reward that must be reckoned according

---

42. Johannes Cocceius, *Summa Doctrinae de Foedere et Testamento Dei* (Leiden, 1654); Willem J. van Asselt, 'The Doctrine of Abrogations in the Federal Theology of Johannes Cocceius (1603–69),' *Calvin Theological Journal* 29 (1994): 101-16; Willem J. van Asselt, *The Federal Theology of Johannes Cocceius (1603–1669)*, trans. Raymond A. Blacketer (Leiden: Brill, 2001); Willem J. van Asselt, 'Expromissio or Fideiusso? A Seventeenth-Century Theological Debate between the Voetians and Coccieans about the Nature of Christ's Suretyship in Salvation History,' *Mid-America Journal of Theology* 14 (2003): 37-57; Willem J. van Asselt, 'Christ, Predestination, and Covenant,' 222-25; Brian J. Lee, *Johannes Cocceius and the Exegetical Roots of Federal Theology: Reformation Developments in the Interpretation of Hebrews 7–10* (Göttingen: Vandenhoeck & Ruprecht, 2009); J. Mark Beach, *Christ and the Covenant: Francis Turretin's Federal Theology as a Defense of the Doctrine of Grace* (Göttingen: Vandenhoeck & Ruprecht, 2007), 272-98.

to what is owed' which 'is usually called merit,' still 'the nature of this merit ... is not condign.' Rather, Cocceius cited Luke 17:10 to the effect that, 'It, therefore, remains that merit is by the covenant.'[43] Even though God does not *intrinsically* owe a creature any reward for obedience, God covenanted with Adam so that Adam could trust that God would provide the expected reward if Adam rendered obedience during his probation in the garden. Since Adam owed everything to God, Adam's merit in this covenant could not be condign but was covenantal. He could earn his reward from God only because God had offered that reward on the basis of the covenant. Keeping in mind the previous chapter's scholastic distinction, Cocceius' formulation entails that the principle of covenantal merit is bound concreatedly into *imago Dei*, representing a situation wherein the works-merit-reward structure of the natural covenant was inherent but not intrinsic.[44]

Cocceius affirmed that this form of covenantal merit could apply to Adam only before his fall into sin. This caveat enabled him to use covenantal merit as a polemic to refute Roman Catholic paradigms of soteriology. First, Cocceius argued that the covenant of works could not be diminished, diluted, or even altered, since it was tied to God's image hardwired into humanity, which reflects God's immutable character:

> The covenant of works is immutable and indispensable because it depends upon God's image, and thus upon God's nature, that is upon eternal uprightness and justice, which is established by him, who is God, and has

---

43. Johannes Cocceius, *Commentarius in Pentateuchum, Josuam, et Librum Judicum* (Amsterdam, 1669), 38 (§124. XII. Homo igitur eo ipso, quod fuit factus ad imaginem Dei, fuit constitutus quasi in foedere Dei. Foedus illud dico sive pactum, conventionem mutua obligatione constantem. quia Deus Adamum obstrinxit ad amandum & quaerendum se ut Deum suum, h[oc].e[st]. desiderandam & in affixione ad Deum atque obedientia per tempus explorationis operandum gloriam aeternam Dei, in ipso manifestandam in vita beatissima: & vicissim Adamo stanti in veritate & rectitudine, & praeceptum explorationis observanti dedit fiduciam sperandi & ab ipso, ut Deo suo, petendi eam gloriae Dei manifestationem in se, & benedictionem in multiplicatione posteritatis cum imagine Dei. Hoc jam ex dictis clare patet. §125. XIII. In hoc pacto consideratur vita coelestis ut merces reputanda κατ᾿ ὀφείλημα. Hoc meritum dici solet. Sed considerandum est, quale id meritum sit. Non ex condigno. Homo nihil Deo potest dare, nihil accipit Deus ex manibus ejus, non sit ditior aut beatior per hominis operam. Homo debet omnia Deo. Vide Luc. 17:10. Restat igitur meritum ex pacto).

44. Bernard Wuellner, SJ, *Dictionary of Scholastic Philosophy* (Milwaukee, MN: The Bruce Publishing Company, 1956), 61, 64.

all divinity; and for that reason, the covenant cannot be changed unless the principal reality is changed.[45]

Cocceius argued that this point about the covenant of works' immutability meant that the category of merit could not be applied after Adam's fall, the contrary being Roman soteriology's shortcoming. Cocceius named John Duns Scotus as a promoter of this idea that merit was a legitimate category for how fallen people might obtain eternal salvation, arguing that this view's results 'confound the covenant of grace and the covenant of works.'[46] Cocceius, therefore, contrasted God's justice with grace, and understood the doctrine of *meritum ex pacto* to be one way to uphold the distinction between the law and the gospel through covenantal categories.

Most pointedly for the value of *meritum ex pacto* as a polemic against Roman Catholic thought, Cocceius leveraged it to attack Robert Bellarmine (1542–1621), the famous Roman apologist. Cocceius thus denied that sinners could still merit after the fall. His starting point was that 'our works in no way merit without covenants.' The covenant assigns the dignity of a work, which cannot be condign since, 'They certainly do not begin to be proportionate and equal, therefore, it is because God has fixed, has prepared, and has promised an eternal reward to them.'[47]

---

45. Cocceius, *Commentarius in Pentateuchum*, 38-39 (§128. XV. Foedus operum est immutabile & indispensabile. Quia nititur imagine Dei, & sic natura Dei, h[oc].e[st]. aeterna veritate & justitia, quae fundatur in eo, quod Deus est, & omnem divinitatem habet; atque ideo foedus mutari non potest, nisi prima veritas mutetur).

46. Cocceius, *Commentarius in Pentateuchum*, 38 (§126. Unde patet, quantopere peccent, qui meritum saltem ex pacto statuunt post lapsum. ut Schola Cantabrigiensis. Virtutum pulchra & speciosa caterva Salutem Aeternam ex pacto quam meruere dabunt. A Joh. Duns id didicerunt. Hoc est confundere foedus gratiae & foedus operum. Sed multo magis delirant, qui debitum ex condigno statuunt sub foedere gratiae).

47. Cocceius, *Commentarius in Pentateuchum*, 76 (§28. In his rursus est discriminanda veritas a mendacio. 1. Verum est, quod opera nostra nullo modo mereantur sine pactos. quod bene Bellarminus. Sed quomodo idem dignitatem personae, & dignitatem operis & communicationem introducit, si sit pactum? Quae plane non consistunt. Non enim incipiunt esse proportionate & aequalia, ideo quia Deus illis destinavit, praeparavit & promisit praemium aeternum. 2. Verum est, quod meritum operum proveniat ex pacto: sed male id pactum confunditur cum promissione Euangelica. Ideo Scriptura legem & promissionem opponit. Gal. 3:17. 3. Pactum illud, a quo est meritum, in ipsa naturae productione fundatum est. Creaturam, quam Deus est dignatus imagine sua, eo ipso etiam dignatus est vocatione ad vitam immarcescibilem: quia se ei quaerendum proposuit. Neque aliter fieri potuit. Atque hac in parte recte sensit ille doctor, cum quo Bellarmino res. Sed plane pessime sensit idem, quod

Thus, Cocceius exemplified our claim that the Reformed have a stronger base ontology than Rome's wherein our position does not require an ontological reproportioning to ground merit but merely a covenant as the judicial solution.

Cocceius pressed his criticism of Bellarmine further to defend justification by faith alone. In anticipation of Rome's appeal to post-fall congruent merit, Cocceius cited Galatians 3:17 to restrict this structure to the covenant of works: 'the merit belonging to works comes into being by the covenant, but it is wicked to confound this covenant with the gospel promise.' Covenantal merit was 'established in itself by the production of nature,' which also establishes 'the calling to everlasting life because God has displayed himself to his image-bearing creature, and it could not be otherwise.' We cannot add this covenantal merit under the structure of the gospel because 'the merit from natural works conflicts with Christ's merit of life.'[48] The proper structure of merit then protects true grace.

---

putavit, etiam post lapsum manere eandem conditionem vitae possibilem; & eam esse factionem boni operis ex regeneratione & justificatione proficiscentem. 4. Bene Bellarm. Christum nobis meruisse vitam immediate. Et quod cum eo pugnet meritum nostrum sine pacto, ex ipsa natura boni operis. quodque alias Christus tantum sit meritus potestatem bene operandi. Sed in eo rursus sibi est contrarius, quod putat cum Christi merito vitae immediate posse conjungi meritum ex pacto. Non enim magis cum Christi merito vitae pugnat meritum ex natura operis, & sic pacto tacito, quam meritum ex pacto verbali. Et falsum est, quod dicit, hoc esse amplioris gratiae & benignitatis ipsius, quod voluerit nos vitam habere non tantum jure haereditatis, sed jure etiam promeritorum. Nam minor est gratia, mereri & aperire quasi viam ad novi pacti conditionem, ut demum si eo pacto steterimus ad vitam perveniamus; quam vitam Christum nobis meritum esse proxime, immediate & sic absolute. Sophisma hic est. Deus nos voluit vitam habere, ut haereditatem & ut compensationem: nempe ut incipiamus hic viventes Deo placere, & sic jam tanquam filii agere, & spem gaudiorum bonis operibus firmare: non vero de Gloria Dei aliquid delibare. 5. De promissione, quae legi opponitur, neuter bene sentit. Nam ea proprie est declaratio Testamenti, quod Deus fecit in Christo, de vita danda propter ipsum eis, qui ipsi dati sunt. Est igitur significatio ejus, quod Christus impetravit. Sic dictum est: Ponam inimicitiam inter semen mulieris & tuum. Et, Ero Deus semenis tui. In Isaaco vocabitur tibi semen. Postulo a me & dabo gentes haereditatem tuam. Patrem multarum gentium dedi te. In semine tuo benedicentur familiae terrae. Haec promissio, quatenus vitam aeternam decernit, singulis per verbum conditionatum applicatur, ut nempe designati haeredes excitentur ad haereditatem quaerendam in Christo; & illi, qui confugiunt ad Christum spem expositam habeant ad eam arripiendum. Hebr. 6:18. Nam sic Testamentum transit in firmitudinem pacti: non autem vitae aeternae promerendae statuitur nova conditio).

48. Cocceius, *Commentarius in Pentateuchum*, 76. Latin included in previous footnote.

Cocceius also reckoned with the issue of disproportionality, posing the solution of covenantal merit. He thought *meritum ex pacto* upheld the distinction between the covenant of works and the covenant of grace, so avoiding the confusion of the law and the promise. God does not set out the hope of everlasting life if we take hold of Christ's merits and add our works to it. Instead, he has ordained that Christ's merits be applied for the everlasting salvation of those whom the Father gave to the Son to redeem. They are then to live the grateful and obedient lives of sons to declare the reality of having received everlasting life. In these respects, Cocceius leveraged covenantal merit to address the issues of both proportionality and the law-gospel distinction. His formulation was thoroughly non-voluntarist, grounding his whole formulation in nature's constituent features, melding but not identically conflating creation and covenant. Cocceius' emphasis on the connection between covenant and the *imago Dei* sets Reformed precedent for our study's defense of the law-gospel distinction from the vantage of the image of God. The next several theologians all have historic links to Cocceius, making his principles a fulcrum in the continual development of *meritum ex pacto* in Reformed theology.

Johannes Braun (1628–1708), once a pupil of Cocceius, taught theology and Hebrew at the university of Groningen. Developing what he learned from Cocceius in a polemic against Arminianism, Braun argued that *meritum ex pacto* structured the covenant of works.[49] Adam's obligation for if he 'performed all things [of the law],' meant that 'he would even have merited, but not by condign merit, as if either his person, or his works would have been worthy of so great a reward.' Braun got straight to the issue of disproportionality, protecting the Creator-creature distinction. Citing a host of biblical passages, Braun affirmed that, 'Nothing is given proportionately between the work of creatures, and the enjoyment of God.' So, Braun, using covenantal merit, aimed to explain how Adam could obtain the beatific vision in the covenant of works to make sense of the proportionality challenge.

Braun also furthered the usual anti-Roman polemic. Adam's reward 'would not even have been by congruent merit, certainly because of the

---

49. Johannis Braunii, *Doctrina Foederum sive Systema Theologiae*, 2 vol. (Amsterdam, 1691), 2.9.11, 24 (citations formatted as part.chapter.section); Piet Steenbakkers, 'Johannes Braun (1628–1708), Cartesiaan in Groningen,' *Nederlands Archief voor Kerkgeschiedenis* 77, no. 2 (Jan 1997): 196-210.

extraordinary gifts, which he had received from God.' He pushed even harder against Rome's view of the nature-grace distinction, refuting the *donum superadditum*: 'Because there was no grace in the case of Adam, the one building favor, when everything he would have was from God.' He concluded, 'Merit, therefore, was to its extent by the covenant, following the stipulation of the covenant, by the mere good pleasure of God.'[50] Affirming that Adam would have merited in the covenant of works had he not sinned, Braun parsed a careful meaning for Adam's merit. Adam's potential merit, which was merit because he genuinely could have earned something from God upon a legal premise, had to have been covenantal. Its basis was that God set terms to Adam and assigned the reward if Adam strictly met them. Braun's denial of grace for Adam is further interesting, entailing that Adam needed to fulfill the covenant by natural strength without supernatural assistance. Braun thereby limited the scope of merit to covenant rather than liciting a situation where grace empowers merit.

Frans Burman (1632–79) was born in Leiden, pastored a church in Hanau, and later taught theology (1662–71) and then history (1671–79) at the University of Utrecht, writing books on theology, biblical commentary, philosophy, and ethics.[51] In his *Synopsis of Theology and Inspection of God's Covenant*, Burman implemented *meritum ex pacto* to explain both the covenant of works and Christ's work. The first reference to the doctrine comes under his treatment of angels, raising the question about their merit.

> Merit indeed is not opposed to the Scripture, if only that merit is
> not founded in the fixed dignity of works, but in the generous divine

---

50. Braunii, *Doctrina Foederum*, 259-60 (Si Adamus stetisset omniaque fecisset, meritus quidem fuisset, sed I. Non ex Condigno, quasi vel ipsius persona, vel ipsius opera tanto praemio digna fuissent. Nulla sane creatura, etiamsi perfectissima, apud Deum mereri potest. (1. quia Deus לא שׂיד Deo Omnia debemus. Luc. 17:10 (2. Deo nullum potest adferri commodum cum sit sufficiens. Genes. 17. Vide Job 22:2. (3. Quicquid homo boni habet, id habet a Deo. Phil. 2:13. Act. 17:28. 1 Cor. 4:7 (4. Nulla datur proportion inter opus creaturae, & fruitionem Dei. Nec etiam II. Meritus fuisset ex congruo, scilicet propter eximia dona, quae a Deo acceperat. (I. quia Deus fuisset acceptor personarum, qui benefaceret ob propria dona, (2. quia in Adama nulla fuit gratia gratum faciens, cum Omnia a Deo habuerit. Ergo meritus ex pacto tantum, secundum stipulationem foederis, ex mero beneplacito Dei).

51. John Watkins, *The Universal Biographical Dictionary*, new ed. (London: Longman, Hurst, Rees, Orme, and Brown, 1821), 302; Alexander Chalmers, *The General Biographical Dictionary*, new ed. (London: J. Nichols and Son, et al, 1813), 7:354-55.

promise; the type of merit is by the covenant, and also the righteousness of works, even as to the first man, if he had continued obeying, then he would be suitable.[52]

Although the connection Burman drew between angels and merit is interesting, the relevant point is his argument for the compatibility of merit, properly understood, with Scripture.

God's relationship with Adam in the covenant of works best illustrates how covenantal merit operates. God's covenant with Adam forged the potential for merit. Flagging a deeply pastoral factor, Burman rejected that merit and love are opposed since 'God's kindness is that he would want to summon the creature, who by default has been subordinated to him and owes him everything by natural obligation, to special communion with him by entering into a covenant, and would want to temper his completely absolute rule with that self-indulgence of love and mutual obligation.'[53] Love and abundant goodness undergird even the covenantal structures of merit. Burman already stated that God's covenant with Adam worked on the premise of *meritum ex pacto* but further outlined God's freedom. He consequently rejected absolute merit by indicating that God was kind to make a covenant with his creature, who had every obligation to obey and no intrinsic right to a reward. This point had the disproportionality issue in view. Once God made that covenant though, it 'impels' him to reward Adam's obedience to the natural law.

---

52. Frans Burman, *Synopsis theologiae et speciatim oeconomiae Foederum Dei, ab initio saeculorum usque ad consummationem eorum*, 2 vol. (Utrecht, 1671–72), 1.46.9 (Quod de merito ipsorum quaeritur, an istud ipsis tribui, ipsorumque remuneratio & vitae aeternae praemium illi adscribi possit; id quidem Scripturae non repugnat, modo meritum id non fundetur in intrinseca quadam operum dignitate, sed in liberali repromissione divina; quale meritum ex pacto, atque operum justitia, etiam homini primo, si obediens permansisset, competivisset).

53. Burman, *Synopsis theologiae*, 2.2.4 (Atque ex hac Dei benignitate est, quod creaturam sibi ultro subditam, ac ex naturali obligatione omnia debentem, inito foedere ad propriorem sui communionem invitare, ac imperium suum plane despoticum ista amoris & mutuae obligationis Ἀκρασία temperare voluerit. Ut jam homo, certissimo aditu ad beatitudinem facto, eam non ex mera solum Dei bonitate, & naturali in creaturas amore, sibi quoquo modo polliceri, verum etiam ex pacto, adeoque propter veritatem & fidelitatem Dei certo expectare possit. Atque infert haec foederis conventio remunerationem ac liberalitatem quandam majorem & abundantiorem, quam homo sibi ex jure Dei per naturam cognito promittere potuisset).

Burman noted how the law was the premise of this covenant and the condition for Adam to have union and communion with God. Connecting legal and relational aspects, he contended that 'God declares by the extensive law the method of perceiving his love and of enjoying union and his communion; and man in return embraces that method prescribed in the covenant, and promises himself for enduring service, and expects reward and payment because of the covenant.'[54] In respect to the condition, he qualified Adam's potential: 'and merit would obtain in only *this human state* [before the fall], but even then not another way than by the covenant and generous promise.'[55] The covenant of works was then the intersection of God's love for Adam and Adam's way to return God's love, all leading to eschatological life.

Burman also employed *meritum ex pacto* for the other motif of explaining Christ's work. Concerning the sponsor of the covenant of grace, he wrote:

> His exaltation had to consist not barely in the payment of eternal life, in so far as it was the reward of the covenant of works, must be conferred to him by justice, but just as he accepted this specific mandate from the Father, so also he initiated a specific covenant with him, in which the reward was likewise promised to him alone, and as the God man's merit is clearly greater than the bare man's, thus also glorious exaltation was owed to him, not by the covenant of works simpliciter, but because of his covenant with the Father.[56]

In this passage, Burman outright formulated the covenant of redemption, wherein the trinitarian persons covenant together concerning the plan of salvation, with Christ earning his glorious (re)exaltation because of

---

54. Burman, *Synopsis theologiae*, 2.2.6 (Foedus Dei est conventio inter Deum & hominem, qua Deus lata lege declarat homini rationem percipiendi sui amoris, & unione ac communione ipsius fruendi; & homo rursus rationem foedere praescriptam amplectitur, ac servaturum sese promittit, & ex foedere remunerationem ac mercedem expectat).

55. Burman, *Synopsis theologiae*, 2.3.21 (Atque in hoc solo hominis statu meritum obtinuisset, sed non aliud quam ex pacto, ac liberli repromissione) (emphasis added).

56. Burman, *Synopsis theologiae*, 2.15.13 (Quae ejus exaltatio non nude consistere debuit in collatione vitae aeternae, quod erat praemium foederis operum cuilibet justo conferendum; sed sicut ille peculiare mandatum a Patre acceperat, & peculiare pactum cum eo inierat, quo singulare etiam praemium ipsi promissum erat; & sicut θεανθρωπος meritum majus plane est merito nudi hominis; ita etiam gloriosior exaltatio ipsi debebatur; non ex foedere operum simplici, sed ex pacto illo cum Patre).

his covenant with the Father. Burman upheld that Christ had genuine condign merit in addition to this covenantal merit: 'Since this exaltation was owed to the Son because of this covenant, there is a reason to call his obedience and subjection truly and properly merit ... and this merit was not only by the covenant, but was also condign.'[57] Burman then incorporated both motifs concerning *meritum ex pacto* into his theology both to explain how Adam could earn a reward in the covenant of works, while polemically excluding Roman notions of post-fall merit, and to explain how Christ earned salvation for his people.

As the seventeenth century wore on, key figures maintained and developed the concept of *meritum ex pacto*. Some very well-known theologians, such as Francis Turretin (1623–87) and Herman Witsius (1636–1708), furthered this notion, more fully tying it into their understanding of the covenant of works. Turretin, who studied in Geneva, Leiden, Utrecht, Paris, Saumur, Montauban, and Nîmes before returning to Geneva as pastor and professor of theology, used *meritum ex pacto* in connection to the covenant of works as a polemical tool against Roman notions of condign and congruent merit.[58] Turretin distinguished strict merit from covenantal merit, underscoring that creatures as such cannot demand a reward from God in a strict and proper sense. Nonetheless,

---

57. Burman, *Synopsis theologiae*, 2.15.14 (Cum autem exaltatio haec Filio ex pacto isto debita fuerit, obedientia & subjectio ejus veri & proprie dicti meriti rationem habuit ... meritum hic fuit non tantum ex pacto, sed etiam ex condigno: tanta enim humiliatio tantae personae gloriae isti & exaltationi proportionata fuit).

58. Emidio Campi, 'FrançoisTurrettini,' *Dictionnaire Historique de la Suisse*, accessed on July 3, 2020 at https://hls-dhs-dss.ch/fr/articles/011337/2012-12-07/; 'Funeral Oration of Benedict Pictet concerning the Life and Death of Francis Turretin,' in Francis Turretin, *Institutes of Elenctic Theology*, trans. George Musgrave Geiger, ed. James T. Dennison, Jr., 3 vol. (Phillipsburg, NJ: P&R, 2007), 3:659-76. For other secondary literature on Turretin's covenant theology and use of *meritum ex pacto*, see Beach, *Christ and the Covenant*, 196-202; Stephen J. Grabill, *Rediscovering the Natural Law in Reformed Theological Ethics* (Grand Rapids: Eerdmans, 2006), 151-74; James F. Bruce, *Rights in the Law: The Importance of God's Free Choices in the Thought of Francis Turretin* (Göttingen: Vandenhoeck & Ruprecht, 2013); HyunKwan Kim, 'Francis Turrretin on Human Free Choice: Walking the Fine Line between Synchronic Contingency and Compatibilist Determinism,' *Westminster Theological Journal* 79 (2017): 25-44; J. Mark Beach, 'Reading Turretin: Some Observations on Francis Turretin's Institutes of Elenctic Theology,' *Mid-America Journal of Theology* 27 (2016): 67-84; B. Hoon Woo, 'The Difference between Scotus and Turretin in Their Formulation of the Doctrine of Freedom,' *Westminster Theological Journal* 78 (2016): 249-69; Lucas W. Sharley, 'Calvin and Turretin's Views of the Trinity in the Dereliction,' *The Reformed Theological Review* 75, no. 1 (April 2016): 21-34.

God can promise a reward to us upon the conditions of a covenant that he makes with us, which undermines the premises for Roman doctrines of condign and congruent merit, especially in regard to the way that sinners can be saved.[59] Furthermore, Turretin used the doctrine of *meritum ex pacto* to address that issue of disproportionality between the works Adam could offer and the reward that he would receive in the covenant of works.[60] Turretin closely followed Cocceius in using *meritum ex pacto* to support the real distinction between works and grace.[61] Thus, Turretin is another example of using *ex pacto* to address the proportionality challenge and to defend the law-gospel distinction.

Turretin connected the covenant of works closely to Adam's created nature, so linking the law's demands to Adam's upright state. This covenant is natural 'because it was established in human nature as it was originally created by God, and in its integrity or abilities.' The covenant is then legal 'because the condition on man's part was the observation of the natural law, which he had stamped into him.'[62] Turretin stated that Adam's reward would have been everlasting life, but the condition was his perfect, personal, and proper obedience.[63] He argued that any help that God gave to Adam 'did not extend to pouring any new virtue into him, but only to revealing the power of that strength which he had received.'[64] Notably, even Adam's virtues, which are fruits of faculties, are not new or superadded to human nature. This point highlights how the Reformed were responding to the Roman view of the nature-grace distinction, by-and-large rejecting the *donum superadditum*.

---

59. Beach, *Christ and the Covenant*, 196-202.

60. Cornelis P. Venema, *Christ and Covenant Theology: Essays on Election, Republication, and the Covenants* (Philipsburg, NJ: P&R, 2017), 88-89, 136 n.86.

61. Beach, *Christ and the Covenants*, 119.

62. Franciscus Turrettinus, *Institutio Theologiae Elencticae*, 3 vol. (Geneva, 1679–85), 8.3.5 (Foedus naturae est, quod Deus Creator cum homine integro, tanquam sua creatura pactus est, de illo felicitate, & vita aeterna donando sub conditione perfectae & personalis obedientiae: Vocatur naturale, non ab obligatione naturali, quae nulla est Dei erga hominam; sed quia in natura hominis, prout primitus a Deo condita est, & in illius integritate, seu viribus fundatur. Dicitur etiam legale, quia conditio ex parte hominis fuit observatio legis naturae, quam sibi habebat insculptam. Et operum, quia operibus, seu obedientia ejus propria nitebatur).

63. Turrettinus, *Institutio*, 17.5.8.

64. Turrettinus, *Institutio*, 8.3.14 (Quod auxilium non tendebat ad virtutem novam aliquam ipsi infundendam, sed tantum ad efficaciam illius virtutis exerendam, quam acceperat).

Turretin maintained some familiar constructions regarding *meritum ex pacto*. He argued that Adam as God's creature had the absolute, inviolable requirement to obey God. God, however, covenanted that this requirement was the meritorious condition, not as such but according to the terms of the covenant, for Adam to earn his reward from God. On man's side, 'the condition was not only according to the covenant, but also absolute and from the nature of the thing.' By founding the principle for Adam to earn reward, however, on God's side, 'the condition was free inasmuch as it depends upon the covenant or free promise, according to which God was bound by an oath, not to the man, but to himself and his own goodness, faithfulness, and truthfulness (Rom. 3:1; 2 Tim. 2:13).' God had no debt to man 'properly speaking' but 'only a debt of faithfulness rising from the promise by which God revealed his constancy and his infallible and immutable truth.' Addressing the major theme of disproportionality, this merit was 'not in respect to the proportion and condignity of the duty that man rendered to God (Rom. 8:18; Luke 17:10), but in respect to God's covenant and covenanted justice, namely faithfulness.'[65] Although God had no natural debt to Adam, his voluntary action of covenanting with Adam forged a condition of 'covenanted justice,' indicating that Turretin thought that the covenant of works was a matter of justice rather than grace.[66]

Turretin further explained that this covenantal arrangement did include a component of merit, not strictly speaking but according to the covenant:

> If, therefore, upright man in that upright state had obtained this merit, it must not be understood properly and rigorously because, since man has

---

65. Turrettinus, *Institutio*, 8.3.16 (XVI. Ex hac vero pactione nascitur obligation mutual partium, quae diversa est pro conditione earum; Nam respectu hominis, non tantum fuit ex pacto, sed absoluta & simplex ex natura rei, tum propter Deum, cui homo tanquam creatura Creatori, beneficiaries benefactor seipsum totum, & quicquid erat Deo debebat, & illum toto corde amare tenebatur. Sed respectu Dei, fuit gratuita, utpote pendens ex pacto seu promissione gratuita, per quam Deus, non ipsi homini, sed sibi, suaeque bonitati, fidelitati, & veracitati obstringebatur Roman. 3.1. 2. Tim. 2.13. nullam ergo fuit debitum proprie dictum, nisi quo homini jus posset nasci, sed tantum fidelitatis debitum, ex promissione ortum, quod ejus constantiam, & veritatem infallibilem & immutabilem ostendit. Quod si Apostolus jus sive debitum videtur agnoscere, Rom. 4.4. non alio sensu intelligendum est, quam respective, non ad proportionem, & condignitatem officii, quod homo praestat Deo Rom. 8.18. Luc. 17.10. Sed Dei pactum, & paciscentis justitiam, id. fidelitatem).

66. Turrettinus, *Institutio*, 17.5.6-7, 25.

everything from God and owed everything to God, he can demand nothing from him as by right, nor can God be a debtor to him. This merit was not according to the condignity of the work and from its intrinsic value because whatever sort it may be, it cannot have any proportion with the infinite reward of life; but by the covenant and God's liberal promise according to which man did have the right of demanding the reward, according to which God had voluntarily obligated himself. And to compare with the covenant of grace, it depends upon only Christ's merit, by which he acquired the right unto life for us, but this covenant antecedently demanded proper and personal obedience, by which he obtained both his own justification before God and life, as the covenanted reward of his labor.[67]

Turretin addressed the issue of disproportion between Adam's work and the reward God offered. The disproportion meant that Adam could not achieve any proper merit.[68] Still, the principle of covenanted justice meant that Adam's covenantal merit even gave him the right to demand his reward if he fulfilled the covenant's conditions.[69]

In implementing *meritum ex pacto* as a polemic against Roman doctrine, Turretin developed the theme also regarding justification. Just as Cocceius had argued that in the covenant of grace sinners must lean entirely upon Christ's merits and not add their own works to it, so too Turretin argued in regard to the link between good works and eternal life that there is 'a relation of order and connection of the sort that is between a means unto the end, of the way unto goal, of the contest unto the crown, of the antecedent unto the consequent.'[70] Turretin was clear that this principle that works lead to eternal life is *not* a description of the

---

67. Turrettinus, *Institutio*, 8.3.17 (emphasis original; XVII. Si quod ergo meritum homo integet in illo statu obtinuisset, non intelligendum est proprie & in rigore, quia cum homo omnia habeat a Deo, & Deo debeat, nihil jure tanquam suum potest ab illo repetere, nec Deus illi debitor esse potest: Non per condignitatem operis, & ex intrinseco ejus valore, quia qualecunque illud sit, nullam proportionem habere potest cum praemio vitae infinito; Sed ex pacto, & liberali Dei promissione, juxta quam jus postulandi praemii homo habuisset, ad quod Deus ultro se obligaverat. Et compare ad foedus gratiae, quod solo merito Christi nititur, quo jus ad vitam nobis acquirit: Hoc vero obedientiam propriam & personalem postulabat antecedenter, ex qua & justificationem suam coram Deo, & vitam obtineret, tanquam mercedem pactam sui laboris).

68. Turrettinus, *Institutio*, 17.5.7, 13.

69. Turrettinus, *Institutio*, 17.5.7, 14, 25.

70. Turrettinus, *Institutio*, 17.5.13 (Fatemur enim dari relationem ordinis & connexionis, qualis est inter medium ad finem, vaie ad metam, certaminis ad coronam, antecedentis ad consequens).

Christian life of sanctification, but of how merit – which can exist only according to the covenant – operates. Such is the role that his statement played in his argument against Roman views of merit.[71] Again similar to Cocceius, in order to explain how sinners can obtain everlasting life if works are the antecedent condition for it, Turretin explained, 'Because Christ most fully merited life and salvation for us, there can then be no place for our merits (Acts 20:28; Heb. 9:12; Acts 4:12).'[72] Turretin was equally clear that humans as God's creatures cannot merit anything from God on intrinsic grounds, and that the covenant's set terms of justice meant that merit remained merit and the conditions could not be diluted.

Witsius, who taught at the universities in Franeker, Utrecht, and Leiden, represents further Dutch use of *meritum ex pacto*, tying it to the doctrine of justification by including it in his understanding of the covenant of redemption.[73] Because 'there is a covenant between the Father and Son,' as Witsius cited Isaiah 53:10, 'By fulfilling the condition, the Son acquired the right to the reward for himself, and thus has merit by the covenant.' Witsius then raised the recurring issue of proportionality, arguing that, 'since this is not a mere man's obedience, but Christ's, the God-man's,' his obedience is 'likewise of infinite value.' So, for his reward, Christ 'has the just proportion corresponding to that highest glory, and to this point is merit, which they call condign, in a way that no mere creature carries.'[74] Witsius' approach was similar to Chamier's and especially Burman's, which further confirms that there were two running themes for *meritum ex pacto* in the early-modern period.

Benedict Pictet (1655–1724), Turretin's nephew, was an important theologian in Geneva in the period of high orthodoxy, playing a

---

71. Turrettinus, *Institutio*, 17.5.14-19, 23.

72. Turrettinus, *Institutio*, 17.5.18 (Quia Christus vitam & salutem nobis plentissime meruit, unde nullus dari potest locus meritis nostris Act. 20.28. Heb. 9.12. Act. 4.12).

73. Fesko, *Covenant of Redemption*, 83-108.

74. Herman Witsius, *De Oeconomia Foederum Dei cum Hominibus*, 3rd ed. (Utrecht, 1694), 2.3.33 (Quum enim hoc pactum inter Patrem & Filium sit, si anima Filii se posuerit victimam pro peccato, videbit semen. Ies. LIII.10. conditione praestita, Filius sibi jus acquisivit ad mercedem, & sic habet meritum ex pacto. Imo quum obedientia haec non meri hominis sit, sed Christi θεανθρωπος, personae infinitae, ipsa quoque infinitae Dignitatis est, consequenter justam proportionem habet ad maximam gloriam illi respondentem, atque hactenus est meritum, quod vocant de condigno, quale in nullam meram creaturam cadit).

significant role as a pastor and instructor in the academy, as well as in other developing institutions.[75] Pictet's work deserves attention as representative of Genevan Reformed thought into the eighteenth century, particularly in reference to his covenant theology. Though the deconfessionalization period began before his ministry, Pictet argued for the Swiss to maintain the Helvetic Formula Consensus as the ecclesiastical confession.

Among the theologians whom we have surveyed, Pictet most clearly explained the connections among the doctrines of justification, the covenant of works, and covenantal merit. He described justification as it theoretically applied to Adam before the fall, arguing that justification can be considered as it related to humanity in different conditions: 'either as innocent and upright, or as a sinner, but repentant and believing, or as regenerate and endeavoring after holiness.'[76] He further explained that Adam before the fall could have merited everlasting life because of 'the free covenant' God made with him. Bringing together two recurring applications of *meritum ex pacto*, Pictet defended the Reformed view of justification by outlining how Adam's potential to merit points to Christ's real merit for us. Pictet's argument is worth quoting in full:

> We say, however, that if the first man would have endured in innocence, then he would have been justified by fulfilling the natural law, which God had imprinted upon his heart, along with the other precepts which God could have prescribed to him, namely that he must perfectly love his God and his neighbor. For if he would have fulfilled this mandate, then he would have been declared righteous, and would have acquired for himself the right to glory, not indeed as if he had properly merited it, because in fact a creature is able to merit nothing from the Creator, except by the free covenant by which God would have rewarded him those things by payment .... The way is most different by which a man could have been justified in the first covenant [of works], and the way by which he is justified in the gospel covenant, and the distinction is between the conditions which

---

75. 'Bénédict Pictet,' *Dictionnaire Historique de la Suisse*, accessed on August 2, 2019 at https://hls-dhs-dss.ch/fr/articles/011291/2010-02-26/; Martin I. Klauber, 'Family Loyalty and Theological Transition in Post-Reformation Geneva: The Case of Benedict Pictet (1655–1724),' *Fides et Historia* 24, no. 1 (Winter/Spring 1992): 54-67; Eugne de Budé, *Vie de Bénédict Pictet, theologien genevois* (1655–1724) (Lausanne: Georges Bridel, 1874).

76. Benedict Pictet, *Theologia Christiana* (Geneva, 1716), 703 (vel ut innocens & Justus, vel ut peccator, sed poenitens & credens, vel ut regenitus & sanctitati incumbens).

God demands in either covenant, and between the foundation because of which a person is justified in either. The way by which God would have justified the innocent person would have been a declaration of the person's holiness and righteousness, and that justification, therefore, can be defined as God's act as judge, by which he grants everlasting life and glory to the perfectly holy person. The way by which God justifies in the gospel covenant, as we will see, is by remitting sins. The requisite condition for the first man was perfect holiness, but the condition afterwards by which a person is justified in the gospel covenant is faith. The foundation of the first type of justification was the merit of good works, although as has been said, nevertheless it cannot properly be called merit. The foundation of justification in the gospel is Christ's death and satisfaction.[77]

Pictet outlined a precise and calibrated covenant theology that accounted for new developments throughout the Reformed world. He posited a covenant between God and Adam that established the principle of merit for Adam to gain his eschatological reward, addressing the challenge of proportionality. His further qualification excluded absolute merit, so that merit could not possibly be a post-fall category, thereby defending the law-gospel distinction. Lastly, he shifted the ground from mere human merit to Christ's merits as the foundation of justification in the covenant of grace, so that all the merit needed for believing sinners to have everlasting communion with God has been achieved for us. Our argument in chapters six and seven may not be much more than a substantiating and updating of Pictet's argument.

---

77. Pictet, *Theologia Christiana*, 704-5 (Dicimus autem quod primus homo, si in innocentia permansisset, justificatus fuisset adimplendo legem naturalem, quam ipsius cordi impresserat Deus, & alia praecepta, quae Deus ipsi praescribere poterat, diligendo perfecte Deum suum & proximum; Nam si haec mandata praestitisset, declaratus fuisset justus, & jus sibi peperisset ad gloriam, non quidem quasi eam proprie meruisset, nihil enim mereri potest creatura a Creatore, sed ex liberali pacto quo Deus ista mercede eum remuneraturus fuisset ... Diversissimus est modus, quo homo justificatus fuisset in primo foedere, & modus quo justificatur in foedere Evangelico, & discrimen est inter conditiones quas Deus in utroque foedere exigit, & inter fundamentum propter quod justificatur in utraquo homo. Modus quo Deus justificasset hominem innocentem, fuisset declaratio sanctitatis & justitiae hominis; unde justification illa definiri potuisset; Actio Dei judicis, qua hominem perfectè sanctum vita donat aterna & gloria. Modus quo Deus justificat in foedere Evangelico, ut videbimus, est remittendo peccata; Conditio requisita in primo homine fuit perfecta sanctitas, At Conditio sub qua justificatur homo in Evangelico foedere est fides; fundamentum justificationis primae fuisset dignitas bonorum operum, quamvis, ut dixi, proprie tamen mereri dici non potuisset; fundamentum justificationis Evangelicae est mors & satisfactio Christi).

Conclusion

This chapter argued that Reformed writers defended Protestant soteriology by using *meritum ex pacto* as a polemic against Roman Catholic paradigms of merit. The theme was not necessarily predominant or centrally important, but some Reformed theologians did implement it. Firstly, they employed it to explain their covenant theology – namely, the covenant of works – by using it to ground the way that God could let Adam earn, even merit, a reward by his works even though creatures cannot intrinsically merit anything from their Creator. Secondly, they applied it to explain Christ's work by using it to establish why the eternal Son of God, whose life was of infinite value and so would have intrinsically condign merit, earned specific things – namely, exaltation for himself and salvation for believers – through his incarnate obedience.

This main argument raises two subsidiary conclusions on the historical side. First, the Reformed writers who used the *meritum ex pacto* concept lived and worked in various places. This chapter examined sources from Germany, the Netherlands, France, and England, showing us that, at least geographically, *meritum ex pacto* was in widespread use. That breadth of occurrence indicates significant intellectual traffic across the Continent and to what is now the United Kingdom. That widespread use also indicates that Reformed writers were implementing this idea apart from a concern to refute any one locally isolated issue. They employed *meritum ex pacto* as a device to support the burgeoning pan-Reformed structures of covenant theology and to explain the obvious shared concern about Christ's work.

Second, just as *meritum ex pacto* was used across the geographical spectrum, so too was it chronologically widespread. The sources examined range from the late-sixteenth to the early-eighteenth century. The at least two centuries of use shows that even if *meritum ex pacto* was a minor theme, it was an enduring one. It was not constructed spontaneously to address a passing issue but remained valuable to some throughout the ongoing development of Reformed theology even after the wane of high orthodoxy. It was, therefore, a genuine feature of the Reformed tradition.

The theological payoff, building at least one directional marker toward our own doctrinal construction in later chapters, is a Reformed trend of using *meritum ex pacto* in the connection between Adam's created nature and our eschatological destiny. As noted throughout this chapter, recurring concerns included the issue of (dis)proportionality of human works to heavenly reward and the integrity of the law-gospel distinction. This historical discussion then helps us see even more why this book angles to defend the law-gospel distinction through the lens of original righteousness in connection to bearing God's image: these concepts are all covenantally grounded according to the internal principles of the Reformed system. Not every Reformed appeal to *meritum ex pacto* was uniform, but the constellation of explanations explored in this chapter provides various footholds that can be synthesized when we come to our own doctrinal construction later in this book. The next two chapters explore the medieval and modern Roman views concerning their paradigm of the orders of nature and grace. In that paradigm, merit is an ontological issue, necessitating grace even before the fall to raise human nature, so that our works would then be inherently meritorious. The medievals drew upon a construct of the nature-grace distinction wherein grace addressed the ontological limits of creaturely nature. This context sets in brighter relief why the Reformed responded by articulating that God addressed the problem of disproportionality before the fall by way of covenant, not ontology.

CHAPTER THREE

Medieval Discussions about Adam's Original Righteousness

The previous chapter's outline of Reformed conceptions of *meritum ex pacto* marked the twofold concern to consider the issue of proportionality and the law-gospel distinction in covenantal terms. That foundation demands further contextualization to determine why covenantal merit would usefully support the Reformed concerns. We need to understand more fully how Reformed and Roman Catholic theologies have opposing views about Adam's created nature concerning his original righteousness that undergird differing concepts of merit. How the nature-grace distinction is parsed then founds any view of merit and works.

The Reformed hold that God, by creating Adam in the divine image, gave the gift of original righteousness to humanity so that it is intrinsic to human nature, being built into God's image as a *concreated* gift (*donum concreatum*). Original righteousness is a gift, in that God gives it to us, but is not a gift distinct from our natural constitution as God's image bearers.[1] Just like the color of a plastic army man is inextricably imbedded in its very makeup, based on the plastic used, so too original righteousness is created intrinsically into human nature as we are made according to the blueprint of *God's* image. For the

---

1. Categorizing original righteousness as a gift entails only that it is *given* by God, not that it is distinct from created human nature; J. V. Fesko, *Adam and the Covenant of Works* (Fearn: Mentor, 2021), 388-91.

Reformed, Adam's natural strength to obey God was then part of human constitution.[2]

By contrast, Roman Catholicism rejects that Adam was created with the *natural* righteousness and holiness sufficient to merit eschatological reward. The development of medieval theology shows that modern Roman theology adopted a specific understanding of the *superadded* gift (*donum superadditum*), teaching that Adam's original righteousness was distinct from and supplemental to basic human nature.[3] Just like paint is applied to furniture in addition to its original constitution, so too Rome views original righteousness as somewhat distinct from human nature.

The Roman tradition concerning grace can be hard for Protestants to understand because of the differing paradigms. Its key feature to know at the outset is that Rome views grace as ontological, meaning it elevates nature. In this scheme, 'sanctifying grace' – distinct from actual grace concerning particular actions – is grace that raises human nature to have supernatural habits or even supernatural faculties of sorts.

This chapter argues that medieval theology developed multiple formulations of this *donum superadditum*, all still suggesting that God elevated Adam's nature as such so that Adam could merit eschatological, supernatural blessings. In the twelfth and thirteenth centuries, Hugh of St. Victor (*c.* 1096–1141) and William of Auxerre (*c.* 1150–1231), both lecturing in Paris, distinguished nature from God's sanctifying grace added to human nature making our works meritorious – merit simply concerns whether someone justly has a right to a reward. These developments were driven by a concern to delineate the natural and supernatural orders more clearly, likely *initially* with Augustinian concerns to delimit grace's precise function.[4]

Centered in the Paris schools, medieval theologians built upon Peter Lombard's ideas to develop the idea of sanctifying grace supplementing nature as the explanatory factor in human merit, albeit the Thomistic and Franciscan traditions shaped this teaching in different ways. This

---

2. Richard A. Muller, *Dictionary of Latin and Greek Theological Terms: Drawn Principally from Protestant Scholastic Theology*, 2nd ed. (Grand Rapids, MI: Baker Academic, 2017), 97-98.

3. Muller, *Dictionary*, 98-99.

4. Alister E. McGrath, *Iustitia Dei: A History of the Christian Doctrine of Justification*, 4th ed. (Cambridge: Cambridge University Press, 2020), 103-8.

ontological outlook wherein nature *per se* needed grace – even prior to Adam's fall – to make our works meritorious characterized, to varying degrees, mainstream medieval theology. We stand in a better position to formulate our own doctrinal stance when we have a clearer picture of the winding roadmap of historical theology.

The Roots of Debate

The later medieval paradigms of merit grow from a more fundamental commitment to the view that human nature must be elevated by grace to be oriented to supernatural ends. The development of that growing discussion throughout the medieval period reveals the conceptual complexities underlying the categories we are investigating: nature, supernature, grace, and merit.[5] The winding trail of medieval thought on these matters follows how they related these categories to one another, illumining why Reformed people should formulate our understanding of the covenant of works in a specific way. That medieval trail begins with Peter Lombard.

Lombard taught theology at Notre Dame in Paris and eventually became bishop of Paris in the year before he died. His magnum opus was *The Sentences in Four Books*, which became the standard theological textbook across the Christian west for centuries.[6] In this work, Lombard collected quotations from the standard authoritative sources, drawing them together under the four headings of the Trinity, Creation, the Incarnation, and the Signs.[7] In later periods of the medieval era, theologians lectured and wrote commentaries on Lombard's *Sentences*.[8]

---

5. Although aimed at a very particular discussion concerning the orders of nature and grace, Lawrence Feingold, *The Natural Desire to See God According to St. Thomas Aquinas and His Interpreter*, 2nd ed. (Faith & Reason: Studies in Catholic Theology and Philosophy; Naples, FL: Sapientia Press, 2010), *passim*.

6. For an excellent survey of university curriculum in Lombard's wake leading to the thirteenth century, see Jacob W. Wood, *To Stir a Restless Heart: Thomas Aquinas and Henri de Lubac on Nature, Grace, and the Desire for God* (Thomistic Ressourcement Series; Washington, DC: Catholic University of America Press, 2019), 37-64.

7. Philipp W. Rosemann, *Peter Lombard* (Great Medieval Thinkers; New York: Oxford University Press, 2004), 3-7.

8. G. R. Evans (ed.), *Medieval Commentaries on the* Sentences *of Peter Lombard Volume 1: Current Research* (Leiden: Brill, 2002); Philipp W. Rosemann (ed.), *Medieval Commentaries on the* Sentences *of Peter Lombard Volume 2* (Leiden: Brill, 2010); Philipp W. Rosemann (ed.), *Medieval Commentaries on the* Sentences *of Peter Lombard Volume 3* (Leiden: Brill, 2015).

As we will see, the medieval commentary tradition on Lombard's *Sentences* was a center of development for the issues of nature, grace, and merit.

The lodestar for the commentary tradition on this intersection of issues was Lombard's discussion of whether Adam needed grace before the fall and whether he had virtues before the fall. Concerning Adam's need for grace, Lombard cited Augustine to argue that Adam required grace before the fall, not to free his will to do good but to enable him to do that good which he was not able to do on his own.[9] In other words, Adam needed grace in order to merit blessing: 'For he was not able to deserve [*mereri*] the good without grace.'[10] Grace was then the precondition for merit: 'there could not have been any merit without grace because, although sin could only have been brought about by free choice, yet the same free choice was not sufficient to have or retain righteousness without the imparting of divine aid.'[11] Lombard then thought Adam needed grace to merit before the fall.[12]

Lombard's answer about whether Adam had virtues before the fall is the discussion that sparked complicated trajectories about human nature spanning the medieval period into the modern day. The commentary tradition on Lombard's statements spawns the whole discussion about 'pure nature' in the sense of humanity divested of original righteousness that relates us to God as fundamentally religious creatures. The distinction between nature and graced-nature-enabled-to-merit is one of our touchpoints to see why covenantal merit is the most effective way to formulate the covenant of works.

What did Lombard say about Adam's original righteousness then? As usual for his *Sentences*, Lombard was reflecting upon quotations and the preceding tradition. He wrote concerning where man had virtues before the fall:

9. Jean-Pierre Torrell, O.P., 'Nature and Grace in Thomas Aquinas,' in Serge-Thomas Bonino, O.P. (ed.), *Surnaturel: A Controversy at the Heart of Twentieth-Century Thomistic Thought*, trans. Robert Williams (Faith and Reason: Studies in Catholic Theology and Philosophy; Ave Maria, FL: Sapientia Press, 2009), 156-57.

10. Peter Lombard, *The Sentences Book 2: On Creation*, trans. Giulio Silano (Toronto: Pontifical Institute of Medieval Studies, 2008), 29.1.2.

11. Lombard, *Sentences 2*, 29.1.2.

12. Wood, *Stir a Restless Heart*, 46-47.

It seems to some that he did not have it, and they strive to prove it by saying as follows: He did not have righteousness, because he held God's command in contempt .... In response to these, we say that he certainly did not have these virtues when he sinned, but that he had them before, and then he lost them.[13]

He concluded his whole argument, 'it is not to be doubted that man before sin shone with the virtues, but he was despoiled of them through sin.'[14] The virtues Lombard had in mind pertained explicitly to *righteousness*, raising the issue of whether Adam was invested with original righteousness as God's image bearer. Often in medieval theology, 'virtue' as a certain perfection of a power was associated with original righteousness in the proper ordering of our faculties.[15] Even when considering man's creation, Lombard connected it to righteousness: 'image is considered in the knowledge of truth, his likeness in the love *of virtue*' so that 'image pertains to form, likeness to nature.'[16] Again, righteousness was tied to the virtues related to Adam's original creation. Lombard, acknowledging that some denied that Adam had righteousness before the fall, affirmed that Adam had virtues before he sinned. He said that Adam lost these virtues, seemingly because of sin.

The lingering question for Lombard is, did God make Adam with that virtuous righteousness or did Adam somehow have to acquire it? Lombard's earlier discussion about man's grace and power before the fall injected this topic with debatable vagueness that fueled discussion across the medieval period about whether God needed to supplement Adam's original constitution to enable him to merit. Lombard certainly argued that Adam needed extra help to perform well enough to obtain eschatological reward, writing that man 'was able in some way to live well through that help [of the strength of his created nature] because he was able to live without sin; but without the additional help of grace, he was not able to live spiritually so as to deserve [*mereri*] eternal life.'[17]

---

13. Lombard, *Sentences 2*, 29.2.1.

14. Lombard, *Sentences 2*, 29.2.2.

15. e.g. St. Thomas Aquinas, *Summa Theologica*, trans. by Fathers of the English Dominican Province, 5 vol. (New York, NY: Benziger Bros., 1948; repr. Notre Dame, IN: Christian Classics, 1981), 1a2ae.55.1

16. Lombard, *Sentences 2*, 16.3.5.

17. Lombard, *Sentences 2*, 24.1.2.

Lombard seemed to plant at least the seed, if not the root, of the later Roman notion of pure nature as a version of human life aimed for earthly purposes, strong enough to avoid sin, but lacking orientation toward supernatural life with God. Although acknowledging that other theologians demurred, Lombard asserted that, 'man would not have been able to make progress or to have merit through the grace of creation.'[18] Adam needed extra grace above the strength which God gave to him by creation to raise his bare nature to the possibility of obtaining spiritual reward.

Medieval theologians differed on this point, as the rest of this chapter argues, developing various constructions of how the *donum superadditum* related to Adam's first condition. Nonetheless, Lombard's connection of original righteousness and the need for grace to merit eschatological life remained a linchpin in that discussion as various theologians reflected upon this matter.[19]

To keep our bearings in this book's argument, we argue that the covenant of works had the condition that if Adam fulfilled his *natural* obligations to the moral law, God would reward him with eschatological life. Hence, Adam's nature was oriented to supernatural communion with God by virtue of the covenant. Humans are fundamentally religious creatures, God having hardwired his image into our constitution, fitting us for the end of spiritual life with him, and creating us with the natural strength to fulfill our duties that had the accompanying prospect of eschatological reward. In other words, in contrast to much medieval theology wherein theologians articulated a need for Adam to receive sanctifying grace to elevate his nature unto spiritual purposes, God created us with supernatural ends and did not need to alter our nature ontologically to orient us toward that purpose.

The Thomist Trajectory

Thomas Aquinas, like Lombard, taught in Paris, leaving his *Summa Theologica* as his magnum opus on doctrinal teaching. Thomas' mature view in the *Summa* was that righteousness was given as part of our

---

18. Lombard, *Sentences 2*, 24.1.6.

19. Concerning the nature-grace discussion during the intervening period after Lombard, especially regarding theologians having direct affect upon the figures discussed here, see the very helpful if not crucial discussion in Wood, *Stir a Restless Heart*, 50-118.

original constitution, although hypothetically distinct, therefore, superadded. Before looking at that mature teaching, which distinguishes Thomas' view from the Franciscan tradition, we need to consider his earlier work centered on the instigating factor for this whole doctrinal trajectory, namely his commentary on Lombard's *Sentences*. By analyzing both sources, we see how Thomas shifted from an earlier semi-Pelagian view to a more Augustinian position.[20]

Before diving into the primary source material, we need to outline what we will call 'the Franciscan Pactum.' Even though this doctrine is more proper to the Franciscan tradition as explored later, introducing it now provides background to understand a lot of the following discussion.[21] This doctrinal axiom teaches that, 'God does not deny grace to those who do what lies within them' (*facientibus quod in se est, Deus non denegat gratiam*). Its point is that our best efforts according to whatever strength is in the nature we have (before and after the fall) to obtain grace.[22] More crassly put, anyone who tries their best will receive grace. One of the theological differences among Roman clerical orders is that Dominicans deny but Franciscans affirm that a person can merit grace. The Franciscan Pactum is a premise for meriting grace, in some cases even from an ungraced state. Dominicans, being more thoroughly Augustinian, insist that God must freely, even sovereignly, bestow grace in all cases. Concerning the whole sweep of our study, Heiko Oberman masterfully demonstrated how this formula came to dominate late medieval views of salvation, largely due to Franciscan influence.[23]

Thomas' commentary on Lombard reveals some mixed, perhaps conflicted, argumentation. He concluded that Adam had grace before the fall, since 'man became injured in nature by sin, and deprived of grace.'[24] Nonetheless, he also argued that Adam lacked this grace by

---

20. Michael Horton, *Justification*, 2 vol. (New Studies in Dogmatics; Grand Rapids, MI: Zondervan, 2018), 1:112-24; Joseph P. Wawrykow, *God's Grace and Human Action: Merit in the Theology of Thomas Aquinas* (Notre Dame, IN: University of Notre Dame Press, 1995), 266-76.

21. McGrath, *Iustitia Dei*, 159-60.

22. McGrath, *Iustitia Dei*, 135-45.

23. Heiko A. Oberman, *The Harvest of Medieval Theology: Gabriel Biel and Late Medieval Nominalism*, 3rd ed. (Grand Rapids, MI: Baker Academic, 2000), 120-84.

24. Thomas Aquinas, *Commentum in Libero II Sententiarum*, dist. 29. q. 1. art. 2, in Stanislai Eduardi Fretté and Pauli Maré (eds.), *Opera Omnia*, 34 vol. (Paris, 1871–80),

nature, so had to obtain it, marking how in his early theology he saw a period in which Adam lacked adequate ability by creation for merit. He reaches this conclusion through some grappling with his preceding tradition, wrestling with positions held by several disagreeing church authorities:

> Others, however, distinguish the state of innocence into two states: for they say that man, at the beginning of his creation, was created without grace in the state of natural gifts alone; but afterwards, before sin, he obtained grace, and according to this distinction the various sayings of the saints and teachers strive to agree. But this does not seem to agree with the sayings of the saints and teachers, who speak of the innocent state as if of one undistinguished state; and therefore this position is not of great authority.[25]

Thomas was aware of the tradition's tension, conceding that the developing gap between nature and grace was at odds with Augustine: 'others say that man was created in grace at the beginning of his creation; and indeed this position seems quite consistent with the opinion of Augustine, who posits that things were at the same time perfected and created in matter and form. But the first opinion seems to be more consistent with the opinion of other saints, who say that, through the succession of time, created things were perfected.'[26] Thomas felt strained to reconcile the Augustinian tradition with the fallout of more Lombardian argumentation.

In his early theology in his Lombard commentary, Thomas attempted this reconciliation by minimizing the temporal gap between Adam's

---

8:388 (Sed contra ... homo per peccatum fuit vulneratus in naturalibus, et spoliatus gratuitis, ut dicitur in Glossa Luc., x. Ergo gratiam habuit.).

25. Thomas, *Commentum in Libero II Sententiarum*, dist. 29. q. 1. art. 2, in *Opera Omnia*, 8:388 (Alii vero distinguunt statum innocentiae in duos status: dicunt enim quod homo in principio creationis suae sine gratia creatus est in naturalibus tantum; postmodum vero ante peccatum gratiam consecutus est, et secundum hanc distinctionem varia dicta sanctorum et doctorum concordare nituntur. Sed istud non videtur convenire dictis sanctorum et doctorum, qui de statu innocentise quasi de uno statu non distincto loquuntur; et ideo haec positio non magnae auctoritatis est.).

26. Thomas, *Commentum in Libero II Sententiarum*, dist. 29. q. 1. art. 2, in *Opera Omnia*, 8:388 (Ideo alii dicunt quod homo in principio creationis suae in gratia creatus est; et haec quidem positio satis congruere videtur opinioni Augustini, qui ponit res simul tempore perfectas fuisse et creatas in materia et in forma. Prima vero opinio magis congruere videtur opinion aliorum sanctorum, qui dicunt per successionem temporis res creatas perfectas fuisse.).

existence in ungraced nature and his obtaining grace. He wrote: 'It is, however, more probable that when man was created in natural integrity, which could not be disengaged, that having turned to God in the first instant of creation, he then obtained grace, and therefore this opinion must be said to be supported.'[27] Trying to harmonize Augustine's view with the event of ungraced nature, argued by later church theologians, he suggested that Adam turned to God to obtain grace in his very first moment of existence.[28] Thus early on, Thomas saw Adam's original state as one in which he needed to take action to order himself to fellowship with God from the state of pure nature. Thomas' early view evidences the semi-Pelagian premise that man could prepare himself for grace, that is, Thomas said man's action toward God prompts God to bestow first grace.[29] Still, even at this point in Thomas' theological career, he saw the need to side with Augustine more than anyone else. He, therefore, affirmed that man did not earn grace by acting according to pure nature: 'But grace is not merited by nature; whence nothing prevents that simultaneously grace is infused into nature.'[30] His rejection of the possibility to merit first grace, even tensely situated next to other ideas in his *Sentences* commentary, developed in his *Summa* to contrast more thoroughly with the Franciscan tradition.[31]

---

27. Thomas, *Commentum in Libero II Sententiarum*, dist. 29. q. 1. art. 2, in *Opera Omnia*, 8:388 (Hoc tamen probabilius est, ut cum homo creatus fuerit in naturalibus integris, quae otiosa esse non poterant, quod in primo instanti creationis ad Deum conversus, gratiam consecutus sit et ideo hanc opinionem sustinendo dicendum est.).

28. Daniel W. Houck, *Aquinas, Original Sin, and the Challenge of Evolution* (Cambridge: Cambridge University Press, 2020), 63-65.

29. Horton, *Justification*, 1:113, citing Bernard Blankenhorn, OP, 'Aquinas on Paul's Flesh/Spirit Anthropology in Romans,' in Matthew Levering and Michael Dauphinais (eds.), *Reading Romans with St. Thomas Aquinas* (Washington DC: The Catholic University of America Press, 2012), 33.

30. Thomas Aquinas, *Commentum in Libero II Sententiarum*, dist. 29. q. 1. art. 2, in *Opera Omnia*, 8:388 (Ad tertium dicendum, quod per gratiam aliquis meretur gloriam, et ideo convenienter gratia tempore gloriam praecedit. Sed per naturam non meretur gratiam; unde nihil impedit ut simul cum natura gratia infundatur.); see also *Commentum in Libero II Sententiarum*, dist. 27. q. 1. art. 4, sol., in *Opera Omnia*, 8:368-69; Wawrykow, *God's Grace and Human Action*, 87–88.

31. For a *detailed* analysis of Thomas' view of merit in his Lombard commentary, which notes the same theological shift, see Joseph P. Wawrykow, 'On the Purpose of "Merit" in the Theology of Thomas Aquinas,' *Medieval Philosophy and Theology* 2 (1992), 101-2; Wawrykow, *God's Grace and Human Action*, 83-91, 143-46; Bernard Lonergan, *Grace and Freedom: Operative Grace in the Thought of St. Thomas Aquinas* (London: Darton, Longman, and Todd, 1971), 6-7.

Thomas developed his view on this matter as he continued to teach and write. In his *Sentences* commentary, he argued an understanding of humanity as lacking the grace needed to obtain supernatural life, although Adam obtained that grace instantly. Later, he directly attacked the notion that man can prepare himself for grace, arguing from Lamentations 5:21 and 2 Corinthians 3:5, that 'we need the help of God's grace to prepare ourselves for grace.' He continued by tackling Pelagianism explicitly, contending that God must dispense grace freely since man cannot move toward God on his own. This contention marks a notable change in his earlier claim that Adam turned toward God in his first moment. He concluded, 'Therefore, people cannot prepare themselves for grace or do anything good without God's help.'[32] This Augustinian premise sets the stage for Thomas' doctrine of *auxilium*, which is discussed more below and becomes important in chapter five for assessing Thomas' relationship to the later Reformed tradition.

Thomas' *Summa* furthers his modified position, showing that he continued to find his earlier view at least somewhat wanting. In the *Summa*, Thomas drew the relationship more tightly between Adam's nature and capacity to merit. Of course, the discussion of righteousness and merit must be kept in the context of the *imago Dei*. Thomas said that God's image, which is not equal to its original because it is merely an analogical imitation, chiefly consists in the intellectual nature.[33] Thomas thought our position as God's image was principally clear in our natural fittingness (*aptitudinem*) 'for understanding and loving God.'[34] Thomas cited Colossians 3:10, where our renewal in God's image centers on knowledge.[35] Knowledge of God was a primary constitutive point of bearing the divine image.

Adam's natural fittingness to know God as his image bearer came with an eschatological orientation toward the beatific vision. Thomas

---

32. Thomas Aquinas, *Quodlibetal Questions*, trans. Turner Nevitt and Brian Davies (New York, NY: Oxford University Press, 2020), quod. I, quest. 4, art. 2 (pp.192-94).

33. Thomas, *Summa Theologica*, 1.93.3. For Thomas' explanation of how man bears God's likeness and image, see Thomas, *Summa Theologica*, 1.93.1, 9; Brian Davies, *Thomas Aquinas's Summa Theologiae: A Guide and Commentary* (New York, NY: Oxford University Press, 2014), 148.

34. Thomas, *Summa Theologica*, 1.93.4; Davies, *Thomas Aquinas's Summa Theologiae*, 148-49.

35. Thomas, *Summa Theologica*, 1.93.6

considered the beatific vision as direct intellectual perception of God's essence.[36] Since knowledge of God was inextricable from bearing the divine image, true beatitude (happiness) is in a consummate vision of the divine essence. Thomas said that Adam did not have this consummate vision because:

> Wherefore no one who sees the Essence of God can willingly turn away from God, which means to sin. Hence all who see God through His Essence are so firmly established in the love of God, that for eternity they can never sin. Therefore, as Adam did sin, it is clear that he did not see God through His Essence.[37]

According to Thomas, Adam's knowledge of God in his innocence was 'between our knowledge in the present state [as sinners], and the knowledge we shall have in heaven, when we see God through His Essence.'[38] Drawing on Augustine's description of humanity's relationship to sin, Thomas saw Adam in the created state as able to sin and able not to sin. If Adam had not sinned, he would have progressed to the beatific vision. Thomas summarized his eschatological understanding of our relation to the divine image, writing: 'Man was happy in paradise, but not with that perfect happiness to which he was destined, which consists in the vision of the Divine Essence.'[39] Thomas connected the divine image to eschatology via a tiered understanding of knowledge according to nature and glory.

For Thomas, our knowledge of God was natural. He stated, 'the first man was established by God in such a manner as to have knowledge of all those things for which man has a natural aptitude.'[40] Thomas had already argued that 'a natural aptitude for knowing God was the primary constituent in bearing God's image according to our intellectual nature, now entailing that we inescapably *do* know God because of that fittingness.'[41] Landing the point to differentiate Adam's

---

36. Carl R. Trueman, *Grace Alone: Salvation as a Gift of God* (The 5 Solas Series; Grand Rapids, MI: Zondervan, 2017), 98.

37. Thomas, *Summa Theologica*, 1.94.1

38. Thomas, *Summa Theologica*, 1.94.1.

39. Thomas, *Summa Theologica*, 1.94.1 ad 1.

40. Thomas, *Summa Theologica*, 1.94.3.

41. Thomas, *Summa Theologica*, 1.93.4.

natural knowledge of God from our fallen condition, Thomas argued: 'there was *no need* for the first man *to attain* to the knowledge of God by demonstration drawn from an effect, such as we need; since he knew God simultaneously in His effects, especially in the intelligible effects, according to his capacity.'[42] Thus, 'the first man was endowed with such a knowledge of these supernatural truths as was necessary for the direction of human life in that state.'[43] Adam did not need to learn knowledge of God because, in his original upright condition, he had knowledge of God that was as immediate as creatures can possess. Thomas' eschatological conception of our knowledge of God was that our natural knowledge of God was merely analogical but our knowledge of God in the beatific vision would be direct and essential. God having made us to know him and fitting us for knowing him in eschatological glory, the question is then how was Adam supposed to realize his eschatological potential?

Thomas taught that God created Adam in original righteousness but superadded sanctifying grace, whereby Adam could merit glory, to that rectitude. Returning to the same tension raised in his *Sentences* commentary, Thomas noted debate about whether Adam was created in grace. In contrast with his earlier work on Lombard, in the *Summa*, Thomas veered more thoroughly Augustinian, omitting the (even minimal) temporal gap between Adam's creation and reception of grace. He affirmed that Adam's first condition of rectitude demands that he was *created in* the condition of being oriented to God, concluding from Ecclesiastes 7:30 that, 'the *very rectitude* of the primitive state, *in which God made man*, seemingly requires that he was created in grace.'[44] Accordingly, 'original righteousness, *in which the first man was created*, was an accident pertaining to the nature of the species, not as caused by the principles of the species, but as a gift conferred by God on the entire human nature.'[45] Original righteousness pertained to our very nature as God's image but was accidental to nature, meaning that it was subsidiary

---

42. Thomas, *Summa Theologica*, 1.94.1 (emphasis added).

43. Thomas, *Summa Theologica*, 1.94.3.

44. Thomas, *Summa Theologica*, 1.95.1 (emphasis added; my translation; Sed quod etiam fuerit conditus in gratia, ut alii dicunt, videtur requirere ipsa rectitudo primi status, in qua Deus hominem fecit, secundum illud Eccle. VII, *Deus fecit hominem rectum*).

45. Thomas, *Summa Theologica*, 1.100.1.

rather than intrinsically essential, in that it was not immutable and could be corrupted by sin.

Upright nature and original righteousness were a concrete reality with sanctifying grace so that there was no graced-elevation apart (if still distinct) from creation.[46] For Thomas, righteousness, or rectitude, entailed the right orientation toward God and toward our supernatural end. To be created in righteousness was to be created with the grace that 'is the principle of merit.'[47] As Hans Boersma has assessed for other categories, 'Aquinas appears intent, at least at this point, to keep heaven and earth, nature and the supernatural, close together.'[48] Some have even understood Thomas to mean that sanctifying grace was included in respect of original righteousness, so much so that modern neo-Thomists had to refute this interpretation to maintain that sanctifying grace is only an extrinsic condition.[49]

Still, the issue of proportionality cracks Thomas' initial formulation. He conceded that Adam's original condition was 'a supernatural endowment of grace,' which drives toward his conception of the relationship of original righteousness, grace, and merit. Thus, Thomas denied that Adam was made 'only in a state of nature' but affirmed that superadded grace was necessary because 'it was not by virtue of the nature wherein he was created that he could advance by merit, but by virtue of the grace which was added.'[50] Thomas' other mature writings confirm that superadded sanctifying grace was distinct from, although protologically joined to, original righteousness, bridging the gap between natural works and supernatural reward.[51] In his mature statement, Thomas argued that the biblical teaching about Adam's original righteousness requisitely entails that he was created as directly endowed with the proper orientation to God, immediately equipped to walk rightly with the Lord, caveating that

---

46. Torrell, 'Nature and Grace in Thomas Aquinas,' 155-67.

47. Thomas, *Summa Theologica*, 1.100.1 ad 2.

48. Hans Boersma, *Seeing God: The Beatific Vision in Christian Tradition* (Grand Rapids, MI: Eerdmans, 2018), 141.

49. e.g. Reginald Garrigou-Lagrange, 'Utrum gratia sanctificans fuerit in Adamo dos naturae an donum personae tantum,' *Angelicum* 2 (1925), 140.

50. Thomas, *Summa Theologica*, 1.95.1 ad 4; Torrell, 'Nature and Grace in Thomas Aquinas,' 168-72.

51. Houck, *Aquinas, Original Sin, and the Challenge of Evolution*, 67-69.

Adam's potential to 'merit glory' owed to superadded grace rather than his original rectitude per se.[52]

While Adam as God's image was upright, superadded grace served to shore up the proportionality problem between creaturely works and heavenly reward. After all, 'Merit thus measured corresponds in degree to the essential reward, which consists in the enjoyment of God.'[53] Thus, proportionality entailed that 'man even before sin required grace to obtain eternal life, which is the chief reason for the need of grace.'[54] In the state of integrity, man 'by his natural endowments' could perform works that were proportionately good to our nature.[55] Although humanity's natural endowment included righteousness, Thomas distinguished this proportionate good from the ability to perform a 'surpassing good,' which requires an infused virtue.[56] Thomas understood this surpassing good as humanity's highest goal, namely 'Eternal happiness is the ultimate and supernatural end.'[57] All the same, tension resides in Thomas' category of natural works proportioned to our nature precisely because he contended that 'God is the last end of man and all other things' and 'happiness means the acquisition of the last end.'[58] Boersma suggests the best resolution by recognizing Thomas' use of Aristotle's scheme of an ultimate end, which is God, and 'subordinate natural ends of earthly happiness.'[59] In this understanding, the two ends are not alternate telic courses. Rather, creaturely life has proximate fulfillment as well as eschatological happiness. A steak dinner is satisfying but not

---

52. Thomas, *Summa Theologica*, 1.95.1 ad 6; Tobias Hoffman, 'Grace and Free Will,' in Eleonore Stump and Thomas Joseph White (eds.), *The New Cambridge Companion to Aquinas* (Cambridge: Cambridge University Press, 2022), 235; Brian Leftow, 'Original Sin,' in *New Cambridge Companion to Aquinas*, 309-10

53. Thomas, *Summa Theologica*, 1.95.4.

54. Thomas, *Summa Theologica*, 1.95.4 ad 1.

55. Thomas, *Summa Theologica*, 1a2ae.109.2; Davies, *Thomas Aquinas's Summa Theologiae*, 224-25.

56. Daria Spezzano, 'Aquinas on Nature, Grace, and the Moral Life,' in Matthew Levering and Marcus Plested (eds.), *The Oxford Handbook of the Reception of Aquinas* (Oxford: Oxford University Press, 2021), 660-69; Wawrykow, *God's Grace and Human Action*, 157-60; Davies, *Thomas Aquinas's Summa Theologiae*, 223.

57. Thomas, *Summa Theologica*, 1.75.7 ad 1.

58. Thomas, *Summa Theologica*, 1a2ae.2.8.

59. Hans Boersma, *Nouvelle Théologie and Sacramental Ontology: A Return to Mystery* (Oxford: Oxford University Press, 2009), 96; Hans Boersma, 'Theology as Queen of Hospitality,' *Evangelical Quarterly* 79 no 4 (2007): 293-97, 299-301.

as satisfying as seeing God in eschatological glory.[60] Thomas himself suggests such a structure: 'Man's happiness is twofold: One is the imperfect happiness found in this life .... The other is the perfect happiness of heaven, where we will see God himself through his essence and the other separate substances.'[61] Elsewhere, Thomas explicitly stated that this twofold aspect belongs to one, singular end: 'The end to which God orders created things is twofold: one which exceeds the proportion and ability of created nature, and this end is everlasting life, which consists in the divine vision ... the other end is proportionate to created nature.'[62] Our singular twofold end pertains penultimately to earthy things and ultimately to supernatural things in knowing God eschatologically. Thomas said that ultimate end surpasses the power of our nature as such, meaning that God must have ordered us in our creation for this supernatural destiny. Thus, this tension of natural and supernatural aspects of our twofold end makes the proportionality issue loom large in Thomas' thought. It drove his whole understanding of merit with the conceptual gap between the value of natural human works and the value of works that, when aided by grace, would obtain eschatological reward.[63]

According to Thomas, Adam's potential for eschatological advancement was contingent upon rendering adequate obedience. Given Adam's prospect to obtain higher communion with God, which he saw as the beatific vision in terms of intellectually seeing (but not comprehending) God's essence, the question was then what would

---

60. Kevin E. Jones, 'Bonaventure on Habitual Grace in Adam: A Change of Heart on Nature and Grace?' *Franciscan Studies* 76 (2018): 58.

61. Thomas Aquinas, *In Boethius de Trinitate*, 6.4 ad 4; cited Christopher M. Cullen, SJ, 'Bonaventure on nature before Grace: A Historical Moment Reconsidered,' *American Catholic Philosophical Quarterly* 85 no 1 (2011): 162n2.

62. Thomas, *Summa Theologica*, 1.23.1 (my translation; Finis autem ad quem res creatae ordinantur a Deo, est duplex. Unus, qui excedit proportionem naturae creatae et facultatem, et hic finis est vita aeterna, quae in divina visione consistit, quae est supra naturam cuiuslibet creaturae, ut supra habitum est. Alius autem finis est naturae creatae proportionatus, quem scilicet res creata potest attingere secundum virtutem suae naturae).

63. Thomas, *Summa Theologica*, 1a2ae.114.1; Wawrykow, *God's Grace and Human Action*, 164n36; Thomas J. Bushlack, 'The Return of Neo-Scholasticism? Recent Criticisms of Henri de Lubac on Nature and Grace and Their Significance for Moral Theology, Politics and Law,' *Journal of the Society of Christian Ethics* (Fall/Winter 2015): 87-88; Peter F. Ryan, 'How Can the Beatific Vision both Fulfill Human Nature and Be Utterly Gratuitous?' *Gregorium* 83 no 4 (2002): 719-23.

make his works have meritorious performance?[64] Thomas' view was that Adam could perform good works, but they could not merit supernatural blessings unless 'sanctifying grace' supplemented their value.[65] In this respect, Thomas thought that 'grace does not destroy nature, but perfects it,' in this sense meaning nature as such – some Protestants later appropriate this dictum, usually meaning that grace perfects *fallen* nature as later chapters consider.[66] The dangling issue was then again when Adam received this grace.

Considering that the debate about pure nature greatly shapes the differences between Reformed and Roman Catholic understandings of sin and our ability after the fall, how does Thomas' view in the *Summa* concerning Adam's original righteousness affect his explanation of our post-fall condition? Strikingly, Thomas never used the phrase 'pure nature' in any of his writings. Those who argue most stridently that he taught the concept as meaning humanity without an innate end in relation to supernatural fellowship with God, all represent an attempt at repristinating neo-scholastic-Thomism. They also all depend on arguments for reading later distinctions forged by Thomas Cajetan and Francisco Suarez back into Thomas as if those concepts truly inhere in Aquinas' words.[67] Those retrojected concepts might indeed

---

64. Thomas, *Summa Theologica*, 1.95.3; 1a2ae.109.5; 1.12.4; 1.62.1; 1a2ae.91.4. For more thorough, theologically oriented analysis, see Boersma, *Seeing God*, 129-62.

65. Rupert Johannes Mayer, 'Man is Inclined to His Last End by Nature, though He cannot Reach It by Nature but Only by Grace: The Principle of the Debate about Nature and Grace in Thomas Aquinas, Thomism and Henri de Lubac. A Response to Lawrence Feingold,' *Angelicum* 88 (2011): 888-92; Houck, *Aquinas, Original Sin, and the Challenge of Evolution*, 59-74. Recently, Marc Cortez, *Resourcing Theological Anthropology: A Constructive Account of Humanity in Light of Christ* (Grand Rapids, MI: Zondervan, 2017) seemingly suggested a similar structure, arguing that the Incarnation was necessary for humanity to achieve eschatological ends, even apart from sin, since otherwise grace would not be necessary to obtain those ends.

66. Thomas, *Summa Theologica*, 1.1.8 ad 2.

67. Santiago Sanz Sanchéz, and John Watson, 'The Revival of Pure Nature in Recent Debates in English Speaking Theology,' *Annales Theologici* 31 (2017): 200-2; Bushlack, 'Return of Neo-Scholasticism?' 86-96; cf. Steven A. Long, *Natura Pura: On the Recovery of Nature in the Doctrine of Grace* (New York, NY: Fordham University Press, 2010); Reinhard Hütter, *Dust Bound for Heaven: Explorations in the Theology of Thomas Aquinas* (Grand Rapids, MI: Eerdmans, 2012); Reinhard Hütter, *Bound for Beatitude: A Thomistic Study in Eschatology and Ethics* (Thomistic Ressourcement Series; Washington, DC: Catholic University of America Press, 2019); Feingold, *Natural Desire to See God*.

resolve tensions in Thomas' writings toward neo-scholastic conclusions. Nevertheless, only the premise that historical conscientiousness is absolute rather than historically conditioned, growing from an idealist understanding of historical theology, demands that the concepts used for later resolution and development must have been present, if implicitly, in the original writings. Hence, neo-scholastic Thomists may represent one plausible and potentially valid interpretive development of Thomas' thought without accurately reflecting what Thomas himself believed. Without getting too far ahead of ourselves in the argument, this space of interpretive development – unshackled from those idealist presumptions – is precisely where the Reformed find grounds to claim Thomas as an antecedent in the Augustinian tradition, whose theology we can appreciate and refine.

For Thomas, the fall damaged Adam's *natural* ability to do good, taking away not only superadded grace but also damaging our original faculties. For Thomas, God created man in righteousness in the sense that Adam's faculties were rightly ordered so 'the lower powers were subjected to the higher,' meaning Adam's godly reason kept his other appetites in check.[68] Sin disordered Adam's faculties, putting reason and desire out of place.[69] Thomas considered human nature as still 'intact,' in that we still possess those faculties, but damaged by an inability to use them rightly apart from renewing grace.[70] Although still capable of some natural goods for earthly life, such as building houses, sinners can no longer perform supernatural goods in relation to God.[71] Thomas' distinction of natural and supernatural goods fueled his argument for a *donum superadditum*. Thus, even in the perfect state, 'man needs a gratuitous strength superadded to natural strength, viz. in order to do and wish supernatural good.'[72] Still, for Thomas, works

---

68. Thomas, *Summa Theologica*, 1.94.1; Houck, *Aquinas, Original Sin, and the Challenge of Evolution*, 61-63.

69. Thomas Joseph White, 'Review of Lawrence Feingold, *The Natural Desire to See God according to St. Thomas Aquinas and his Interpreters*, 2nd ed.,' *The Thomist* 74 no 3 (July 2010): 466.

70. Trueman, *Grace Alone*, 98-100.

71. Thomas, *Summa Theologica*, 1a2ae.109.2; Wawrykow, *God's Grace and Human Action*, 165n38, 191-93; Spezzano, 'Aquinas on Nature, Grace, and the Moral Life,' 667.

72. Thomas, *Summa Theologica*, 1a2ae.109.2; 1a2ae.91.4.

can merit supernatural blessings before and after the fall if someone has the proper superadded strength.[73] The difference, for Thomas, is that sinners require more grace. Since God had sovereignly superadded grace to human nature to make Adam capable of meriting the beatific vision, only another sovereign act of grace could restore our ability to merit.[74]

At a more fundamental level concerning the ongoing structures of merit in developing medieval theology, Thomas explicitly rejected the Franciscan Pactum. Citing the axiom as an objection to his own view, Thomas outlined his opponents' stance that 'man prepares himself for grace by doing what is in him to do, since if man does what is in him to do God will not deny him grace,' arguing his own view instead as, 'Man can do nothing unless moved by God, according to John 15:5: "Without Me, you can do nothing." Hence when a man is said to do what is in him to do, this is said to be in his power according as he is moved by God.'[75] Even before the Franciscan Pactum came to its fullest expression in the later medieval period, Thomas in his mature writings found it and its insistence that even sinful man can make the first move to procure God's grace to be Pelagian. He insisted instead on the priority of grace to move sinners to God.[76] Despite how he, to some degree, flattened the pre- and post-fall situations concerning grace's necessity, Thomas emphasized God's sovereignty in dispensing grace to refute the semi-Pelagianism of his day, which distinguished him from other medieval trajectories wherein humans before and after the fall have ability to merit first grace by exercising their natural abilities.[77] Thomas, therefore, is a true member of the Augustinian lineage of the priority of God's sovereign grace in salvation.

---

73. Thomas, *Summa Theologica*, 1a2ae.114.2

74. Wawrykow, *God's Grace and Human Action*, 187-90; Davies, *Thomas Aquinas's Summa Theologiae*, 88-91; E. Towers, 'Actual Grace,' in George D. Smith, *The Teaching of the Catholic Church: A Summary of Catholic Doctrine*, 2 vol. (Waterloo, Canada: Arouca Press, 2021), 1:601-12, 617-20. Thanks to Camden Bucey for helping me identify this Smith volume.

75. Thomas, *Summa Theologica*, 1a2ae.109.6; also 1a2ae.112.1-5.

76. Joseph P. Wawrykow, '*facienti quod in se est*,' in *The Westminster Handbook to Thomas Aquinas* (Louisville, KY: Westminster John Knox, 2005), 54-56; Wawrykow, 'On the Purpose of "Merit"', 101-2; Wawrykow, *God's Grace and Human Action*, 15-17, 141-42, 210-16, 268-76.

77. Horton, *Justification*, 1:100-29.

The determinative factor that preserves Thomas' Augustinianism concerning grace, despite his endorsement that sinners can by grace merit salvation after the fall, is his doctrine of *ordinatio*, that is predestination. For Thomas, God's sovereign election and guiding providence was foundational to creatures having and obtaining their supernatural ends: 'Now it belongs to providence to direct things toward their end ... . Hence the type of the aforesaid direction of a rational creature towards the end of life eternal is called predestination.'[78] God's predestination of some individuals to salvation then 'implies a relation to grace, as cause to effect, and of act to its object.'[79] God will give the necessary grace to those creatures whom he has ordained to salvation so that they may reach their end, even by merit. In other words, God predestined that some would obtain merit to everlasting life but does not elect on the basis of foreseen merit.[80]

Thomas' view of grace's relationship to merit for the salvation of sinners emphasizes God's loving and sovereign involvement to bring the elect to everlasting life by the necessary means. Sometimes Thomas is misread incorrectly as if his doctrine of *ordinatio* means that God ordained that certain works would be meritorious, essentially amounting to congruent merit.[81] John Duns Scotus later taught a doctrine of *acceptatio* wherein 'God decides freely to treat certain acts done under certain conditions (that is, in grace and charity) as meritorious.'[82] By contrast, Thomas' doctrine of *ordinatio* is not God's commitment to this voluntarist economy of merit but God's wise plan to bring the elect to their ordained end of salvation.[83] As Joseph Wawrykow summarized, 'Merit is possible because God has chosen the person to attain God and in this light moves the person through grace to God.'[84] For Thomas,

---

78. Thomas, *Summa Theologica*, 1.23.1.

79. Thomas, *Summa Theologica*, 1.23.2 ad 4; 1.23.3-7.

80. Thomas, *Summa Theologica*, 1.23.5.

81. For a survey of various interpretations of Thomas' view, including helpful analysis, see Wawrykow, *God's Grace and Human Action*, 1-59.

82. Wawrykow, *God's Grace and Human Action*, 189.

83. Francis 'Kunle Adedara, 'The Possibility of Merit Before God According to Thomas Aquinas,' *Bodija Journal* 9 (Oct. 2015): 46-59; Wawrykow, *God's Grace and Human Action*, 182-200.

84. Wawrykow, *God's Grace and Human Action*, 183.

following Augustine, God's predestination takes no account of foreseen merit but brings it about as effects of his grace.[85] Thus, he unequivocally denied that man can merit grace in the first place: 'Man's every good work proceeds from the first grace as from its principle.'[86] The link of merit more directly to God's predestinarian work establishes man's means to his ordained end: 'man's merit with God exists only on the presupposition of the Divine ordination, so that man obtained from God as a reward of his operation, what God gave him the power of operation for.'[87] In this way, because our works have meritorious character only on account of God's predestining ordination, 'it does not follow that God is made our debtor simply, but His own, inasmuch as it is right that His will should be carried out.'[88] Thomas aimed to prevent his doctrine of merit from making God subservient to the creature by defining the value of merit in relation to God's own decree rather than directly in God's relation to the creature. Although the Reformed explain the point very differently, Thomas seemingly suggested nothing more than Augustine's own predestinarian axiom of grace and works: 'If, therefore, your good merits are God's gifts, then God does not crown your merits as your merits, but as his gifts.'[89] Further, Thomas also denied that sinners even merit perseverance, which is by grace too; since perseverance 'depends solely on the Divine motion,' then 'God freely bestows the good of perseverance, on whomsoever He bestows it.'[90] God

---

85. Pasquale Porro, '"Rien de Personnel": Notes sur la question de l'*acceptio personarum* dans la théologie scolastique,' *Revue des Sciences philosophiques et théologiques* 94 no 3 (July–Sept 2010): 485-502; Pasquale Porro, 'Divine Predestination, Human Merit and Moral Responsibility: The Reception of Augustine's Doctrine of Irresistible Grace in Thomas Aquinas, Henry of Ghent and John Duns Scotus,' in Pieter d'Hoine and Gerd van Riel (eds.), *Fate, Providence and Moral Responsibility in Ancient, Medieval and Early Modern Thought: Essays in Honor of Carlos Steel* (Leuven: Leuven University Press, 2014), 553-62.

86. Thomas, *Summa Theologica*, 1a2ae.114.5.

87. Thomas, *Summa Theologica*, 1a2ae.114.1.

88. Thomas, *Summa Theologica*, 1a2ae.114.1ad3; cf. Stephen Ozment, *The Age of Reform, 1250–1550: An Intellectual and Religious History of Late Medieval and Reformation Europe* (New Haven, CT: Yale University Press, 1980), 31-34.

89. Augustine, *De Gratia et Libero Arbitrio*, 6.15, in Jacques Paul Migne (ed.), *Patrologia Cursus Completus: Series Latina*, 221 vol. (Paris, 1844–64), 44:891 (Si ergo Dei dona sunt bona merita tua non Deus coronat merita tua tanquam merita tua, sed tanquam dona sua).

90. Thomas, *Summa Theologica*, 1a2ae.114.9; Wawrykow, *God's Grace and Human Action*, 269.

in grace ordained sinners to their saving end, directing them there in grace by providence.[91] Even though the Reformed later reject some of Thomas' ways of working out and applying the Augustinian paradigm, he certainly carried forward a baseline Augustinianism that Reformed theologians would pick up and that we still share with him.

The Franciscan Trajectory

In contrast to Thomas' view wherein God gave the needed righteousness, sanctified by grace, to merit eschatological reward in humanity's original constitution, Franciscan theologians argued that Adam needed to obtain that supernaturally infused grace by first performing works of strictly natural good.[92] As a key difference from Dominican (and more robustly Augustinian) theologians, Franciscans argued that we can merit first grace from the state of pure nature. This position forges two tiers of merit wherein merit according to pure nature obtains sanctifying grace followed by graced merit toward supernatural reward.

Bonaventure of Bagnoregio (1221–74), who taught at the University of Paris, understood sanctifying grace (*gratia gratum faciens*) as that necessary help which humanity needs from God for acquiring merit to reach the everlasting condition. Bonaventure's understanding of humanity's telos also revolved around the beatific vision, grounding Adam's need for sanctifying grace in an ultimately eschatological ordering.[93] In *Breviloquium*, he explained various aspects of Adam's creation in relation to his end and merit: 'a twofold end was prepared for the man, namely one visible and the other invisible, one temporal and the other everlasting, one of the flesh and the other of the spirit. Moreover, according to these goods, God gave one and promised the other so that one might be possessed freely but the other acquired by merit.'[94] On account of man's 'defective nature' that made him liable

---

91. John Meinert, 'St. Thomas Aquinas, Perseverance, and the Nature/Grace Debate,' *Angelicum* 93 no 4 (2016): 828-35; Hoffman, 'Grace and Free Will,' 237-40, 245; Davies, *Thomas Aquinas's Summa Theologiae*, 88-90, 229; Trueman, *Grace Alone*, 102-6; Wawrykow, 'On the Purpose of "Merit",' 109-12.

92. Henri de Lubac, *Augustinianism and Modern Theology*, trans. Lancelot Sheppard (Milestones in Catholic Theology; New York, NY: Crossroad Publishing, 2000), 215-24.

93. Jones, 'Bonaventure on Habitual Grace in Adam,' 40, 53-55.

94. Bonaventure, *Breviloquium*, 2.11; in A.C. Peltier (ed.), *S.R.E Cardinalis S. Bonaventure … Opera Omnia*, 15 vol. (Paris: Ludovicus Vivès, 1864–71), 7:269 (ideo duplex

to fall, God gave him a fourfold help: 'twofold of nature and twofold of grace.' In this help, 'the twofold perfection of grace was also superadded,' including 'grace freely given' (*gratiae gratis datae*) and 'sanctifying grace' (*gratiae gratum facientis*). The first pertained to Adam's faculties and the second clothed those faculties in divine grace.[95]

For Bonaventure, sanctifying grace, which supplemented the grace given to Adam's natural faculties, undergirded his doctrine of merit. He wrote, 'Moreover, grace is properly called the gift of divine help that results in meriting, which certainly is called the gift of sanctifying grace [*gratiae gratum facientis*] that makes one acceptable, without which no one is able to merit, nor accomplish good, nor arrive at everlasting blessing.'[96] In contrast to Thomas who saw sanctifying grace as elevating the *work* to a meritorious level, Bonaventure saw sanctifying grace as making the graced *person* acceptable to God, facilitating the possibility of merit on the premise of this grace.[97] According to Bonaventure, since this sanctifying grace is needed in order to merit: 'no man is able to merit that [everlasting blessing] by a condign merit, but does merit to be strengthened in the way to it, so that by being strengthened he merits also to be perfected in fatherly and everlasting glory by God himself, which is imparted grace to be strengthened and perfected, according to

---

bonum praeparatum est homini, unum scilicet visibile, et alterum invisibile; unum temporale, et aliud aeternum; unum carni, et alterum spiritui. Ex his autem bonis Deus unum dedit, alterum promisit, ut unum gratis possideretur, alterum vero per meritum acquireretur). Thanks to Ryan McGraw for referring me to look at 2.11 further.

95. Bonaventure, *Breviloquium*, 2.11; in *Opera*, 7:269 (Et quoniam homo, ratione natura defectivae ex nibilo formatae, nec per gloriam confirmatae, poterat cadere; benignissimus Deus quadruplex contulit ei adjutorium, scilicet duplex naturae, et duplex gratiae. Duplicem enim indidit rectitudinem ipsi naturae: videlicet unam ad recte judicandum, et haec est rectitudo conscientiae; aliam ad recte volendum, et hæc est rectitudo synderesis, cujus est remurmurare contra malum, et stimulare ad bonum. Duplicem etiam superaddit perfectionem gratiae: unam gratiae gratis datae, quae fuit scientia illuminans intellectum ad cognoscendum seipsum, et Deum suum, et mundum istum, qui factus fuerat propter ipsum; aliam vero gratiae gratum facientis, quae fuit charitas habilitans affectum ad diligendum Deum super omnia, et proximum sieut seipsum. Et sic ante lapsum homo perfecta habuit naturalia, supervestita nihilominus gratia divina. Ex quo manifeste colligitur, quod si cecidit, non aliunde fuit, nisi ex sua culpa, quia obedire contempsit).

96. Bonaventure, *Breviloquium*, 5.2; in *Opera*, 7:297 (proprie vero gratia dicitur adjutorium datum divinitus ad merendum quod quidem dicitur donum gratiae gratum facientis, sine quo nullus potest mereri, nec in bono proficere, nec ad aeternam pervenire salutem).

97. Jones, 'Bonaventure on Habitual Grace in Adam,' 46, 61-62.

our will's cooperation, and according to the intention or good pleasure of eternal predestination.'[98] So, Bonaventure argued that a person can merit strengthening grace, which strengthens him to merit further along the road to condign merit for supernatural blessing.[99]

Despite a similar premise of sanctifying grace's necessity for merit, Bonaventure's understanding of grace and merit should already appear significantly different from Thomas' mature view of flatly denying that man can merit grace. Further, he differed from Thomas concerning sanctifying grace's relationship to Adam's original condition. In his commentary on Peter Lombard's *Sentences*, Bonaventure argued that Adam was created *without* that sanctifying grace which would enable him to merit the beatific vision, aiming for a sharper distinction between the natural and supernatural orders.[100] Reflecting on Lombard's claim that 'man was able, on account of grace's assistance in creation, to resist evil but not to accomplish good,' Bonaventure explained, 'If [Adam] had possessed sanctifying grace to make him acceptable [*gratiam gratum facientem*] from creation's outset, he would have been capable of both resisting evil and perfectly accomplishing good. If, therefore, he was not able to perfectly accomplish good, he is exposed.'[101] These statements suggest that Bonaventure saw the principle of merit as a truly righteous work made meritorious as it is performed by a person in the state of sanctifying grace. On one hand, for Bonaventure in contrast to Thomas, merit's premise pertains to the *person* having sanctifying grace. On the other hand, Bonaventure in agreement with Thomas maintained that the *work* performed by the person in the state of sanctifying grace had to be a

---

98. Bonaventure, *Breviloquium*, 5.2; in *Opera*, 7:297 (Unde nullus ipsam mereri potest merito condigni; sed ipsa meretur augeri a Deo in via, ut aucta mereatur et perfici in patria et gloria sempiterna ab ipso Deo, cujus est gratiam infundere, augere et perficere, secundum cooperationem voluntatis nostrae, et secundum propositum sive beneplacitum praedestinationis aeternae).

99. Christopher M. Cullen, *Bonaventure* (Great Medieval Thinkers; Oxford: Oxford University Press, 2007), 153-64.

100. Cullen, 'Bonaventure on nature before Grace,' 163, 166-68; Torrell, 'Nature and Grace in Thomas Aquinas,' 155-58.

101. Bonaventure, *Commentary on the Sentences*, bk.2, dist. 29, art. 2, q. 2, rat. 5; in *Opera*, 3:316 (Item Magister dicit supra: 'Poterat homo per auxilium gratiae creationis resistere malo, sed non perficere bonum.' Sed si habuisset gratiam gratum facientem ab exordio creationis, potuisset utrumque: ergo si non potuit perficere bonum, patet, etc.).

truly righteous act. Later Franciscans would articulate a more voluntarist principle concerning what works could be counted as meritorious.

Bonaventure did appear as a clear fountainhead for later Franciscan ideas by distinguishing Adam's creation from his later reception of superadded, sanctifying grace. He argued, 'Likewise, the gift of grace is unfruitful unless recognized to be from God because no one in himself can hold onto grace unless being grateful to God for it. If, therefore, [Adam] possessed the order of grace to a greater degree, namely as superadded to natural abilities, than that which is naturally given, then it is clear that the gift of grace was conveyed to the man not by creation itself but after.'[102] Bonaventure concluded, 'in the state of innocence, two moments can be distinguished, specifically there was a certain time in which he had only the natural [abilities], but another certain time in which he had both natural and grace-given [abilities].'[103] Indeed he said, 'the Lord willed to give grace after nature even when he was able to give them simultaneously' because there is an ascending order of wisdom, good, and righteousness. For this arrangement:

> For this order of righteousness, God required namely a particular disposition and preparation on our part according to what the law requires, with respect to which he infused grace into them ... therefore grace was not concreated in man but was postponed until man disposed himself to receive it by the act and use of reason in a certain way, as so is confirmed by Augustine with regard to the first man.[104]

---

102. Bonaventure, *Commentary on the Sentences*, bk.2, dist. 29, art. 2, q. 2, rat. 5; in *Opera*, 3:316 (Item donum gratiae infructuosum est, nisi a Deo esse recognoscatur; nemo enim in se gratiam reservare potest, nisi pro illa Deo gratus existat: igitur si magis tenet rationem gratuiti quod est naturalibus superadditum, quam quod est naturaliter inditum, et donum gratiae est mere gratuitum; ergo videtur quod non ab ipsa creatione, sed post, donum gratiæ fuerit homini collatum).

103. Bonaventure, *Commentary on the Sentences*, bk.2, dist. 29, art. 2. q. 2, conc.; in *Opera*, 3:316 (Unde secundum hanc in statu innocentiae distinguuntur duo tempora: quoddam enim fuit tempus, in quo tantum habuit naturalia, quoddam vero in quo habuit et naturalia, et gratuita).

104. Bonaventure, *Commentary on the Sentences*, bk.2, dist. 29, art. 2, q. 2, rat. 5; in *Opera*, 3:316-17 (Ratio autem, quare Dominus voluit post naturalia dare gratiam, cum posset dare simul, sumitur ex triplici ordine, videlicet ab ordine sapientiae, bonitatis, et justitiae ... Ordo etiam iustitiae hoc requirebat: Deus enim secundum legem communem requirit aliquam dispositionem et praeparationem a parte nostra, ad hoc quod infundat alicui gratiam, sive in eo cui infundit, ut adulto, sive in alio adjuvante, secundum quod contingit in parvulo: et ideo gratia non fuit homini concreata, sed dilata fuit quousque

Bonaventure emphasized man's preparatory role in receiving grace.

Although Thomas squirmingly took a similar position in his own *Sentences* commentary, as we saw above, his Augustinian impulses made him uneasy with the temporal, therefore real, gap between Adam's creation and his obtaining of grace. On the one hand, Thomas argued in his *Summa*, quite possibly to refute Bonaventure, that God granted sanctifying grace, which ordered Adam to the supernatural blessing, *by creation* namely in that 'in the state of innocence man in a certain sense possessed all the virtues ... the virtues are nothing but those perfections whereby reason is directed to God, and the inferior powers regulated according to reason.'[105] On the other hand, Bonaventure said that Adam had to obtain that superadded righteousness by doing good works performed in pure nature to orient himself to God.[106] After Adam had sanctifying grace superadded to nature, he would have been equipped so that his works performed from natural powers would merit everlasting blessing.[107] This last point seems to confirm that a requirement for merit, according to Bonaventure, was in the work being truly righteous. Bonaventure borrowed much of his argumentation from his Order's collaborative work, *Summa Fratris Alexandri*.[108]

Starkly marking their disagreement on this point, Thomas and Bonaventure both cited the exact same phrase from Augustine to support their position: 'Therefore, the one who made you without you will not justify you without you.'[109] Bonaventure interpreted Augustine to mean that man must cooperate with God to receive virtues unto justification. In

homo per actum et usum rationis quodam modo se disponeret ad illam suscipiendam, ut sic verificaretur illud Augustini in primo homine).

105. Thomas, *Summa Theologica*, 1.95.3. Thomas wrote the *Summa* after years of reading Bonaventure, parts of it seeming to aim at response to him; Wood, *Stir a Restless Heart*, 211, 243, 249.

106. Cullen, 'Bonaventure on nature before Grace,' 166-68

107. Cullen, 'Bonaventure on nature before Grace,' 173-74.

108. Jones, 'Bonaventure on Habitual Grace in Adam,' 45-52; concerning collaborative Franciscan works and Bonaventure as a representative theologian, see Lydia Schumacher, *Early Franciscan Theology: Between Authority and Innovation* (Cambridge: Cambridge University Press, 2019), 2-12.

109. Thomas, *Summa Theologica*, 1a2ae.55.4; Bonaventure, *Commentary on the Sentences*, bk.2, dist. 29, art. 2, q. 2, rat. 5; in *Opera*, 3:316-17; Augustine, *Sermon 169: De verbis Apostoli, Philipp. Cap. III, 3–16*, §11; in Migne, *Patrologia ... Latina*, 38:923 (Qui ergo fecit te sine te, non te justificat sine te).

other words, even Adam needed to obtain the higher sort of righteousness adequate to perform supernaturally worthy merit by performing purely natural works, which is the sense in which Bonaventure saw justification in the state of innocence. In contrast, Thomas took Augustine to mean that 'Infused virtue is caused in us by God without any action on our part, but not without our consent.'[110] Thomas seems to be on firmer ground, since Augustine explained his meaning:

> Therefore he who made the ignorant, justifies the willing. However, he justifies that it may not be your righteousness, that you may not return to damnation, detriment, and excrement, to be found in him not having your own righteousness, which is by the law, but righteousness by faith in Christ, which is from God: righteousness by faith that is to know him and the power of his resurrection and communion with his sufferings. And this will be your virtue: communion with Christ's sufferings will be your virtue.[111]

The point is not whether any of these statements were theologically correct, especially within a Reformed assessment, but whether Thomas or Bonaventure was historically more properly Augustinian. Even as Augustine and Thomas argue that God justifies the willing, they also affirm that this work owed to the priority of God's grace, not our personal righteousness, directly in contrast with Bonaventure. That said, concerning this particular issue, Bonaventure still maintained Augustinian credentials by affirming a solid predestinarianism and the fall's real effects upon our nature.[112] Bonaventure would strongly object to the idea that we can know nature apart from God, since he posed God as our first object of knowledge.[113] Later Franciscans developed Bonaventure's ideas on the

---

110. Thomas, *Summa Theologica*, 1a2ae.55.4 ad 6.

111. Augustine, *Sermon 169*, §11; in Migne (ed.), *Patrologia… Latina*, 38:923 (Ergo fecit nescientem, justifcat volentem. Tamen ipse justificat, ne sit justitia tua, ne redeas ad damna, ad detrimenta et stercora, invenire in illo non habens justitiam tuam, quae ex lege est, sed justitiam per fidem Christi, quae est ex Deo: justitiam ex fide, ad cognoscendum eum, et virtutem resurrectionis ejus, et communicationem passionum ejus. Et ipsa virtus tua erit; communicatio passionum Christi, virtus tua erit.).

112. Bonaventure, *Breviloquium*, 1.8; in *Opera*, 7:255-58; Nathaniel Gray Sutanto, 'Questioning Bonaventure's Augustinianism?: On the Noetic Effects of Sin,' *New Blackfriars* 102 no 1099 (May 2021): 401-17.

113. N. Gray Sutanto, '*Gevoel* and Illumination: Bavinck, Augustine, and Bonaventure on Awareness of God,' *Pro Ecclesia* 30 no 3 (2021): 265-78. Thanks to Gray Sutanto for his insight, including these caveats, on Bonaventure, as well as his recommendations for sources.

nature-grace relation in even less Augustinian directions, departing from his Augustinianism on these other basic issues as well.[114]

Later Franciscans followed Bonaventure, opposing Thomas' views on original righteousness.[115] John Duns Scotus, who also taught in Paris (as well as Oxford), argued that the righteousness sufficient to perform supernaturally meritorious works is not natural to humanity but a supernatural gift – a *donum superadditum* – in a multi-tiered way. Compared to Bonaventure, Scotus similarly distinguished pure nature from superadded righteousness for humanity even prior to the fall. Dissimilarly, he was not explicit as to whether this distinction was merely conceptual or a real difference in Adam's experience.[116] Even then, for Scotus, original righteousness is not identical with the sanctifying grace that makes works meritorious. Drawing on Lombard, he argued that Adam needed infused grace even in addition to superadded original righteousness to advance to supernatural communion with God. Thus, Scotus shows a developing Franciscan pattern of rejecting that God originally built human nature with the righteousness needed to reach supernatural communion with God. He instead argued for a paradigm in which Adam had to obtain infused grace by which he would *then by grace* merit everlasting blessing.

Scotus surpassed Bonaventure in furthering a trajectory that clashed with real Augustinian principles. Richard Cross, a renowned Scotus expert, commented that Scotus' account of original sin 'is in every respect weaker than the standard Augustinian one accepted by most of his contemporaries.'[117] Scotus also curtailed the significance of unfallen humanity's supernatural gifts so that 'their loss has only the smallest effect on human existence.'[118] This position drastically minimizes the difference between our unfallen and fallen states, making sin of little consequence.

---

114. Carl A. Vater, *God's Knowledge of the World: Medieval Theories of Divine Ideas from Bonaventure to Ockham* (Washington, D.C.: Catholic University of America Press, 2022); Justus, H. Hunter, *If Adam Had Not Sinned: The Reason for the Incarnation from Anselm to Scotus* (Washington D.C.: Catholic University of America Press, 2020).

115. Richard Cross, 'Duns Scotus and William of Ockham,' in *Oxford Handbook of the Reception of Aquinas*, 53-66.

116. Ernesto Dezza, 'John Duns Scotus on Human Beings in the State of Innocence,' *Traditio* 75 (2020): 294-95; cf. Horton, *Justification*, 1:138.

117. Richard Cross, *Duns Scotus* (Great Medieval Thinkers; New York, NY: Oxford University Press, 1999), 83.

118. Cross, *Duns Scotus*, 83.

The discussion of whether the *person* with sanctifying grace or the *act* performed is the determinative factor in if a work is meritorious becomes again significant in Scotus' thought. Disagreeing even with Bonaventure, Scotus thought that sin lacked rectitude in an *act* but indicated no necessary lack of rectitude in the *person* sinning; the human soul can never lose its essential rectitude, its right ordering.[119] In some ways like Bonaventure but fully unlike Thomas, his position concentrated merit in the acceptability of the person not the work.[120] On the one hand, we will see that he followed Bonaventure's principle that merit's basis was in God's acceptance of the *person* in possession of sanctifying grace. On the other, Scotus was not as firm that this meritorious *act* had to be *truly* righteous. In this vein, Scotus denied that original righteousness was natural to us, making original righteousness not even about being rightly ordered to God sufficiently to obtain eschatological glory but about a supernatural, superadded quality inhering in the soul. The loss of original righteousness returned us to our purely natural state, which had its own essential and unassailable rectitude.[121]

Scotus distinguished three concepts of pure nature, original righteousness, and sanctifying grace. Commenting on the same discussion from Lombard's *Sentences* that drove Thomas' and Bonaventure's thoughts on nature and grace, Scotus took up the question, 'Is it necessary to posit that the original righteousness in Adam was some supernatural gift?'[122] Throughout his discussion, Scotus' voluntarism shows in his concern about whether *the will* can bring the other appetites in line regarding righteousness and sin.[123] For Scotus, original righteousness was *the result* of 'perfect tranquility' among the appetites, meaning that original righteousness was not any inherent attribute tied to our image bearing status but a harmony of our desires

---

119. Cross, *Duns Scotus*, 95.

120. John Duns Scotus, *Quaestiones Quodlibetals*, 17.4, in *Opera Omnia*, editio nova, 26 vol. (Paris, 1891–95), 26:206 (Non enim actus alicujus acceptatur ut dignus praemio, nisi persona operans sit accepta).

121. Cross, *Duns Scotus*, 97.

122. John Duns Scotus, *Questiones in Librum Secundum Sententiarum*, 2.29.1, in *Opera*, 13:267 (Utrum justitiam originalem in Adam, necesse sit ponere aliquod donum esse supernaturale?).

123. e.g. Scotus, *Questiones*, 2.29.1.4, in *Opera*, 13:272.

effected by our will.[124] At least hypothetically, Scotus implied Adam's need to merit original righteousness itself by willing his appetites into proper order by pure nature: 'Natural rectitude or original [righteousness] is separable from sanctifying grace, *if the opposite (viz. original sin) does not pre-exist* in the person.'[125] For Scotus, original sin was just a privation of the supernatural gift of ordered appetites.[126] Adam could have original righteousness by avoiding sin, suggesting that some action was required to obtain the first tier *donum superadditum* of Scotus' anthropology.[127] Thus, perhaps more radically than his contemporaries but aligning with his stronger voluntarism, Scotus outright states that 'this righteousness was a supernatural gift.'[128] For Scotus, even the concept of original righteousness itself is just a state of affairs concerning the will.[129]

Giving credence for why Scotus was called the *doctor subtilis*, the instances where Scotus might appear to say otherwise concerning grace's relation to original righteousness involve some carefully parsed issues. For example, in his defense of Mary's immaculate conception – the dogma wherein it is claimed that Mary was born without the stain of original sin and that she was preserved from all actual sin – Scotus contended:

> I declare the first [that Mary was never in original sin] because grace is equivalent to original righteousness to the degree that it concerns divine acceptance, with the result that on account of this grace, original sin does

---

124. Scotus, *Questiones*, 2.29.1.4, in *Opera*, 13:272-73 (Si igitur in primo homine fuit ille effectus, scilicet perfecta tranquillitas, et erit effectus originalis justitie); Dezza, 'Scotus on Human Beings in the State of Innocence,' 294-301; Cross, *Duns Scotus*, 97.

125. John Duns Scotus, *Reportatio Parisiensis*, 4.1.5, n 4; cited in Cross, *Duns Scotus*, 98 (emphasis added).

126. Cross, *Duns Scotus*, 99.

127. Horton, *Justification*, 1:138.

128. Scotus, *Questiones*, 2.29.1.4, in *Opera*, 13:273 (illa justitia fuit donum supernaturale, quia fecit Deum delectabiliorem voluntati quam aliquod appetibile sensibile, quod non potuit esse ex aliquo dono naturali ipsius voluntatis).

129. Nominalism's seeds are present in Scotus' voluntarism when he denied that *ex puris naturalibus tantum* we can know 'the characteristics of separated substances,' meaning that our reason cannot form abstract ideas from concrete particulars; H. van der Laan, 'Nature and Supernature according to Duns Scotus: An Analysis of the First Part of Duns Scotus' Prologue to his "Ordinatio",' *Philosophia Reformata* 38 no 1 (1973): 69-70. For considerations on Scotus' view of knowledge, see William E. Mann, 'Duns Scotus on Natural and Supernatural Knowledge of God,' in Thomas Williams (ed.), *The Cambridge Companion to Duns Scotus* (Cambridge: Cambridge University Press, 2003), 238-62.

not belong to the soul possessing it. God is able at the first instant to infuse grace into this soul to such a degree as was given to other souls in circumcision or baptism. Therefore, in the first instant, the soul would not have original sin, just as someone would not have it after when he became a baptized person.[130]

In this passage, Scotus equated grace with original righteousness but only upon certain conditions. Just above, we quoted Scotus' *Reportatio* argument that original righteousness is *separable from* sanctifying grace on the condition that original sin was not a pre-existing factor.[131] In this defense of Mary's immaculate conception, he equated grace with original righteousness inasmuch as *this grace* results in removing original sin – seemingly both by prevention (for Mary) or by forgiveness (via the sacraments) – as a pre-existing factor in the soul. This premise opens a few considerations.

Scotus' defense of the immaculate conception confirms our understanding of his division of pure nature, original righteousness, and sanctifying grace. It also shows how intricate his reasoning on these matters was. In Scotus' thought, Mary is the example in addition to Adam that seemingly establishes the threefold division of pure nature, original righteousness, and sanctifying grace as being *really* rather than hypothetically distinct. For Mary, according to Scotus, *this* grace prevented her from having original sin, creating that condition where original sin did not stain her. For *this situation* wherein Mary, as a descendent from Adam, would normally be liable to original sin, the grace which sanctified Mary for acceptance equated to original righteousness because this grace *resulted* in original sin not infecting Mary.[132]

The potential confusion is that, for Scotus, there are situations wherein sanctifying grace equates to original righteousness, specifically when sanctifying grace removes the liability to original sin. This set of affairs, as is

---

130. John Duns Scotus, *Four Questions on Mary*, trans. Allan B. Wolter, OFM (Saint Bonaventure, NY: The Franciscan Institute, 2000), 42 (Question Two: The Immaculate Conception of the Blessed Virgin; Primum declaro, quia gratia aequivalet iustitiae originali quantum ad acceptationem divinam, ut propter hanc animae habenti gratiam non insit peccatum originale; potuit Deus in primo instanti illius animae infundere sibi gratiam tantam quantam alii animae in circumcisione vel baptismo; igitur in primo instanti animae non habuisset peccatum originale, sicut nec habuisset postea quando fuisset persona baptizata).

131. Scotus, *Reportatio Parisiensis*, 4.1.5, n 4.

132. Duns Scotus, *Four Questions on Mary*, 35-39.

clear in the quoted passage, applies also to how God works in the sacrament of baptism (or circumcision in the Old Testament). So, in the experience of sinners, sanctifying grace and original righteousness come together as that grace removes original sin in the moment that the sacrament is administered.

This factor – wherein the exclusion of a usual liability to original sin, applying to everyone since Adam – differentiates the typical state of affairs from Adam's own situation. Adam was not liable to original sin as if he had a natural reason to contract it. Thus, according to Scotus, for Adam, sanctifying grace was separable from original righteousness. As we will see in more detail below, this premise entailed that God gave Adam this sanctifying grace which enabled Adam to merit the condition of original righteousness. The noteworthy factor, unpacked at more length shortly, is how Scotus contended that grace qualified even someone who was not in the state of righteousness to merit by working in accord with the base principles of pure nature.

The passage defending Mary's immaculate conception shows a few other interesting features of Scotus' thought. First, his appeal to circumcision and baptism shows how Scotus thought of the sacraments as occasions but not causes of grace. For Scotus, God did not endue the sacramental element with any instrumentality, but merely used the administration of the sacrament as an opportunity to act in grace immediately.[133] Scotus' occasionalism is confirmed in his defense of the immaculate conception as he appealed to the occasion of circumcision or baptism as the moment wherein God gave grace in parallel to how God supposedly used the first instant of Mary's existence as the occasion for providing grace. That Scotus saw a direct parallel between God's immediate action upon Mary apart from any sacramental element, and his action when a sacramental element is involved confirms that Scotus did not view the element as having instrumentality in conveying grace. This observation pertains to our wider discussion because it underscores Scotus' voluntarism inasmuch as, even concerning the sacraments, Scotus emphasized the priority of God's direct will rather than any connection to the nature of the thing.

Second, Scotus' defense of Mary's immaculate conception helps to confirm our wider argument that the Roman tradition developed in

---

133. Cross, *Duns Scotus*, 136-38.

favor of the Franciscan trajectory. Although Roman apologists have long sought to explain Thomas' argument away, he clearly rejected the notion of Mary's immaculate conception:

> If the soul of the Blessed Virgin had never incurred the stain of original sin, this would be derogatory to the dignity of Christ, by reason of His being the universal Savior of all. Consequently after Christ, who, as the universal Savior of all, needed not to be saved, the purity of the Blessed Virgin holds the highest place. For Christ did not contract original sin in any way whatever, but was holy in His very Conception, according to Luke 1:35: *The Holy which shall be born of thee, shall be called the Son of God.* But the Blessed Virgin did indeed contract original sin, but was cleansed therefrom before her birth from the womb.[134]

Appealing to the honor of Christ and his exclusive role in bringing salvation to *everyone* who is saved, Thomas asserted that Mary did have original sin at conception and was later cleansed from it. Far from a glitch, the University of Paris expelled all Thomists in 1387 on account of their rejection of Mary's immaculate conception.[135] Although the Marian dogmas were not ratified until Vatican I, clearly Scotus' legacy had already in the fourteenth century set pace for the development of Roman theology to follow the Franciscan trajectory. The same would hold true on matters of pure nature, original righteousness, and sanctifying grace.

Pressing ahead, Scotus also disconnected original righteousness from sanctifying grace, posing the latter as the basis of merit. Scotist commentators extrapolated that 'sanctifying grace alone cannot be called original righteousness,' positing it as *a* righteousness, although it is 'another thing to be called *original* righteousness.'[136] Grace adds more to pure nature than even righteousness: 'it is impossible to say that sanctifying grace is original righteousness insofar as it has greater

---

134. Thomas, *Summa Theologica*, 3.27.2 (italics original).

135. Denis R. Janz, 'Late Medieval Theology,' in David Bagchi and David C. Steinmetz (eds.), *The Cambridge Companion to Reformation Theology* (Cambridge: Cambridge University Press, 2004), 6.

136. Scotus, *Questiones*, 2.29.1.7.comm., in *Opera*, 13:275 (emphasis added; ergo gratia sanctificans non potest se sola vocari justitia originalis, potest quidem vocari justitia, qua fideles justi formaliter redduntur, sed aliud est vocari justitiam, aliud vocari justitiam originalem).

power than original righteousness has alone.'[137] In Scotus' theology, pure nature is *very* basic, devoid both of original righteousness, which is the supernatural harmonious order of appetites, and of sanctifying grace which is a different supernatural righteousness.

Scotus' position, forging the widest gap between nature and supernature so far, has perhaps more significance than might be immediately obvious. By separating sanctifying grace from original righteousness, he made it possible for a person to have sanctifying grace as the basis of merit without having the righteous ordering of our nature. Put a different way, someone can have sanctifying grace, which establishes his ability to merit, without having true personal righteousness, or even the forgiveness of sin in the case of sinners.[138] The implication is that a sinner can have the ability to merit by having *a* righteousness of sanctifying grace without having *the* original righteousness of properly ordered and implemented faculties. Scotus' view puts in sharp relief why this book argues that Adam's concreated original righteousness was natural to him, including the strength to render perfect obedience according to the powers of his *natural* faculties, which would fulfill the covenant of works. In this way, we see Scotus follow Bonaventure's principle that merit is based on the *person* possessing sanctifying grace. It also suggests that Scotus was much weaker than Bonaventure on how truly righteous the meritorious *act* must be.

Scotus' way of addressing the distinction of natural and supernatural orders concerning the problem of proportionality also reveals his voluntarist, incipiently nominalist, notion of merit.[139] The principal characteristic of such a notion would be that a work is labeled as meritorious despite not having a real righteousness to it. Applying his distinction of sanctifying grace as a different sort of righteousness than original righteousness (which was also supernatural), Scotus posited that a supernatural gift must be the sort of grace that grounds merit,

---

137. Scotus, *Questiones*, 2.29.1.7.comm., in *Opera*, 13:275 (non potest did quod gratia sanctificans sit justitia originalis, quatenus majorem haberet virtutem, quam modo habet).

138. Horton, *Justification*, 1:141.

139. The point of calling Scotus' view of merit incipiently or proleptically nominalist is not to cast him wholesale as a proto-nominalist, but only to establish the connection on this particular issue concerning merit; Daniel P. Horan, OFM, *Postmodernity and Univocity: A Critical Account of Radical Orthodoxy and John Duns Scotus* (Minneapolis, MN: Fortress Press, 2014), 16-17.

writing that 'if there be any supernatural gift,' it is not necessarily 'the principle of merit' since 'it relates to grace, which is the principle of merit, as exceeding and excess.' So, grace is 'indeed exceeding because he [God] joined the will more firmly to the ultimate end than to grace.'[140] The human will wants our final end inescapably but does not necessarily have the grace needed to achieve it.[141] At creation, in contrast to Thomas, 'Scotus's Adam was spiritually underdeveloped, unable to perform meritorious actions.'[142] According to Scotus, Adam received the supernatural gift of original righteousness to order his appetites but never acted upon that gift sufficiently to obtain sanctifying grace, which would enable him to merit.

Sanctifying grace is then, for Scotus, the supernatural supplement that grounds human works as meritorious. Scotus distinguished natural and supernatural acts 'because a meritorious act is a supernatural act.'[143] Hence, natural and supernatural acts are of different sorts because 'the act of meritorious affection is elicited by means of a supernatural habit, such as love.'[144] Scotus then thought that a work was meritorious because it was performed from the supernatural habit of sanctifying grace, meaning that the same act – for example giving to the poor – can be non-meritorious if performed in a natural state or meritorious if performed while possessing sanctifying grace.[145] Wawrykow explained, 'In Scotus, God decides freely to treat certain acts done under certain conditions (that is, in grace and charity) as meritorious.'[146] Scotus posits grace as the underlying principle making works meritorious.

---

140. Scotus, *Questiones*, 2.29.1.7, in *Opera*, 13:282 (Ad quartum dico, quod si fuerit aliquod donum supernaturale, non tamen oportet quod sit principium merendi; se enim habet ad gratiam, quae est principium meriti, sicut excedens et excessum. Excedens quidem, quia fini ultimo conjunxit firmius voluntatem quam gratia).

141. Feingold, *Natural Desire to See God*, 47-65.

142. Cross, *Duns Scotus*, 99.

143. Scotus, *Quaestiones Quodlibetals*, 17.3, in *Opera*, 26:204 (id est, quod titulus qugestionis debet magis intelligi de actu naturali distincto contra actum supernaturalem, quia actus meritorius est actus supernaturalis).

144. Scotus, *Quodlibetals*, 17.1, in *Opera*, 26:202 (actus autem dilectionis meritoriae elicitur mediante habitu supernaturali, puta charitate; naturale autem et supernaturale differunt specie).

145. Cross, *Duns Scotus*, 103-11; Horton, *Justification*, 1:140-44.

146. Wawrykow, *God's Grace and Human Action*, 189.

Scotus further applied his voluntarist principles to the notion of merit. Scotus' doctrine of *acceptatio* is key for shoring up the proportionality problem, locating his solution in God's *will* to accept a work as meritorious. He argued, 'a meritorious act is an act specially accepted by God, as being worthy of a reward for that act.' In one sense, God 'accepts all things with a general acceptance,' appreciating whatever goodness is present to order them to himself as the end. Still, 'he specially accepts a meritorious act into a class that results in the return of some blessing for it.' So then, 'merit adds a double relation upon the act, one concerning the will as accepted, and the other concerning that blessing to which the will, having accepted it, ordains it.'[147] Scotus' interpreters confirmed, 'merit is an act *accepted* by God as worthy of reward.'[148] With particular clarity, Scotus expressed a voluntarist, proleptically nominalist, view of merit's ground: 'neither relation imported on account of merit is real because it does not agree with the act by the nature of any real thing in the act, but only by an act of the will, by which the act is accepted.'[149] The condition for merit is that 'the act itself must be related to a supernatural pattern,' namely its operative power must be 'grace or love.'[150] Ultimately for Scotus, a work is meritorious because God chooses to accept it as such, regardless of its true perfection or if the person has even had the remission of sins.[151] Hence, Scotus went much further

---

147. Scotus, *Quodlibetals*, 17.4, in *Opera*, 26:205 (De secundo dico, quod actus meritorius actus Deo specialiter acceptus, tanquam scilicet dignus praemio reddendo pro illo actu. Specialiter dixit, quia omnia acceptat acceptatione generali, diligendo ea secundum bonitatem suam, et ordinando ea ad seipsum, ut ad finem, sed actum meritorium specialiter acceptat in ordine ad aliquod bonum juste reddendum pro eo. Meritorium igitur addit supra actum duplicem relationem, unam ad voluntatem ut acceptam, et aliam ad illud bonum ad quod voluntas acceptus illud ordinat).

148. Scotus, *Quodlibetal*, 17.3, in *Opera*, 26:204 (Secundum dictum hujus articuli merilum est actus a Deo acceptatus, ut dignus praemio).

149. Scotus, *Quodlibetals*, 17.4, in *Opera*, 26:205 (Neutra autem relatio importata per meritorium est realis, quia non competit actui ex natura alicujus realis in actu, sed tantum per actum voluntatis, quo actus acceptur).

150. Scotus, *Quodlibetals*, 17.4, in *Opera*, 26:205-6 (Alia autem habitudo requiritur ipsius actus ad formam supernaturalem, qua acceptatur ipsa persona, vel potentia operans, quae ponitur esse gratia, vel charitas); Antonie Vos, *The Theology of John Duns Scotus* (Studies in Reformed Theology; Leiden: Brill, 2018), 243-49.

151. Vos, *Theology of John Duns Scotus*, 249-53 (although Vos underestimates Scotus' voluntarist principles); J. Pohle, 'Merit,' in Charles G. Herbermann, Edward A. Pace, Condé B Pallen, Thomas J. Shahan, John J. Wynne (eds.), *The Catholic Encyclopedia*,

than Bonaventure in a voluntarist direction. This voluntarist basis for merit is perhaps the obvious entailment of Scotus' voluntarist notion of the natural law, wherein – against Thomas' view that God's *nature* grounds the whole natural law which is summarized in the Decalogue – God's *will* determines what is good and right.[152] Far from Thomas' objectivity wherein God ordains the elect to obtain real righteousness, Scotus posited merit as the premise of willed acceptability.

The Nominalist Turn

The Franciscan paradigm flourished in the late medieval period, arguably albeit partially, setting the exact context for the Reformation.[153] Although departing from the Parisian lineage, a major precipitating development was the teaching of William of Ockham (1285–1347), a notable Franciscan who helped develop a more full-orbed nominalist outlook where value and meaning were hyper-voluntaristically assigned. As Laurence Renault has demonstrated, Ockham, more so than any before him, emphasized that anything that cannot be known and achieved according to the very principles of a given nature must belong to another nature. This emphasis broadened the real gap between the natural and supernatural orders since God and the beatific vision are not of the same exact order of nature, and cemented a version of pure nature wherein religious life is thoroughly extraneous to human existence.[154]

On the issue of nature, grace, and merit, Ockham radicalized the Franciscan trajectory of increasing voluntarism in respect to the moral law. Bonaventure had said that God would accept a truly righteous *act* as meritorious if performed by a *person* with sanctifying grace. Scotus was ambiguous about whether the act itself had to be *truly* righteous for God to accept it as meritorious, if performed by a person with sanctifying grace. Ockham applied his thoroughgoing voluntarism to the law,

---

special ed., 15 vol. (New York, NY: The Encyclopedia Press, 1913), 10:206-7; Cross, 'Duns Scotus and William of Ockham,' 65; Wawrykow, *God's Grace and Human Action*, 188-89; McGrath, *Iustitia Dei*, 164; Horton, *Justification*, 1:141.

152. Cross, 'Duns Scotus and William of Ockham,' 61.

153. McGrath, *Iustitia Dei*, 116-17.

154. Laurence Renault, 'William of Ockham and the Distinction between Nature and Supernature,' in *Surnaturel*, 191-202.

therein showing his nominalism, in rejecting the deeper connection between God's character and the natural law. In this connection, on one hand, Scotus had held that the natural law was somewhat mutable since all but the first two commandments could be changed. On the other hand, Ockham's radicalizing nominalism again shows, as he taught, that God's law was entirely arbitrary and fully mutable so that God could even command humans to hate him, and it would be righteous. In this way, Ockham located the foundation for the righteousness of our duties to God entirely in divine choice.[155] Thus, Ockham's voluntarist and nominalist metaphysics in application to the law entailed that no realist premise for what acts are *truly* righteous even exists.[156]

This context of shifting ideas produced controversy in the late-thirteenth and early-fourteenth centuries over whether God can recognize a person's acts as meritorious apart from grace.[157] That debate distinguishes between what God *can* do and what God *will* do: Is God able to save apart from grace versus has God decided to save apart from grace? Drawing upon the distinction of God's absolute and ordained power, Ockham contended that ordained power 'must be understood in this way that God's power for something is sometimes taken as in accord with the laws ordained and instituted by God, and God is said to be able to do these things by his ordained power.'[158] In application to this issue, God decides the contingent working principles of salvation and then works within his own ordained structures.[159] On this premise, keeping in mind that for Ockham 'created charity' was the infused grace related to salvation, 'a person can be saved according to God's absolute power

---

155. Hannes Möhle, 'Scotus's Theory of Natural Law,' in *Cambridge Companion to Duns Scotus*, 315-16; A. S. McGrade, 'Natural Law and Moral Omnipotence,' in Paul Vincent Spade (ed.), *The Cambridge Companion to Ockham* (Cambridge: CUP, 1999), 273-301; Francis Oakley, 'Medieval Theories of Natural Law: William of Ockham and the Significance of the Voluntarist Tradition,' *Natural Law Forum* (1960): 68-72.

156. Barrett, *Reformation as Renewal*, 251-56.

157. Marilyn McCord Adams, *William Ockham*, combined edition (South Bend, IN: University of Notre Dame Press, 1989), 1259, 1263-65.

158. William of Ockham, *Quodlibeta* (Leiden: Janon Carcain, 1488), 6.1.1 (fol. n3v; Sed est sic intelligenda quod posse deum aliquod quandoque accipitur secundum leges ordinatas et institutas a deo et illa dicitur deus posse facere de potentia ordinata); also William of Ockham, *Quodlibetal Questions: Volumes 1 and 2: Quodlibets 1-7*, trans. Alfred J. Freddoso and Francis E. Kelley (New Haven, CT: Yale University Press, 1991), 491-92.

159. Ozment, *Age of Reform*, 38-40.

without created charity.'[160] Set in terms used by preceding theologians, Ockham thought that God could save apart from sanctifying grace although he has chosen not to do so.[161]

Ockham then applied his voluntarist denial of grace's necessity to his principle of merit, which was equally voluntarist and nominalist as was his view of the law. In striving to uphold God's freedom, Ockham argued: 'God can give everlasting life to someone who does a good work without such grace.'[162] The key factor is that a good work is still required for salvation, but that work can be performed without God infusing grace into the person. Harking back to Scotus, Ockham implicitly conceded that created love is normally required as the 'habit of a previous power that is the principle for meriting.' Still, he contended that 'God can give to him everlasting life without any grace of the kind under investigation, which is the principle of merit.'[163] Ockham's complexity is in how he has argued that 1) the infused love is not necessary for salvation according to God's absolute power, 2) that infused love is the principle of merit, and 3) a good work is still required for salvation even if God has not granted that infusion of grace as the principle of merit.[164]

That complexity reveals how his voluntarism and nominalism come to fruition in his doctrine of pure nature. He argued that 'a [person's] will constituted in only natural aspects is able according to God's absolute power to perform a meritorious act.'[165] In this respect, 'In addition,

---

160. Ockham, *Quodlibeta*, 6.1.2.1 (fol. n3v; Circa secundum articulum dico primo quod homo potest salvari sine caritate creata de potentia dei absoluta); Ockham, *Quodlibetal Questions*, 492.

161. Ockham, *Quodlibeta*, 6.1.2.1 (fol. n3v); Ockham, *Quodlibetal Questions*, 492. Concerning Ockham's application of absolute power to grace and justification, see Horton, *Justification*, 1:144-46.

162. Ockham, *Quodlibeta*, 6.1.2.1 (fol. n3v; Ergo potest dare vitam eternam alicui facienti bonum opus sine tali gratia); Ockham, *Quodlibetal Questions*, 492.

163. Ockham, *Quodlibeta*, 6.1.2.1 (fol. n3v; Preterea quod potest dari non tantus premium pro merito potest sibi dari de potentia dei absoluta sine omni habitu potentia previo qui est principium merenda: sed actus beatificus dabatur paulo in suo raptu. Quia tunc vidit essentia dei non tanque premium merito ergo potest sibi dare: vitam eternam sine tali gratia que[tione] est principia merenda); Ockham, *Quodlibetal Questions*, 492-93.

164. Adams, *William Ockham*, 1277-78.

165. Ockham, *Quodlibeta*, 6.1.2.1 (fol. n3v; Ergo voluntas in solus naturalibus constituta per potentiam dei absolutam potest in actum meritoriam); Ockham, *Quodlibetal Questions*, 493.

nothing is meritorious except that which is in our power. Therefore, an act is meritorious principally on account of that grace but also on account of free will causing it. Therefore, God could accept such an act elicited by the will without such grace.'[166]

For Ockham, the principle of merit depends upon our ability to perform the act, including in reference to created love. Hence, because free will exercised according to our natural ability contributes to merit, God can decide to accept a work as meritorious of everlasting life if it is performed without grace according to our natural capacities.[167] Ockham's view was that if a person has power to will a demeritorious act, then he also has power to will a meritorious act.[168]

In all these respects, Ockham was speaking according to God's absolute power. On the other hand, according to Ockham, in God's ordained power, no one can be saved without grace or perform a meritorious act apart from grace.[169] In one way, in connection to his use of absolute power, Ockham went even further than Scotus by denying that sanctifying grace was necessary to merit salvation.[170] Ockham concluded: 'I say that God can forgive a sinner of all punishment without infused grace.'[171] He supported that claim with two arguments from the greater to the lesser, explaining:

> I prove this thus and in this way that God can accept a person as if worthy of everlasting life without any created grace infused, then he can forgive all their guilt without any created grace. But since God, according to his

---

166. Ockham, *Quodlibeta*, 6.1.2.1 (fol. n3v–n4r; Preterea nihil est meritorium nisi quod est in potestate nostra, ergo actus est meritorious principaliter propter illam gratiam sed propter voluntatem libere causantem. Ergo posset deus talem actum elicitum a voluntate acceptare sine tali gratia); Ockham, *Quodlibetal Questions*, 493. Freddoso and Kelly seem to have translated an edition of Ockham's Latin that included phrases not in the early modern edition used here. Their translation supplies a minor premise and highlights Ockham's Pelagian priority of our free will over grace.

167. 'Similarly, love is laudable for how much it is the cause and principle of a meritorious work.' Ockham, *Quodlibeta*, 6.2 (fol. n4v; Similiter caritas est laudabilis pro quanto est operis meritorii causa et principium).

168. Ockham, *Quodlibeta*, 6.1.2.1 (fol. n3v); Ockham, *Quodlibetal Questions*, 493; Adams, *William Ockham*, 1270–73.

169. Ockham, *Quodlibeta*, 6.1.2 (fol. n4r); Ockham, *Quodlibetal Questions*, 493.

170. Ockham, *Ordinatio*, I.17.3; cited in Cross, 'Duns Scotus and William of Ockham,' 65.

171. Ockham, *Quodlibeta*, 6.4.1 (fol. n5v; dico quod deus potest peccatori remittere omnem penam sine gratie infusione); Ockham, *Quodlibetal Questions*, 501.

absolute power, if it were pleasing to him, could accept a sinner to everlasting life without grace, therefore he could forgive his sin without grace.[172]

This forgiveness returns someone to pure nature: 'God can forgive sin and restore to a state of innocence or establish in pure nature.'[173] In another way, Ockham realized that his voluntarist claims left him susceptible to severe criticisms, so applied ordained power as a counter-balance.

Recognizing that his concession that a sinner, according to God's absolute power, could merit salvation apart from grace could be perceived as Pelagian, Ockham attempted to disassociate his view from that heresy by doubling down on his voluntarist premise. In that regard, he thought he avoided Pelagianism by arguing that, although God *can* accept a work as meritorious if performed without grace, he is not *required* to do so. Thus, Ockham argued:

> Although it is said that the first conclusion is Pelagius' error, I respond that it is not because Pelagius supposed that in fact grace is not required in order to have everlasting life and that an act elicited from the state of pure nature is condignly [meritorious] of everlasting life. I, however, suppose that it will be meritorious only on account of God's absolute power if he wills to accept it. [174]

Ockham attempted to differentiate his view from Pelagianism on the slim premise that Pelagius rooted merit in necessity, but he appealed to God's absolute and ordained power, so preserving God's freedom.[175] Accordingly, Ockham equivocated on what love in connection to grace is: 1) using it to refer to an infused quality that makes us acceptable, in which

172. Ockham, *Quodlibeta*, 6.4.1 (fol. n5r; Hoc probo sic quecunque deus potest acceptare tanquam dignum vita eterna sine omni gratia creata infusa: illa potest remittere omnem culpam sine omni gratia creata: sed deus de potentia sua absoluta si sibi placeret posset peccatonem acceptare ad vitam eternam sine gratia. ergo potest remittere sibi &c); Ockham, *Quodlibetal Questions*, 500.

173. Ockham, *Quodlibeta*, 6.4.3 ad arg. (fol. n5v; Deus posset remittere peccatum et reducere ad statum innocentie sive ponere in puris naturalibus); Ockham, *Quodlibetal Questions*, 502.

174. Ockham, *Quodlibeta*, 6.1.2 (fol. n4r; Etsi dicatur quod prima conclusio error est Pelagii. Respondeo quod non quia Pelagius posuit quod de facto non requiritur gratia ad vitam eternam habendam et quod actus ex puris naturalibus elicitus est condignus vitae eternae. Ego autem pono quod solum erit meritorius per potentiam dei absolutam si velit acceptare); Ockham, *Quodlibetal Questions*, 493.

175. Adams, *William Ockham*, 1279-97; Horton, *Justification*, 1:146-49; cf. Rega Wood, 'Ockham's Repudiation of Pelagianism,' in *Cambridge Companion to Ockham*, 350-73.

way it is unnecessary; 2) as God's acceptance in which way this grace is necessary. In this way, he tried to avoid saying that some inherent quality forces God to find a person acceptable and to affirm God's control over the saving process.[176] Nonetheless, as we saw above, a good work is still necessary for salvation even apart from grace and can be achieved by the power of free will. Hence, only Ockham's voluntarist caveat, wherein he posited that God chooses to accept a work as meritorious, distinguished his teaching from blatant Pelagianism, wherein God *must* reward even a sinner's good work with everlasting life because of the intrinsic worth in the act. Certainly, later Augustinians, even those sympathetic to nominalist methodology, suspected Ockham of Pelagianism.[177] Ockham thought that his rejection of the *condignity* of a meritorious work and his rejection of the absolute necessity that God accept a work as meritorious saved him from Pelagianism.[178] These very rejections in some ways opened the door, as Stephen Ozment has shown, to radicalize the doctrine of congruent merit wherein a sinner can by imperfect works earn grace and salvation, which still left Ockham liable to the charge of Pelagianism.[179]

As important as Ockham was for mainstreaming the nominalism that undergirded late-medieval soteriology, Gabriel Biel is likely most significant for nominalism's upshot concerning nature, grace, and merit. Biel was a prominent lecturer at the University of Tübingen, championing the 'modern way' (*via moderna*), which had roots in opposition to Thomism – Thomism being essentially the 'old way' (*via antiqua*).[180] Although Biel belonged to the Brethren of the Common Life rather than the Franciscan order, the modern way was forged in Ockham's nominalist teaching.[181] Biel's work was in some ways paradigmatic of late medieval theology, crystalizing the issues around grace and merit that were ready kindling for Reformation doctrine.

---

176. Ockham, *Quodlibeta*, 6.1.2.2 ad arg. (fol. n4r); Ockham, *Quodlibetal Questions*, 494; Wood, 'Ockham's Repudiation of Pelagianism,' 353-58.

177. William J. Courtenay, *Ockham and Ockhamism: Studies in the Dissemination and Impact of His Thought*, (Leiden: BRILL, 2008), 349-57; Barrett, *Reformation as Renewal*, 260-63.

178. Ockham, *Quodlibeta*, 6.2.2 (fol. n4r); Ockham, *Quodlibetal Questions*, 496

179. Ozment, *Age of Reform*, 40-42.

180. Oberman, *Harvest of Medieval Theology*, 12-21.

181. Barrett, *Reformation as Renewal*, 266-67.

In his lectures upon Lombard's *Sentences*, Biel argued for the same positions about pure nature and the *donum superadditum* as has been noted throughout the Franciscan tradition. He explained that 'pure nature does not exclude God's general influence ... but the purely natural things mean the soul's nature or substance with the qualities and consequent actions arising, excluding the habits and gifts supernaturally infused by God alone.'[182] Biel's view of pure nature was then that it lacked supernatural gifts, which he applied to 'the state of innocence – for man could then be in pure natural things without grace and without guilt.'[183] Addressing Lombard's next distinction, the same section whereupon Bonaventure and Scotus developed their views of pure nature, Biel also asked 'whether in the state of innocence man was accepted by God without the gift of grace.'[184] Quoting Bonaventure himself, Biel distinguished the acceptance of pure nature from the acceptance elevated by the *donum superadditum*, truly encapsulating the Franciscan premise that Adam would need to earn the *donum superadditum* before then earning eschatological reward: 'The first type of acceptance does not require the *donum superadditum* of grace beyond those things that are from the natural condition. The second type, however, cannot be accepted thereupon both on account of God's gracious condescension and on account of the creature's exaltation beyond nature's limits.'[185] So, he inferred, 'Therefore, neither nature's consecration nor adoption, nor the soul's union with God is effected through some natural property but through some gift of grace

---

182. Gabriel Biel, *Sentences*, bk. 2, dist. 28, q. 1, art. 1, not. 2; in *Collectorium circa quattuor libros Sententiarum*, ed. Wilfridus Werbeck and Udo Hofman, 6 vol. (Tübingen: Mohr Siebeck, 1973–92), 2:536-37 (Secundo notandum quod, cum loquimur de puris naturalibus, non excluditur generalis Dei influentia ... Sed per pura naturalia intelligitur animae natura seu substantia cum qualitatibus et actionibus consequentibus naturam, exclusis habitibus ac donis supernaturaliter a solo Deo infusis).

183. Biel, *Sentences*, bk. 2, dist. 28, q. 1, art. 1, not. 3; in *Collectorium*, 2:537 (in statu innocentiae – tunc enim potuit homo esse in puris naturalibus sine gratia et sine culpa).

184. Biel, *Sentences* bk. 2, dist. 29. q. 1, art. 3, dub. 3; in *Collectorium*, 2:551 (Utrum homo in statu innocentiae absque dono gratiae fuerit acceptus Deo).

185. Biel, *Sentences* bk. 2, dist. 29. q. 1, art. 3, dub. 3; in *Collectorium*, 2:552 ('Primum acceptationis genus non requirit superadditum donum gratiae ultra ea, quae sunt de condicione naturae. Secundum vero genus non potest non esse gratui tum tum propter gratuitam Dei condescensionem, tum propter creaturae super naturae terminos exaltationem.').

superadded to nature.'[186] Drawing his final conclusion, he brought the point full circle back to our concerns for Adam's original righteousness: 'It might be doubted whether Adam was created in grace.'[187] In sum, like Bonaventure, Biel concluded that Adam existed in a pure nature prior to possessing original righteousness, which is necessary for obtaining blessings that transcend the faculties of pure nature.[188]

Clarifying how this theological trajectory affects soteriology, Biel attacked Gregory of Rimini (1300–58), an Augustinian who taught in Oxford, concerning pure nature after the fall. Biel argued that even though God applies sanctifying grace to pure nature after the fall to enable man to perform meritorious works, those works could have been performed naturally even without sanctifying grace: 'Secluding sanctifying grace from pure natural endowments, God's general influence remains standing. Man can dispose himself to grace, dispose of an obstacle, and become infirm or excellent. Indeed man is able by pure nature to stand by God's general help or by God's general grace is able to do what is within him.'[189] Remember that Biel understood God's general influence as merely providence in pure nature apart from original righteousness, meaning man can obtain sanctifying grace to earn everlasting life by his own even fallen strength.[190] If man does 'what is within him' specifically without the help of grace, he attains this higher good.[191] In other words, according to Biel, sinners can congruently merit first grace, which then enables them to merit condignly.[192]

---

186. Biel, *Sentences* bk. 2, dist. 29. q. 1, art. 3, dub. 3; in *Collectorium*, 2:552 (Ideo nec consecration nec adoptatio naturae nec unio animae ad Deum fit per aliquam proprietatem naturae, sed per aliquod donum gratiae naturae superadditum).

187. Biel, *Sentences* bk. 2, dist. 29. q. 1, art. 3, dub. 3; in *Collectorium*, 2:553 (Posset moveri dubium, utrum Adam creatus esset in gratia).

188. Oberman, *Harvest of Medieval Theology*, 47-50.

189. Gabriel Biel, sermon 87, in *Sermones dominicales Gabrielis biel Spirensis Hyemales Estiuales De Tempore* (Hagenua, 1510), fol. 127 (Ex puris naturalibus seclusa gratiam gratum facientem: stante generali influentia dei: potest homo sese ad gratiam disponere: obicem disponere: et infirmatis seu lectum potestare. Potest enim homo ex puris naturalibus stante adiutorio dei generali seu gratia dei generali facere quod in se est).

190. Oberman, *Harvest of Medieval Theology*, 135-41.

191. Oberman, *Harvest of Medieval Theology*, 132-39; McGrath, *Iustitia Dei*, 135-45.

192. Denis Janz, 'A Reinterpretation of Gabriel Biel on Nature and Grace,' *Sixteenth Century Journal* 8, no. 1 (April 1977): 104-8.

This formulation of the Franciscan Pactum encapsulated the distinctly late-medieval covenant theology. Concerning its broad scope, Matthew Barrett outlined the order in Biel's soteriology as: 'moral effort,' 'infusion of grace as an appropriate reward,' 'moral cooperation,' and 'reward of eternal life as a just due.' Given his premises of pure nature outlined above, Biel was furthering the Franciscan idea that a person can merit first grace, specifically by their best natural efforts. Hence, Biel viewed human nature as affected by sin but not so corrupted in pure nature that we cannot perform meritorious acts without grace.[193] In this respect, Biel followed Ockham in asserting that: 'There is no human merit that does not depend partly on free will. The principal cause of meritorious moral action, however, is attributed to grace. But grace does not determine the will.'[194] The combination of grace with the determining factor of free will shows Biel's dependence on Ockham's voluntarist construction of the necessity of grace.[195] Biel's premise then began with human effort in pure nature to earn grace by the use of free will.

Drawing our attention back to the doctrine of the *donum superadditum*, Biel plainly outlined the stages in his order of salvation as the sinner acquiring infused (sanctifying) grace unto initial justification that then enables the performance of meritorious deeds that will lead to everlasting life. The connection shows us how Biel considered sanctifying grace:

> Now we must see just what this grace is by which the sinner is justified and what is accomplished in us. The grace of which we speak is a gift of God supernaturally infused into the soul. It makes the soul acceptable to God and sets it on the path to deeds of meritorious love.[196]

Biel categorized the effects of grace as: '(a) making acceptable, (b) justifying, and (c) making the works which result meritorious and

---

193. Barrett, *Reformation as Renewal*, 267-69.

194. Gabriel Biel, 'The Circumcision of the Lord,' in Heiko A. Oberman, *Forerunners of the Reformation: The Shape of Late Medieval Thought* (London: Lutterworth Press, 1967; repr. Cambridge: James Clarke & Co., 2002), 170.

195. Barrett rightly noted how Biel followed Lombard on this combination; Barrett, *Reformation as Renewal*, 270. A likely more proximate source, especially important for tracing our trajectory, was Ockham, *Quodlibeta*, 6.1.2.1 (fol. n3v–n4r); Ockham, *Quodlibetal Questions*, 493.

196. Biel, 'Circumcision of the Lord,' 168.

worthy of eternal life, of grace and glory.'[197] These three effects of grace reveal how Biel followed the Franciscan trajectory of locating merit in relation to the *person* in possession of sanctifying grace.

As he explained those three effects of grace, Biel's use of the *donum superadditum* as the ontological elevation of our nature to enable becomes clear. First, citing Scotus, Biel contended that, 'grace is an enrichment of nature that is pleasing to God's will.' This grace adorns human nature as 'that special acceptation by which man is according to God's decision ordained toward eternal life.'[198] In this respect grace pertains to Scotus' doctrine of *acceptatio* and functions as the supplement to our nature that relates us to the supernatural order. Second, this *transformative* grace as an elevation of our nature makes a sinner acceptable to God unto justification, which highlights how Biel's soteriology nominalist was a far cry from the later Reformed view of forensic imputation.[199] Accordingly, Biel affirmed that grace is an infused habit that 'elevates human power beyond itself' so that our works can be meritorious as sin is weakened in us.[200] Third, grace as the *donum superadditum* for initial justification enables us to merit possession of that supernatural order to which grace ordered us:

> Thus God makes these our works meritorious and acceptable for eternal reward, not actually all our works but only those which have been brought forth by the prompting of grace. It is assumed of a meritorious work that the person who performs it is accepted, since the acts of a person who has not been accepted or of an enemy cannot please God.[201]

Biel herein clarified how works are meritorious on account of a *person* in possession of sanctifying grace performing them.[202] Thus, Biel followed the developing Franciscan trajectory for categorizing merit in conjunction to the *person* without specific respect to the true righteousness of the *work*, as had been the case with Thomas. This use of sanctifying grace relativized the

---

197. Biel, 'Circumcision of the Lord,' 168.

198. Biel, 'Circumcision of the Lord,' 168.

199. Biel, 'Circumcision of the Lord,' 169; McGrath, *Iustitia Dei*, 81.

200. Biel, 'Circumcision of the Lord,' 171.

201. Biel, 'Circumcision of the Lord,' 169.

202. For more thorough analysis of this point in Biel's more technical writings, see Oberman, *Harvest of Medieval Theology*, 160-68.

requirement of true righteousness for merit, opening the door to a greater application of voluntarism for what works God would accept for obtaining both initial justification and final justification. Others have effectively explored how Biel's doctrine comes to fruition in a Pelagian doctrine of justification, so we will turn our attention to focus on the narrower scope of how Biel's use of the Franciscan Pactum connected to merit.[203]

Biel's use of the Franciscan Pactum applied to merit followed Ockham in distinguishing his view from Pelagianism only by the slim premise that God *chose* to – rather than had to – accept works as meritorious. We have already explored how Biel emphasized 'that which is in him,' or our best efforts according to pure (ungraced) nature as the basis for merit. Following Ockham in rejecting the necessity of grace as an infused quality, Biel asserted that God 'could have simultaneously made us His friends and accepted our work as meritorious *without this gift of grace*.'[204] Leaning upon his premise that a person in pure nature is not so damaged by sin that he cannot turn himself to God, Biel brought home his voluntarist to the premise of merit: 'Thus God established the rule [covenant] that whoever turns to Him and *does what he can* will receive forgiveness of sins from God.' Biel's illustration of a lenient king only reinforces that his view of grace requires the sinner to make the first move toward God to receive grace and then to keep performing grace-empowered works of love to merit eschatological reward.[205] In Biel's paradigm, works of pure nature merit first grace and works performed in sanctifying grace then merit final grace unto glory, making it a works-based scheme from top to bottom wherein grace – as for Ockham – amounts to God's decision to accept imperfect, even sin-stained works, as meritorious.[206] In grace, God made a covenant to accept our works even from pure nature as meritorious of first grace, of the increase of grace, and of entry to glory.[207]

---

203. Matthew Barrett, 'Can this Bird Fly? Repositioning the Genesis of the Reformation on Martin Luther's Early Polemic against Gabriel Biel's Covenantal, Voluntarist Doctrine of Justification,' *Southern Baptist Journal of Theology* 21.4 (2017): 61-101; Barrett, *Reformation as Renewal*, 263-83; Oberman, *Harvest of Medieval Theology*, 120-84; Horton, *Justification*, 1:150-62.

204. Biel, 'Circumcision of the Lord,' 173 (emphasis added).

205. Biel, 'Circumcision of the Lord,' 173.

206. Oberman, *Harvest of Medieval Theology*, 140-41, 167.

207. Oberman, *Harvest of Medieval Theology*, 169-74; McGrath, *Iustitia Dei*, 97-100.

Lest a thread be left untied, Biel applied his voluntarism in Ockhamist fashion to the law as well. Biel excludes the realist and intellectualist premises that Thomas used to explain the moral law, instead hanging the standard of righteousness entirely upon God's choice:

> Because nothing to do is worthy except that you choose to declare it worthy according to your dignity and merciful will. For God does not will something because it is good or just. Rather, because God wills, therefore it is good and just. Indeed, the divine will does not depend upon our goodness, but our goodness depends upon the divine will. Nor is something good except because it is thus accepted by God.[208]

In connection to the Franciscan Pactum, Biel's view of the law entails that God can appoint any human work whatsoever – at least in accord with God's ordained will as long as it is performed in sanctifying grace – as a meritorious act. Franciscan voluntarism flowered in Biel so that even righteousness is a nominalist matter of God arbitrarily naming what is good and evil so to decide whether it becomes meritorious.[209]

Significant debate has taken place regarding whether Biel was ultimately Pelagian. Oberman argued that Biel implemented Pelagian explanations of the relation of free will and grace for their respective contribution to meritorious acts. Because Biel thought that even a sinful person did not need the aid of grace to act right and held that, according to God's absolute power, grace is not necessary for a meritorious act, Oberman concluded that Biel's soteriology was ultimately Pelagian. Biel viewed grace simply in terms of God's ordained power as the decree to accept every act performed by a person possessing sanctifying grace as condignly meritorious. The upshot is that the person is responsible for an act's true goodness while grace is responsible for making that act meritorious.[210]

Biel's voluntarist outlook has persuaded some that he implemented a more thoroughgoing doctrine of grace. Challenging Oberman, Alistair

---

208. Gabriel Biel, *Sacri Canonis Missae Lucidisse Expositio* (Brescia: Thomas Bozzolam, 1576), Lect. 23E (Pg. 143; quia nihil fieri dignum est, nisi quod de tua dignitate, et misericordia voluntate dignum iudicare volueris: neque enim quia bonum, aut iustum est aliquid, ipsum deus vult: sed quia deus vult, ideo bonum est et iustum. Voluntas namque divina non ex nostra bonitate: sed ex divina voluntate bonitas nostra pendet: nec aliquid bonum: nisi quia a deo sic acceptum).

209. McGrath, *Iustitia Dei*, 100-2.

210. Oberman, *Harvest of Medieval Theology*, 164, 166-68, 170, 175-77.

McGrath has contended that Biel's appeal to God's covenant to accept a work performed even without grace as meritorious protected him from Pelagianism. As we saw above, Ockham differentiated his teaching from Pelagius' teaching that God *necessarily* had to accept works as meritorious in that his view rested upon God's *choice* to accept a work as meritorious. McGrath accepted the validity of Ockham's premise and applied it to Biel as rescuing him from outright Pelagianism. He then defended Biel on historical grounds by suggesting that Biel's contemporaries would not have considered him a Pelagian as measured by the councils of Carthage (418), Ephesus (431), and Orange (521).[211]

Biel's development of Ockham's theology complicates the matter. Ozment recounts how Ockham argued that a sinner who does the best that he could do from natural ability (*ex puris naturalibus*) without the assistance of grace can merit first grace from God. As we saw above, Ockham himself recognized this view's liability to the accusation of Pelagianism, prompting him to address that accusation preemptively.[212] Ozment and Oberman further document how Augustinians such as Gregory of Rimini and Thomas Bradwardine considered Ockham to be a Pelagian.[213]

Inasmuch as Biel's position matched Ockham's in differing from Pelagius only on account of God's choice, the historical grounds for defending Biel from the charge of Pelagianism disappear. McGrath seems to have mistakenly missed how the accusations of Pelagianism from among Biel's contemporaries against Ockham would likewise have applied to Biel. Their assessments of Ockham as Pelagian entail that they would find Biel to be Pelagian too. Vindicating Oberman, Barrett not only brought Ozment's historical framing to bear but also highlighted how McGrath downplayed the role of free will in Biel's view of justification. Namely, although Biel's view of the covenant had an 'outer structure' of grace in God's decision to accept a work as meritorious, its 'inner structure' ultimately depends upon a person doing what is in them according to pure nature. Works have priority as the final causality in Biel's system wherein final salvation is determined by

---

211. McGrath, *Iustitia Dei*, 124-25. On Augustinianism at these councils, see Ozment, *Age of Reform*, 29.

212. Ockham, *Quodlibeta*, 6.1.2; Ockham, *Quodlibetal Questions*, 493.

213. Ozment, *Age of Reform*, 37-42; Oberman, *Harvest of Medieval Theology*, 196-206.

our best efforts in cooperation with God's leniency. Biel and his grace-lacquered paradigm of works ultimately proves to be truly Pelagian and a leading instigation of Reformation soteriology.[214]

The Henrician Exception

As we have seen, the Parisian theologians drove the discussion about how to construct a theological understanding of human nature, noting that Lombard, Thomas, Bonaventure, and Scotus all spent time teaching in Paris. Henry of Ghent (c. 1217–93), who taught in Paris after Thomas, introduced a complicating factor into this discussion, which proves to be an important precedent for how Reformed theology should formulate human nature in relation to eschatological reward in the covenant of works.

Henry fully rejected the *donum superadditum*, instead affirming that Adam was *naturally* righteous before the fall. His question was, 'whether original righteousness included in itself another infused gift.'[215] He concluded:

> Hence because original righteousness, inasmuch as it includes a gift, by necessity simultaneously also includes natural uprightness, but inasmuch as it merely establishes natural uprightness it does not necessarily include a gift, therefore the simpler and naturally first is the explanation of original righteousness, so that it establishes only the uprightness of nature which thus includes the gift.[216]

Henry saw the gift of original righteousness as intrinsic to human nature (*donum concreatum*). Cross labelled Henry's view of natural righteousness as 'the extreme Augustinian line,' marking it as a highly palatable option for Protestants looking for a view with historical precedent regarding the *imago Dei* to support their burgeoning soteriology of grace.[217]

Like Thomas, Henry, when describing pure nature, simply meant nature undefiled by sin since God made it with *natural* or concreated original righteousness:

---

214. Barrett, *Reformation as Renewal*, 276-83.

215. Henry of Ghent, Quodlibet VI, question 11; in *Aurea Quodlibeta*, 2 vol. (Venice, 1613), 1:350v (Utrum iustitia originalis includat in se aliquod donum infusum).

216. Henry, Quodlibet VI, question 11; in *Aurea Quodlibeta*, 1:352r (Vnde quia originalis iustitia secundum quod includit donum, necessario simul & includit rectitudinem naturalem, non necessario includit donum, simplicior ergo & prior naturaliter est ratio originalis iustitiae, ut ponit solam naturae rectitudinem, quod ut includit donum).

217. Cross, *Duns Scotus*, 96-97; Horton, *Justification*, 1:138.

Moreover, the will ought to preserve that righteousness which it received by a natural gift in the state of pure nature, lest it should lose it, just as one would keep the members of the body from harm, so also he sins by not taking heed and by not guarding against harm, thus he would have sinned by willingly distorting himself and by losing that natural righteousness.[218]

Scotus attacked Henry's views on precisely these issues.[219] Scotus' response shows how Franciscan theology opposed joining original righteousness directly to human nature. Respecting the fall, Scotus argued against Henry, contending that the first sin damaged the superadded righteousness but 'has not created a wound in the natural condition of human persons.'[220] Nonetheless, Henry said righteousness was a natural gift bound intrinsically into pure nature, displaying that his version of pure nature simply meant unfallen. By contrast, the Franciscans continued to advocate that humanity's supernatural orientation was extrinsic to our nature, at least one effect being that Henry had a stronger view of sin's effects than many Franciscans.

Henry is not a standalone precedent in the wider tradition. Others in the wider tradition seem to take an Augustinian stance more akin at least to Thomas or even Henry than Bonaventure, for instance John of Damascus (c. 675–749) explained: 'God made man innocent, straightforward, virtuous, free from pain, free from care, ornamented with every virtue, and adorned with all good qualities.'[221] Throughout the medieval era, however, theologians drifted further and further from the tight relationship between human nature and the righteousness needed for living life with God.

---

218. Henry, *Quodlibet VI*, question 11; in *Aurea Quodlibeta*, 1:351r (Voluntas autem illam iustitiam, quam naturali dono accepit, conservare debuit in statu purae naturae, ne eam amitteret, sicut & membra corporis a nocumento custodire, & sicut peccat illa non custodiendo, neque nocumenta praecauendo, sic peccasset voluntarie se obliquando, & illam naturalem iustitiam amittendo).

219. Scotus, *Questiones*, 2.29.1, in *Opera*, 13:268, 273; Dezza, 'Scotus on Human Beings in the State of Innocence,' 291-94; Cross, 'Duns Scotus and William of Ockham,' 53-66, likewise highlighted Franciscan disagreement with Henry.

220. Dezza, 'Scotus on Human Beings in the State of Innocence,' 308.

221. John of Damascus, *An Exact Exposition of the Orthodox Faith*, 2.12, in *The Fathers of the Church: St. John of Damascus: Writings*, trans. Frederic H. Chase, Jr. (Washington, D.C.: The Catholic University of America Press, 1958), 235. Damascus did seemingly believe that the human will is intact after the fall, since he said that God does not determine all things; *Orthodox Faith*, 2.30 in *Writings*, 263-66. Thanks to Ryan McGraw for this second reference.

Henry's Augustinianism is less strident concerning merit and grace. He agreed with Thomas' Augustinianism that we cannot merit first (sanctifying) grace but differed by affirming that we can merit grace's increase and fulfillment.

> For after first sanctifying grace [*gratam gratum facientem*] whatever increase of grace in the present, and its consummation in the future, has in us a meritorious cause from worth [*digno*], namely a work elicited from free will in accordance with the assistance of preceding grace up to first sanctifying grace, which has no meritorious cause in us all because it is freely given to forgive sins and precedes free will's first meritorious movement.[222]

Henry applied this principle even to predestination, posing some foreseen merit as a motivating factor in God's election.[223] Henry's view is complicated because he attempted to balance Augustinian sensibilities with his inclination that some congruence must exist between God's election and its object.[224] As Pasquale Porro explains: 'when God elects someone to grace, he elects him to the most perfect grace that can occur in this life, and when he destines that someone to such grace, he elects him in the not-yet-perfect grace which is to be realized; and, insofar as he elects him to the latter, he elects him by grace freely given [*gratia gratis data*]' and yet 'he who uses the first grace correctly by his free will receives the second, and, if he uses it well, the third, until reaching the glory which is the end ultimate to which God has predestined him.'[225]

---

222. Henry, Quodlibet IV, question 19; in *Aurea Quodlibeta*, 1:196v (Post primam enim gratam gratum facientem quodlibet gratiae augmentum in praesenti, et consummatio eius in futuro causam habet in nobis meritoriam de digno, opus scilicet elicitum a libero arbitrio in adiutorio gratiae praecedentis usque ad primam gratiam gratum facientem. Illa enim non habet in nobis causam meritoriam ullam omnino, quia gratis data condonat peccata et praecedit primum motum liberi arbitrii meritorium).

223. Porro, 'Divine Predestination, Human Merit and Moral Responsibilty,' 562-67, 569.

224. Cf. Henry, Quodlibet VIII, question 5; in *Aurea Quodlibeta*, 2:9r (Ad hoc dicunt aliqui, q[uod] Deus quicquid operatur circa creaturas, ex mera liberalitate, et solo beneplacito suae voluntatis operatur, et faciendo quod facit, et non faciendo quod non facit, et faciendo modo, quo facit, et non faciendo modo, quo non facit, ut super hoc non sit aliqua alia ratio, vel causa petenda, vel investiganda aut merita praeterita praesentia, vel futura, vel dispositio ulla ex parte recipientium).

225. Porro, 'Rien de Personnel,' 505 (Ainsi, selon le premier point de vue, quand Dieu élit quelqu'un à la grâce, il l'élit à la grâce la plus parfaite qui puisse advenir en cette vie, et quand il destine ce quelqu'un à une telle grâce, il l'élit dans la grâce non encore parfaite qui doit être réalisée; et, en tant qu'il l'élit à cette dernière, il l'élit à la *gratia gratis data*,

Henry then made some room for foreseen merits within the full remit of predestination, even if not for the reception of first grace.[226]

Henry's view on the principle of merit is difficult to ascertain. He clearly emphasized his predestinarianism, marking him as a real Augustinian even if he conceded points that were in tension with that fundamental commitment. Like Thomas, he subsumed the whole structure of grace and merit under God's sovereign decree: 'predestination's whole effect concerning grace's substance and habit as well as the essence of the whole meritorious operation, inasmuch as the whole is the effect of grace, the whole belongs to the effect of predestination.'[227] Unlike Thomas and Scotus, he seemed holistically preoccupied with this discussion of predestination. He affirmed the priority of God's grace in predestination while trying to coordinate merit to predestination's effect, more than explaining his criteria for merit. It is then not clear whether he grounded merit along Thomas' realist lines or with Scotus' *acceptatio* principle. His emphasis on predestination might suggest a kinship to Thomas' *ordinatio*, but the detailed analysis required to substantiate that conjecture is beyond this discussion's scope.

Conclusion

This chapter surveyed the landscape of medieval discussions about Adam's original nature from Peter Lombard through late medieval theologians like Gabriel Biel. Medieval theology was in premise committed to Augustine's priority of grace, but the differences between Thomist and Franciscan thinkers reveal how various explanations greatly strained – even broke – that consensus.[228] Notably, Thomas and the Franciscans all suggested that even Adam required grace to obtain his

---

et ainsi à rebours, jusqu'au grade initial qui est offert à tous. Dans l'exécution, l'ordre est inversé: celui qui utilise correctement la première grâce dans son libre arbitre, reçoit la seconde, et, s'il l'utilise bien, la troisième, jusqu'à atteindre la gloire qui est la fin ultime à laquelle Dieu l'a predestine).

226. Porro, 'Rien de Personnel,' 502-8.

227. Henry, Quodlibet VIII, question 5; in *Aurea Quodlibeta*, 2:11v (Et potest dici secundum praedicta, quod licet effectus totus praedestinationis quo ad substantiam, et habitum gratiae, et essentiam operationis meritoriae totius, inquantum totum est effectus gratiae, totum pertinet ad effectum praedestinationis).

228. Jaroslav Pelikan, *The Growth of Medieval Theology (600–1300)* (Chicago, IL: University of Chicago Press, 1978), 9-105.

eschatological reward. On the one hand, Thomas argued that God created Adam with superadded grace, enabling him to merit the beatific vision, so that this grace was given to man by an act of pure divine good pleasure. On the other hand, Franciscans argued that Adam needed to obtain that initial grace by performing good works from pure nature. These theologians differed concerning the dispensation of grace itself – Thomas in God's sovereign gift, the Franciscans in man's earning. Thomas, affirming that 'grace is not acquired by one's merits,' argued 'as the first man had original [righteousness] from the beginning by God's gift, not by his own merit, so also, and far less, was he able to merit it after his sin by repenting or performing any other work.'[229] Still, all suggested that Adam needed the empowering of grace to have the original righteousness required to merit eschatological blessings.[230]

The evidence shows that theologians following the Franciscan trajectory increasingly separated Adam's created state from his ability to perform obedience that would obtain supernatural, eschatological communion with God. Many theologians argued that Adam had to cooperate with natural abilities in order to achieve an orientation toward supernatural realities. Although Thomas Aquinas still articulated some conceptual distinction between natural and supernatural ends, his later position sided with Augustine that Adam was created properly oriented toward God from the outset with the gift of original righteousness given in the act of creation. This later position amounted to a view functionally of *donum concreatum*.

If it need be said, this book focuses on one specific set of issues pertaining to original righteousness and merit, meaning that *this* topical lineage we are tracing toward a Reformed view has little to no bearing upon how the medieval figures discussed here might feature in a trajectory concerning *other* doctrines. Although this chapter obviously charts a certain course concerning Reformed appropriation of these theologians' ideas on this topic, they found at least Bonaventure more helpful on other issues than on this one. The Reformed eclectically drew from their antecedent sources, synthesizing from various parts of

---

229. Thomas Aquinas, *Compendium of Theology*, trans. Richard J. Regan (New York, NY: Oxford University Press, 2009), 149 (§198).

230. Karim Schelkens and Marcel Gielis, 'From Driedo to Bellarmine: The Concept of Pure Nature in the 16th Century,' *Augustiniana* 57 no 3/4 (2007): 431-34.

the tradition as suited their purposes. Even concerning the covenant of works, the Reformed were not uniform in what building blocks they used concerning voluntarist and intellectualist ideas.[231] Nonetheless, this chapter's outline of medieval theology helps Reformed theology find its bearings about why we need to formulate the issue of grace in the covenant of works so carefully. The notion that Adam needed grace to perform his original duties quickly suggests, as in various medieval views, that he was not naturally oriented toward supernatural communion with God. The teaching about sanctifying grace always concerned the supplementing of Adam's nature *ontologically* to make him fit to pursue eschatological ends. Although complexities exist in our tradition, as we will see, our confessional heritage favors rejecting this need for ontological elevation in support of seeing the covenant of works as what orders us to our natural orientation of a supernatural end.

---

231. Harrison Perkins, *Catholicity and the Covenant of Works: James Ussher and the Reformed Tradition* (New York, NY: Oxford University Press, 2020), 87-103.

CHAPTER FOUR

The Road to (Modern) Rome

The previous chapter delved into the medieval legacy about the natural and supernatural orders, finding that, according to the medievals, sanctifying grace was the key concept to explain how a finite creature could earn an infinitely valuable reward. In that paradigm, God provided a way for humanity to merit eschatological glory by using sanctifying grace to address the problem of proportionality. Although the principle of sanctifying grace as that which ontologically elevated human nature to enable us to merit remained consistent, the explanations relating nature to grace and of grace's necessity varied. Still, the story of those ideas continued past the medieval period.

This chapter explores how the nature-grace distinction in relation to merit continued to develop in Roman theology up into the modern period. Because of the breadth of sources, this discussion is more selective than chapter three's, which was itself minimal. Nonetheless, the purpose is to sketch how these issues have remained live in Roman theology until today, informing aspects of Protestantism's lingering disagreement with Rome. Although modern Roman theology could not have informed the development of Reformed theology in the period of confessionalization, this survey clarifies why a retrieval, refinement, and application of early modern Reformed theology's categories related to our status as God's image bearers remain pertinent to our defense of the law-gospel distinction that undergirds our soteriology.

Early Modern Roman Trajectories

The Franciscan position regarding nature and grace set Rome's theological trajectory across the board. Across the centuries, consensus settled in preferring a stronger divide between the natural and supernatural orders.[1] The stated purpose was to protect grace's gratuitousness within the Roman ontological scheme. The doctrinal lines did not remain confined within clerical orders. Dominicans began to interpret Thomas Aquinas by developing distinctions to fit Thomas' formulations more cleanly into the ongoing development of their nature-grace paradigm.[2] As Roman scholars have noted, the early modern discussion attempted to resolve Thomas' ambiguities over the proportionality problem in having a natural eschatological end. This early modern development shifted the question about pure nature from primarily concerning capacities to obtain a true supernatural end to whether humanity had a self-contained natural end. That self-contained natural end conceived of our nature as fulfilled apart from any relation to eschatological satisfaction in the beatific vision.[3] This section considers snapshots of Roman theology from the early modern period, especially as relevant to early Reformation and Reformed Orthodox theology.

Thomas' early modern interpreters, especially Cardinal Thomas Cajetan (1469–1534), heavily emphasized his distinction between natural and supernatural ends. In this understanding, Adam's natural ability related merely to civil goods, such as 'to build dwellings, plant vineyards and the like.'[4] To acquire the beatific vision, Adam would require supplemental infused grace to make his works adequately valuable. This interpretation stressed Thomas' argument that even in the perfect state,

1. Henri de Lubac, *Augustinianism and Modern Theology*, trans. Lancelot Sheppard (Milestones in Catholic Theology; New York, NY: Crossroad Publishing, 2000), 147-83.

2. Lawrence Feingold, *The Natural Desire to See God according to St. Thomas Aquinas and his Interpreters*, 2nd ed. (Naples, FL: Sapientia Press, 2001), 101-65, 211-76.

3. Karim Schelkens and Marcel Gielis, 'From Driedo to Bellarmine: The Concept of Pure Nature in the 16th Century,' *Augustiniana* 57 no 3/4 (2007): 425-26, 434-36, 446-47; Alexander S. Rosenthal, 'The Problem of the *Desiderium Naturale* in the Thomistic Tradition,' *Verbum* 6 no 2 (2004): 335-44; Peter F. Ryan, 'How Can the Beatific Vision both Fulfill Human Nature and Be Utterly Gratuitous?' *Gregorium* 83 no 4 (2002): 723-25.

4. St. Thomas Aquinas, *Summa Theologica*, trans. by Fathers of the English Dominican Province, 5 vol. (New York, NY: Benziger Bros., 1948; repr. Notre Dame, IN: Christian Classics, 1981), 1a2ae.109.2.

'man needs a gratuitous strength superadded to natural strength, viz. in order to do and wish supernatural good.'[5] Cajetan, however, never merely repeated Thomas but sought to defend Thomas' main principles and apply them to contemporary debates, often accepting less important premises from Scotist theology to refute more fundamental principles in Scotism.[6] Accordingly, Cajetan interpreted Thomas' view of the *donum superadditum* in a way that was more consistent with the burgeoning Franciscan theology that predominated late-medieval theology in the *via moderna*.[7]

The complexity of Thomas' distinction between natural and supernatural ends easily facilitated multiple readings, including Cajetan's.[8] Nonetheless, Cajetan's commentary on Thomas' *Summa* became historically and lastingly significant in the Roman interpretation of Thomas. In Thomas' own view, the *donum superadditum* was conceptually distinct from human nature but infused by God with creation when he made Adam. This functional concreatedness of sanctifying grace tied Adam's natural strength to merely natural ends but his infused strength to supernatural ends. In this respect, when Thomas himself referred to 'pure nature,' he simply meant human nature as unaffected by sin.[9] On the other hand, Cajetan appealed to Thomas' conceptual distinction between human nature and the *donum superadditum* to separate the order of natural morality from the order of grace, leaving room for the former to be linked to human capacities

---

5. Thomas, *Summa Theologica*, 1a2ae.109.2.

6. Cajetan Cuddy, OP, 'Sixteenth-Century Reception of Aquinas by Cajetan,' in Matthew Levering and Marcus Plested (eds.), *The Oxford Handbook of the Reception of Aquinas* (Oxford: Oxford University Press, 2021), 146-53.

7. Jacob W. Wood, *To Stir a Restless Heart: Thomas Aquinas and Henri de Lubac on Nature, Grace, and the Desire for God* (Thomistic Ressourcement Series; Washington, DC: Catholic University of America Press, 2019), 380-90, 426; Rupert Johannes Mayer, 'Man is Inclined to His Last End by Nature, though He cannot Reach It by Nature but Only by Grace: The Principle of the Debate about Nature and Grace in Thomas Aquinas, Thomism and Henri de Lubac. A Response to Lawrence Feingold,' *Angelicum* 88 (2011): 892-901.

8. Joseph P. Wawrykow, *God's Grace and Human Action: Merit in the Theology of Thomas Aquinas* (Notre Dame, IN: University of Notre Dame Press, 2016), 1-59.

9. Thomas, *Summa Theologica*, 1a2ae.109.4; Philip McCosker, 'Grace,' in Philip McCosker and Denys Turner (eds.), *The Cambridge Companion to the Summa Theologiae* (Cambridge: Cambridge University Press, 2016), 211-12; P. J. Donnelly, 'The Gratuity of the Beatific Vision and the Possibility of a Natural Destiny,' *Theological Studies* 11 (1950): 384-86.

of a supposed 'pure nature' disconnected from original righteousness.[10] Cajetan argued:

> The rational creature can be considered in two ways: the first way is absolutely; the other way is as ordained unto happiness. If the rational creature is considered in the first way, absolutely, then his natural desire is not for something beyond his natural faculties, and thus I concede that he does not *naturally* desire the vision of God absolutely in himself. On the other hand, if the rational creature is considered in the second way, as ordained unto happiness, then he naturally desires the vision of God because as such he knows certain effects, namely pure grace and glory, of which God is the cause, since God is self-contained in himself, not as the universally efficient cause.[11]

Cajetan articulated an understanding of pure nature in which humanity is not oriented or ordered toward eschatological life with God.[12]

Cajetan exposits merit in a strict but voluntarist fashion, keeping some Thomist ideals but also drawing upon prevailing Franciscan and nominalist principles. In affirming that, 'God has revealed to us in the sacred writings that human works merit something with God,' he also correlated merit and reward so that each concept entailed the other: 'wherever God promises a reward to man, it must be understood as merit in that reward and merit are correlative. Indeed, merit is the merit of a reward, and a reward is a reward of merit.'[13] Thus, Cajetan posed a strict relationship wherein our merit is required to receive God's blessing.

---

10. Rosenthal, 'Problem of the *Desiderium Naturale*,' 337-38; Schelkens and Gielis, 'Driedo to Bellarmine,' 434.

11. Thomas Cajetan, *Summa Sacrae Theologiae… Commentariis*, 3 vol. (Bergamo: Comini Venturae, 1590) 1:114 (commentary on Thomas' *Summa*, 1.12.1; emphasis added; Ad euidentia horum scito, quod creatura rationalis pot[est] dupliciter considerari: uno modo absoluté; alio modo ut ordinata est ad felicitate. Si primo modo co[n]sideretur, sic naturale eius desiderium non se extendit ultra naturae facultate. & sic concede, q[uod] non naturaliter desiderat visionem Dei in se absoluté. Si vero secundo modo co[n]siderat visionem Dei: quia ut sic nouit quosdam effectus, pura gratiae, & gloriae: quorum causa est De[us], ut Deus est i[p]se absoluté, non ut universal agens).

12. Paul Helm, *Calvin at the Centre* (New York, NY: Oxford University Press, 2010), 325-26; Mayer, 'Man is Inclined to His Last End by Nature, though He cannot Reach It by Nature but Only by Grace,' 887, 892.

13. Thomas de Vio Cajetan, *de Fide et Operibus adversus Lutheranos*, ch. 7, in *Opuscula Omnia* (Lyon, 1562), 290 (Revelavit Nobis Deus in sacris literis humana opera mereri apud Deum aliquid. Et ne occupemur in exponendis singulis sacre scripturae locis de hoc scito, quod ubicunque promittit Deus homini mercedem, ibidem cointelligitur meritum:

Nonetheless, he reckoned with the well-worn problem of proportionality. He acknowledged that we cannot merit 'simply and absolutely from God' (*simpliciter et absolutè*). Rather, drawing on Franciscan style voluntarism, he related the premise of merit entirely to God covenanting to grant a reward to some work in purely contractual fashion:

> Therefore, a man cannot merit anything from God in such way that it is owed to the man by right, unless the right is so much weakened so that it is greatly less than the right of a master to a servant and of a son to a father. This so weakened right is not found absolutely between man and God (since, absolutely speaking, man's every good work is owed voluntarily to God, and the more superior and many good works a man performs internally or externally, the more he owes to God, because God himself works in us both to will and to accomplish all our works) but this weakened right between man and God is by divine ordination, by which God has ordered our works to this end even if without merit from God.[14]

God in his authority determines a work's result, even overcoming their disproportionality. Contrary to Thomas' paradigm of grace enabling truly righteous and fitting works, attained as God predestined, Cajetan locates a work's relation to its reward in God's will. Merit is not a real correspondence but a convention: 'it is presupposed by an agreement [*conventio*] made between God and man concerning something, for instance, how among men, if a master makes a pact with his servant about something, a right is thence born between master and servant. Thus, if God deems to make a pact with a man, a right is born between the man and God concerning the thing about which he made a pact.'[15]

---

eo quod merces & meritum, correlativa sunt. meritum enim est mercedis meritum, et merces est meriti merces et propterea absque alia declaration cum leges in sacra Scriptura Deum promittere mercedem homini, cointellige meritum hominis respectu illius mercedis a Deo reddenda).

14. Cajetan, *de Fide et Operibus*, ch. 6, in *Opuscula Omnia*, 290 (Non potest igitur homo mereri aliquid a Deo sic quod iure debeatur homini, nisi iure tam attenuato, ut sit longe minus quam ius domini ad servum et filii ad patrem. Nec hoc tam attenuatum ius invenitur inter hominem et Deum absolute (quonia, absolute loquendo omnis bona operatio voluntaria hominis debetur Deo et quanto potioribus et pluribus bonis operibus internis vel externis pollet homo, tanto plus Deo debet, quia ipse Deus operatur in nobis et velle et perficere et omnia opera nostra) sed hoc attenuatum ius est inter hominem et Deum ex divina ordinatione, qua Deus ordinavit opera nostra ad hoc ut sine meritoria a Deo).

15. Cajetan, *de Fide et Operibus*, ch. 6, in *Opuscula Omnia*, 290 (Et haec sunt vera et indubitata simpliciter et absolute loquendo, secus autem est praesupposita conventione

Further, 'For it is clear from these events that merit's condition can be found even legally in our works related to the first thing about which an agreement [*conventio*] was made with God.'[16] Cajetan's voluntarist principle of merit is God's pact to accept (*acceptatio*) notably *some* work as sufficient for salvation, solidifying the notion of congruent merit in the Roman consensus.

Cajetan's move concerning the acceptance of the *work* rather than the *person* proves important in the overall trajectory of Roman theology on this doctrine. It marks a turning point wherein even Thomist theology moves in a Franciscan direction, setting the stage for Gabriel Biel's nominalist soteriology to get synthesized into mainstream Roman doctrine. In one respect, Cajetan's focus on the *work* kept him somewhat in the Thomistic orbit since, as chapter three documented, Thomas himself had argued that the work was the central concern for what is meritorious. On the other hand, Cajetan mitigated Thomas' concern for true righteousness (realism) by applying the Franciscan notion of *acceptatio* to the work rather than to the person. As the previous chapter explored, Franciscans like Bonaventure had maintained an Augustinianism by arguing that the truly good work of a *person* in possession of sanctifying grace would be meritorious on account of that grace by which God accepted the person. Later Franciscans diluted that Augustinianism by lessening the concern that the work had to be truly righteous, incorporating more voluntarist principles. Cajetan redirected the Thomist tradition in a Franciscan direction by shifting the principle of *acceptatio* from the person to the work. This shift brought the doctrine of congruent merit into Dominican theology in a new way, setting pace for a new mainstream understanding in Roman doctrine. In this case, it also kept open the possibility of the Franciscan Pactum that if we do *whatever* is within us, God will grant grace.

The Franciscan-leaning consensus nature of Cajetan's view becomes obvious from his argumentation. We should not dive too far into the tangential debate about whether we have an innate natural desire to see

---

facta inter Deum et hominem de aliquo nam quemadmodum inter homines si dominus pactum aliquod cum servo suo facit, nascitur inde ius inter servum et dominum: ita si Deus dignatur pactum facere cum homine, nascitur ius inter hominem et Deum quo ad illud de quo pactum est).

16. Cajetan, *de Fide et Operibus*, ch. 6, in *Opuscula Omnia*, 290 (Ex his enim manifestum sit, quod ratio meriti etiam iure potest inveniri in operibus nostris relatis ad primum, de quo conventio facta est cum Deo).

God, which was a key feature in Roman debates about protecting the distinction of the natural and supernatural orders. At the same time, the categories that Cajetan used to interpret Thomas notably came from Franciscan sources. Drawing upon the *Summa Fratris Alexandri*, a medieval Franciscan doctrinal synthesis manual, he implemented new distinctions about our faculties' potency in order to smooth out passages in Thomas' works where he seemed to suggest a natural, that is innate, orientation toward our supernatural end.[17] That Cajetan leveraged these Franciscan categories to refute Scotus does not undermine, but in fact furthers, the present claim that his tactic represents a maneuver owing to greater consensus between the various clerical orders on these topics. The claim becomes concrete as later Roman theologians, such as Dominican Domingo Bàñez (1528–1604) and Jesuit Francisco Suàrez (1548–1617), adopted Cajetan's approach.[18]

At one of the arguably most significant moments for Reformed theology's relationship to Roman doctrine, the Council of Trent's decrees remained ambiguous on the particular point of the relationship of nature and grace.[19] According to the pronouncement about original sin, Adam 'immediately lost the holiness and righteousness in which he had been constituted [*constitutus*].'[20] The ambiguity lies in the meaning of the verb *constitutus*, which could refer to the first creation so that Adam was created in holiness and righteousness, or to a more general establishment in rectitude for which case the timing of Adam's constitution in righteousness is not named. The decree could then be read to mean that Adam lost the righteousness with which he was imbued from creation, leaning in a more Thomistic direction. On the other hand, it could be read to mean that Adam lost the superadded grace of righteousness 'which he received from God' at some point subsequent to his creation, leaning in a more Franciscan direction.[21] As with many

---

17. Feingold, *Natural Desire to See God*, 105-14.

18. Feingold, *Natural Desire to See God*, 211-76.

19. Herman Bavinck, *Reformed Dogmatics*, ed. John Bolt, trans. John Vriend, 4 vol. (Grand Rapids, MI: Baker Academic, 2003–2008), 2:541.

20. Council of Trent, Fifth Session, §1, in Philip Schaff (ed.), *The Creeds of Christendom*, 3 vol. (New York, NY: Harper and Brothers, 1877), 2:84 (statim sanctitatem et justitiam, in qua constitus fuerat, amisisse).

21. Council of Trent, Fifth Session, §2 in Schaff, *Creeds of Christendom*, 2:85 (acceptam a Deo).

confessional documents, Trent was a consensus statement phrased broadly enough to include an acceptable range of views, avoiding a resolution to this particular debate.[22]

Trent was clearer on the relationship among grace, merit, and justification. As in Rome's consistent note, grace enables merit: 'Hence everlasting life must be delivered to those *who work well* and to those who hope in God all the way to the end, both as grace mercifully promised to God's sons on account of Christ Jesus and *as recompense faithfully rendered to their good works and merits* from by the promise of God himself.'[23] Since Christ 'continually infuses strength into those justified,' then 'they are considered, by those very works which are performed in God, to have fully satisfied the divine law according to the state of this life, and, if they die still in grace, to have truly merited everlasting life, following in its own time.'[24] Further, the good works of justified people are 'God's gifts,' relating then to grace, 'and also the good merits of the justified one,' meaning that grace enables meritorious works. In this sense, a justified person does 'truly merit the increase of grace, everlasting life, and the attainment of that everlasting life if he dies still in grace.'[25] Regardless of its exact configuration of grace to nature, Trent nonetheless clearly posited that grace was the principle

---

22. Christian D. Washburn, 'The Shaping of Modern Catholic Anthropology in the Context of the Counter-Reformation: St. Robert Bellarmine and the Transformative Power of Grace,' in Bertram Stubenrauch and Michael Seewald (eds.), *Das Menschenbild der Konfession – Achillesferse der Ökumene?* (Freiburg: Herder, 2015), 221n13; Swafford, *Nature and Grace*, 41-49.

23. Council of Trent, Sixth Session, ch. 16, in Schaff, *Creeds of Christendom*, 2:107 (emphasis added; Atque ideo bene operantibus usque in finem, et in Deo sperantibus proponenda est vita aeterna, et tanquam gratia filiis Dei per Christum Jesum misericorditer promissa, et tanquam merces ex ipsius Dei promissione bonis ipsorum operibus et merits fideliter reddenda).

24. Council of Trent, Sixth Session, ch. 16, in Schaff, *Creeds of Christendom*, 2:108 (in ipsos justificatos jugiter virtutem influat; nihil ipsis justificatis amplius deesse credendum est, quo minus plene illis quidem operibus, quae in Deo sunt facta, divinae legi pro hujus vitae statu satisfecisse, et vitam aeternam suo etiam tempore (si tamen in gratia decesserint), consequendam, vere promeruisse censeantur).

25. Council of Trent, Sixth Session, canon 32, in Schaff, *Creeds of Christendom*, 2:117-18 (Si quis dixerit hominis justificati bona opera ita esse dona Dei, ut non sint etiam bona ipsius justificati merita; aut ipsum justificatum bonis operibus, quae ab eo per Dei gratiam et Iesu Christi meritum, cujus vivum membrum est, fiunt, non vere mereri augmentum gratiae, vitam aeternam, et ipsius vitae aeternae, si tamen in gratia decesserit, consecutionem atque etiam gloriae augmentum: anathema sit).

of merit so that justified persons can progress to merit everlasting life by their works.[26] Even then, implicitly drawing upon Biel's theology of pure nature and congruent merit, Trent allowed for the possibility of meriting first grace congruently.[27] Trent's facilitation of these categories represents the official flowering of the more Franciscan trajectory as the prevailing Roman view.[28]

Rome's view clarified when Pope Pius V (1504–72), in his papal bull *ex omnibus afflictionibus* (1567), condemned Michael Baius (1513–89), a Franciscan professor in Louvain. The papal condemnation applied to Baius' teaching – among other things – that sin had damaged human nature so fundamentally that grace is necessary even to perform 'natural' works properly.[29] Baius contended that a right doctrine of 'human nature's corruption' and 'its restoration because of Christ's grace' required a proper understanding of the *imago Dei*.[30] Thus, 'the first man, in whom the nature of the whole human race was created, was originally established upright.'[31] Baius described original righteousness:

---

26. Washburn, 'Shaping of Modern Catholic Anthropology,' 240-41. For a historical-theological account of the formulation of canon 32, which did have some relevant background debate, see Christian D. Washburn, 'The Transformative Power of Grace and Condign Merit at the Council of Trent,' *The Thomist* 79 (2015): 173-212.

27. Heiko A. Oberman, 'Das tridentinische Rechtfertigungsdekret im Lichte spätmittelalterlicher Theologie,' *Zeirschrift für Theologie und Kirche* 61, no. 3 (1964): 251-82, esp. 268-78; Heiko A. Oberman, 'Duns Scotus, Nominalism, and the Council of Trent,' in Heiko A. Oberman (ed.), *The Dawn of the Reformation: Essays in Late Medieval and Early Reformation Thought* (Grand Rapids, MI: Eerdmans, 1992), 204-33. Even if correct that Oberman 'over interpreted' Trent's use of the verb *promereri* specifically as an explicit endorsement of the Franciscan approach, Alister McGrath likely underestimated the council's consensus use of terms to *facilitate* the Franciscan categories; Alister E. McGrath, *Iustitia Dei: A History of the Christian Doctrine of Justification*, 4th ed. (Cambridge: Cambridge University Press, 2020), 326-28. Christian Washburn interestingly highlighted how Trent's use of *proprie, improprie, vere*, and *verum* convey the same meaning as condign and congruent merit without invoking the scholastic terms, substantiating Oberman's basic claim that the categories are present; 'Grace and Condign Merit at the Council of Trent,' 173-212.

28. Michael Horton, *Justification*, 2 vol. (Grand Rapids: Zondervan, 2018), 1:332-52.

29. Karim Schelkens and Marcel Gielis, 'Driedo to Bellarmine: The Concept of Pure Nature in the 16th Century,' *Augustiniana* 57 no 3/4 (2007): 438-43; Helm, *Calvin at the Centre*, 326-28; Feingold, *Natural Desire to See God*, 277-78, esp. 278n3.

30. Michael Baius, *de Prima Hominis Iustitia*, praefatio, in *Opera*, 2 vol. (Cologne, 1696), 1:47 (humanae naturae corruption; ejusdem per Christi gratiam reparation).

31. Baius, *Prima Hominis*, 1.2, in *Opera*, 1:49 (Primum hominem, in quo omnium hominum natura concreata est, initio fuisse conditum rectum).

Now, the integrity of the first righteousness, which we believe was given to man at the beginning, consisted not only in how he clung to his Creator with his mind by perfect knowledge of the law, and with his will by full obedience, saying with the Psalmist 'But it is good for me to cling to God, and to put my hope in God,' but also in how the soul's lower parts served the higher and the body's every member instantly served the will's command.[32]

Baius saw this righteousness 'did not owe to an elevation of human nature but to its natural condition.'[33] In this respect, he followed Henry of Ghent, whom the previous chapter described.

Concerning the principle of merit, Baius argued that merit requires that works be truly righteous obedience. He acknowledged the diversity of views, noting that 'some establish merit's basis in a sharing in the divine nature, but others measure its whole condition by obedience to the precept.'[34] This difference describes the Thomists and Franciscans respectively. Capturing the difference between these traditions, the question that the difference raises is: 'whether everlasting life is due to good works, that is, from the object, end, and remaining circumstances on account of all things in agreement with the divine law, from their quality and nature because they are obviously obedience to the divine law, or from the precursory dignity of the worker.'[35] Baius was pinpointing the issue of whether merit was located in the *work* or the *person*. For Thomas, merit was based on the performance of a truly righteousness work.[36] Cajetan and other Dominicans such as Domingo de Soto (1484–

---

32. Baius, *Prima Hominis*, 1.3, in *Opera*, 1:54 (Consistebat autem primae rectitudinis integritas, quam initio homini datam credimus, non tantum in hoc, quod mente per integram legis notitiam, et voluntate per plenam obedientiam suo creatori adhaerebat, dicens cum Psalmista: Mihi autem adhaerere Deo bonum est, et ponere in Deo spem meam: sed etiam in eo, quod inferiores animae partes superioribus, et omnia corporis membra voluntatis imperio ad nutum serviebant).

33. Baius, *Prima Hominis*, 1.4, in *Opera*, 1:55 (Quod primae creationis integras non fuerit indebita naturae humanae exaltatio, sed naturalis ejus conditio).

34. Michael Baius, *De Meritis Operum Liber Secundus*, 1, in *Opera*, 1:35 (quod alii fundamentum meriti statuant divinae naturae consortium, alii vero totam ejus rationem ex obedientia praecepti metiantur).

35. Baius, *Meritis Operum Secundus*, 1, in *Opera*, 1:35 (An bonis operibus, id est, ex objecto, fine et reliquis circumstantiis per omnia divinae legi consentaneis, ex sua qualitate & natura, quia videlicet sunt divinae legis obedientia, an solum ex praevia operantis dignitate, vita debeatur aeterna).

36. Thomas, *Summa Theologica*, 1.114.1 (Man merits, inasmuch as he does what he ought).

1560) followed this view.[37] For Scotus, God does not accept a good work as meritorious, regardless of its content, unless he has accepted the person, making a work's merit relationally relative.[38] Expressing his own view on merit in contrast to Scotus, Baius affirmed that 'eternal life is due to a good work, not because of any precursory dignity of the worker, but because of the good work's nature and quality, which constitutes the quality of the worker, because it agrees with God's standard.'[39] In other words, merit demands perfect obedience before the Lord.[40] On the other hand, our obedience to the natural law entailed that God must reward us with the beatific vision.[41] Again, the disagreement about whether merit concerns the person or the work proves a fundamental issue in the development of Roman doctrine.

Baius' theology contains the interesting feature that he rejected any need for Adam to have sanctifying grace before the fall to perform righteous works. Rather God gave Adam the righteousness he needed for merit concreated with his nature. Further, the fall greatly damaged our ability to render righteousness so as now after the fall we need God's grace to perform ethically.[42] Even modern Roman theologians have called this view 'extreme Augustinianism.'[43] Baius' successor developed this trajectory.

Cornelius Jansenius (1585–1638), a Jesuit who also taught at Louvain and drew upon Baius' ideas that had provoked formal papal disapproval, vigorously objected to the Roman doctrine of pure nature. He rejected

---

37. Washburn, 'Grace and Condign Merit at the Council of Trent,' 177.

38. John Duns Scotus, *Quaestiones Quodlibetals*, 17.4, in *Opera Omnia*, editio nova, 26 vol. (Paris, 1891–95), 26:206 (Non enim actus alicujus acceptatur ut dignus praemio, nisi persona operans sit accepta).

39. Baius, *Meritis Operum Secundus*, 2, in *Opera*, 1:36 (Igitur bono operi, non ex praevia aliqua dignitate operantis, sed ex natura et qualitate boni operis quae qualitatem facit operantis, quia videlicet Dei ordinationi consentit, vita debetur aeterna).

40. de Lubac, *Augustinianism and Modern Theology*, 8. One Roman theologian, Ambrogio Catarino (1484–1553), formulated God's relationship with Adam in covenantal terms; Aaron C. Denlinger, *Omnes in Adam ex Pacto Dei: Ambrogio Catarino's Doctrine of Covenantal Solidarity and Its Influence on Post-Reformation Reformed Theologians* (Reformed Historical Theology; Göttingen: Vandenhoeck and Ruprecht, 2010).

41. Jacob W. Wood, 'Henri de Lubac, *Humani Generis*, and the Natural Desire for a Supernatural End,' *Nova et Vetera*, English ed., 15 no 4 (2017): 216-17;

42. Schelkens and Gielis, 'Driedo to Bellarmine,' 438-43.

43. Wood, *Stir a Restless Heart*, 399-400.

any hypothetical human existence where we are not ordered to the vision of God.[44] Jansenius recognized an historical complication in how this doctrine was used and had veered in a Pelagian direction. On one hand, he saw that earlier uses of pure nature aimed to explain the freeness of grace by distinguishing the natural and supernatural orders. On the other hand, he perceived that, by contrast, especially the late medieval nominalists such as Gabriel Biel used it to argue that our present condition after the fall remains supposedly pure nature, fully intact. Jansenius, therefore, contested the state of pure nature particularly in that sense, because he saw that sin has damaged our present natural state. Jansen strongly critiqued the implications of pure nature for the fall: 'For among them [the scholastics], nothing differs between a pure nature and a vitiated one, except that a naked one differs from a despoiled one.'[45] Drawing on Augustine, he associated pure nature with original righteousness, affirming that sin wrecked pure nature: 'Since, therefore, pure nature does not at all survive the fall in the freedom to do good, but rather is bound by a greater propensity and necessity to sin, it will be clear, according to Augustine's teaching, that no work at all, even if morally good, can manifest pure nature, but that in each act it will sin by inescapable necessity.'[46] Clarifying his view on the relation of nature and grace, he argued, 'that necessity for sinning … is not grounded in some lower rank of fallen nature to a supernatural state or in some special worth of good works.' Rather, we necessarily sin because without grace we lack ability to love God as the purpose of our good works and are imprisoned in concupiscence, lacking power to free ourselves.[47] Although Roman theologians have described Jansenius as

---

44. Feingold, *Natural Desire to See God*, 277-78.

45. Cornelius Jansenius, *de Statu Purae Naturae*, 2.9, in *Augustinus, seu Doctrina Sancti Augustini de Humanae Naturae Sanitate*, 3 vol. (Paris, 1641), 2:352 (Nihil enim apud eos pura natura a vitiata nisi quod nudus a spoliato discrepat).

46. Jansenius, *de Statu Purae Naturae*, 2.10, in *Augustinus*, 2:354 (Cum ergo pura natura nihil omnino lapsam in benefaciendi libertate superet, sed potius maiori peccandi pronitate atque necessitate deuineta teneatur, perspicuum erit iuxta doctrinam Augustini nihil omnino operis etiam moraliter boni puram naturam praestare posse, sed in singulis actibus ineluctabili necessitate peccaturam).

47. Jansenius, *de Statu Purae Naturae*, 2.10, in *Augustinus*, 2:354 (Nam illa necessitas peccandi, iacturaque laudabilis libertatis, non in aliqua naturae lapsae subiectione in supernaturalem statum, vel in aliqua peculiari operum bonorum dignitate fundata est, sed partim in eo quod creatura rationalis cum Deum sine vera gratia tanquam finem

denying pure nature entirely, his view more accurately was a rejection of the possibility of pure nature *after the fall*, believing that sin inherently damaged our originally pure nature.[48]

Jansenius argued from his understanding of our sinful condition that merit is impossible on this side of the fall. Speaking in the sense of the view he opposed, he noted, 'in pure nature, as in regard to the fall, there can be no natural happiness, but only true and great misery,' which precludes a place to merit supernatural blessing.[49] Targeting at least the most extreme versions of the Franciscan Pactum, Jansenius concluded that the idea that 'one can attain the state of an intact nature by the merits from pure nature,' meaning that congruent merit could obtain the sanctifying grace of original righteousness then enabling merit of supernatural reward, 'entails much greater absurdities.'[50] Lining up three arguments, he claimed first that this view violates the disproportionality of natural merit and supernatural reward, 'because it follows that a reward that surpasses all strength of nature can be obtained by natural works.'[51] This critique took aim at how the Franciscan Pactum posed that we can obtain a supernatural orientation by purely natural, even sinful, works as long as we perform that which is within us. Bringing his position to bear on the idea of natural ends, he concluded, 'since it is quite clear that pure nature cannot merit attaining the integrity of nature, there cannot be hope of attaining natural happiness according to purely natural things without grace,' meaning that we cannot attain the telic happiness of even our earthly endeavors because of our sin.[52]

---

operis boni non possit suis viribus diligere, necessario in creaturae dilectione requiescere debebit: quod ei aeterna lege vetitum est; partim in concupiscentia captivum tenente arbitrium voluntatis, a cuius vinculo se expedire non potest).

48. Feingold, *Natural Desire to See God*, 277-93.

49. Jansenius, *de Statu Purae Naturae*, 2.9, in *Augustinus*, 2:352 (in pura natura sicut in lapsa, nullam naturalem esse posse beatitudinem, sed veram tantum magnamque miseriam).

50. Jansenius, *de Statu Purae Naturae*, 2.9, in *Augustinus*, 2:352 (An forte meritis purae naturae statum integrae naturae consequi potest? ... Hoc vero multo est in solentius multoque maiores absurditates secum trahit).

51. Jansenius, *de Statu Purae Naturae*, 2.9, in *Augustinus*, 2:353 (Primo quia sequitur naturalibus operibus praemium obtineri posse, quod omnes naturae vires superat).

52. Jansenius, *de Statu Purae Naturae*, 2.9, in *Augustinus*, 2:353 (Cum igitur satis liquido constet non posse in pura natura esse meritum, quo ad integritatem naturae peruchi possit, nulla etiam spes in naturalibus puris erit consequendae beatitudinis naturalis sine gratia).

Jansenius' argument from proportionality highlights how he understands the principle of merit. For Jansenius, our obedience to the natural law as such did not obligate God to grant the beatific vision, but God was obliged to create us with whatever grace was needed to obtain our final end.[53] As Lawrence Feingold explained, Jansenius addressed the disproportion between nature and supernatural reward by locating God's freeness from any strict debt to a creature in his free decision to create humanity as a creature with such nature that we could find ultimate rest only in a supernatural end.[54] Jansenius did not evacuate the category of sanctifying grace entirely but redefined it. He outlined sin's effects: 'the guilt and vice which he contracted by slipping away from that first state of condition, and because of which he is in no way healthy and safe, is especially centered in that he lost that sanctifying grace.'[55] As we saw above, however, Jansenius had no category for an intact pure nature after the loss of sanctifying grace. In other words, aligning with Feingold's assessment, Jansenius saw sanctifying grace as synonymous with concreated original righteousness, which sin fundamentally damaged.[56] Affirming original nature's integrity, he affirmed that 'all such [supernatural] works, and therefore also the very trust and love for God, could be done by him by free will, so that God's grace did not bestow them upon him.'[57] However Jansenius would define merit, it rested upon his understanding of Adam's natural original righteousness. Sin damaged that righteousness, excluding the possibility of real merit after the fall.[58]

---

53. Wood, 'Henri de Lubac, *Humani Generis*, and the Natural Desire for a Supernatural End,' 1216-17, 1222.

54. Feingold, *Natural Desire to See God*, 287-88.

55. Cornelius Jansenius, *de Statu Naturae Innocentis, seu de Gratia Primi Hominis et Angelorum*, ch. 1, in *Augustinus*, 2:21 (Iam vero culpa et vitium, quod ab illo prima conditionis statu prolabendo, contraxit, et propter quodiam nullo modo sanus & saluus est, in eo maxime situm est, quod gratiam illam sanctificantem amisit).

56. Jansenius, *de Statu Naturae Innocentis*, ch. 1, in *Augustinus*, 2:31-34. Although Pelagius essentially equated sanctifying grace with our nature, Jansenius differs from him greatly by affirming that sin fundamentally damaged our nature.

57. Jansenius, *de Statu Naturae Innocentis*, ch. 7, in *Augustinus*, 2:44 (Nos igitur his asserimus tanquam sine dubitatione verissumum, iuxta doctrinam sancti Augustini et Ecclesiae, omnia huiusmodi opera, adeoque et ipsam fidem et dilectionem Dei, ab eo potuisse per arbitrii libertatem fieri, sic ut ea non donaret ei gratia).

58. Jansenius, *de Statu Naturae Innocentis*, ch. 7, in *Augustinus*, 2:47.

Jansenius' explanation of merit was then sharply limited, contrasting to some degree with grace, compared to his other Roman forebearers and contemporaries. Following the lineage of Henry of Ghent, he applied his view of Adam's *natural* original righteousness so that Adam did not need grace to elevate his original nature to be oriented and equipped for supernatural life. Drawing again upon Augustine, Jansenius posited grace and merit as two opposing principles: 'For in the first place, if we want a premise of grace, he expressed it when, after he taught that immortality would be conferred upon Adam because of merit, wherein he seemed to exclude grace on account of merit.'[59] He even referred to 'that antithesis of grace and merit,' although appealing to Augustine as precedent for his identification of original righteousness with sanctifying grace.[60] Regarding Adam's potential to obtain supernatural reward, Jansenius once again leveraged Augustine, positing: 'he calls Adam's merit *natural* because it could be had because of nature, so because of free will given naturally in creation, not by grace producing it so it occurred but only in helping it so without it, it would not have occurred.'[61] Almost mirroring Protestants, as Roman theologians have historically noted, he claimed that for sinners, 'Because where there is no such thing as a good work by the strength of pure nature, it is plain that there can be no merit except for damnation.'[62] Jansenius followed Thomas in seeing that merit rested on a real principle of a truly good and worthy work, but demurred from Thomas by denying that extra-natural grace was needed to equip Adam to perform such works and

---

59. Jansenius, *de Statu Naturae Innocentis*, ch. 10, in *Augustinus*, 2:52 (Nam in primis, si rationem gratiae desideramus, expressit illam cum, postquam Adamo per meritum conferendam esse docuisset immortalitatem, quo meriti nomine gratiam exclusisse videbatur).

60. Jansenius, *de Statu Naturae Innocentis*, ch. 11, in *Augustinus*, 2:54 (Sed cum vereretur, ne ex illa antithesi gratiae et meriti, suspicaretur aliquis merita tunc sine gratia haberi potuisse, attexit illico: quamvis sine gratia nec tunc ullum meritum esse potuisset).

61. Jansenius, *de Statu Naturae Innocentis*, ch. 16, in *Augustinus*, 2:68 (Ubi meritum Adae naturam vocat, quia per naturam haberi poterat, seu per naturalem in creatione datum arbitrii libertatem, gratia non dante illud, ut fieret, sed tantummodo adiuuante, ut sine ille non fieret).

62. Jansenius, *de Statu Purae Naturae*, 2.10, in *Augustinus*, 2:334 (Ubi enim nullum esse potest purae naturae viribus opus bonum, ibi nec meritum nisi damnationis esse posse manifestum est); also Jansenius, *de Statu Naturae Innocentis*, ch. 4, in *Augustinus*, 2:38; J. Pohle, 'Grace, Controversies on,' in Charles G. Herbermann, Edward A. Pace, Condé B. Pallen, Thomas J. Shahan, John J. Wynne (eds.), *The Catholic Encyclopedia*, special ed., 15 vol. (New York, NY: The Encyclopedia Press, 1913), 6:710.

by affirming that the fall so badly damaged our nature that a sinner could never perform such a work.[63] As recent scholarship has shown, Jansenius' legacy sits as one extension of Thomistic thought that gets as close to Protestant theology as occurs in the ongoing Roman tradition.[64]

---

63. Arguably, Jansenius still had some room for Roman categories of soteriological merit, wherein a renewed sinner could perform some meritorious deeds. In one passage for which I do not understand his full meaning well enough to provide analysis, especially in the main text, he contended that an upright nature (original righteousness) cannot be obtained by the merits of pure nature, arguing:

> First because it would follow that a reward can be obtained by natural works, which surpasses all the natural powers. Nevertheless, since merit and reward must be of the same order, then there can be no merit before God unless they are born from God's love. That is to say, the love of a creature that is not returned to God is a defective love and cannot be the true merit of that happiness.

Jansenius, *de Statu Purae Naturae*, 2.9, in *Augustinus*, 333-34 (An forte meritis purae naturae statum integrae naturae consequi potest? Nam et hoc aliquis comminisci posset, hominem in pura natura constitutum bonis operibus praesentis vitae hoc apud Deum adipisci posse, ut ei in futura vita velut praemium virtutis naturalis illa beatitudo reddatur. Hoc vero multo est insolentius multoque maiores absurditates secum trahit. Primo quia sequetur naturalibus operibus praemium obtineri posse, quod omnes naturae vires superat. Cum tamen meritum et praemium eiusdem ordinis esse debeant. Deinde non potest esse meritum apud Deum nisi ex Dei amore nascantur. Amor enim creaturae, qui non retorquetur in Deum vitiosus amor est, neque verum beatitudinis illius meritum esse potest).

The question turns on whether *amor creaturae* is objective or subjective. If objective, Jansenius may have meant something like Ockham that God's love for the creature can create what is required for merit. Theologically, however, Jansen would be suggesting that *God's* love was defective, which seems problematic. If *creaturae* is a subjective genitive, Jansenius meant that the love belonging to a creature is faulty unless directed toward God. This reading seems more likely, but then suggests something along Franciscan lines from Scotus and Ockham that love is the virtue that makes works meritorious. The concession seems to run against his other principles. Regardless, he excluded Ockham's actual view that grace was unnecessary for merit in the state of pure nature: 'Therefore, every good merit in pure nature is utterly impossible without the help of grace, especially to achieve something so great and at such a distance that exceeds all natural powers.' Jansenius, *de Statu Purae Naturae*, 2.9, in *Augustinus*, 333 (Omne igitur meritum bonum in pura natura, sine gratiae adiutorio prorsus impossibile est, praesertim ad adipiscendam rem tantam tantoque interuallo excedentem omnes naturae vires).

64. Eric J. DeMeuse, '"The World is Content with Words": Jansenism between Thomism and Calvinism,' in Jordan J. Ballor, Matthew T. Gaetano, and David S. Sytsma (eds.), *Beyond Dordt and De Auxiliis: The Dynamics of Protestant and Catholic Soteriology in the Sixteenth and Seventeenth Centuries* (Leiden: Brill, 2019), 245-76; cf. Aza Goudriaan, 'Defending Grace: References to Dominicans, Jesuits, and Jansenists in Seventeenth-Century Dutch Reformed Theology,' in *Beyond Dort and De Auxiliis*, 277-96; cf. Ralph Keen, 'The Critique of Calvin in Jansenius's *Augustinus*,' in Maria-Cristina Pitassi and Daniela Solfaroli Camillocci (eds.), *Crossing Traditions: Essays on the Reformation and Intellectual History in Honour of Irena Backus* (Leiden: Brill, 2017), 405-14.

Some evidence among Reformed writers themselves evidences attempts to appropriate and modify Jansenius' work.[65]

In the Counter-Reformation, Robert Bellarmine, a Jesuit and Rome's leading apologist against Protestantism, doubled down on the doctrine of pure nature requiring sanctifying grace for merit. Contextually, he studied and taught at Leuven during Baius' time, forging a correlation between his initial opposition to Baianism and later its similarities in Protestantism.[66] Bellarmine unequivocally affirmed that original righteousness itself was the *donum superadditum*: 'this rectitude with which Adam was created, and without which after his fall all people are born, was a supernatural gift.'[67] Bellarmine qualified that, in a few senses, original righteousness was natural. Most pertinently for our purposes, 'it helps nature and perfects it respecting natural works, and not elevates it to any supernatural works. In this way original righteousness, if being understood as distinct from sanctifying grace [*gratia gratum faciente*], can be called a natural gift.'[68] In other words, Biel's view of sanctifying grace as distinct from that supernatural grace that elevates us to supernatural works means that original righteousness is natural as it helps a person perform natural works. He also demurred from earlier Franciscan and nominalist views that had posed a temporal gap between Adam's creation and the reception of the *donum superadditum*, arguing that Adam received sanctifying grace in creation.[69]

Nevertheless, according to Bellarmine, original righteousness is properly supernatural: 'In itself, it is called supernatural because by its kind it is not suitable to proceed from principles of nature .... In its accidents, it is called supernatural because it is sometimes obtained by

---

65. Theophilus Gale, *The True Idea of Jansenisme both Historick and Dogmatick* (London, 1669). Thanks to Ryan McGraw for alerting me to this source.

66. Schelkens and Gielis, 'Driedo to Bellarmine,' 443-45; Ryan, 'How Can the Beatific Vision both Fulfill Human Nature and Be Utterly Gratuitous?' 723-25.

67. Robert Bellarmine, *de Gratia Primi Hominis*, 1.5, in *De Controversiis Christianae Fidei, tomus quartus* (Sartorius, 1601), 15 (Rectitudo illa cum qua Adam creatus fuit, et sine qua post eius lapsum homines omnes nascuntur, donum supernaturale fuit).

68. Bellarmine, *de Gratia Primi Hominis*, 1.5, in *De Controversiis ... quartus*, 16 (Tertio dicitur naturale, quod tametsi donum fit gratuitum, tamen naturam iuuat, ac perficit in operibus naturalibus, neque eam elevat ad opera ulla supernaturalia. Et hoc modo iustitia originalis, si distincta esse intelligatur a gratia gratum faciente donum naturale dici potest).

69. Bellarmine, *de Gratia Primi Hominis*, 1.3, in *De Controversiis ... quartus*, 7-12; Washburn, 'Shaping of Modern Catholic Anthropology,' 221n13.

a divine miracle, though otherwise it usually proceeds from principles of nature.'[70] He explicitly contrasted his position with Protestant arguments: 'Thus, original righteousness, which restrained that rebellion of the flesh, *according to our adversaries' opinion*, pertained to man's *natural* constitution, not to supernatural gifts.'[71] Bellarmine codified a response to Protestantism, affirming that original righteousness, which was needed to perform works worth a supernatural reward, was superadded.[72] Even if Adam did not exist in true pure nature, lacking superadded grace before sin (which seems debatable), the fall brought us into the state of pure nature where nature as such is fully intact and undamaged but not equipped for supernatural life.[73]

Perhaps expectedly, Bellarmine discussed merit within his refutation of the Protestant doctrine of justification by faith alone, denying justification is by faith alone because other causes also contribute – especially love. He affirmed that *initial* justification is entirely by grace, although not excluding the possibility of a congruously merited initial justification.[74] For Bellarmine, in contrast to Protestants, infused righteousness precedes good works which increase justification itself. Bellarmine tied this discussion to Protestantism's law-gospel distinction, arguing against any antithesis of law and gospel even in justification because the law is part of the gospel. In this way, he cast the law-gospel distinction more as a redemptive-historical contrast than a principle distinction.[75] Expanding upon Trent, Bellarmine contended that an initially justified person must then render good works to complete his or her justification and enter everlasting life.[76]

---

70. Bellarmine, *de Gratia Primi Hominis*, 1.5, in *De Controversiis … quartus*, 16 (Per se dicitur supernaturale, quod ex genere suo non est aptum fluere ex principiis naturae, qualis fuit ascensio Helie igneo curru in coelum, robur Samsonis, et alia id genus. Per Accidens supernaturale vocatur quod interdum obtinetur divino miraculo, licet alioqui ex naturae principiis fluere soleat)

71. Bellarmine, *de Gratia Primi Hominis*, 1.1, in *De Controversiis … quartus*, 4 (emphasis added; originalis igitur iustitia, quae rebellionem illam carnis coercebat, ex adversariorum sententia, ad naturalem hominis constitutionem, non ad dona supernaturalia pertinebat)

72. Washburn, 'Shaping of Modern Catholic Anthropology,' 219-22.

73. Schelkens and Gielis, 'Driedo to Bellarmine,' 446-47.

74. Washburn, 'Shaping of Modern Catholic Anthropology,' 232-35.

75. Washburn, 'Shaping of Modern Catholic Anthropology,' 235-38.

76. Robert Bellarmine, *de Justificatione Impii, et nobis Operibus Generatim*, 2.3-5 in *De Controversiis … quartus*, 1033-50; Washburn, 'Shaping of Modern Catholic Anthropology,' 240-47.

When explaining merit directly, Bellarmine avoided equivocation but relied on voluntarist premises. Concerning the reality of merit, he contended, 'the good works of the righteous are truly and properly merit, and not merit for *some* sort of reward, but for everlasting life itself.'[77] Almost quoting the very words of Cajetan's principle of the correlative relationship of merit and reward, Bellarmine asserted that any reward we receive must owe to our merit: 'a reward and merit are relative: for rewards are paid on account of merits, just as grace is given freely. Thus, since the recompense of works is so often and so plainly called rewards, no doubt should exist that in fact works themselves, following the manner of speaking in the Scriptures, are properly called merits.'[78] In Bellarmine's view, any notion of reward demands the concept of merit.

For Bellarmine, Christ enables his people to merit. In his view, works are not automatically meritorious, as the work on its own is not the ground for merit. Rather, 'not just any sort of grace is required' but the sort that makes someone 'a living member of Christ's body' to provide sanctifying grace that elevates pure nature just like before the fall.[79] In other words, at least one of Bellarmine's premises for merit harks back to Scotus' position that God accepts an act as meritorious only from a person whom he has accepted as pleasing, relativizing the standard of merit according to what a justified person can perform. One must have a relation to Christ in order to merit because, if our works are meritorious on their own, there is risk that Christ's works would be no greater than ours. Bellarmine's foundation of the necessity for Christ so that we might merit protects the basis of grace in *initial* justification, which must be followed by works that secure our final entry into everlasting life.[80]

---

77. Bellarmine, *de Justificatione Impii*, 5.1, in *De Controversiis … quartus*, 1253-54 (Nos igitur probabim us id, quod habet communis Catholicorum omnium sententia, opera bona iustorum vere, ac proprie esse merita, et merita non cuiuscunque praemii, sed ipsius vitae aeternae).

78. Bellarmine, *de Justificatione Impii*, 5.2, in *De Controversiis … quartus*, 1255 (At merces, et meritum, relativa sunt: merces enim meritis redditur, sicut gratia gratis datur. Igitur cum tam saepe, et tam perspicue praemium operum dicatur merces, dubium esse non debet, quin ipsa opera secundum morem loquendi Scripturae, recte dicantur merita).

79. Bellarmine, *de Justificatione Impii*, 5.12, in *De Controversiis … quartus*, 1289 (Requiritur igitur ad fructum, id est, ad bona opera facienda, non quaecunque gratia, sed ea, quae facit hominem esse vivum membrum corporis Christi).

80. Washburn, 'Shaping of Modern Catholic Anthropology,' 242-43. Notably, Cajetan and Bellarmine's principle of correlativity for merit and reward helpfully informs present

Bellarmine's voluntarist concept of merit appears clearly in his consideration of works themselves. For Bellarmine, God must graciously promise to reward a morally good work and must bestow supernatural virtue to perform it. The proportionality problem reappears, as Bellarmine wrote that God 'willed nothing other except that our merit is not condign, or from absolute justice, but only from the postulate, that is, valued in God's liberal promise' and 'entirely wills that our merit be from God's grace proceeding and getting value from the promise, yet not such that it is owed reward from justice but from God's liberality alone.'[81] He elaborated: 'the good works of the righteous are condignly meritorious for everlasting life by reason of a pact, and of the work likewise, certainly not respectively without a pact, or then a good work does not have by acceptance [*acceptatione*] a proportion to eternal life, but because God is not bound to accept a good work for that reward, however equal and for equal reward, unless the agreement [*conventio*] intervenes.'[82] Although Christian Washburn argued that this statement blends Thomist realism – because the work itself is a reason – and Scotus' voluntarism, only the latter is prominent. Seemingly following Cajetan again, Bellarmine rests his doctrine of merit on a divine convention,

conversations about the role of works at the final judgment. Some Protestant theologians assert that although (initial) justification is by faith alone, our works are included in the basis for receiving final salvation. They attempt to ward off the accusation of Roman Catholicism by insisting that those works are not meritorious and are empowered by grace. Cajetan and Bellarmine show that to affirm the necessity of works as a condition for receiving final salvation but to deny that those works are merit is just a game of nominalism – rejecting the title but endorsing the concept. The correlativity principle asserts that if final salvation is a reward for something we do, then those deeds are meritorious. All the more, the Roman tradition throughout affirms that God gives grace to empower the justified to perform those deeds needed for final salvation. The paradigm becomes remarkably similar.

81. Bellarmine, *de Justificatione Impii*, 5.16, in *De Controversiis … quartus*, 1306 (Quod vero attinet ad rem ipsam, Durandi sententia, si nihil aliud vellet, nisi merita nostra non esse ex condigno, sive ex iustitia absolute, sed tantum ex hypothesi, id est, posita liberali Dei promissione non esset reprobanda. Caeterum videtur omnino velle, merita nostra ex gratia Dei procedentia et posita promissione, adhuc non esse talia, ut eis ex iustitia debeatur merces, sed ex sola Dei liberalitate.

82. Bellarmine, *de Justificatione Impii*, 5.17, in *De Controversiis … quartus*, 1309-10 (opera bona iustorum meritoria esse vitae aeternae ex condigno ratione pacti, et operis simul, non quidem quod sine pacto, vel acceptatione non habeat opus bonum proportionem ad vitam aeternam, sed quia non tenetur Deus acceptare ad illam mercedem opus bonum, quamvis par, et aequale mercedi, nisi conventio interveniat).

establishing the ground for God accepting a work as proportional for eschatological reward primarily in a pact.

Rome's early modern trajectory followed the Franciscan tradition in holding that the *donum superadditum* is the gift of original righteousness entirely supplemental to basic human nature.[83] Cajetan's more Franciscan interpretation of Thomas bridged the gap as Rome's presiding view, affirming that Adam's sin forfeited that superadded gift of righteousness, still leaving natural human nature fundamentally undamaged.[84] With Bellarmine, who was both Rome's foremost intellectual weapon against Protestantism as well as Protestants' foremost target, the Franciscan view of pure nature became the magisterium's definitive teaching, thereby the required interpretation of Thomas as well.[85] Furthermore, the Franciscan Pactum had reached full ascendance, controlling the prevailing views of merit with lasting effects until today.

Modernity and Neo-Thomism

The intervening centuries undoubtably contain many relevant developments and arguments pertaining to our discussion, but forward motion and selectivity demands that we jump closer to the modern period. Roman thought in the modern period confirms the basic stability of the established early modern consensus. In the nineteenth century, Pope Leo XIII (1810–1903) set the course for modern Roman theology and the shape of variegated Thomism with his encyclical *aeterni patris* (1879), which declared Thomism to be Rome's official philosophy.[86] This Leonine decree has several interesting implications.

---

83. e.g. Alexander of Hales, *Summa Theologiae, Pars Secunda* (Venice: Franciscum Franciscium, 1575), 192-202, 222-23 (these sections are questions 91 and 96, membrum 1 of Hales' pars secunda but cited as page numbers because the interior numbering of questions is inconsistent); Bonaventure, *Breviloquium*, 2.11-12; in A.C. Peltier (ed.), *S.R.E Cardinalis S. Bonaventure … Opera Omnia*, 15 vol. (Paris: Ludovicus Vivès, 1864–71), 7:268-70; Martin Becanus, *Summa Theologiae Scholasticae* (Rouen, 1652), 1.5.3.1-2.

84. Henri de Lubac, *A Brief Catechesis on Nature and Grace*, trans. Richard Arnandez (San Francisco, CA: Ignatius Press, 1984), 122; Richard Cross, *Duns Scotus* (Great Medieval Thinkers; New York, NY: Oxford University Press, 1999), 103-7; Helm, *Calvin at the Centre*, 325.

85. Bellarmine, *de Gratia Primi Hominis*, 1.5, in *De Controversiis*, 15; Schelkens and Gielis, 'Driedo to Bellarmine,' 445-47.

86. Pope Leo XIII, *Aeterni Patris*, at *The Holy See*; August 4, 1879; accessed on May 29, 2024 at https://www.vatican.va/content/leo-xiii/en/encyclicals/documents/hf_l-xiii_enc_04081879_aeterni-patris.html, §31; Fergus Kerr, *After Aquinas: Versions of Thomism*

First, it required all Roman theologians to be Thomists, regardless of how much they agree with Thomas himself. This shift launched a renaissance of interpreting Thomas. All Roman theology had to square with Thomas' principles, and, from the other direction, Thomas had to square with Roman dogma and consensus. This context establishes a complicating but limiting factor wherein we must measure more carefully *how* ideas count as Thomistic. For our purposes, the upshot is that we take modern Roman claims about the nature of true Thomism with a grain of salt, realizing the rhetorical driving forces. Our concern is not in tediously measuring the lines of which theologians are truly Thomistic. To put it another way, although the early modern strands of interaction with Thomas were fundamentally theological claims in interaction with Thomas, the Leonine decree meant that thenceforth historical claims about Thomas/Thomism in relation to modern viewpoints were theological arguments. Roman theologians could not disconnect historical investigations from dogmatic concerns because they *had* to square their view with Thomas' – or square his theology with theirs.[87] This extra layer to Thomistic historiography means that we must consider Roman historical theology of Thomas in two respects: 1) as a real argument about the historical interpretation of Thomas, and 2) as a theological argument about Thomas' natural or interpreted relationship to later dogmatic standards.

Second, although many Reformed thinkers have been highly critical of Thomas/Thomism as rationalistic, perceiving a claim that we must climb from *tabula rasa* to knowledge of God by pure reason alone unaided by divine revelation, the historical moment of Leonine Thomism demands some caveats. Developing philosophical trends, perhaps culminating in Immanuel Kant (1724–1804) and his noumena-phenomena divide wherein we *cannot* access the supernatural, set the stage for modernism.

(Oxford: Blackwell Publishing, 2002), 17-19; also Jörgen Vijgen, 'Biblical Thomism: Past, Present and Future,' *Angelicum* 95 no 3 (2018): 373-85.

87. cf. Richard A. Muller, 'Reflections on Persistent Whiggism and Its Antidotes in the Study of Sixteenth- and Seventeenth-century Intellectual History,' in Alister Chapman, John Coffey, and Brad S. Gregory (eds.), *Seeing Things Their Way: Intellectual History and the Return of Religion* (Notre Dame: University of Notre Dame Press, 2009), 134-53; Quentin Skinner, 'Introduction: Seeing things their way,' in *Visions of Politics: Volume 1: Regarding Method* (Cambridge: Cambridge University Press, 2002), 1-7; Richard A. Muller, *Calvin and the Reformed Tradition: On the Work of Christ and the Order of Salvation* (Grand Rapids, MI: Baker Academic, 2012), 16-24.

This philosophical advent was a major problem for all Christian thought including Rome. Almost undoubtedly, Kant's distinction of pure reason, practical reason, and each with its own self-contained principles helped strengthen an intellectual milieu where the notion of self-contained pure nature with its distinctly proportionate principles could flourish.[88] Leonine Thomism's appeal to Thomas as *the* philosopher of Rome was not a *de novo* interpretation but a response to modernism.

Thomas' use of reason has been subject to multiple interpretations. Although our purpose is not to settle those debates, one consideration demonstrates our contextual point about modern Roman theology. Neo-Thomism interpreted Thomas as working with pure reason to reach knowledge of God. Although Reformed theologians should judge this theological position incorrect, we might sympathize with its motivation when we realize that Kant posed that it was basically impossible to know anything about the supernatural. The neo-Thomist response was to assert a reading of Thomas wherein we can reason our way to God.[89] In sum, it was a flat denial of the premise in the Kantian problem.[90]

While Leonine Thomism posed a strong faith-reason division with certain *preambula fidei* as doctrines that must be reached by reason without revelation before faith, Thomas' own view was not quite so fitting within modernity.[91] Thomas' 'five proofs' of God's existence serve as a useful example. These proofs should be understood as situated within a theological framework such as *Summa* rather than as positivist arguments truly intended for bringing unbelievers to know God. In this context, Thomas' reasoning is about demonstrating that we can know God truly though not exhaustively. The truth about God makes sense to people made in his image. The five proofs aim to verify our contingent nature as creatures who are always dependent on God who is distinct from the creature.[92] After all, Thomas affirmed that 'certain truths

---

88. David Bentley Hart, *You Are Gods: On Nature and Supernature* (Notre Dame, IN: University of Notre Dame Press, 2022), 36-38.

89. Reginald Garrigou-Lagrange, *Grace: Commentary on the Summa Theologica of St. Thomas 1a2ae q.109–14*, trans. the Dominican Nuns (St. Louis: B. Herder Book Co. 1952), 44-46.

90. Kerr, *After Aquinas*, 35-38.

91. Kerr, *After Aquinas*, 52-61.

92. Kerr, *After Aquinas*, 61-72.

which exceed human reason should be made known to him by divine revelation.' Moreover, 'those truths about God which human reason could have discovered, it was necessary that man should be taught by a divine revelation.'[93] Just as other disciplines implement rather than argue for their basic principles, theology 'does not argue in proof of its principles, which are the articles *of faith*, but from them it goes on to prove something else.' Holy Scripture is necessary because 'there are no longer any means of proving the articles of faith by reasoning.'[94] Thomas presumed a thorough dependence on revelation and Scripture, using reason to clarify what is made known on theological principles.[95]

Although Thomas was no modern, neo-Thomists developed interpretive lines consistent with reigning ecclesiastical standards. Perhaps the most renowned neo-Thomist of the classical stripe was Cardinal Reginald Garrigou-Lagrange (1877–1964), a Dominican who maintained Thomas' Leonine heritage. Garrigou-Lagrange manifested a rationalist penchant in interpreting Thomas. As Joseph Wawrykow noted, he denied any development in Thomas' thought on merit, particularly between the *Sentences* commentary and the *Summa*, so contending that Thomas always affirmed congruent merit and the Franciscan Pactum premise of merit. Wawrykow excoriated Garrigou-Lagrange's historiographical method as revealing 'the lengths to which certain students of Thomas have gone to bring Thomas in line with what they take to be the requirements of later Church doctrine.'[96] In Wawrykow's estimation, Garrigou-Lagrange's view that Thomas held something similar to Scotus' *acceptatio* rather than God's sovereign *ordinatio* of individuals to salvation by obtaining merit 'should be dismissed as wishful thinking.'[97] Wawrykow's criticism lands in a patently obvious way for Garrigou-Lagrange's suggestion that Thomas used the distinction of God's antecedent and consequent will to decree a universal salvation, received by those who do their part, rather than the election of individuals to everlasting life. Garrigou-Lagrange explicitly aimed at distancing Thomas from 'Calvinism,' branding his

---

93. Thomas, *Summa Theologica*, 1.1.1.

94. Thomas, *Summa Theologica*, 1.1.8.

95. Concerning the pertinence for Reformed theology, see J. V. Fesko, 'The Scholastic Epistemology of Geerhardus Vos,' *Reformed Faith and Practice* 3.3 (2018): 21-45.

96. Wawrykow, *God's Grace and Human Action*, 16-17.

97. Wawrykow, *God's Grace and Human Action*, 32.

historical interpretation with the Whiggish marks of attempting to align a past theologian with his own dogmatic concerns.[98] Garrigou-Lagrange's commentary on Thomas serves our purposes by giving theological insight into Garrigou-Lagrange's teaching as the leading twentieth-century neo-Thomist, not by shedding real historical light on Thomas himself.

Garrigou-Lagrange followed Cajetan's 'pure nature' interpretation of Thomas, arguing that we must maintain the real distinction of the natural and supernatural orders.[99] He did reckon with the fall's real effects, arguing that in the fallen condition we cannot love God or act rightly without grace.[100] Neo-Thomism then opposed the Pelagian model of Gabriel Biel and the nominalists, taking issue even with Cajetan. Garrigou-Lagrange defended the category of sanctifying grace as that which renders a person justified or pleasing to God.[101] Merit is then the effect of sanctifying grace.[102] Acknowledging that the proportionality problem means that man cannot merit from God strictly speaking, Garrigou-Lagrange appealed to divine ordination as the principle of merit, wherein God bestows man with supernatural power to perform meritorious works.[103] Garrigou-Lagrange drew upon Thomas' realism to argue that only Christ's merits have condign merit, explicitly distancing himself from Scotus and nominalists who hold that God's *acceptio* of a work even in fallen condition makes its condignly meritorious.[104] Garrigou-Lagrange, however, posed that a person *without grace* can merit something congruently.[105] Nonetheless, this merit cannot pertain to everlasting life.[106] Condign merit is needed

98. Garrigou-Lagrange, *Grace*, v.

99. Réginald Garrigou-Lagrange, 'La possibilité de la vision béatifique peut-elle se démonstrer?' *Revue Thomiste* 38, no. 80 (1933): 669-88; Roger W. Nutt, 'The Reception of Aquinas in Early Twentieth-Century Catholic Neo-Scholastic and Historical Theologians,' in *Oxford Handbook of the Reception of Aquinas*, 392-406; Donnelly, 'Gratuity of the Beatific Vision,' 374-404; Mayer, 'Man is Inclined to His Last End by Nature,' 887-88.

100. Garrigou-Lagrange, *Grace*, 61-64.

101. Garrigou-Lagrange, *Grace*, 150-54

102. Garrigou-Lagrange, *Grace*, 363.

103. Garrigou-Lagrange, *Grace*, 363-66.

104. Garrigou-Lagrange, *Grace*, 266-68.

105. Garrigou-Lagrange, *Grace*, 369.

106. Garrigou-Lagrange, *Grace*, 369-71; cf. Garrigou-Lagrange, *Grace*, 384-90.

for everlasting life which is attained because initial justification means that 'the works of the just, inasmuch as they proceed from sanctifying grace and the movement of the Holy Ghost, are proportionate in justice to the excellence of eternal life.'[107] Once again, superadded grace bridges the gap between the natural and supernatural orders so that, explicitly in opposition to Scotus, sanctifying grace inherently proportions our works to merit a supernatural reward.[108] The principles in Garrigou-Lagrange's explanation show a mixture of ideas from Thomas and Franciscans concerning the issue of whether the work or the person is of chief concern in merit.

Tackling the issue of nature and grace more pointedly in regard to Adam, Garrigou-Lagrange asked whether sanctifying grace was a quality of innocent nature or a gift exclusively to the person.[109] His position confirms part of our interpretation of Thomas, but also incorporates a true place for pure nature. Regarding pure nature, he interpreted the Council of Trent as *unambiguously* teaching that Adam received superadded grace after creation.[110] He appealed to Thomas' commentary on Lombard's *Sentences* to support that Adam was created without grace but turned himself to God in his first instant.[111] In this respect, Garrigou-Lagrange ignored the diachronic development of Thomas' thought. Although our argument differs from Garrigou-Lagrange's by recognizing that Thomas' later view bound original righteousness to human nature by creation, the similar conclusion is that grace is not the extrinsic principle of original righteousness, since sanctifying grace was included in original righteousness.[112] Thus, Garrigou-Lagrange's own position is that sanctifying grace 'was not an exclusively personal gift to Adam but an endowment to [his] nature, since "original righteousness includes sanctifying grace."'[113] Garrigou-Lagrange then saw original

---

107. Garrigou-Lagrange, *Grace*, 373.

108. Garrigou-Lagrange, *Grace*, 372-83.

109. Reginald Garrigou-Lagrange, 'Utrum gratia sanctificans fuerit in Adamo dos naturae an donum personae tantum,' *Angelicum* 2 (1925), 133-44.

110. Garrigou-Lagrange, 'gratia sanctificans,' 133-35.

111. Garrigou-Lagrange, 'gratia sanctificans,' 138-39.

112. Garrigou-Lagrange, 'gratia sanctificans,' 139-42.

113. Garrigou-Lagrange, 'gratia sanctificans,' 144 (Ex his omnibus satisclare constat gratiam sanctificantem et secundum S. Thomam et secundum rei veritatem, fuisse

righteousness as the *donum superadditum* that included the sanctifying grace that proportions our works to merit supernatural reward.

Apart from Garrigou-Lagrange as the formidable example of neo-Thomism, the modern presentation of the traditional view also manifests in collaborative publications in the twentieth century. More specifically collected essays and encyclopedia entries represent the center mainstream of Roman theology. *The Catholic Encyclopedia* represents a major synthesis of Roman thought, digesting a mainstream understanding of their doctrine and practice. Interestingly, the same author, J. Pohle, wrote the articles both on grace and merit. According to this *Encyclopedia*, although 'the so-called state of pure nature' wherein a supernatural capacity did not exist, actual grace – in its first respect to sinners – elevates a person to the supernatural order to perform supernatural acts.[114] Thus, actual grace produces sanctifying grace, which is equivalent to initial justification.[115] This justification amounts to the infusion of supernatural virtues and the Spirit's indwelling presence. Sanctifying grace, as a permanent quality rather than pertaining to discreet acts as is the case in actual grace, is the supernatural order, allowing one to obtain second justification and the increase of grace.[116]

Following what had become the mainstream Roman tradition, Pohle described merit as 'that property of a good work which entitles the doer to receive a reward (*proemium, merces*) from him in whose service the work is done.' Supernatural merit has ground only in God's 'infallible promise' and 'root in gratuitous grace.'[117] Condign merit has 'equality between service and return' by commutative justice for a *real* claim to reward.[118] Given the proportionality problem, however, condign merit's twofold basis is 'the intrinsic value of the good work' and 'the free acceptance and gratuitous promise of God.'[119] Congruous merit is characterized by

---

in Adamo innocente non donum personale *tantum*, sed dotem naturae, nam 'iustitia originalis includit gratiam gratum facientem.').

114. J. Pohle, 'Grace,' in *Catholic Encyclopedia*, 6:691.

115. Pohle, 'Grace,' 6:701.

116. Pohle, 'Grace,' 6:707-8.

117. J. Pohle, 'Merit,' in *Catholic Encyclopedia*, 10:202.

118. Pohle, 'Merit,' 10:202

119. Pohle, 'Merit,' 207.

'its inadequacy and the lack of intrinsic proportion.'[120] Aligning with the Franciscan stream and its voluntarist principles, sanctifying grace is then the background that relates a *person* to the supernatural order, wherein he or she can perform good works, which God accepts as condignly meritorious on the basis of his choice. Although enabled by actual grace (as the key to avoiding *outright* Pelagianism), the performance of congruous merit orders a person to the supernatural by obtaining sanctifying grace. In this structure, congruous merit depends entirely upon God's decision to accept someone's grace-enabled best efforts as meritorious, since proportionally sinners cannot perform a work of intrinsic proportion.

Canon George D. Smith gathered essays into a collection aimed at summarizing teachings on the whole of Roman theology, including essays on anthropology, grace, and merit. These articles maintain the division of the natural and supernatural orders, contending that grace enables merit. In this view, as B. V. Miller argued, original righteousness itself was superadded to Adam's pure nature in that 'the word *justice*, as here used, means first and principally the supernatural gift of sanctifying grace, which raised Adam to a higher state and nobler dignity, which put him into a relationship of real friendship with God in this life, and gave him the pledge of eternal happiness in the closest union with him in the next.'[121] Moreover, 'immortality *and integrity*, are called preternatural gifts' because 'these qualities did not belong to Adam by virtue of his human nature,' meaning that they were not part of our physical constitution and rational faculties. Manifesting Biel-style distinctions, even superadded integrity 'did not put him, as grace did, into a different and altogether higher order of existence.'[122] Rome's standard category of the need for grace to elevate nature is plain.

Several things bear significantly upon our discussion already. First, righteousness itself was then *supernatural* to human nature, added by sanctifying grace. Second, the paradigm of pure nature comes to a new moment of flourishing as this supernatural grace that supplied a 'nobler dignity' than humanity had by creation was necessary not only for Adam

---

120. Pohle, 'Merit,' 202.

121. B. V. Miller, 'The Fall of Man and Original Sin,' in George D. Smith (ed.), *The Teaching of the Catholic Church: A Summary of Catholic Doctrine*, 2 vol. (Waterloo, Canada: Arouca Press, 2021), 1:322 (italics original).

122. Miller, 'Fall of Man and Original Sin,' 1:322.

to be oriented to an eschatological end but even for him to have a 'real friendship with God in this life.' In other words, Adam was by creation a base, non-religious creature. Everything that made us Godward creatures had to be superadded to human nature. That superaddition which ordered us to God both for this life as well as eschatologically first concentrated on the supplement of original righteousness that we lacked by nature. Hence why this book's argument contends that God constituted Adam in original righteousness as that premise connecting us to God as his image bearers and linking our covenantal obligations to our eschatological end.

In Smith's collection of articles, E. Towers shed light on the modern Roman view of sanctifying grace as having superadded and ontological character. More than just an estate without sin, 'grace is a positive reality *superadded* to the glorious natural endowment of the soul ... it is the possession of this additional glory, rather than the mere absence of mortal sin, which constitutes the state of grace.'[123] Again, the issue of proportionality rises but is addressed by grace that elevates the work to supernatural capacity: 'When we say, then, that grace gives us the power of performing supernatural actions ... we mean that we become capable of performing actions which are not in any sense miraculous but are *intrinsically elevated* so as to become *in themselves* of a higher order and value.'[124] Thus, 'no man can really merit before God unless he be in the state of grace.'[125] This essay emulates what we saw in Garrigou-Lagrange concerning the mixture of traditionally Dominican and Franciscan emphases concerning whether merit concentrates in the work or in the person. Further, although siding with the Dominicans on the Augustinian premise that we cannot merit first grace, it quite clearly elaborated how grace is the premise of merit.[126]

In connection to Miller's explanation of human nature, Towers' view of sanctifying grace helped to protect an untainted human nature even after the fall. Hence, if Adam's superadded immortality and

---

123. E. Towers, 'Sanctifying Grace,' in *Teaching of the Catholic Church*, 1:550, 551-54 (emphasis added).

124. Towers, 'Sanctifying Grace,' 1:568 (emphasis added).

125. Towers, 'Sanctifying Grace,' 1:577.

126. Towers, 'Sanctifying Grace,' 1:579.

uprightness 'were natural, then, since by his sin he lost them both for himself and for us, it will follow that man's nature now is intrinsically and essentially vitiated by being deprived of some elements originally proper to it.' The *donum superadditum* eased the dilemma in wanting to preserve human nature from any real damage due to sin, entailing that despite its loss 'human nature remains complete, in essence unimpaired by original sin, intrinsically whole and good in itself.'[127] Adam's sin lost him 'all his supernatural and preternatural gifts' but nothing 'belonging to his nature as man.'[128] In sum, 'Adam's sin did not deprive him of any of his purely natural endowments; after it, as before, his manhood was intrinsically whole and perfect.'[129] Rome's view contrasts with Protestantism's 'denial of the reality of sanctifying grace as a supernatural gift,' necessitating that after the fall, Adam's 'nature was intrinsically depraved and corrupted, and a thing evil in itself.'[130] Hence from a Reformed perspective, Miller seems basically Pelagian in how intact and *perfect* our nature remains despite sin.

The same relation of sanctifying and actual grace also appears. Sanctifying grace is the 'elevation of our nature to the divine sonship' making it 'a real quality infused into the soul and making it Godlike.' In this respect, it is permanent. On the other hand, 'actual grace is a supernatural help given by God for the special purpose of enabling us to perform some particular action which tends toward our salvation.'[131] In other words, sanctifying grace orients the person to the supernatural order while actual grace facilitates individual acts that tend toward the supernatural order. This premise again manifests the mixed view regarding whether the person or the work has focal concern.

The proportionality problem again surfaces concerning merit and our supernatural end. Expectedly, an ontological solution bridges nature and glorious reward, directly raising the issue of merit in that 'for the preparation for and meriting of this supernatural end God gave Adam *a new nature and life*, the supernature and supernatural life of sanctifying

---

127. Miller, 'Fall of Man and Original Sin,' 1:326.

128. Miller, 'Fall of Man and Original Sin,' 1:333.

129. Miller, 'Fall of Man and Original Sin,' 1:335.

130. Miller, 'Fall of Man and Original Sin,' 1:333.

131. E. Towers, 'Actual Grace,' in *Teaching of the Catholic Church*, 1:584.

grace.'[132] Because God cannot strictly owe a debt to a creature, 'apart from his promise' there is 'no right to a return for what I have done.' [133] Christ empowers our meriting as we must be in the graced state to do so, making sanctifying grace 'a condition for all real merit before God.'[134] Thus, as in the Franciscan Pactum, we must do our best, sincerely performing that which is within us, because to 'merit an increase of grace our actions must reach a certain degree of *fervor*' relating to grace already received.'[135] The exact premise of merit follows the voluntarist trajectory as God's command to Adam threatened the loss of superadded gifts, meaning 'an implied pact or covenant between God and Adam, the observance of which by Adam was a grave obligation, for God's will is the highest law, and it was his will that Adam should pass from this life into the beatific vision.'[136] The mainstream consensus then followed the lineage of the Franciscans, Cajetan, and Bellarmine in asserting that God's will, rather than his character of true righteousness, determines what merits reward.

Nouvelle Théologie and Vatican II Settlement

The modern period contains considerable intra-Roman debates about the relationship of the natural and supernatural orders. These debates primarily owe to a reinterpretation of Thomas' understanding of our natural desire for the beatific vision. Mainly among French-speaking theologians, the *nouvelle théologie* school rose to prominence as a *ressourcement* movement, prioritizing reading Thomas in his historical context rather than as an abstract theologian and advocating for a more dynamic recovery of traditional sources.[137] Étienne Gilson

---

132. Miller, 'Fall of Man and Original Sin,' 1:327 (emphasis added).

133. Towers, 'Sanctifying Grace,' 1:577.

134. Towers, 'Sanctifying Grace,' 1:577.

135. Towers, 'Sanctifying Grace,' 1:579 (emphasis added).

136. Miller, 'Fall of Man and Original Sin,' 1:329-30; Towers, 'Sanctifying Grace,' 1:579-80.

137. Hans Boersma, *Nouvelle Théologie and Sacramental Ontology: A Return to Mystery* (Oxford: Oxford University Press, 2009); Jürgen Mettepenningen, *Nouvelle Théologie – New Theology: Inheritor of Modernism, Precursor of Vatican II* (London: T&T Clark, 2010); John O'Malley, *What Happened at Vatican II* (Cambridge, MA: Belknap Press of Harvard University Press, 2008); Jürgen Mettepenningen, '*Nouvelle Théologie*: Four Historical Stages of Theological Reform Towards *Ressourcement*,' in Gabriel Flynn and Paul D. Murray (eds.), *Ressourcement: A Movement for Renewal in Twentieth-Century Catholic Theology* (New York, NY: Oxford University Press, 2012), 172-84.

(1884–1978), renowned historian of medieval philosophy, contended that commentators had distorted Thomas' teaching. He saw Cajetan himself as 'the consummate example of a *corruptorium Thomae*' – the corruption of Thomas.[138] Following a similar historical line, Henri de Lubac (1896–1991) argued that Thomas understood the human desire for a supernatural vision of God as intrinsically built into our nature.[139] The sum effect was that *nouvelle* theologians shed the idealist assumptions of post-Enlightenment rationalism, which had proliferated in Leonine neo-Thomism, and recognized that theological formulations are historically conditioned rather than absolute.

The roots for *nouvelle* thinking have always been disputed. Many of its neo-Thomist contemporaries perceived it as an attempt to make room for modernism in Roman theology. They thought it challenged the manualist doctrinal stance in favor of contextualized theology in order to relativize doctrine.[140] On the other hand, the French Revolution had so asserted nature over and against any place for the supernatural, resulting in mass bloodshed particularly of clergy, that *French* theologians of the *nouvelle* school likely perceived far more at stake in the natural-supernatural divide than simply theoretical theological categories.[141] Hence their concern to reconnect theology to everyday life, hoping to avoid the pitfalls and dangers of opposing natural and supernatural orders. This context of the French Revolution indisputably informed the historical, political, and ecclesiastical situation in the neighboring Netherlands, arguably providing impetus for parallel theological

---

138. Étienne Gilson, *Letters of Étienne Gilson to Henri de Lubac* (San Francisco, CA: Ignatius Press, 1988), 24-25; cited in Bernard N. Schumacher, 'The Reception of Thomas Aquinas by the Neo-Scholastic Philosophers in the First Half of the Twentieth Century,' in *Oxford Handbook to the Reception of Aquinas*, 381; Francesca Aran Murphy, 'Gilson and the *Ressourcement*,' in *Ressourcement*, 51-64.

139. Henri de Lubac, 'Duplex hominis beatitude (Saint Thomas, 1a2ae, 1.62, a.1,' *Recherches de Science Religieuse* 35 (1948): 200-99; Santiago Sanz Sanchéz, and John Watson, 'The Revival of Pure Nature in Recent Debates in English Speaking Theology,' *Annales Theologici* 31 (2017): 171-82; Mayer, 'Man is Inclined to His Last End by Nature,' 901-6; Alexander S. Rosenthal, 'The Problem of the *Desiderium Naturale* in the Thomistic Tradition,' *Verbum* 6 no 2 (2004): 338-44; Horton, *Justification*, 1:135-36.

140. Gerard Loughlin, '*Nouvelle Théologie*: A Return to Modernism?' in *Ressourcement*, 36-50; cf. the more accurate Hans Boersma, 'Analogy of Truth: The Sacramental Epistemology of *Nouvelle Théologie*,' in *Ressourcement*, 157-71.

141. Swafford, *Nature and Grace*, 17-19, 28-36.

concerns about the nature-supernature relationship among *nouvelle* and Dutch neo-Calvinist theologians.[142] The present point is not to affirm or deny the truthfulness of either camp, pertaining chiefly to whether their insights are biblical. The point is that our theologizing as contingent creatures is necessarily conditioned historically as well as driven and refined by the perspective that our contextual events provide for doctrinal claims. The recognition of our historically conditioned existence possibly prompted similar concerns among Reformed and Roman theologians sharing an outlook on disastrous past events.[143]

For our purposes, de Lubac's challenge against the neo-scholastic doctrine of pure nature is the *nouvelle théologie*'s main contribution. Although the *nouvelle* theologians seemed to have less to say to connect grace and merit, de Lubac was firmly set against a dichotomy of the natural and supernatural order. Although still affirming that sanctifying

---

142. James Bratt, 'Abraham Kuyper and the French Revolution,' in James Eglinton and George Harinck (eds.), *Neo-Calvinism and the French Revolution* (London: T&T Clark, 2014), 1-12; George Harinck, 'Herman Bavinck and the Neo-Calvinist Concept of the French Revolution,' in *Neo-Calvinism and the French Revolution*, 13-30; Ewout Klei, 'Dutch Orthodox Protestant Parties and the Ghost of the French Revolution,' in *Neo-Calvinism and the French Revolution*, 115-26; Hugo den Boer, 'Another Revolution: Towards a New Explanation of the Rise of Neo-Calvinism,' in *Neo-Calvinism and the French Revolution*, 177-94; James Eglinton, *Bavinck: A Critical Biography* (Grand Rapids, MI: Baker Academic, 2020), 3-11.

143. That historical context of course makes some neo-Calvinist principles unwieldy to transpose, especially directly, into other contexts (as is the case with any doctrine wedded closely to a contextual need). This issue of trans-cultural transposition possibly explains some of the tensions within Dutch Reformed theology in the American context concerning the development and use of the doctrine of antithesis, as well as difficulties in its reception within the wider Presbyterian and Reformed community in America. Unless we account for how social contexts informed particular uses of doctrines, we cannot understand how to implement them well in differing social contexts, since cultural concerns will not be identical in shifting contexts. Some may leap to defend these ideas as *purely* biblical, although to deny *any* historical considerations behind even the best doctrinal development instantly places us in the realm of idealism's understanding of history and is aligned with the rationalism of Leonine neo-Thomism that stands in stark contrast to Reformed theology's epistemological *principia*. My present point is not a blunt denial of the biblical grounding for antithesis but to provide new framework considerations to clarify and advance these discussions. The insistence upon special revelation, perceived at times to be contrary to a use of natural theology, makes full sense against a background where the appeal to nature grounded an attempt to evacuate religion from society entirely; Hans Burger, 'Kuyer's Anti-Revolutionary Doctrine of Scripture,' in *Neo-Calvinism and the French Revolution*, 1217-42. Thanks to Gray Sutanto for his insight on neo-Calvinist sources.

grace orders us to our supernatural end, he contested this extrinsic model of our orientation to a consummate experience of God because he thought it leads to secularism.[144] De Lubac's interpretation seized upon Thomas' view that superadded righteousness was given *with* creation to emphasize continuity between natural and supernatural ends.[145] According to this view, grace encompasses the whole of human life, and our ends are intrinsically toward the beatific vision with no neutral category of 'pure nature' so that humanity's supernatural ends, not being limited to the gifts 'superadded' to human nature in creation, raise us to an end that is disproportionate to but still built into how God made us.[146] As de Lubac contended, the supposition of 'another me' that is called to something other than a supernatural destiny posits an entirely different being. For de Lubac, speculation about beings called to other ends than our own clarifies very little about the existing concrete state of affairs.[147]

De Lubac's reading sparked great controversy in Roman Catholic theology, producing a huge and still growing body of literature wherein many perceive de Lubac as undermining the gratuitousness of grace.[148]

144. Henri de Lubac, *Surnaturel: études historiques* (Théologie; Paris: Aubier-Montaigne, 1946); Henri de Lubac, *A Brief Catechesis on Nature and Grace*, trans. Richard Arnandez (San Francisco, CA: Ignatius Press, 1984); Henri de Lubac, *The Mystery of the Supernatural*, trans. Rosemary Sheed (Milestones in Catholic Theology; New York, NY: Crossroad Publishing, 1998); de Lubac, *Augustinianism and Modern Theology*, 262-77; Boersma, *Nouvelle Théologie and Sacramental Ontology*, 86-115; Sanchéz, and Watson, 'Revival of Pure Nature,' 175-82; Wood, *Stir a Restless Heart*, 422.

145. de Lubac, *Catechesis on Nature and Grace*, 25-30, 41-44.

146. Hans Urs von Balthasar, *The Theology of Henri de Lubac* (San Francisco, CA: Ignatius Press, 1991), 63-73; Adam G. Cooper, 'The Reception of Aquinas in *Nouvelle Théologie*,' in *Oxford Handbook of the Reception of Aquinas*, 437-40.

147. de Lubac, *Mystery of the Supernatural*, 62-63.

148. e.g. J. P. Donnelly, 'Discussions on the Supernatural Order,' *Theological Studies* 9, no. 2 (1948): 213-49; J. P. Donnelly, 'The Supernatural: Father de Lubac's Book,' *The Review of Politics* 10, no. 2 (April 1948): 226-32; J. P. Donnelly, 'The *Surnaturel* of P. Henri de Lubac, S.J.,' *Catholic Theological Society of America Proceedings* 3 (1948): 108-21; J. P. Donnelly, 'The Gratuity of the Beatific Vision and the Possibility of a Natural Destiny,' *Theological Studies* 11, no. 3 (1950): 374-404; Feingold, *Natural Desire to See God*, 295-395; Guy Mansini, 'Henri de Lubac, the Natural Desire to See God, and Pure Nature,' *Gregorianum* 83, no. 1 (2002): 89-109; Kerr, *After Aquinas*, 134-48; Raymond Moloney, SJ, 'De Lubac and Lonergan on the Supernatural,' *Theological Studies* 69 (2008) 509-27; Nicholas J. Healy, 'Henri de Lubac on Nature and Grace: A Note on Some Recent Contributions to the Debate,' *Communio* 35 (Winter 2008): 535-64; Mayer, 'Man is Inclined to His Last End by Nature, though He cannot Reach It by Nature but Only by Grace,' 892-901; David Grummett, 'Eucharist, Matter and the Supernatural: Why de

A general openness to de Lubac's insights levied against the scholasticism of neo-Thomism abides in much modern Roman thought.[149] On the other hand, the pure nature emphases of Neo-Scholasticism has also seen reinvigorated argumentation.[150]

This debate shapes even modern pronouncements from the Roman magisterium. Although de Lubac contended that his exact theology did not fall under the declaration, Pope Pius XII's encyclical *Humani Generis* (1950), aiming to end dispute, seemed to denounce his view directly: 'Others destroy the gratuity of the supernatural order, since God, they say, cannot create intellectual beings without ordering and calling them to the beatific vision.'[151] Karl Rahner (1904–84), a Jesuit, became a prominent

Lubac Needs Teilhard,' *International Journal of Systematic Theology* 10, no. 2 (April 2008): 165-78; David Grummett, 'De Lubac, Grace, and the Pure Nature Debate,' *Modern Theology* 31, no. 1 (Jan 2015): 123-46; Henry Donneaud, OP, '*Surnaturel* through the Fine-Tooth Comb of Traditional Thomism,' in Serge–Thomas Bonino, OP, *Surnaturel: A Controversy at the Heart of Twentieth-Century Thomistic Thought*, trans. Robert Williams (Faith and Reason: Studies in Catholic Theology and Philosophy; Ave Maria, FL: Sapientia Press, 2009), 41-57; Christopher M. Cullen, 'The Natural Desire for God and Pure Nature: A Debate Renewed,' *American Catholic Philosophical Quarterly* 86, no 4 (2012): 705-30; Sean Larsen, 'The Politics of Desire: Two Readings of Henri de Lubac on Nature and Grace,' *Modern Theology* 29, no. 3 (July 2013): 279- 310; Neil Omerod, 'The Grace-Nature Distinction and the Construction of a Systematic Theology,' *Theological Studies* 75, no. 3 (2014): 515-36; Swafford, *Nature and Grace*, 87-139; John Meinert, 'St. Thomas Aquinas, Perseverance, and the Nature/Grace Debate,' *Angelicum* 93, no 4 (2016): 823-42; Randall S. Rosenberg, *The Givenness of Desire: Human Subjectivity and the Natural Desire to See God* (Toronto, Buffalo, London: University of Toronto Press, 2017).

149. e.g. Peter F. Ryan, 'How Can the Beatific Vision both Fulfill Human Nature and Be Utterly Gratuitous?' *Gregorium* 83, no 4 (2002): 717-54; John Millbank, *The Suspended Middle: Henri de Lubac and the Renewed Split in Modern Catholic Thought*, 2nd ed. (Grand Rapids, MI: Eerdmans, 2005); Matthew Kuhner, 'The Lesser Light is not Dimmed: On the Significance of Thomas Aquinas's Treatise on the Incarnation for the Relationship between Nature and Grace,' *Angelicum* 93, no 4 (2016): 751-84; Wood, *Stir a Restless Heart*, 423-38; Wood, 'Henri de Lubac, *Humani Generis*, and the Natural Desire for a Supernatural End,' 1209-41; Sánchez and Watson, 'Revival of the Notion of Pure Nature,' 189-94, 212-18.

150. e.g. Steven A. Long, *Natura Pura: On the Recovery of Nature in the Doctrine of Grace* (New York, NY: Fordham University Press, 2010); Reinhard Hütter, *Dust Bound for Heaven: Explorations in the Theology of Thomas Aquinas* (Grand Rapids, MI: Eerdmans, 2012); Reinhard Hütter, Bound for Beatitude: A Thomistic Study in Eschatology and Ethics (Thomistic Ressourcement Series; Washington, DC: Catholic University of America Press, 2019); Feingold, *Natural Desire to See God*; Sánchez and Watson, 'Revival of the Notion of Pure Nature,' 195-200, 207-12, 218-26.

151. Pius XII, 'Encyclical *Humani Generis*,' *The Holy See*; August 12, 1950; accessed on May 9, 2023 at https://www.vatican.va/content/pius-xii/en/encyclicals/documents/

voice in attempting to reconcile de Lubac's opposition to an extrinsicist view of humanity, wherein our supernatural destiny is artificially bolted onto pure nature, with traditional Roman principles.[152] With implied critique of neo-Thomism, Rahner posited 'the offer of grace as constitutive of the actual condition of human existence' so that humanity, having no self-contained pure nature, is entirely graced, dissolving the church-world divide so that everything is the kingdom of grace.[153]

These tensions fed into the Second Vatican Council (1962–65), arguably shaping the Council's stance on a number of issues.[154] Following *nouvelle théologie*'s emphasis on *ressourcement*, many of Vatican II's major documents indicate a greater return to creative retrieval of patristical, liturgical, and traditional sources, as well as renewed biblical studies, for the sake of revitalizing the church's present theology and practice.[155] A new perspective on the nature-grace distinction made room for Rome to recognize the supernatural outside their own confines, even acknowledging in *Lumen Gentium* other churches as Christian without being in communion with the Bishop of Rome.[156] This view's foundation,

---

hf_p-xii_enc_12081950_humani-generis.html, §26; Joseph A. Komonchak, '*Humani Generis* and *Nouvelle Théologie*,' in *Ressourcement*, 138-56.

152. Karl Rahner, 'Concerning the Relationship between Nature and Grace,' in *Theological Investigations Volume* 1 (New York, NY: Seabury Press, 1974), 297-317 (thanks to Camden Bucey for helping me obtain this source); Sánchez and Watson, 'Revival of the Notion of Pure Nature,' 185-89; Richard Lennan, 'The Theology of Karl Rahner: An Alternative to *Ressourcement*?' in *Ressourcement*, 405-22; for Reformed assessment of Rahner concerning the particular issues in our focus, see Camden M. Bucey, *Karl Rahner* (Great Thinkers; Phillipsburg, NJ: P&R, 2019), 22-38.

153. Roger Haight, 'Sin and Grace,' in Francis Schüssler Fiorenza and John P. Galvin (eds.), *Systematic Theology: Roman Catholic Perspectives*, 2nd ed. (Minneapolis, MN: Fortress Press, 2011), 404; on more recent developments related to Rahner's views, see Ryan McAnally-Linz, 'Extrinsic Grace and Eccentric Existence,' *Modern Theology* 31 no 1 (Jan 2015): 179-94; Aaron Pidel, SJ, 'Erich Przywara on Nature-Grace Extrinsicism: A Parallax View,' *Modern Theology* 37 no 4 (Oct 2021): 865-87.

154. For historical background to Vatican II, see John W. O'Malley, *What Happened at Vatican II* (Cambridge, MA: The Belknap Press of Harvard University Press, 2008).

155. Gerald O'Collins, '*Ressourcement* and Vatican II,' in *Ressourcement*, 372-91.

156. 'Dogmatic Constitution on the Church *Lumen Gentium*,' *The Holy See*; November 21, 1964; accessed on May 9, 2023 at https://www.vatican.va/archive/hist_councils/ii_vatican_council/documents/vat-ii_const_19641121_lumen-gentium_en.html, §8, 15. For issues in interpreting this constitution, see Guy Mansini, 'Lumen Gentium,' in Matthew L. Lamb and Matthew Levering (eds.), *The Reception of Vatican II* (New York, NY: Oxford University Press, 2017), 48-80.

as outlined in *Ad Gentes*, is the recognition of the universal revelation of the Son to all humanity in creation, preparatorily grounding the church's missionary calling.[157] That widened sphere of natural orientation to the supernatural prompted a new, open disposition to even non-Christian religions where salvation was available outside the visible church, as *Nostra Aetate* declared in interpreting *Lumen Gentium* §14–16.[158] Vatican II at least lowered the walls between the natural and supernatural orders.

Although Vatican II itself produced no documents directly addressing the issue of grace and merit, the *Catechism of the Catholic Church* provides insight into Rome's post-Vatican II views. Picking up the language of Trent, the *Catechism of the Catholic Church* more overtly ties original righteousness to our creational condition, arguing 'Adam and Eve, were constituted in an original "state of holiness and justice."'[159] Original holiness was a 'grace' wherein 'The inner harmony of the human person, the harmony between man and woman, and finally the harmony between the first couple and all creation, comprised the state called "original justice."'[160] All the same, the catechism, albeit understated in the ethos of Vatican II, maintains the distinction of natural and supernatural orders.[161]

The *Catechism of the Catholic Church*, a document spearheaded by Joseph Ratzinger who became Pope Benedict XVI, is a key source as the proportionality problem again appears. According to Rome's catechism, 'Merit is relative to the virtue of justice, in conformity with the principle of equality which governs it.'[162] In the absolute sense, therefore, 'With

---

157. 'Decree *Ad Gentes* on The Mission Activity of The Church,' *The Holy See*; accessed on May 9, 2023 at https://www.vatican.va/archive/hist_councils/ii_vatican_council/documents/vat_ii_decree_19651207_ad-gentes_en.html. On interpretation of this decree, see Ralph Martin, 'Ad Gentes,' in *Reception of Vatican II*, 266-91; O'Collins, '*Ressourcement* and Vatican II,' 388-90.

158. 'Declaration on the Relation of the Church to Non-Christian Religions *Nostra Aetate*,' *The Holy See*; October 28, 1965; accessed on May 9, 2023 at https://www.vatican.va/archive/hist_councils/ii_vatican_council/documents/vat-ii_decl_19651028_nostra-aetate_en.html. For interpretation of this declaration, see Gavin D'Costa, 'Nostra Aetate,' in *Reception of Vatican II*, 425-58.

159. *Catechism of the Catholic Church*, 2nd ed. (Washington DC: United States Conference of Catholic Bishops – Libreria Editrice Vaticana, 1997), §375.

160. *Catechism of the Catholic Church*, §376.

161. *Catechism of the Catholic Church*, §1998, 2000, 2005.

162. *Catechism of the Catholic Church*, §2006.

regard to God, there is no strict right to merit on the part of man. Between God and us there is an immeasurable inequality, for we have received everything from him, our Creator.'[163] Potentially omitting congruent merit in the state of pure nature, the catechism grounds human merit in God's grace: 'The merit of man before God in the Christian life arises from the fact that God *has freely chosen to associate man with the work of his grace.*'[164] Although contending that 'Filial adoption, in making us partakers of the divine nature, can bestow *true merit* on us as a result of God's gratuitous justice,' still, 'Since the initiative belongs to God in the order of grace, *no one can merit the initial grace* of forgiveness and justification, at the beginning of conversion.'[165] In stating that adoption makes us partake of the divine nature thereby enabling our merit, the catechism affirms the standard Roman premise that grace must elevate our nature so that merit is possible because of this ontological supplement, reinforcing the distinction of the natural and supernatural orders concerning proportionality. All the same, the catechism formally sides with Thomas against Franciscan theology by affirming that no one can merit first grace.[166] Nevertheless, it also seems to take the more traditionally Franciscan view of locating merit in the *person* in possession of sanctifying grace rather than the work.

Admitting that hot debate exists over the proper interpretation and application of Vatican II, one understanding of its principles is simply a return to Gabriel Biel's understanding of pure nature and congruent merit. In *Lumen Gentium*, cooperation with whatever is in us, even apart from Christ and the gospel, can lead to salvation: 'Those also can attain to salvation who through no fault of their own do not know the Gospel of Christ or His Church, yet sincerely seek God and moved by grace strive by their deeds to do His will as it is known to them through the dictates of conscience.'[167] More practically, *Nostra Aetate*, seemingly echoing Rahner's theology, outlined how saving grace is always causally dependent upon Christ but nonetheless available to

---

163. *Catechism of the Catholic Church*, §2007.

164. *Catechism of the Catholic Church*, §2008 (italics original).

165. *Catechism of the Catholic Church*, §2009, 2010.

166. *Catechism of the Catholic Church*, §2026–2027.

167. 'Lumen Gentium,' §16

adherents of other religions.[168] This principle informs the *Catechism*'s position that merit requires grace, in reality facilitating merit from the state of pure nature – at least in a sense – because Christ's grace is, in effect, at least partly universal.

The modern connection to Biel and the Franciscan Pactum is apparent in the teaching of Bishop Robert Barron, a significant popular-level conveyer of the Roman faith. Barron is a highly gifted communicator, and at least his recent stand on moral issues ought to be admired. As to our topic, he has contended that following your conscience, if done with *sincerity*, can lead to salvation even for an atheist. Although qualifying that Christ is the 'privileged route' to salvation and that all salvation is at least 'indirectly' through Christ, Barron articulated:

> Vatican II clearly teaches that someone outside the explicit Christian faith can be saved. Now, they're saved through the grace of Christ indirectly received. So, I mean the grace is coming from Christ. But it might be received according to your conscience. So, if you're *following your conscience sincerely*, or in your [Ben Shapiro's] case if you're following the commandments of the law *sincerely*, yeah you can be saved .... So, even an atheist, Vatican II teaches, *of good will* can be saved.[169]

Since Barron rejected this statement's potential for relativism, the relevant emphasis is the *sincerity* of following your conscience or doing your best to keep God's commands.

Albeit framed in more accessible terms, Barron's emphasis on sincerity amounts to the Franciscan Pactum. That connection is clear as he posed our best efforts (sincerity) at acting according to our conscience (what is within us) as one path to saving grace. Continuing his application for the mechanics of salvation, Barron resolved: 'So, we use the language of cooperation with grace, that grace comes first, accepted in faith. Luther was right to that extent. If Luther had said "gratia prima," we'd be fine – "grace first".' Reflecting on our response of love required by our reception of grace, he comments that, 'it's grace and then cooperation with grace, which manifests itself in a life of love, and that's what salvation consists

---

in.'[170] Aligned with Biel, the operative principle in Barron's view is that grace is God's acceptance of our sincere best efforts, even apart from the specific grace of conversion, as sufficient to obtain salvation. Hence, grace includes God's imputation of meritorious value to our cooperation with whatever grace we might possess.

Contemporary Roman theology is full of complexity. Barron may well represent the emphatic shift toward intrinsicism that rose to prominence after Vatican II, prompting even de Lubac's pushback against a perceived drift toward a universalism wherein grace was so equivalent to nature that saving grace had to be present within other religions – likely a cause for the recent resurgence of pure nature theology.[171] Barron's position, specifically concerning how salvation relates to those outside the Christian faith, has not gone uncriticized within the Roman communion. Still, he demonstrates that contemporary Roman theology still gravitates toward traditionally Franciscan formulations, even among those who are formally Thomistic proponents.

Eastern Orthodoxy?

Readers might wonder why these chapters have so greatly focused on the western theological tradition. The simple answer is that Eastern Orthodoxy does not have an equivalent trajectory for the discussion of nature, supernature, and grace. Even recent Eastern theologians mark their tradition's trend of rejecting the two orders of nature and grace, concerning how we are oriented to God. John Meyendorff (1926–92) denies that the 'divine spark' which imbues divine qualities into humanity is superadded, but naturally makes us 'dynamically oriented toward further progress in God.'[172] Our image bearing capacity entails a relation to God but also a '*function* and *task*' in creation.[173] According to Meyendorff, who stated that Augustinian thought has 'exercised practically no influence' in Eastern theology, Adam's sin had no effects on our nature besides rendering us mortal.[174] Likewise distancing himself from Augustinian views, Kallistos

---

170. Barron, Interview, 19:09–56.

171. Swafford, *Nature and Grace*, 20-21, 25-28, 55-66, 87-88.

172. John Meyendorff, *Byzantine Theology: Historical Trends and Doctrinal Themes* (New York, NY: Fordham University Press, 1979), 139.

173. Meyendorff, *Byzantine Theology*, 140 (emphasis original).

174. Meyendorff, *Byzantine Theology*, 143-46.

Ware (1934–2022) affirmed that humanity was made naturally for fellowship with God, but our station as God's image means that 'the gulf between creature and Creator is not impassable,' allowing for confusion of the Creator-creature distinction. Accordingly, with arguable *formal* similarity to Roman views of nature and grace, ameliorated by explicit synergism of another sort, Ware outlined that we are irrevocably God's image but must acquire his (moral) likeness as our (eschatological?) goal by the increase of virtue, assisted by grace.[175] As John Anthony McGuckin has explained, Pelagius and his teachings have never bothered Eastern theological sensibilities as was the case in the Augustinian west, leaving them very open to his view of nature and works, and seeing salvation as ontological ascent into God.[176]

Along far more radical (and pluralist) lines, in his recent collection of essays on nature and supernature from an Eastern Orthodox perspective, David Bentley Hart lamented the modern resurgence of 'two-tier' neo-Thomism with its insistence on the distinction of natural and supernatural orders.[177] Rather, nature and supernature are 'varying intensities within a single transcendent act.'[178] Bearing some similarity to de Lubac's argument, Hart contended that the imposition of an extrinsic supernatural order upon pure nature essentially eviscerates the creature that we were, making some new sort of being.[179] In his view, no spiritual creature, such as humanity, *can* have a purely natural end, since spirituality entails a relation to God that cannot rest in something purely natural.[180] Although falling into a rut whereby Eastern Orthodox theologians continually abjure certain western criticism that supposedly always misunderstand their Essence-Energies distinction, Hart's position – wherein 'we are gods in the process of becoming God' because our participation in divinity, since nothing but God exists, grounds our constitution – contains an

---

175. Timothy Ware, *The Orthodox Church: An Introduction to Eastern Christianity*, new ed. (Milton Keynes, UK: Penguin Random House UK, 2015), 212-15.

176. John Anthony McGuckin, *The Path of Christianity: The First Thousand Years* (Downers Grove, IL: IVP Academic, 2017), 451-55; also Ware, *Orthodox Church*, 215-31.

177. Hart, *You Are Gods*, xi-xviii, 2-9, 30-31.

178. Hart, *You Are Gods*, xvii.

179. de Lubac, *Mystery of the Supernatural*, 62-63.

180. Hart, *You Are Gods*, 9-18, 25.

'implicit univocity.'[181] Before Reformed theologians too quickly ascribe univocity to every Roman implementation of the nature-supernature distinction, we must note that Hart denied the distinction of natural and supernatural orders. His purpose was to blur the Creator-creature distinction, eschewing western trinitarian metaphysics that rule out the descending ladder of being that begins with the Father and declines through the personal processions of the Son and Spirit to creation 'at the termination of that continuum,' making it '"located" nowhere but *within* the very life of God *as* God.'[182] Moreover, 'Our being in God and God's being in us are both also and more originally God's being as God.'[183] The Eastern Orthodox repudiation of the natural and supernatural orders facilitates an understanding of our supernatural end that is in no way eschatological but is an entire conflation of nature into God's being. It produces a correlativity of the highest rank wherein history amounts to the incarnation of God and the deification of creation.[184] Hart's position proves that Reformed theology does need guardrails for our own criticism of the Roman distinction of natural and supernatural orders when we come to formulate the covenant of works.

Conclusion

The development of the Roman tradition from the early modern period to the present day concerning the issue of grace and merit shows how the history of this doctrine is complicated and cannot be reduced to simple differences between Protestants and Roman Catholics on any of the involved issues. Nonetheless, the overall trajectory demonstrates that Roman theology increasingly gave place to a real moment of pure nature in Adam's existence. Drawing upon nominalist principles developed in the late medieval tradition, works of pure nature had the potential for merit even after the fall. Arguably flowering into a more robust but flexible paradigm after Vatican II, these principles remain active in contemporary Roman thought so that those who do what is in them and cooperate with whatever grace they may have can attain salvation even without knowing the gospel of Christ directly.

181. Hart, *You Are Gods*, 32-33, 102.

182. Hart, *You Are Gods*, 102 (italics original).

183. Hart, *You Are Gods*, 105.

184. Hart, *You Are Gods*, 102-24.

The discussion about the historical development of Roman thought on nature and grace, which has run throughout chapters three and four, is in no way exhaustive nor a definitive history of these matters. Nearly every figure treated warrants a whole monograph even on the narrow issues raised. The purpose has been to familiarize Reformed theology afresh with an awareness of the issues involved in the discussion about original righteousness, merit, nature, grace, and supernature and to provide contours in our perspective on how past theologians have related these issues in very different ways. The next chapter reckons with how these Roman discussions intersect *historically* with the development of Reformed theology, culminating in an outline of how that intersection affects the current landscape of the Reformed use of the law-gospel distinction.

Roman Views of Original Righteousness, Grace, and Merit

The following chart summarizes how the figures surveyed in the preceding history of Roman thought explained the major aspects of how the distinction of natural and supernatural orders pertain to the topics of original righteousness, grace, and merit.

	Original Righteousness	Grace's Function	Merit's Principle
Peter Lombard	Ambiguous as to whether Adam was created with grace-infused virtues or had to obtain them. Sin caused the loss of original righteousness	Supplemented human nature itself	Ambiguous: Sanctifying grace enabled meritorious performance
Thomas Aquinas	Given as part of Adam's created constitution. Was supernatural in the sense that righteousness was the right ordering of appetites that reside within faculties that remain as part of human nature	Superadded to elevate human nature to perform truly meritorious *acts*	Realism: The *work* must be truly righteous and worthy of merit

179

	Original Righteousness	Grace's Function	Merit's Principle
Bonaventure of Bagnoregio	Adam created in pure nature from which he had to obtain the sanctifying grace of original righteousness	Elevated human nature so that the *person* is accepted by sanctifying grace	Realism: The *work* must be truly righteous and worthy of merit
John Duns Scotus	Adam's original righteousness was superadded to his nature. In addition to original righteousness, Adam had to obtain sanctifying grace, which would make works meritorious	Elevated human nature so that the *person* is accepted by sanctifying grace	Voluntarism: God accepts a good work as meritorious because it is performed by a person acting in the state of sanctifying grace
William of Ockham	Ambiguous in some respects, but clear that neither original righteousness nor sanctifying grace are absolutely necessary to merit	Optional, since even a sinner in a purely natural state could perform works to merit everlasting life	Nominalism: God by sheer will names a work as meritorious, since universal (realist) standards for righteousness do not exist. This denial of any universal premise for true righteousness also excludes God's own nature, since God's will determines what is right
Gabriel Biel	Adam was created in pure nature, having to obtain original righteousness and sanctifying grace	Optional, since even a sinner in a purely natural state could perform works to merit everlasting life	Nominalism: God by sheer will names a work as meritorious, since universal (realist) standards for righteousness do not exist. This denial of any universal premise for true righteousness also excludes God's own nature, since God's will determines what is right

	Original Righteousness	Grace's Function	Merit's Principle
Henry of Ghent	Adam had original righteousness naturally as a concreated part of his nature	Sanctifying grace makes a *work* meritorious	Ambiguous: emphasis on predestination may suggest kinship to Thomas' doctrine of *ordinatio*, which had the realist premise of a truly righteous work
Thomas Cajetan	Adam's pure nature required the *donum superadditum* to relate him to the supernatural order and to eschatological life	Grace adds the supernatural order to our nature and undergirds the covenant that makes a good *work* meritorious	Voluntarism: God covenants to accept *some* (truly righteous) *work* of his choosing as meritorious
The Council of Trent	Ambiguous	Grace infuses strength into the justified to perform meritorious works	Ambiguous
Michael Baius	Adam was created with original righteousness as natural	Grace, at least sanctifying grace, was unnecessary before the fall	Realism: The *work* must be truly righteous and worthy of merit
Cornelius Jansenius	Original righteousness belonged to pure nature	Sanctifying grace was equivalent to natural original righteousness	Realism: The *work* must be truly righteous and worthy of merit; merit after the fall is impossible
Robert Bellarmine	Original righteousness was the *donum superadditum*	Grace added the supernatural order to pure nature; sanctifying grace restores and elevates human nature so that the *person* is accepted	Voluntarism: God covenants to accept *some* (truly righteous) *work* of his choosing as meritorious

	Original Righteousness	Grace's Function	Merit's Principle
Modernist Neo-Thomism	Adam was created in pure nature and received superadded grace after creation. Original righteousness then was the *donum superadditum* that included sanctifying grace	Sanctifying grace makes a *person* acceptable to God, enabling them to perform condignly meritorious *works*; a person without grace can perform works of congruent merit	Realism: The *work* must be truly righteous and worthy of merit; an accompanying voluntarist premise is often added that God wills to accept the *work* as truly meritorious
Post-Vatican II	Mixed, but characterized by a concern to reject extrinsicism	Grace ontologically supplements nature to enable merit. Although formal Roman teaching denies that we can merit first grace, some theologians hold that grace is universal and available even through other religions	Ambiguous and presumably mixed

CHAPTER FIVE

An Ongoing Reformed Conversation

With some familiarity with the historical issues surrounding nature and supernature as well as grace and merit in place, we need to lean back toward theological construction. To proceed, we need some clearer direction for the way forward. Before turning to outright theological formulation in chapters six and seven, therefore, this chapter serves the transitionary role of relating Reformed theology to what we have seen in the medieval and Roman traditions. We begin by noting that the Reformed tradition contains diversity concerning the relationship of the natural and supernatural orders. The simple fact is, there is no one Reformed view on this issue of these orders. Consequently, when we turn to articulate our position, we must pick a certain trajectory within Reformed theology and argue in its favor. The second section then analyzes how early modern Reformed theologians engaged the medieval tradition and their early modern Roman Catholic counterparts on these issues, opening greater historical clarity on how they responded on the ground to particular aspects of this discussion. The final section surveys modern instances wherein Protestant theologians have ordered grace before works even for Adam, inverting the traditional law-gospel relationship, with the usual result of undermining justification by faith alone. This closing section re-orients us to what is at stake theologically in these historical investigations before we shift to develop our own doctrinal conclusions.

Reformed Diversity

Although this book favors one trajectory within the Reformed tradition, diversity exists among our theologians. John Calvin basically maintained a medieval outlook of the natural and supernatural orders concerning the faculties of human nature, albeit emphasizing the fall's effects in good Augustinian fashion. Calvin affirmed 'that the natural gifts were corrupted in man through sin, but that his supernatural gifts were stripped from him.' He explained the supernatural gifts as: 'the light of faith as well as righteousness, which would be sufficient to attain heavenly life and eternal bliss.'[1] Calvin seemed to own the Thomistic heritage that supernatural capacities, even related to original righteousness, were needed to obtain the beatific state.[2]

Francis Junius (1545–1602) may represent a mediating position containing some inconsistencies. On the one hand, he tied our nature closely to aspects of the supernatural order by relating the divine image to 'the law of creation, or our created nature as it was first created by God.' In this instance, he further seemed to equate grace with the *renewal* of that image that occurs in regeneration.[3] On the other hand, when as a professor in Leiden he exchanged (eventually published) correspondence with Jacob Arminius (1560–1609) about the nature of predestination, he articulated a basically medieval view of the nature-grace issue. On one side of that exchange, Arminius went beyond the Thomistic outlook, articulating essentially Robert Bellarmine's view: 'God's image is in man not by nature but by supernatural grace, not having respect to natural happiness but to supernatural life.'[4] Pushing back, Junius sided with Thomas against Bellarmine by contending that nature is twofold having relation to the physical world and the spiritual

---

1. John Calvin, *Institutes of the Christian Religion*, trans. Ford Lewis Battles, ed. John T. McNeill, 2 vol. (The Library of Christian Classics; Louisville, KY: Westminster John Knox, 1960), 2.2.12.

2. J. V. Fesko, *Adam and the Covenant of Works* (Fearn: Mentor, 2021), 84-87.

3. Francis Junius, Πρωτοκτισα (Heidelberg, 1589), 53 (Deinde imaginem Deo dupliciter considerari necesse est: Primum, in nobis secundum creationis legem, sive in natura nostra, ut primum, a Deo create est: deinde vero secundum instaurationis legem, vel gratiam Dei, prout in Christo indies renovator, et perfectionem summam adeptura est).

4. Jacob Arminius, *Amica cum Francisco Iunio de praedestinatione per literas habita collatio* (Leiden: 1613), 99 (Quae imago Dei non est natura in homine, sed supernaturalis gratia; non habens respectum ad faelicitatem naturalem, sed supernatural vitam).

world.[5] Whereas Arminius claimed that no man was ever created in a purely natural state, Junius went further than Thomas by denying that man has supernatural endowments and by affirming that God made even Adam in a purely natural state before bestowing supernatural grace: 'God contemplated man in pure nature upon whom he will confer supernatural aspects by his decree.'[6] Even in his distinction of pure nature and supernatural aspects, Junius affirmed the image of God as natural to human nature in righteousness and holiness. These supernatural endowments, therefore, do not pertain to Adam's image bearing status as such.[7] This caveat demands more reflection inasmuch as it shows that Junius' use of pure nature differed from the meaning that developed by the time of early modern Roman theology.

Junius clarified the relation of these supernatural additions to the image of God to our natural and supernatural ends. Thus, he explained his view of our supernatural end: 'The future of his nature in its integrity was natural happiness, although, so to speak, afterward to be absorbed into the supernatural on account of God's grace. This happiness was as much as the natural end of man's integrity and its natural limit.'[8] Drawing on the Thomistic view of ends, he posited: 'nature is the foundation of the supernatural.'[9] Coordinating the twofold ends, he denied that the subordinate natural end was at variance with the supernatural end, stating that the issue concerned the means of obtaining each end: 'Adam was able to strive for the former by nature, but able to be exalted to the latter on account of grace.'[10] Junius outlined essentially a Reformed Thomist view of the nature-grace paradigm, resisting what he saw to be weaknesses in Arminius' view of original nature – owing to Jesuit theology – but still holding to a real distinction of the natural and

---

5. Arminius, *de praedestinatione*, 100.

6. Arminius, *de praedestinatione*, 102 (Immo vero, mi frater, hominem Deus in puris naturalibus contemplatus est, cui supernaturalia conferret decreto suo).

7. Arminius, *de praedestinatione*, 102-15.

8. Arminius, *de praedestinatione*, 151 (Naturae enim integrae sua fuerat futura naturalis felicitas, licet in supernaturali per Dei gratiam post absorbenda, ut ita loquamur: Atque haec foelicitas tamquam naturalis finis hominis integri, & illius extremum naturale fuit).

9. Arminius, *de praedestinatione*, 152 (At duo spectari in causa hac oportuit; unum felicitatem naturalem esse praestructam supernaturali; alteram, substructam esse).

10. Arminius, *de praedestinatione*, 152 (Ad illum per naturam poterat Adam contendere: ad hunc per gratiam ab illo evehi).

supernatural orders.[11] Junius' view of natural and supernatural ends might more effectively be categorized as subordinate and ultimate ends since he did not suggest that our supernatural end was superadded. Junius thought that grace enabled Adam to seek that ultimate end but did not state that grace added it to nature.

John Owen (1616–83) took a position on the divine image that very closely resembled Thomas Aquinas' distinction of natural and supernatural capacities. In describing how the Holy Spirit immediately sanctified Christ's human nature so to make the Son's human nature entirely spotless and without any stain of original sin, he also drew the connection to Adam:

> … let the natural faculties of the soul, the mind, will, and affections, be created pure, innocent, undefiled, – as they cannot be otherwise immediately created of God, – yet there is not enough to enable any rational creature to live to God; much less was it all that was in Jesus Christ. There is, moreover, required hereunto supernatural endowments of grace, superadded unto the natural faculties of our souls. If we live unto God, there must be a principle of spiritual life in us, as well [as] of life natural. This was the image of God in Adam, and was wrought in Christ by the Holy Spirit.[12]

For Owen, Adam's principle of spiritual life was in the *imago Dei*, which surpasses the soul's natural faculties of the mind, will, and affections. In other words, the sanctification of human nature relates to its endowment with the divine image as our connection to supernatural life for living unto God. Even the phrase 'supernatural endowment of grace' comes directly from Thomas Aquinas.[13] In this respect, however, Owen employed the category of 'supernatural endowments' to refer to our constitutive elements that relate us to God, and used 'grace' seemingly

---

11. Jordan J. Ballor, "'In the Footsteps of the Thomists': an Analysis of Thomism in the Junius-Arminius Correspondence,' in Jordan J. Ballor, Matthew T. Gaetano, and David S. Sytsma (eds.), *Beyond Dordt and* De Auxiliis: *The Dynamics of Protestant and Catholic Soteriology in the Sixteenth and Seventeenth Centuries* (Leiden: Brill, 2019), 142-47; Fesko, *Adam and the Covenant of Works*, 93-94; partly refining Harrison Perkins, *Catholicity and the Covenant of Works: James Ussher and the Covenant of Works* (Oxford Studies in Historical Theology; New York, NY: Oxford University Press, 2020), 61-64.

12. John Owen, Πνευματολογια, 2.4, in *The Works of John Owen, D.D.*, ed. William H. Goold, 20 vol. (Edinburgh: T&T Clark, 1862), 3:168-69.

13. St. Thomas Aquinas, *Summa Theologica*, trans. by Fathers of the English Dominican Province, 5 vol. (New York, NY: Benziger Bros., 1948; repr. Notre Dame, IN: Christian Classics, 1981), 1.95.1 ad 4.

in a broad sense of God's empowering a person to exercise the capacities of human nature unto spiritual ends.

Owen drew this connection to our wider topic of the covenant of works by connecting the law principle to the reason for the sabbath. After explaining that the sabbath set forth the prospect of eschatological rest, he turned to consider the nature of the sabbath command.[14] For Owen, Adam's creation with faculties to know God and to be fit for eschatological destiny meant that 'the order of his nature, called "the image of God," inclined and enabled him' to love, to fear, to obey, and to trust God as his preserver and rewarder.[15] In this connection, Adam had necessary obligations of obedience by virtue of his nature having the image-bearing relationship to God's nature, which included setting aside due time for the performance of worship.[16] Accordingly, he described the covenant of works' superadded features:

> Man in his creation, with respect unto the ends of God therein, was constituted under a covenant. That is the law of his obedience was attended with promises and threatenings, rewards and punishments, suited unto the goodness and holiness of God; for every law with rewards and recompenses annexed hath the nature of a covenant. And in this case, although the promise wherewith man was encouraged unto obedience, which was that of eternal life with God, did in strict justice exceed the worth of the obedience required, *and so was a superadded effect of goodness and grace*, yet was it suited unto the constitution of a covenant meet for man to serve God in unto his glory; and, on the other side, the punishment threatened unto disobedience, in death and an everlasting separation from God, was such as the righteousness and holiness of God, as his supreme governor, and Lord of him and the covenant, did require. Now, this covenant belonged unto the law of creation …[17]

Although Owen saw the covenant of works as belonging to nature inasmuch as it cohered with the natural law, nonetheless superadded grace was necessary to address the problem of proportionality. This passage is

---

14. John Owen, *Exercitations concerning the Name, Original, Nature, Use, and Continuance of a Day of Sacred Rest*, 3.9–19, in *Works*, 19:333-40.

15. Owen, *Exercitations concerning … a Day of Sacred Rest*, 3.10, in *Works*, 19:336.

16. Owen, *Exercitations concerning … a Day of Sacred Rest*, 3.10, in *Works*, 19:336-37.

17. Owen, *Exercitations concerning … a Day of Sacred Rest*, 3.10, in *Works*, 19:337 (emphasis added).

not clear as to whether Owen saw the superadded grace in this instance as simply the making of the covenant to overcome the disproportionality issue, or as the superadded endowments of grace that he mentioned in the earlier quote about the sanctification of Christ's human nature. If the latter, it is hard to distinguish Owen's view from the medieval paradigm of using sanctifying grace as the ontological solution to the proportionality problem.[18] The issue involved, however, was that Owen thought that the idea that Adam could obey in his own strength would make Adam an independent creature, since man was created to depend on the Spirit.[19] Owen's assumption might overlook important nuances concerning the concept of *auxilium* and concursus, which is discussed below.

This book's remaining arguments enlist representatives of our preferred view, so will not roll out extensive historical evidence for the issue's other side now. Intellectual integrity and academic honesty have been the point for presenting this multiform cast of the Reformed tradition even on important issues like this one. Nonetheless, the later Reformed Orthodox seemed more emphatically against the older separation of natural and supernatural orders, emphasizing nature and covenant more than nature and grace.

Francis Turretin mounted an ardent argument against the *donum superadditum* both as to human nature as such and to Adam's covenant-keeping ability. Contending against Bellarmine, Turretin denied even the hypothetical possibility of Adam's existence in pure nature.[20] Drawing a critically helpful distinction, he posed that original righteousness was thoroughly natural in respect to the created order but now is supernatural inasmuch as grace restores it to corrupt sinners.[21] So, he concluded that God's freedom in how he might create humanity did not mean that original righteousness was supernatural to the way that he did make us in his likeness:

> However much original righteousness can rightly be called 'grace' or 'a gratuitous gift,' and therefore not owed from God's part in the same manner

---

18. Fesko, *Adam and the Covenant of Works*, 98.

19. Thanks to Ryan McGraw, an Owen expert, for clarifying this point in understanding Owen's position.

20. Franciscus Turrettinus, *Institutio Theologiae Elencticae*, 3 vol. (Geneva, 1679–85), 5.9.1–11; 5.11.5.

21. Turrettinus, *Institutio*, 5.11.4–6.

also that nature itself was created by him, it does not for that reason follow that it was supernatural, or undue to upright nature's perfection, because although God owed nothing to man, nevertheless having posited that he willed to create man according to his own image, he owed to create him righteous and holy.[22]

Turretin continued the same trajectory in discussing Adam's ability in the covenant of works. Although the covenant even intensified Adam's obligation to obey God, any help God gave Adam 'did not extend to pouring any new virtue into him but only to revealing the power of that strength which he had received.'[23] Turretin's anti-Roman polemic had an important role for nature's integrity even in relation to supernatural realities.

Petrus van Mastricht (1630–1706), professor of theology in Utrecht, represents a more guarded use of terminology, emphasizing Adam's natural aspects in the covenant of works. He affirmed that original righteousness is 'natural to man' and that 'man was creature not only innocent, but also endowed with original righteousness.'[24] In one respect, he aligned with Thomas: 'Original righteousness is ... that most ordered uprightness and harmony of the intellect, will, and affections.'[25] Still, he connected the divine image and original righteousness intrinsically – 'man insofar as in his original righteousness he bears the image of God' – rather than posing this properly ordered state of affairs as supernatural.[26] Thus, he saw our supernaturally oriented faculties as natural to our nature. Within the covenant, Mastricht argued that Adam's natural strength, rather than grace-enabled and supernatural obedience, was required. As the condition, 'God stipulated from man

---

22. Turrettinus, *Institutio*, 5.11.16 (Quamvis Iustutia originalis recte dici possit *Gratia*, seu *donum gratuitum*, atque adeo indebitum a parte Dei, quemadmodum et natura ipsa, quae ab ipso creata est; Non sequitur propterea esse supernaturalem, vel indebitam ad perfectionem naturae integrae, quia licet nihil debuerit Deus homini, posito tamen quod voluit creare hominem ad imaginem suam, debuit illum creare justam et sanctum).

23. Turrettinus, *Institutio*, 8.3.14 (Quod auxilium non tendebat ad virtutem novam aliquam ipsi infundendam, sed tantum ad efficaciam illius virtutis exerendam, quam acceperat). These observations clarify and strengthen Fesko's interpretation of this passage, which had less analysis of *auxilium*; *Adam and the Covenant of Works*, 101-2.

24. Petrus Van Mastricht, *Theoretical-Practical Theology*, trans. Todd M. Rester, ed. Joel R. Beeke, 7 vol. (Grand Rapids, MI: Reformation Heritage Books, 2017–), 1.3.9.51, 52, 54.

25. Mastricht, *Theoretical-Practical Theology*, 1.3.9.52.

26. Mastricht, *Theoretical-Practical Theology*, 1.3.11.5.

an obedience that was perfect in every way, one that was to be *offered in his own strength*, which condition Adam also received.'[27] Further, 'intrinsically, he was equipped with a perfect principle of obeying, namely, original righteousness.'[28] In Turretin and Mastricht, we find representatives of a Reformed construal of our nature in relation to obtaining our supernatural end that depended on premises that were more covenantal than ontological, which is precisely the view we argue.

A Reformed Reflection on Roman Views

The preceding chapters painted a complex portrait of medieval and Roman theology concerning nature, grace, and merit. Some bearings amidst the various views and issues seem helpful for moving forward as we take account of even the Reformed tradition's historical eclecticism. Although Thomas was no proto-Protestant, in several ways the Reformed were nearer to him than to other medieval figures, mainly due to shared Augustinian concerns.[29] Even Martin Luther specifically named John Duns Scotus and Gabriel Biel as targets as he lambasted scholasticism.[30] This section analyzes certain key features explored in our historical survey to see how early modern Reformed writers engaged these issues. The point is not that the Reformed were all full-blown Thomists. The point is that Thomas was the theologically *closer*, which does not suggest identical, historical antecedent on these issues because he was a stronger Augustinian theologian. The inverse way of stating this historical upshot is that the Reformed were committedly Augustinian even in their eclectic appropriation of the prior tradition.

First, Thomas bound the *imago Dei* to human constitution, closely aligning our relationship with God to creation itself. Citing Augustine, Thomas argued that man is fundamentally the image and likeness of God. Binding image and likeness together, he wrote, 'likeness is essential to an image; and that an image adds something to likeness – namely, that it is copied from something else.' For Thomas, image indicates a closer resemblance to the original than mere likeness, and

---

27. Mastricht, *Theoretical-Practical Theology*, 1.3.12.17.

28. Mastricht, *Theoretical-Practical Theology*, 1.3.12.19.

29. John Patrick Donnelly, SJ, 'Calvinist Thomism,' *Viator* 7 (1976): 441-55.

30. Martin Luther 'Disputation Against Scholastic Theology,' in *Luther's Works Volume 31* (Philadelphia, PA: Fortress Press, 1957), §6.

'man is said to be both *image* by reason of the likeness; and to be the *image* by reason of the imperfect likeness,' by which he meant that the Son is the only perfect likeness of God.[31] Thomas located our image-bearing, which included likeness, in our rational nature that allows us to imitate God in understanding and loving God.[32] By creation, then, we have 'a *natural* aptitude for understanding and loving God,' highlighting how we were made for fellowship with God even apart from our eschatological end.[33] In other words, Thomas posed a fundamentally religious purpose to our *whole* constitution, posing image and likeness as no more than inflections on the same notion that we resemble God in our makeup.

By contrast, Bellarmine separated the concepts of image and likeness. Leveraging his reading of the patristics, he argued that the likeness of God referred to abilities superadded to God's image given in human nature, 'From this host of patristic evidence, we are compelled to admit that *the image and likeness are not entirely the same*. Rather, the image pertains to nature, the likeness to abilities.'[34] For Bellarmine, differing from Thomas, not everything belonging to our role and charge to reflect God at the creaturely level is constitutive of human nature. Thus, Bellarmine followed Bonaventure's interpretation that image and likeness differ 'according to mode' in that 'image is in the order of natural things, and likeness in the order of things belonging to grace.'[35] Bonaventure's distinction then separates naturally implanted faculties from supernatural virtues.[36] Bellarmine's appropriation of Bonaventure's

---

31. Thomas, *Summa Theologica*, 1.93.1.

32. Thomas, *Summa Theologica*, 1.93.4, 9.

33. Anthony A. Hoekema, *Created in God's Image* (Grand Rapids, MI: Eerdmans, 1986), 36-42.

34. Robert Bellarmine, *de Gratia Primi Hominis*, 1.2, in *De Controversiis Christianae Fidei, tomus quartus* (Sartorius, 1601), 6 (emphasis added; Ex his igitur tot Patrum testimoniis cogimur admittere non esse omnino idem imaginem, & similitudinem, sed imaginem ad naturam, similitudinem ad virtutes pertinere: proinde Adamum peccando non imaginem Dei, sed similitudinem perdidisse).

35. Bonaventure, *Commentary on the Sentences*, bk.2, dist. 16, art. 2, q. 3, resp., in A. C. Peltier (ed.), *S.R.E Cardinalis S. Bonaventure... Opera Omnia*, 15 vol. (Paris: Ludovicus Vivès, 1864–71), 2:647 (Secundus modus distinguendi est, quod imago est in naturalibus, et similitudo in gratuitis).

36. Bonaventure, *Itinerarium Mentis in Deum*, §4, in *Opera Omnia*, 12:13-16; Denys Turner, *The Darkness of God: Negativity in Christian Mysticism* (Cambridge: Cambridge

interpretation further confirms our thesis that the Franciscan legacy concerning the *imago Dei*, original righteousness, and merit came to predominate the Roman tradition.

Geerhardus Vos picked up this issue in his taxonomy of views about the *imago Dei*. He tagged that 'Bellarmine held that "image" designated the natural and "likeness" the supernaturally added.'[37] To force Vos' critique to apply to Thomas, someone must supply the assumed but obviously incorrect middle premise that Bellarmine agreed with Thomas on this issue. Thomas' view falls within Vos' statement that the true position is that image and likeness both 'serve to describe one and the same concept from two sides.'[38] Moreover, when Vos contended that the Reformed view means that 'the image of God comprises both the intellectual and the moral nature of man,' it seems to encompass Thomas' position that our image bearing binds us to understanding and loving God.[39] The Reformed then more aligned with Thomas that bearing God's image is concreated with human nature.

Second, Reformed theology has closer affinity to Thomas' position that God created Adam with that original righteousness. It further clarifies that this original righteousness was a fundamental part of bearing God's image, so that it was inseparably, rather than superadded, *concreated* with our nature.[40] According to Thomas, God gave original righteousness, which for him was a properly ordered subjection of the lower appetites to the spiritual faculties, with creation, although conceptually superadded to human nature.[41] David Pareus (1548–1622), professor of Old and New Testament at Heidelberg, provides Reformed precedent for our interpretation that Thomas' view contained some ambiguities on this issue, explaining that Thomas' position 'is

University Press, 1995), 110-11; Hans Boersma, *Seeing God: The Beatific Vision in Christian Tradition* (Grand Rapids, MI: Eerdmans, 2018), 204.

37. Geerhardus Vos, *Reformed Dogmatics*, 5 vol. (Bellingham, WA: Lexham Press, 2012–14), 2:11.

38. Vos, *Reformed Dogmatics*, 2:11.

39. Vos, *Reformed Dogmatics*, 2:11; Thomas, *Summa Theologica*, 1.93.4. Note Thomas' inclusion of *love* means that in some way he does factor the will into the divine image.

40. Richard A. Muller, *Dictionary of Latin and Greek Theological Terms: Drawn Principally from Protestant Scholastic Theology*, 2nd ed. (Grand Rapids, MI: Baker Academic, 2017), 97-98.

41. Thomas, *Summa Theologica*, 1.95.1.

obscure because he did not explain what he means by sanctifying grace [*gratiam gratum facientem*]. Thomas called grace "that which by man is united to God."[42] Junius observed the same ambiguity.[43] Notably, Pareus employed Thomas to refute Bellarmine, even though Bellarmine followed Thomas that Adam received sanctifying grace at creation.[44] Pareus ultimately understood Thomas to mean, in contrast to Bellarmine's thorough doctrine of pure nature, that 'Everlasting happiness, according to Thomas, was man's natural end. Natural means, therefore, also existed to attain it. These means, however, were man's original rectitude and righteousness.'[45] Pareus named Lombard and Scotus as those making original righteousness something separate from sanctifying grace, and others, such as Thomas Aquinas and Albert Magnus, as saying that 'original righteousness is conjoined with sanctifying grace [*gratia gratum faciente*].'[46] Compared with some of the multiform medieval options then, many Reformed have *a* proximity to Thomas. Pareus even sets historical precedent within our tradition for this book's interpretation of the various medieval trajectories in relation to Reformed theology.

---

42. David Pareus, *Roberti Bellarmini … de Gratia Primi Hominis* (Heidelberg, 1612), 36 (Obscura, quia non explicat, quid velit per gratiam gratum facientem. Thomas vocat gratiam, per quam homo conjungitur Deo).

43. Arminius, *de Praedestinatione*, 198-200.

44. Bellarmine, *de Gratia Primi Hominis*, 1.3, in *De Controversiis … quartus*, 7-12; Washburn, 'Shaping of Modern Catholic Anthropology,' 221n13; describing Bellarmine, Pareus, *de Gratia Primi Hominis*, 36 (Primum hominem non quamlibet animi rectiitudnem, sed ipsam etiam gratiam gratum facientem accepisse). From an Eastern perspective, David Bentley Hart noted that Thomas' own view contains ambiguities and unresolved tensions on the nature-supernature relation; *You Are Gods: On Nature and Supernature* (Notre Dame, IN: University of Notre Dame Press, 2022), 17

45. Pareus, *de Gratia Primi Hominis*, 90 (Finis hominis naturalis supponebat media naturalia in homine ad eum assequendum: alioqui rebus omnibus esset infelicior homo. Aeterna beatitudo iuxta, Thomam fuit finis hominis naturalis. Ergo ad eam etiam erant media naturalia. Media autem erant hominis rectitudo & iustitia originalis).

46. Pareus, *de Gratia Primi Hominis*, 37 (Dissidium Sophistarum explicaturus dicit, quosdam (Lombardum, Scotum) justitiam originalem primo parenti in creatione concessam, separare a gratia gratum faciente: ac docere, Adamum accepisse quidem habitum quendam, qui partem inferiorern subijceret superiori: non tamen accepisse gratiam gratum facientem, quae amicos Dei efficit, quaeque ad *promerendam* vitam aeternam sit necessaria: Alios (Thomam, Alb. Magnum) justitiam originalem cum gratia gratum faciente ita conjungere, ut obedientia inferioris partis a gratia gratum velut a radice et fonte dependeret: quos dicit se sequi).

This aspect of Reformed theology's closer alignment to Thomas is perhaps more complicated than the first. Pareus' position – which the next chapter will show to match the confessional consensus – was that 'original righteousness itself pertains to God's image, as part to the whole.'[47] In this respect, the Reformed most resemble Henry of Ghent, who saw that the gift of original righteousness is intrinsic to human nature (*donum concreatum*).[48] Martin Luther himself seemed to articulate Henry's exact point.[49] At least Theodore Beza noted Henry as also one of the sounder scholastics from the medieval period.[50] Like Thomas, Henry, when describing pure nature, simply meant nature undefiled by sin since God made it with *natural* or concreated original righteousness. Notably, Scotus explicitly attacked Henry's views on precisely these issues, placing the strongest critique of the view most similar to the Reformed within the Franciscan camp.[51] The later medieval and early modern Roman tradition only expanded the doctrine of pure nature to be a linchpin of the doctrinal system.

Third, the Reformed are closer to Thomas than the Franciscans concerning the fall's effects. For Thomas, sin damaged Adam's very nature, requiring God's grace for restoration. By creation, Adam had natural ability to love God but lost it in the fall. On the one hand, 'man, in the state of integrous nature, was able, by the strength of his nature, to perform the good that is connatural to him without the superadded gift of grace, although not without God's help [*auxilio*] for moving, but

---

47. Pareus, *de Gratia Primi Hominis*, 39 (Nos rectius, justitiam originalem habere se ad imaginem Dei, ut partem ad totum).

48. Henry of Ghent, Quodlibet VI, question 11; in *Aurea Quodlibeta*, 2 vol. (Venice, 1613), 1:350v–52r; Richard Cross, *Duns Scotus* (Great Medieval Thinkers; New York, NY: Oxford University Press, 1999), 96-97; Michael Horton, *Justification*, 2 vol. (New Studies in Dogmatics; Grand Rapids, MI: Zondervan, 2018), 1:138.

49. As noted by Herman Bavinck, *Reformed Dogmatics*, ed. John Bolt, trans. John Vriend, 4 vol. (Grand Rapids, MI: Baker Academic, 2003–2008), 2:548-49; Fesko, *Adam and the Covenant of Works*, 89.

50. David S. Sytsma, 'Sixteenth-Century Reformed Reception of Aquinas,' in Matthew Levering and Marcus Plested (eds.), *The Oxford Handbook of the Reception of Aquinas* (Oxford: Oxford University Press, 2021), 132.

51. e.g. John Duns Scotus, *Questiones in Librum Secundum Sententiarum*, 2.29.1, *Opera Omnia*, editio nova, 26 vol. (Paris, 1891–95), 13:268, 273; Ernesto Dezza, 'John Duns Scotus on Human Beings in the State of Innocence,' *Traditio* 75 (2020): 291-93; Richard Cross, 'Duns Scotus and William of Ockham,' in *Oxford Handbook of the Reception of Aquinas*, 53-66 likewise highlighted Franciscan disagreement with Henry.

to love God above all things is something connatural to man.'[52] We will return to Thomas' concept of *auxilio* shortly, which is an important factor in this discussion. Before that, Thomas, on the other hand, argued that the fall did real damage to our nature as such, so that whereas we had connatural ability to love God supremely, 'in the state of corrupt nature man is insufficient for this according to the rational will's appetite, which, because of nature's corruption, pursues the deprivation of good, unless healed by God's grace.'[53] Showing his Augustinian commitments, Thomas stated that sin damaged our connatural faculties for relating to God with the result that we could pursue him only if God renewed those faculties by grace. Given Thomas' doctrine of *ordinatio*, his assertion of the necessity for renewing grace at least resembles the Reformed doctrine of God's sovereign regeneration.[54]

Thomas, aware that these issues needed explanation in more principle terms, related sin's corruption to a detailed breakdown of human nature. He began by stating the three relevant aspects of human nature as our faculties, our inclination to virtue, and the gift of original righteousness:

> The good of human nature is threefold. First, there are principles of which nature is constituted, and the properties that flow from them, such as the powers of the soul, and so forth. Secondly, since man has from nature an inclination to virtue, as stated above (Q. 60, A. 1; Q. 63, A. 1), this inclination to virtue is a good of nature. Thirdly, the gift of original justice [*donum originalis iustitiae*], conferred on the whole human nature in the person of the first man, may be called a good of nature.[55]

Given that this article was about sin's effects upon nature, his discussion of nature concerned pure nature *as Thomas intended the concept*, meaning unfallen and uncorrupted human nature. In that upright condition, our

---

52. Thomas, *Summa Theologica*, 1a2ae.109.3 (my translation; homo in statu naturae integrae poterat operari virtute suae naturae bonum quod est sibi connaturale, absque superadditione gratuiti doni, licet non absque auxilio Dei moventis. Diligere autem Deum super omnia est quiddam connaturale homini).

53. Thomas, *Summa Theologica*, 1a2ae.109.3 (my translation; Sed in statu naturae corruptae homo ab hoc deficit secundum appetitum voluntatis rationalis, quae propter corruptionem naturae sequitur bonum privatum, nisi sanetur per gratiam Dei).

54. Karim Schelkens and Marcel Gielis, 'From Driedo to Bellarmine: The Concept of Pure Nature in the 16th Century,' *Augustiniana* 57 no 3/4 (2007): 431-32. For Thomas' view of *ordinatio*/predestination, see the discussion in chapter three.

55. Thomas, *Summa Theologica*, 1a2ae.85.1.

faculties have the *natural* impulse to act rightly before God.[56] We also had the gift of original righteousness. In that respect, we should keep in mind that all agree that original righteousness is a gift from God. The debated issue for our discussion is whether it is a superadded or concreated gift.

Thomas explained how sin affects each of these aspects of human nature. His explanation is telling for how we should understand his relation to the later Roman tradition. He continued: 'Accordingly, the first-mentioned good of nature is neither destroyed nor diminished by sin. The third good of nature was entirely destroyed through the sin of our first parent. But the second good of nature, viz. the natural inclination to virtue, is diminished by sin.'[57] By saying that our nature's first good is not destroyed or diminished, he was referring to the remaining existence of our faculties. That humanity retains the basic functionality of faculties, meaning that we still have an intellect and a will, is not disputed between Rome and Protestants. Concerning original righteousness, Thomas resembled most Reformed theologians by affirming that sin wiped out original righteousness. We must, of course, remember that this matter is not the same as whether the image of God remains in us. In Reformed theology, although the divine image is *distorted* in us, sin means that we 'fell from [our] originall righteousnesse and communion with God, and so became dead in sin, and wholly defiled in all the faculties and parts of soul and body.'[58] Although our faculties then remain, the sinfulness of our fallen estate includes 'the want of original righteousness, and the corruption of our whole nature.'[59] Thus, Reformed theology aligns with Thomas on both these points.

The remaining issue then concerns our natural inclination toward virtue. Thomas' position was that sin 'diminished' this inclination. He elaborated his rationale:

> The good of nature, that is diminished by sin, is the natural inclination to virtue, which is befitting to man from the very fact that he is a rational

---

56. Vos, *Reformed Dogmatics*, 2:49.

57. Thomas, *Summa Theologica*, 1a2ae.85.1.

58. Westminster Confession of Faith 6.2; John R. Bower, *The Confession of Faith: A Critical Text and Introduction* (Principal Documents of the Westminster Assembly; Grand Rapids, MI: Reformation Heritage Books, 2020), 203.

59. Westminster Shorter Catechism 18; Philip Schaff (ed.), *The Creeds of Christendom*, 3 vol. (New York, NY: Harper and Brothers, 1877), 3:679.

being; for it is due to this that he performs actions in accord with reason, which is to act virtuously. Now sin cannot entirely take away from man the fact that he is a rational being, for then he would no longer be capable of sin. Wherefore it is not possible for nature to be destroyed entirely.[60]

His telling point was that sin is completely irrational in creatures who bear God's image. That connection is clear because as we saw above, Thomas focused his understanding of the divine image in our rational capacity.[61] Regardless of whether we agree with Thomas that the *imago Dei* centers in the rational faculty, Reformed theology agrees that we remain God's image bearers after the fall, albeit distorted. Further, we agree that all sin is completely irrational and contrary to nature. It ought not to be what we do, and it was not how our original wiring inclined us. Thomas reasoned that because that aspect of bearing God's image remains as part of our natural constitution, sin could not wipe it entirely. Reformed theology's potential disagreement with Thomas about sin's effects then concerns the degree to which sin diminished this inclination.

Despite Thomas' affirmation that sin damaged our connatural faculties for relating to God, some may object that he did not do justice to how the fall corrupted our overall abilities. After all, he held that we still maintain ability to work toward natural ends, such as planting vineyards and building houses.[62] In other words, he counted sin as destroying our ability to function proper in our supernatural relations but not in our capacity to understand and engage nature, general revelation, with accuracy.[63] Although that criticism is interesting to pursue for some discussions, it does not put him outside the realm of Reformed commitments. Jerome Zanchi (1516–90), professor of theology in Heidelberg, explicitly aligned himself with Thomas about fallen human freedom, weaponizing Thomas even against the Council of Trent.[64] Louis Berkhof (1873–1957) argued much the same as Thomas concerning our remaining ability for earthly activities:

---

60. Thomas, *Summa Theologica*, 1a2ae.85.2.

61. Thomas, *Summa Theologica*, 1.93.4, 9.

62. Thomas, *Summa Theologica*, 1a2ae.109.2.

63. Although see Brian Leftow, 'Original Sin,' in Eleonore Stump and Thomas Joseph White (eds.), *The New Cambridge Companion Aquinas* (Cambridge: Cambridge University Press, 2022), 317-19.

64. Hieronymius Zanchius, *Operum Theologicorum*, 8 vol. (Geneva, 1649), 4:92-93, 101-3; Donnelly, 'Calvinist Thomism,' 451.

> Man did not lose any of the constitutional faculties necessary to constitute him a responsible moral agent. He still has reason, conscience, and the freedom of choice. He has ability to acquire knowledge, and to feel and recognize moral distinctions and obligations .... Moreover, he has the ability to appreciate and do many things that are good and amiable, benevolent and just, in the relations he sustains to his fellow beings.[65]

Even if arguing for a greater degree, the Reformed follow Thomas in holding that sin damaged our nature itself and our natural capacities to know and to love God.[66]

The Roman tradition overall wanted to preserve even fallen human nature from sin's effects, often denying that the fall wrecked any of our *natural* faculties. Although most agree that our faculties themselves, especially our faculty of the intellect and our faculty of the will, remain after the fall, disagreement pertained to our faculties' enduring propensity for good. In the Franciscan lineage, Scotus suggested that humanity's natural condition remains essentially the same before and after the fall.[67] For Scotus, humanity before the fall needed to merit original righteousness by 'ungraced' nature. He thought that, despite an increased difficulty, we remain able after the fall to perform works of pure nature for meriting the investiture of righteousness with which we further cooperate to merit justification.[68] Bellarmine applied his anthropology to his view of sin so that the fall damaged only humanity's supernatural faculties, not our natural ability, arguing in contrast to Thomas that 'all humanity became wicked on account of Adam's sin, yet nevertheless, neither free will nor the other natural gifts were ruined, but *only the supernatural ones*.'[69] Using his separation of image and likeness, he distinguished which aspects of human nature that sin did and did

---

65. Louis Berkhof, *Systematic Theology*, expanded ed. (Edinburgh: The Banner of Truth, 2021), 2:247.

66. Arvin Vos, *Aquinas, Calvin, and Contemporary Protestant Thought: A Critique of Protestant Views on the Thought of Thomas Aquinas* (Washington, DC: Christian University Press, 1985), 147-52.

67. Cross, *Duns Scotus*, 83, 95-100.

68. Horton, *Justification*, 1:138.

69. Bellarmine, *de Gratia Primi Hominis*, 1.1; in *De Controversiis ... quartus*, 2 (emphasis added; Docent enim Adae peccatum totum hominem vere deteriorem esse factum; & tamen nec liberum arbitrium, neque alia naturalia dona, sed solum supernaturalia perdidisse).

not damage: 'Hence, by sinning, Adam totally ruined, *not* God's image, but the likeness.'[70] Sin's effects damaged only our supernaturally added likeness to God, leaving free will and rationality intact even if minimally wounded.[71] Rome's codification of this view is most obvious, as explored in chapter four, in the official, papal condemnation of Michael Baius and Cornelius Jensenius, who had argued for a natural orientation toward the supernatural and the accompanying doctrine that sin damaged even our natural faculties. Many Roman theologians perceived their teaching to be akin to Calvin's view.[72] Modern Roman Catholic theology has primarily followed this Franciscan trajectory, as some even argued that sin damaged only our supernatural endowments, but pure nature remained 'intrinsically whole and perfect' after the fall.[73]

Protestants indisputably rejected and still reject that dilution of sin's corrupting power upon our nature and faculties. Still, for our historical concerns, we must recognize that this trend in Roman theology to preserve the full intactness of even fallen nature followed a particular line of theology growing from the early Franciscan tradition into late medieval scholasticism most represented by William of Ockham and Gabriel Biel. In articulating principles of natural theology, Vos criticized 'the pursuit of the scholastics' as related to semi-Pelagianism 'whenever the human race and human reason are not viewed as entirely corrupt.'[74] In light of our explorations

---

70. Bellarmine, *de Gratia Primi Hominis*, 1.2; in *De Controversiis ... quartus*, 6 (emphasis added; Ex his igitur tot Patrum testimoniis cogimur admittere non esse omnino idem imaginem, & similitudinem, sed imaginem ad naturam, similitudinem ad virtutes pertinere: proinde Adamum peccando non imaginem Dei, sed similitudinem perdidisse).

71. Christian D. Washburn, 'The Shaping of Modern Catholic Anthropology in the Context of the Counter-Reformation: St. Robert Bellarmine and the Transformative Power of Grace,' in Bertram Stubenrauch and Michael Seewald (eds.), *Das Menschenbild der Konfession – Achillesferse der Ökumene?* (Freiburg: Herder, 2015), 222-30.

72. J. Pohle, 'Grace,' in Charles G. Herbermann, Edward A. Pace, Condé B Pallen, Thomas J. Shahan, John J. Wynne (eds.), *The Catholic Encyclopedia*, special ed., 15 vol. (New York, NY: The Encyclopedia Press, 1913), 6:693; J. Pohle, 'Grace, Controversies on,' in *Catholic Encyclopedia*, 6:710.

73. B. V. Miller, 'The Fall of Man and Original Sin,' in George D. Smith (ed.), *The Teaching of the Catholic Church: A Summary of Catholic Doctrine*, 2 vol. (Waterloo, Canada: Arouca Press, 2021), 1:335; see Gregg R. Allison, *Roman Catholic Theology and Practice: An Evangelical Assessment* (Wheaton, IL: Crossway, 2014), 46-55.

74. Geerhardus Vos, *Natural Theology*, trans. Albert Gootjes (Grand Rapids, MI: Reformation Heritage Books, 2022), 8.

in chapter four and throughout this chapter, his attack aims most forcefully against late medieval scholasticism in the likes of Ockham and Biel. In Vos' late-nineteenth context for these lectures, Roman theology's prevailing view was Leonine Thomism on the way to the modern neo-Thomist synthesis in Cardinal Reginald Garrigou-Lagrange, which more closely followed the Franciscan trajectory that continued through early modern pure-nature theologians. That historically conditioned interpretation shows how Protestants' relationship to Thomas himself about the fall's effects was quite another matter.

Fourth, before tackling the relationship of the Reformed to medieval views of sanctifying grace proper, we need to consider some metaphysical categories and how they fit within this discussion. In this respect, the Creator-creature distinction is primary. We must grapple with the concepts of univocity and analogy considering the relationship between God and creatures. For brevity, this discussion will be somewhat crass, missing nuances that philosophers would want to maintain.[75] For our purposes, we need these concepts only to help us understand more central matters to our discussion. In a univocal understanding of the Creator-creature distinction, God and creatures differ basically in quantity rather than intrinsic quality. God differs from creatures by having *more* being, *more* knowledge, *more* power, etc.[76] For example, God and humans know things in the same way, but God has infinitely more knowledge. On the analogical view, God and creatures differ qualitatively, so that God's being, knowledge, power, etc. is foundational while creatures' is derivative.[77] On the one hand, God knows as the Creator, having his own divine ideas immediately in his mind as the template of creation and foreordained history. On the other hand, we know in creaturely fashion understanding by

---

75. For a more expansive account, see Andrew Davison, *Participation in God: A Study in Christian Doctrine and Metaphysics* (Cambridge: Cambridge University Press, 2019), 176-79, 182-93.

76. Lydia Schumacher, *Early Franciscan Theology: Between Authority and Innovation* (Cambridge: Cambridge University Press, 2019), 65-67, 133-37, 139-41; Colmán ó Huallacháin, 'Duns Scotus and 13th Century Philosophy,' *University Review* 1, no. 10 (Autumn 1956): 30-43; Cross, *Duns Scotus*, 31-46.

77. Christopher Shields and Robert Pasnau, *The Philosophy of Aquinas*, 2nd ed. (New York, NY: Oxford University Press, 2016), 137-48.

revelation and acquired knowledge from nature rather than accessing the divine idea itself.[78]

Scotus, explicitly targeting Henry of Ghent's explanation of analogy which amounted to equivocation, understood the Creator-creature distinction univocally, meaning that God and creatures exist in the same way.[79] In the traditional reading, Scotus thought that 'a single unified notion of being' applies in reference to God and creatures alike, grounding metaphysics.[80] Scotus was Kant's apparent more proximate precursor than Thomas was, introducing an interesting factor in evaluating Leonine Thomist epistemology. Accordingly, Scotus' metaphysics entailed that we either cannot know God at all, or that we must accept the creatures' being is univocal with God's. Scotus favored the latter option.[81] Through an array of complex metaphysical distinctions about modality in infinite

---

78. Richard A. Muller, 'Calvinist Thomism Revisited: William Ames (1576–1633) and the Divine Ideas,' in Kathleen M. Comerford, Gary W. Jenkins, and W. J. Torrance Kirby (eds.), *From Rome to Zurich, between Ignatius and Vermigli: Essays in Honor of John Patrick Donnelly, SJ* (Leiden: Brill, 2017), 103-18.

79. Martin Pickavé, 'Henry of Ghent on Metaphysics,' in Gordon A. Wilson (ed.), *A Companion to Henry of Ghent* (Leiden: Brill, 2011), 159-66; Steven P. Marrone, 'Henry of Ghent and Duns Scotus on the Knowledge of Being,' *Speculum* (Jan 1988): 22-57; Giorgio Pini, 'Before Univocity: Duns Scotus' Rejection of Analogy,' in Giorgio Pini (ed.), *Interpreting Duns Scotus: Critical Essays* (Cambridge: Cambridge University Press, 2022), 204-14. Scotus held that univocity and analogy might be compatible but 'defends the univocity of "being" at length'; Peter King, 'Scotus on Metaphysics,' in Thomas Williams (ed.), *The Cambridge Companion to Duns Scotus* (Cambridge: Cambridge University Press, 2003), 58n13; Roland J. Teske, *Essays on Philosophy of Henry of Ghent* (Milwaukee, WI: Marquette University Press, 2012), ch. 10–11.

80. Etienne Gilson, 'Avicenne et le point de depart de Duns Scot,' *Archives d'histoire doctrinale et littéraire du moyen âge* 2 (1927): 89-149; Timotheus A. Barth, 'Die Stellung der univocatio im Verlauf der Gotteserkenntnis nach Lehre des Duns Skotus,' *Wissenschaft und Weishei* 5 (1938): 235-54; Timotheus A. Barth, 'De univocationis entis Scotisticae intent principali necnon valore critico,' *Antonianum* 28 (1953): 83-94; William E. Mann, 'Duns Scotus on Natural and Supernatural Knowledge of God,' in *Cambridge Companion to Duns Scotus*, 246-47; King, 'Scotus on Metaphysics,' 18; Pini, 'Before Univocity,' 214-22; Garrett R. Smith, 'Analogy after Duns Scotus: The Role of the *analogia entis* in the Scotist Metaphysics at Barcelona, 1320–1330,' in *Interpreting Duns Scotus*, 224-26; Hans Boersma, 'Accommodation to What? Univocity of Being, Pure Nature, and the Anthropology of St Irenaeus,' *International Journal of Systematic Theology* 8, no. 3 (July 2006): 271-75; Hans Boersma, 'Theology as Queen of Hospitality,' *Evangelical Quarterly* 79, no 4 (2007): 301.

81. King, 'Scotus on Metaphysics,' 18; Thomas Joseph White, O.P., 'How Barth Got Aquinas Wrong: A Reply to Archie J. Spencer on Causality and Christocentrism,' *Nova et Vetera*, English ed. 7, no. 1 (2009): 241-69.

and finite being, Scotus maintained divine transcendence and avoided real pantheism as well as programmatic nominalism.[82] He preserved some sense of true universals.

A recent lacuna in Scotus scholarship concerning the Reformation's relationship to Scotus deserves a brief excursus. First, this mainstream understanding of Scotus himself as holding a thoroughgoing univocity has come under some scrutiny as some scholars have argued that Scotus' univocity applied only to semantics rather than to ontology itself.[83] Second, other scholars, most notably in the movement of Radical Orthodoxy but others as well, have slated Scotus' metaphysics with all the woes of modernity and blamed the Reformation for developing the Scotist heritage into principles responsible for modern secularism.[84] The pushback on this 'Scotus story' may have *some* validity insofar as, even according to Michael Horton and Matthew Barrett, certain particular metaphysical problems that trailed into the Reformation are less directly attributable to Scotus as to the holistic and radical nominalism of William of Ockham and Gabriel Biel.[85]

---

82. King, 'Scotus on Metaphysics,' 21-57; Smith, 'Analogy after Duns Scotus,' 243-44. James Salladin argued that Jonathan Edwards held a view of creatures' ontological participation in God that, if correct, suggests semblance to univocity unlike other, more Thomistic, articulations; 'Nature and Grace: Two Participations in the Thought of Jonathan Edwards,' *International Journal of Systematic Theology* 18, no. 3 (July 2016): 290-303.

83. Daniel P. Horan, OFM, *Postmodernity and Univocity: A Critical Account of Radical Orthodoxy and John Duns Scotus* (Minneapolis, MN: Fortress Press, 2014), 157-88; Domenic D'Ettore, *Analogy After Aquinas: Logical Problems, Thomistic Answers* (Thomistic Resssourcement Series; Washington, DC: Catholic University of America Press, 2019), 18-32; Thomas M. Ward, *Ordered by Love: An Introduction to John Duns Scotus* (Brooklyn, NY: Angelico Press, 2022), 26-38; Richard Cross, 'Where Angels Fear to Tread: Duns Scotus and Radical Orthodoxy,' *Antonianum* 76 (2001): 7-41; Robert Sweetman, 'Univocity, Analogy, and the Mystery of Being according to John Duns Scotus,' in James K. A. Smith and James H. Olthuis (eds.), *Radical Orthodoxy and the Reformed Tradition: Creation, Covenant, and Participation* (Grand Rapids, MI: Baker Academic, 2005), 73-87.

84. e.g. John Millbank, *Theology and Social Theory: Beyond Secular Reason*, 2nd ed. (Oxford: Blackwell, 2006); John Millbank, *Beyond Secular Order: The Representation of Being and the Representation of the People* (Oxford: Wiley-Blackwell, 2014); Brad S. Gregory, *The Unintended Reformation: How a Religious Revolution Secularized Society* (Cambridge, MA: The Belknap Press of Harvard University Press, 2012); Boersma, 'Accommodation to What?' 272n18; cf. Horan, *Postmodernity and Univocity*, 15-58.

85. Horton, *Justification*, 1:152-53; Matthew Barrett, *The Reformation as Renewal: Retrieving the One, Holy, Catholic, and Apostolic Church* (Grand Rapids, MI: Zondervan Academic, 2023), 245.

Complications apply to both points in these recent scholarly developments. On the one hand, Ockham and Biel's radical theology did not come from nowhere since Scotus paved the way for them.[86] Our investigations in chapter three made this connection clearest as Scotus related his voluntarism to his soteriology.[87] Further, the scholars contending that Scotus did not hold a thoroughgoing univocity are not mere historians but are committed to Scotus' philosophy.[88] Their historical arguments are then in fact defenses aiming to undo the damage associated with Scotus' metaphysics, especially as Radical Orthodoxy, Brad Gregory, and Hans Boersma have pinpointed Scotus as the beginning of the end in the development of secularism's philosophical underpinnings.

On the other hand, the Reformation's supposed Scotist connection must be questioned from two vantages. One vantage concerns the truth in the Scotus Story insomuch as it pertains to Scotus' own views and whether Scotus should get blamed for the intellectual underpinnings of secular modernity. In this regard, even if Scotus focused on semantics, *something* in his theology truly suggests univocity of being.[89] The second, arguably more important, vantage concerns our present focus, specifically that the Reformed were *not* Scotists.[90] Even given the first vantage, the Reformed were not advocates of the ideas wherever whence they came – even as Gregory and others have seen those ideas as Scotist – supposedly leading to modernity. The historical point in our view

---

86. Hans Boersma, *Heavenly Participation: The Weaving of a Sacramental Tapestry* (Grand Rapids, MI: Eerdmans, 2011), 68-76

87. Barrett, *Reformation as Renewal*, 239-43.

88. e.g. Thomas Williams, 'The Doctrine of Univocity is True and Salutary,' *Modern Theology* 21 (2005): 575-85; Thomas Williams, 'Reason, Morality and Voluntarism in Duns Scotus: A Pseudo-Problem Dissolved,' *Modern Schoolmen* 74 (1997): 73-94; Richard Cross, 'Duns Scotus and Suarez at the Origins of Modernity,' in Wayne J. Hankey and Douglas Hedley (eds.), *Deconstructing Radical Orthodoxy: Postmodern Theology, Rhetoric and Truth* (Aldershot: Ashgate, 2005), 65-80.

89. Matthew Levering, *Participatory Biblical Exegesis: A Theology of Biblical Interpretation* (Notre Dame, IN: University of Notre Dame Press, 2008), 18-25; Gregory, *Unintended Reformation*, 36-39; Cross, *Duns Scotus*, 33-39; Barrett, *Reformation as Renewal*, 234-39, 247-50.

90. Richard A. Muller, 'Not Scotist: Understandings of Being, Univocity, and Analogy in Early-Modern Reformed Thought,' *Reformation and Renaissance Review* 14 no 2 (2012): 127-50.

concerning these debates over Scotus is that the Reformed aligned more with an analogical rather than a univocal metaphysic, undermining one foundational premise of the narrative that blames the Reformation with continuing the Scotist ideals responsible for secularism. Thus, even if the recent reinterpretations of Scotus hold, the present argument that the Reformed opposed nominalism and univocity entails that at least Gregory's thesis has no remaining legs on which to stand, being in that case undermined from the Roman and Protestant sides.[91]

Returning to our main argument on the other side of that excursus about recent debates over Scotus, the main point is that the Reformed generally sided with an analogical understanding of the Creator-creature distinction. In contrast to Scotus, Thomas held an analogical view, affirming a qualitative rather than quantitative difference between Creator and creature.[92] The analogical view associated with Thomas paved the way for later Reformed theologians to build our understanding of archetypal and ectypal knowledge.[93] Based on his doctrine of creation

91. Jared Michelson, 'Reformed and Radically Orthodox?: Participatory Metaphysics and Radical Orthodoxy's Critique of Modernity,' *International Journal of Systematic Theology* 20, no. 1 (Jan 2018): 104-28; Muller, 'Not Scotist,' 146.

92. Thomas Aquinas, *Summa Contra Gentiles*, 4 vol. (Notre Dame, IN: University of Notre Dame Press, 2009), 1.32.6-7; Thomas, *Summa Theologica*, 1.13.5; David B. Burrell, 'Analogy, Creation, and Theological Language,' in Rik van Nieuwenhove and Jospeh Wawrykow (eds.), *The Theology of Thomas Aquinas* (Notre Dame, University of Notre Dame Press, 2005), 79-83; Rik van Nieuwenhove, *An Introduction to Medieval Theology* (Cambridge: CUP, 2012), 232-35; John F. Wippel, 'Metaphysics,' in Norma Kretzmann and Eleonore Stump (eds.), *The Cambridge Companion to Aquinas* (New York: CUP, 1993), 89-99; George Lindbeck, 'Nominalism and the Problem of Meaning as Illustrated by Pierre D'Ailly on Predestination and Justification,' *Harvard Theological Review* 52 no 1 (1959): 43-60; William J. Courternay, 'The King and the Leaden Coin: The Economic Background of "Sine Qua Non" Causality,' *Traditio* 28 (1972): 185-209; William J. Courtenay, 'Nominalism and Late Medieval Thought: A Bibliographical Essay,' *Theological Studies* 33 no 4 (1972): 716-34; David Steinmetz, 'Medieval Nominalism and the *Clerk's Tale*,' *The Chaucer Review* 12 no 1 (1977): 38-54; Jeffrey Combs, 'The Possibility of Created Entities in Seventeenth-Century Scotism,' *Philosophical Quarterly* 43 no 173 (Oct 1993): 447-59; Ralph McInerny, *Aquinas and Analogy* (Washington DC: Catholic University of America Press, 1996); Boersma, 'Accommodation to What?,' 272-73; Barrett, *Reformation as Renewal*, 248-49.

93. Johann Heinrich Alsted, *Theologia Naturalis* (Frankfurt, 1615), 32 (Non univoce; quia creaturae non recipient eandem entitatis formalitem a Deo, quae in Deo est. Thomas, contr. Gent. 6.23 .... Relinquitur igitur, ens de Deo & creaturis enunciari analogice); Francis Junius, *A Treatise on True Theology*, trans. David C. Noe (Grand Rapids, MI: Reformation Heritage Books, 2014), 107-20; Ballor, 'In the Footsteps of the Thomists,' 127-39.

ex nihilo, Thomas recognized an intrinsic difference at the ontological level that rules out univocity.[94]

That qualitative difference concerning the Creator-creature distinction also applies to the nature of divine and human action, which raises the topic of causality and brings us back to Thomas' doctrine of *auxilium*. As mentioned above, Thomas held that man with his connatural faculties could love God as a creature fundamentally related to him, 'although not without God's help [*auxilio*] for moving.'[95] Thomas' *auxilium* might at first seem at odds with our wider argument that man was naturally equipped to perform the law without superadded grace, primarily because many Roman theologians have referred to *auxilium* as 'actual grace.'[96] In truth, *auxilium* is a necessary aspect of the fundamentally Christian understanding of the Creator-creature distinction because this 'help' is an assertion of God as first cause of all our good deeds. It is a conceptual lodestone for rejecting that we can act autonomously apart from God. For Thomas, *auxilium* is not even about exclusively supernaturally oriented acts or faculties, nor about elevating nature, but about the operating cause of humanity acting properly toward God in any capacity.[97] As he reflected on our condition in integrity and as corrupt, Thomas noted that 'in both states human nature needs the help of God [*auxilio divino*] as

94. Laurence Paul Hemming, '*Analogia non Entis sed Entitatis*: The Ontological Consequences of the Doctrine of Analogy,' *International Journal of Systematic Theology* 6, no. 2 (April 2004): 118-29. The scope of fitting Hemming's ontological point to the apparatus of analogy is beyond our scope.

95. Thomas, *Summa Theologica*, 1a2ae.109.3 (my translation; homo in statu naturae integrae poterat operari virtute suae naturae bonum quod est sibi connaturale, absque superadditione gratuiti doni, licet non absque auxilio Dei moventis. Diligere autem Deum super omnia est quiddam connaturale homini).

96. Thomas, *Summa Theologica*, 1a2ae.62.1; Pohle, 'Grace,' 6:689; Pohle, 'Grace, Controversies on,' 6:710-13; Vos, *Aquinas, Calvin, and Contemporary Protestant Thought*, 142.

97. Tobias Hoffman, 'Grace and Free Will,' in *New Cambridge Companion Aquinas*, 233, 241-43, 244-46; Reginald M. Lynch, OP, 'Divine Causality and Human Freedom: Aquinas, Báñez, and Premotion after Descartes,' in *Beyond Dordt and De Auxiliis*, 219-44. In this respect, Bonaventure concurred with this basic Augustinian premise of the necessity of God's general influence; Jacob Schmutz, 'The Medieval Doctrine of Causality and the Theology of Pure Nature (13th to 17th Centuries),' in Serge-Thomas Bonino, O.P. (ed.), *Surnaturel: A Controversy at the Heart of Twentieth-Century Thomistic Thought*, trans. Robert Williams (Faith and Reason: Studies in Catholic Theology and Philosophy; Ave Maria, FL: Sapientia Press, 2009), 215-17.

First Mover, to do or wish any good whatsoever.'[98] Respectively, as it was often synonymous with *motio divina*, *auxilio* is not about a deficiency in human nature but about how God is the prime cause in directing creatures to his foreordained ends, especially in the Thomist system.[99] Joseph Wawrykow documented how Thomas, shifting position between his earlier *Sentences* commentary and his *Summa*, developed his view of *auxilium* as containing the notion of operative grace – remembering that in Roman theology *all* supernatural action belongs to the order of grace. Thomas' use of *auxilium* was grounded in 'distinctively Augustinian ideas' referring 'not only to God causing human action but indeed to God causing *correct* human action' so that *auxilium* is God's sufficiency in bringing his *ordinatio* to pass by his sovereign action.[100] Thomas' predestinarianism was the extension of his Augustinian heritage.[101] The Reformed would later share that heritage and often leveraged Thomas and other medieval Augustinians, such as Gregory of Rimini, against more Pelagian tendencies in the trajectory of Gabriel Biel.[102]

---

98. Thomas, *Summa Theologica*, 1a2ae.109.2 (emphasis added).

99. Schmutz, 'Medieval Doctrine of Causality and the Theology of Pure Nature,' 207-11; Reginald Garrigou-Lagrange, *Grace: Commentary on the Summa Theologica of St. Thomas 1a2ae q.109–14*, trans. the Dominican Nuns (St. Louis: B. Herder Book Co. 1952), 42, 53-54; Richard A. Muller, *Dictionary of Latin and Greek Theological Terms: Drawn Principally from Protestant Scholastic Theology*, 2nd ed. (Grand Rapids, MI: Baker Academic, 2017), 50 (auxilium sine quo non), 223-24 (motus); Pohle, 'Grace,' 6:689, 692-93.

100. Joseph P. Wawrykow, *God's Grace and Human Action: 'Merit' in the Theology of Thomas Aquinas* (Notre Dame, IN: University of Notre Dame Press, 1995), 172, 172-77, 231, 249-54; Francis 'Kunle Adedara, 'The Possibility of Merit Before God According to Thomas Aquinas,' *Bodija Journal* 9 (Oct 2015): 39-41 (italics original).

101. Henri de Lubac, *Augustinianism and Modern Theology*, trans. Lancelot Sheppard (Milestones in Catholic Theology; New York, NY: Crossroad Publishing, 2000), 40-53.

102. Richard A. Muller, *Divine Will and Human Choice: Freedom, Contingency, and Necessity in Early Modern Reformed Thought* (Grand Rapids: 2017), 211-57, 283-310, 324; Jordan J. Ballor, Matthew T. Gaetano, and David S. Sytsma, 'Introduction: Augustinian Soteriology in the Context of the *Congregatio De Auxiliis* and the Synod of Dordt,' in *Beyond Dordt and* De Auxiliis, 1-18; David S. Sytsma, 'Vermigli Replicating Aquinas: An Overlooked Continuity in the Doctrine of Predestination,' *Reformation & Renaissance Review* 20, no. 2 (2018): 155-67; David S. Sytsma, 'Aquinas in Service of Dordt: John Davenant on Predestination, Grace, and Free Choice,' in *Beyond Dort and de Auxiliis*, 169-99; Sytsma, 'Sixteenth-Century Reformed Reception of Aquinas,' 121-43; Ballor, 'Footsteps of the Thomists,' 139-47.

The Reformed alignment with Thomas' view of *auxilium*, at least regarding its operative aspect, is a necessary bulwark against Pelagianizing tendencies.[103] The idea is typical decretal theology as in Westminster Confession 3.1:

> God from all eternity did, by the most wise and holy Counsell of his own Will, freely, and unchangeably ordaine whatsoever comes to passe: yet so as thereby neither is God the Author of sin, nor is violence offered to the will of the Creatures, nor is the Liberty or contingencies of second Causes take away, but rather established.[104]

As standard Reformed theology, God's sovereign decree stands behind all events. Still, God does not bring about his decree in such a way that he is the operative cause *of sin*, meaning he gives no *auxilium* or sufficient causality to evil human acts even if he has actively decreed to permit them.[105] He is, however, the operative cause of good things as their first cause without damaging the true place of secondary, proximate causes or contingency.[106] As Heiko Oberman highlights, Biel argued that God's predestining act established humanity's autonomously free will, enabling us to merit without grace or assistance. Biel's Pelagian doctrine of predestination said that God chose the elect based upon merits foreseen in them, introducing contingency into God by making him dependent upon creatures' actions.[107] Concerning *auxilium*, Biel

---

103. Calvin, *Institutes*, 2.2.6; Mastricht, *Theoretical-Practical Theology*, 1.2.3.9, 13-17; Bavinck, *Reformed Dogmatics*, 2:608-19; Anthonius Thysius, 'On Free Choice,' in *Synopsis Purioris Theologiae/Synopsis of a Purer Theology*, gen. eds. Willem J. van Asselt, William den Boer, and Reimer A. Faber, 3 vol. (Leiden: Brill, 2015–20), 1:415; Turrettinus, *Institutio*, 6.4.5; Samuel Rutherford, *Disputatio Scholastica de Divina Providentia* (Edinburgh, 1649), 401-2 (Turretin and Rutherford noted in Muller, *Divine Will and Human Freedom*, 75n96).

104. Bower, *Confession of Faith*, 199.

105. For a generally excellent account of how this point relates to wider metaphysical concerns, see Davison, *Participation in God*, 239-59.

106. Calvin, *Institutes*, 1.16.8; J. V. Fesko, *The Theology of the Westminster Standards: Historical Context and Theological Insights* (Wheaton, IL: Crossway, 2014), 101-16; Chad Van Dixhoorn, *Confessing the Faith: A Reader's Guide to the Westminster Confession of Faith* (Edinburgh: The Banner of Truth Trust, 2014), 43-46; Robert Letham, *The Westminster Assembly: Reading Its Theology in Historical Context* (Phillipsburg, NJ: P&R, 2009), 174-84.

107. Heiko A. Oberman, *The Harvest of Medieval Theology: Gabriel Biel and Late Medieval Nominalism*, 3rd ed. (Grand Rapids, MI: Baker Academic, 2000), 132-34, 189-90, 192-96; also Horton, *Justification*, 1:153-58.

explicitly disagreed with Gregory of Rimini, Thomas, and Bonaventure but followed Ockham. Thus, he denied the necessity of *auxilium* even for sinners. This denial of God as the true first cause, exalting man's autonomy, was part of a return to a Pelagian notion of God and his decree as dependent upon the creatures' actions.[108]

Biel set the trajectory for the sixteenth-century clash on this very issue between Dominicans, following Thomas' more full-throated Augustinianism, and Jesuits, such as Robert Bellarmine. This controversy motivated the middle knowledge theory of Jesuit Luis de Molina (1535–1600).[109] Even Thomist theologian Domingo de Soto downplayed Thomas' predestinarianism in the same way as was appropriated by later Jesuits.[110] Given de Soto's prominent contribution to soteriological debates at the Council of Trent, even the claim that the Council leaned upon Thomas' *Summa* must be filtered through how these re-readings of Thomas were prevailing interpretations.[111] Although drawing heavily upon Jesuit theology, even Jacob Arminius defended the *auxilium* model:

> Concerning man's freewill, I perceive thus: man in his first state of creation was fitted with knowledge, holiness, and strengths of such sort that he was able to understand, to assess, to consider, to will, and to accomplish true good, just as certainly he had been commanded. But nevertheless, he could not do this *except by the help of God's grace.*[112]

---

108. Gabriel Biel, *Sentences*, bk. 2, dist. 28, q. 1, A; in *Collectorium circa quattuor libros Sententiarum*, ed. Wilfridus Werbeck and Udo Hofman, 6 vol. (Tübingen: Mohr Siebeck, 1973–92), 2:528-33; Schmutz, 'Medieval Doctrine of Causality and the Theology of Pure Nature,' 223-29; Oberman, *Harvest of Medieval Theology*, 139-41; Horton, *Justification*, 1:155.

109. Schmutz, 'Medieval Doctrine of Causality and the Theology of Pure Nature,' 205-7, 211-15, 230-32, 235-50; R. J. Matava, 'A Sketch of the Controversy *de auxiliis*,' *Journal of Jesuit Studies* 7 (2020): 417-46; Thomas M. Osborne Jr., 'Spanish Thomists and the Need for Interior Grace in Acts of Faith,' in *Beyond Dort and de Auxiliis*, 79-85.

110. de Lubac, *Augustinianism and Modern Theology*, 119-25.

111. Stephen Gaetano, 'Domingo Báñez and His Dominican Predecessors: the "Dominican School" on the Threshold of the Controversy *De Auxiliis*,' in *Beyond Dort and de Auxiliis*, 35-65; Schmutz, 'Medieval Doctrine of Causality and the Theology of Pure Nature,' 229

112. Jacobus Arminius, *Opera Theologica* (Leiden, 1629), 121-22 (emphasis original; De Libero arbitrio hominis ita sentio; hominem in primo statu creationis suae ejuscemodi notitia, sanctitate iisque viribus instructum fuisse, ut verum bonum intelligere, aestimare, considerare, velle & perficere valuerit, prout quidem ei mandatum erat: sed hoc tamen non nisi cum *auxilio gratiae Dei*); Jacobus Arminius, *Verclaringhe Jacobi Arminii Saliger Ghedachten* (Leiden, 1610), 39.

Applying the point to sinners, he argued: 'And in this way, I ascribe to grace the initiation, continuation, and consummation of all good, even to such extent, that an already regenerate man without this prevenient and exciting, following and cooperating grace is absolutely not able to think, will, or do good, nor able to resist any temptation for evil.'[113] Arminius even named Thomas, presumably in self-conscious opposition to his own position, as representing views held 'among the doctors of our Church' for how God efficaciously brings his elect to their decreed everlasting life.[114] Nevertheless, Arminius' understanding of God's decree rested upon Molina's logic of middle knowledge, entailing that the Synod of Dort (1618–19) tackled problems concerning God as in some way contingent upon creatures, since denying *auxilium* introduces true human autonomy into God's sovereignty over whatsoever comes to pass.[115]

Individual Reformed writers demonstrate the significance of this *auxilium* category, specifically in refuting Roman teaching. At a more basic level, Casper Olevianus (1536–87) commented on the Apostles' Creed that the Creator 'gives movement and everything else to creatures, so that they can do nothing except as they are moved by the Creator.'[116] Pareus criticized Bellarmine, who argued that 'The first man, clothed in original righteousness and sanctifying grace, did not need special help [*auxilio speciali*], by which he would be incited to performing good or to avoiding sin.'[117] In other words, Bellarmine thought that sanctifying grace meant that man did not need God as the operative cause of his good deeds, amounting to a denial

---

113. Arminius, *Opera Theologica*, 122 (Atque hoc modo gratiae adscribo *initium, continuationem atque consummationem omnis boni*; etiam eousque, ut homo jam regeneratus sine hac praeveniente & excitante sequente & cooperante gratia, bonum prorsus neque cogitare, velle aut facere possit, ac ne quidem ulli tentationi malae resistere.); Arminius, *Verclaringhe*, 39-40.

114. Jacob Arminius, *Amica ... collatio*, 4 (inter doctores Ecclesiae nostrae).

115. Richard A. Muller, 'Arminius's "Conference" with Junius and the Protestant Reception of Molina's *Concordia*,' in *Beyond Dort and de Auxiliis*, 115-26; Eef Dekker, 'Was Arminius a Molinist?' *Sixteenth Century Journal* 27, no. 2 (1996): 337-52; Keith D. Stanglin, '*Scientia Media*: the Protestant Reception of a Jesuit Idea,' in *Beyond Dort and de Auxiliis*, 148-68.

116. Casper Olevianus, *An Exposition of the Apostles' Creed*, trans. Lyle D. Bierma (Classic Reformed Theology; Grand Rapids, MI: Reformation Heritage Books, 2009), 42.

117. Bellarmine, *de Gratia Primi Hominis*, 1.4, in *De Controversiis ... quartus*, 12 (Primus homo iustitia originali, et habita gratia gratum facientis ornatus non eguit auxilio speciali, quo excitaretur ad bene operandum, vel ad vitanda peccata).

of God as the first cause. Bellarmine's position clarifies that *auxilium* is not about grace elevating nature and is about God's sovereignty, which the Reformed avidly protect. Pareus responded: 'That which Bellarmine contends is, therefore, false, that it was in man's power to live well without God's support, so that he did not need God's special assistance [*auxilio*].'[118] We saw above that Pareus equally fought against Bellarmine's affirmation of Adam's need for sanctifying grace before the fall.[119]

Zanchi provides a most pointed example as he advocated the necessity of *auxilium* as a refutation of semi-Pelagianism after the Council of Trent, perceiving Thomas' Dominican position as a weapon against later Roman dogma. He took up the question of 'Whether man can on his own account, without God's grace, understand, will, and do any good and good actions,' noting the necessity of 'the threefold distinction of actions, of grace, of power.'[120] After distinguishing three sorts of actions, he explained how 'grace, or God's help [*auxilium*]' has threefold necessity in the present.[121] Although the second and third senses of grace concern the Spirit's general gifting of people and the proper grace of redemption in Christ, grace's first sense concerns us as *auxilium* 'for the general divine motion and action by which he moves and directs all things according to at least its own nature and innate quality, about which Acts 17:28: "In him we live, move and have our being."'[122] Although fallen man retains ability to know and to choose

---

118. Pareus, *de Gratia Primi Hominis*, 50 (Falsum igitur, quod Bellarminus contendit, sine adjutorio Dei bene vivere in hominis fuisse potestate, ut speciali Dei auxilio non indigeret).

119. This section clarifies, refines, and to some degree corrects my previous argument wherein I did not thoroughly understand the nature of *auxilium* in relation to the Reformed rejection of the *donum superadditum*; Harrison Perkins, *Catholicity and the Covenant of Works: James Ussher and the Reformed Tradition* (Oxford Studies in Historical Theology; New York, NY: Oxford University Press, 2020), 61-66. Especially, this clarified place for *auxilium* in Reformed theology as related to metaphysical causality, rather than original righteousness, relieves the previously perceived tension between Pareus and Anthony Burgess (1600–64), at least on this particular emphasis concerning divine assistance (*auxilium*).

120. Zanchius, *Operum Theologicorum*, 4:95 (An homo possit per se, sine gratia Dei, quiduis boni bonarumque actionum intelligere, velle, et facere: ic circo antequam ad quaestionis explicationem veniamus, quo felicius id fiat, notanda est in primis triplex distinctio actionum, gratiae, potentiae).

121. Zanchius, *Operum Theologicorum*, 4:95 (gratia, sive auxilium Dei, quantum in praesentia cognitu necessarium est, trifariam accipi potest).

122. Zanchius, *Operum Theologicorum*, 4:95 (Aliquando pro motione et actione divina generali qua omnia movet et agit, secundum suam tamen quidque naturam et ingenium,

natural truths and actions, he cannot do any of it 'without God's general help [*auxilio*].'[123] Zanchi meant, much like Thomas, that our ability to act toward earthly and civic ends remained after the fall.[124] Zanchi invoked the Augustinian tradition as the whole church, including Gregory of Rimini and Thomas Aquinas, in attesting to the same truth of *auxilium*.[125]

Major synthesizers of Reformed orthodoxy furthered the same argument. Bringing even more clarity to our earlier analysis of Turretin's denial that any help God gave Adam in the covenant of works amounted to superadded infusion, his point was precisely to distinguish with crystal clarity this very category of *auxilium* from any notion of grace that adds new powers or elevates human nature in some superadded way: 'that assistance [*auxilium*] did not extend to pouring any new virtue into him but only to revealing the power of that strength which he had received.'[126] Mastricht connected original righteousness and the concept of *auxilium* more definitively, arguing that original righteousness made man 'born fit to be subject to God and to persist in perfect obedience to him, that

---

de qua Actor. 17. In ipso vivimus, movemur et sumus. Et ad Heb.1. Portansque ommia verbo virtutis sua. Vocatur hoc auxilium Dei a Scholasticis quidem superfluxus generalis: a nostris praesertim a Luthero, actio omnipotentiae: et communis est etiam animantibus omnibus, imo et rebus inanimis).

123. Zanchius, *Operum Theologicorum*, 4:96 (Homo, etsi etiam post lapsum vis relicta sit tum intelligendi in eius intellectu, tum eligendi in eius voluntate, tum operandi in eius anima atque corpore, qua res actionesque naturales et intelligere et eligere ac persequi possit: tamen neque quicquam horum sine gerali Dei auxilio, neque alia vel plura, quam quae et quot Domino visum fuerit percipere, eligere efficereve potest).

124. Zanchius, *Operum Theologicorum*, 4:98, 101 (Tanta est hominis non renati naturalis corruptio atque cacitas, ut licet ex solo generali Dei auxilio, multa civilem humanamque vitam pertinentia, et intellectu assequi, et voluntate eligere possit: disciplinas tamen ipsas, aut etiam artes, sive speciali Dei auxilio per sese percipere et consequi non valeat: sed ubicunque sunt ibi singularia Dei dona sint … Etsi per hoc auxilium Dei peculiar, potest homo non Renatus morales actiones praestare, moralesque virtutes consequi).

125. Zanchius, *Operum Theologicorum*, 4:111 (Hanc vero fuisse doctrinam totius Ecclesiae, abunde demonstrat Gregorius Arimin. in secundum sentent. Dist. 16. q. 2. art. 1 et dist. 29. q.1 art. 2. ex August. Hieronymo, Gregorio Bernhardo, Beda & aliis Patribus. Quin et Thomas Aquinas in prima secundae q. 109 art.4. quaestionem proponit, an homo sine gratia possit praecepta legis per sese implere: et concludit, non posse). Interestingly, Zanchi cited Rimini's commentary on the section of Lombard's *Sentences* that drove the discussion in most of our previous chapter.

126. Turrettinus, *Institutio*, 8.3.14 (Quod auxilium non tendebat ad virtutem novam aliquam ipsi infundendam, sed tantum ad efficaciam illius virtutis exerendam, quam acceperat). These observations clarify and strengthen Fesko's interpretation of this passage, which had less analysis of *auxilium*; *Adam and the Covenant of Works*, 101-2.

is, if he should will,' and yet 'the willing itself, and this the act itself of persisting, *required in addition another kind of second grace, one whereby that first grace would be excited, and would pass from potency into act*, and be conserved, for God causes both to will and to work (Phil. 2:13).'[127] Using grace in reference to all supernatural activity, Mastricht invoked a second kind of grace as the efficient cause of Adam acting rightly upon the abiding quality of original righteousness.[128] Thomas' doctrine of *auxilium* vitally manifests the Reformed continuity with him on the Creator-creature distinction in rejecting all divine-human correlativity.[129]

The *auxilium* debate pertains to our wider topic of nature's relationship to supernatural realities because the repudiation of concursus was (and remains) a key factor in a completed doctrine of pure nature. The doctrine of concursus affirms that the acts of all contingent beings occur under God's providence in such a way that he does not, apart from miracles and extraordinary acts, contravene free, contingent, or necessary secondary causes. Rather, God's own action as first mover works in accord with, even upholding, secondary causes.[130] The denial of concursus, which is bound into the denial of *auxilium*, suggests a relative autonomy to created order and to human decisions. Without *auxilium* as a premise for divine providence, human acts occur apart from God's supervening work. Thus, the natural order becomes a closed-off, self-contained system that is sufficient on its own principles without divine co-action. In other words, it becomes pure nature. God's supervening acts of providence no longer cohere with the structure of the natural order but supplement if not supplant it.[131] The *auxilium* debates demonstrate the historical point that the Roman paradigm of pure nature came to full fruition in the early modern period.[132] Protestants

---

127. Mastricht, *Theoretical-Practical Theology*, 1.3.9.34 (emphasis added).

128. Mastricht, *Theoretical-Practical Theology*, 1.4.1.7; 1.4.2.11.

129. Johannes Scharpius, *Cursus Theologicus* (Geneva, 1620), 546-47; Aza Goudriaan, 'Defending Grace: References to Dominicans, Jesuits, and Jansenists in Seventeenth-Century Dutch Reformed Theology,' in *Beyond Dort and* De Auxiliis, 277-96; Matthew T. Gaetano, 'Calvin against the Calvinists in Early Modern Thomism,' in *Beyond Dort and* De Auxiliis, 297-320.

130. Muller, *Dictionary*, 73-74.

131. Wood, *Stir a Restless Heart*, 149-51, 257.

132. Henri de Lubac, *The Mystery of the Supernatural*, trans. Rosemary Sheed (Milestones in Catholic Theology; New York, NY: Crossroad Publishing, 1998), 7-9, 37, 140-66;

rejected this notion of an autonomous and closed off system of pure nature, affirming nature's intrinsic need for God's concursus.[133]

Finally, we must reckon with the Reformed relation to various preceding models of sanctifying grace. As this book drives toward a prescriptive theological argument, we cannot foist our dogmatic concerns upon historical interpretation but must let past voices speak for themselves. No medieval theologian precisely aligned with our coming argument that God oriented humanity naturally to his supernatural end so much so that grace – not as in *auxilium* but in the sense of making up a deficiency in nature – was not necessary before the fall for Adam to merit according to our ordering in the covenant of works. Nonetheless, we can see a few coordinates of correspondence or greater dis-alignment.

The contrast of Roman clerical orders guides the trajectories of agreement. In the Franciscan tradition and much of the Jesuits, original righteousness was in no way natural but was entirely supernatural as was sanctifying grace. Man in pure nature had to turn himself to God to be ordered to him as his superadded end. For Thomas, man was connaturally related to God with the faculties of knowledge and love for that relationship. Unlike in later Roman theology, Thomas did not pose original righteousness and our relation to God as entirely supernatural. Rather, sanctifying grace elevated nature precisely for the purpose of proportioning our works to be meritorious of eschatological reward. Respectively, Thomas' doctrine of the *donum superadditum* was aimed entirely at the proportionality problem, explaining how creaturely works can obtain a reward of infinite, heavenly value. Thomas used sanctifying grace, not to address a lack in human nature as such, but solely to shore up the proportionality gap between creaturely works and heavenly reward. Although our argument is that the covenant of works more adequately addresses the proportionality problem, we can sympathize with how Thomas, in his contemporary ontologically preoccupied milieu, reduced the function of sanctifying grace to solving the proportionality problem rather than fitting it within a wider notion of pure nature where we are not created as ordered toward God as our supernatural end.

Louis Dupré, 'Introduction to the 2000 Edition,' in de Lubac, *Augustinianism and Modern Theology*, xii-xiv.

133. For a generally poignant account of how concursus relates to our status as analogical creatures who are dependent on God, see Davison, *Participation in God*, 217-38.

That then raises the premise of merit. For Thomas, in contrast to Scotus, righteousness and sanctifying grace were united, so that someone with original righteousness had what was needed to obtain eschatological glory. Thus, God gave sanctifying grace at creation at least functionally concreated. For Thomas, the need for sanctifying grace to elevate the value of our works to be truly proportional to supernatural reward shows that his premise for merit is *real* righteousness. For Thomas, merit is ontologically grounded, meaning that the undergirding righteousness is truly worthy of its reward. There is a true, not willed, ground to what righteousness is and thereby what could be counted as merit.[134] This objectivity in Thomas – that merit must be truly righteous – corresponds more to the concerns in Reformed covenantal merit outlined in chapter two and defended in chapter seven. The Reformed use of *meritum ex pacto* then eclectically combined aspects of Thomas' premise of real righteousness with other understandings of pacted righteousness. Nonetheless, unlike late medieval and early modern Roman views, Reformed covenantal merit never compromised the requirement of true righteousness as if God would accept even sinful best efforts as meritorious.

Preserving Law and Gospel

The preceding discussion brings us to one of the major concerns raised in chapter one: protecting the law-gospel distinction from the vantage of the *imago Dei*. Although our next two chapters take up this connection theologically, the remainder of this chapter outlines how the need to address this concern rises from a widespread confusion of law and gospel in contemporary theology. In traditional Reformed theology's paradigm, the covenant of works and covenant of grace frame redemptive history so that grace, properly speaking, addresses sin rather than nature as such. In contrast, many modern theologians have insisted that grace as such must always, before and after the fall, precede works. This section's purpose is to recount some prevailing trajectories concerning the relationship of grace and works. Our focus must be at the academic level and cannot trace how these arguments trickle into popular-level discourse. These views vary in how thorough their tension is with Reformed theology's

---

134. Alister E. McGrath, *Iustitia Dei: A History of the Christian Doctrine of Justification*, 4th ed. (Cambridge: Cambridge University Press, 2020), 161-63.

law-gospel distinction but do all manifest an ordering of grace and works that bears similarity to medieval structures.

This ordering facilitates problematic structures similar to medieval thought wherein Adam's prelapsarian need for grace to merit transposed after the fall so that sinners just need more grace to merit heavenly reward. Bellarmine and the subsequent Roman tradition mitigated sin's effects upon human nature by suggesting it damaged only our supernaturally added likeness to God, consisting in abilities, but not God's image itself, leaving free will and rationality intact. In this respect, Calvin unsurprisingly affirmed that God's image and likeness are basically interchangeable concepts, rejecting that the fall ruined only Adam's supernaturally added gifts.[135] The Roman denial of the seriousness of the fall's effects allowed them to continue the same paradigm of grace-enabled merit wherein initial justification preceded the need to earn the increase of grace unto final justification.

Modern theologians, particularly those stating allegiance to the Reformed tradition, who argue that justification is by faith alone but that glorification requires a consideration of our works often deny that their paradigm correlates to the Roman paradigm of merit. They appeal to the grounds that God's initial grace encompasses the whole process. This denial misses that the whole Roman paradigm of final justification by works is *grace-enabled* merit, as was always the case even before the fall. We might remember Henry of Ghent's struggle between a commitment to the Augustinian principle that nothing in us can cause God to give us at least first grace but also having this unquenchable sense that there must be *some* congruence between the elect person and his or her final arrival at the reward of glory. The arguments to order grace before the law – implicitly undermining the hard distinction between the covenants of works and grace – result in highly varied degrees of confusion of the law-gospel distinction, sometimes not coming to fruition in the problems just noted for relating justification and glorification. The purpose of the following discussion is to account for growing paradigmatic confusion related to the law-gospel distinction, not to claim that every theologian treated made equally grievous errors in applying his order of grace before law.

---

135. Calvin, *Institutes*, 1.15.3.

Although subsequent Reformed theologians relate to him in different ways, Karl Barth (1886–1968) was arguably the fountainhead of the modern rejection of the covenant of works, leading to an inversion of the law-gospel distinction to order grace before law. While Barth praised their attention to the historical dimension of revelation, specifically in recognizing the dynamic nature of redemptive history, he criticized early modern federal theologians for describing a series of covenants rather than reducing history to one covenantal event.[136] Barth contended that the distinction between the covenants of works and grace was destructive to Reformed theology, arguing instead for one covenant of grace before and after the fall with the law as the description of our response to grace.[137] For Barth – and critical in our wider discussion – federal theology's problem was that 'Nature and grace are both on the same historical level, and confront one another as the principles of individual covenants.'[138] Barth at times talked about God's 'general grace' in creation and providence pertaining to the Christian message of 'God with us.' Nonetheless, he found Reformed federal theology as he understood it to be problematic because he focused grace in God's act of salvation, posed as an *ontological* need: 'Created being as such needs salvation, but does not have it ... The coming of this salvation is the grace of God.'[139] By God's determination to be for us in Jesus Christ, 'grace is not only the basis and essence, the ontological substance of the original relationship between God and man which we have described as the covenant between them willed and instituted and controlled by God. The recognition of this original covenant is also grace and therefore a free divine favor.'[140] Explicitly disagreeing with Luther, Barth upended the Protestant law-gospel distinction: 'In Scripture we do not find the Law alongside the

136. Karl Barth, *Church Dogmatics*, ed. G. W. Bromiley and T. F. Torrance, trans. G. W. Bromiley, 14 vol. (Peabody, MA: Hendrickson, 1936–77), IV.1:54-56.

137. Barth, *Church Dogmatics*, IV.1:58-66. For analysis, see Michael S. Horton, 'Covenant,' in Michael Allen and Scott R. Swain (eds.), *The Oxford Handbook of Reformed Theology* (Oxford: Oxford University Press, 2020), 441-43.

138. Barth, *Church Dogmatics*, IV.1:59.

139. Barth, *Church Dogmatics*, IV.1:8, 6-12. Seemingly the same view is argued in Ian A. McFarland, 'Rethinking Nature and Grace: The Logic of Creation's Consummation,' *International Journal of Systematic Theology* 24, no. 1 (Jan 2022): 56-79.

140. Barth, *Church Dogmatics*, IV.1:44.

Gospel but in the Gospel.'[141] Barth placed grace before law in reference to the covenant, denying the covenant of works altogether, leading, according to Hans Küng, to a doctrine of justification very similar to the Roman Catholic view.[142]

Barth's arguably most pre-eminent followers were J. B. Torrance (1923–2003) and T. F. Torrance (1913–2007). Following Barth, the Torrance school was highly critical of the covenant of works on account of how this covenant placed law before grace.[143] Perhaps not coincidentally, Barth's followers shifted the emphasis of Christ's satisfaction from fulfilling the terms of a covenant to an 'ontological representation,' marking a similarity between these rejections of federal theology and medieval explanations of salvation.[144] Barth's pivotal role in modern theology sent echoes of his grace-law paradigm reverberating throughout Reformed theology.[145]

---

141. Barth, *Church Dogmatics*, II.1:363.

142. Hans Küng, *Justification: The Doctrine of Karl Barth and a Catholic Reflection*, 40th Anniversary ed. (Louisville, KY: Westminster John Knox, 2004); Paul Helm, 'Nature and Grace,' in Manfred Svensson and David VanDrunen (eds.), *Aquinas Among the Protestants* (Hoboken, NJ: Wiley Blackwell, 2018), 239-45; James J. Cassidy, 'Francis Turretin and Barthianism: The Covenant of Works in Historical Perspective,' *The Confessional Presbyterian* 5 (2009): 203-13, 323; R. Michael Allen, *Reformed Theology* (London: T&T Clark, 2010), 46-51.

143. e.g. J. B. Torrance, 'Covenant or Contract? A Study of the Theological Background of Worship in Seventeenth Century Scotland,' *Scottish Journal of Theology* 23 (1970): 51-69; T. F. Torrance, *Scottish Theology: From John Knox to John McLeod Campbell* (Edinburgh: T&T Clark, 1996), 125-53; Holmes Rolston III, *John Calvin Versus the Westminster Confession* (Richmond: Westminster John Knox Press, 1972). Likely because he studied under T. F. Torrance for his doctoral work, although differing from these Barthian proposals in many ways, Douglas F. Kelly outlined a similar view to Herman Hoeksema's that the pre- and post-fall contexts are really one covenant, although adding that God also made a law covenant with Adam within the context of the overarching grace covenant; *Systematic Theology: Grounded in Holy Scripture and Understood in Light of the Church*, 3 vol. (Fearn: Mentor, 2008-21), 1:387-400. Aligning his view, at least formally, with the problematic structures of medieval thought already considered, Kelly differentiates Adam's situation from Genesis 2 and 3 in that prelapsarian grace did not include the forgiveness of sin, so that Adam's relationship with God was grace followed by law; Kelly, *Systematic Theology*, 1:396. For charitable critique of Kelly's position, see Ryan McGraw, 'Review of Douglas F. Kelly, *Systematic Theology: Grounded in Holy Scripture and Understood in Light of the Church, Volume 1*,' *Westminster Theological Journal* 72 no 1 (Spring 2010): 195-96.

144. Kevin J. Vanhoozer, 'Redemption Accomplished: Atonement,' in *Oxford Handbook of Reformed Theology*, 481-84.

145. For more detail and critique of Barth, see Fesko, *Adam and the Covenant of Works*, 409-12.

In the twentieth century, continental Reformed theology saw a widespread rejection of the covenant of works, gaining following in related communities in North America. Criticizing Geerhardus Vos, Klass Schilder (1890–1952) denied that the covenant of works was a different covenant from the covenant of grace, repudiating that Adam had any prospective reward and arguing that the covenant before and after the fall always demanded faith and concomitant obedience.[146] Emphasizing that God's covenant with creatures must be unilateral, Herman Hoeksema (1886–1965) contended that covenant was imbedded in Adam's creation as God's image but that covenant required no reciprocal action from Adam to fulfill the covenant for realizing higher blessing than the original covenantal fellowship, which amounts to a rejection of the covenant of works.[147] Resembling medieval tendencies of equating all God's *ad extra* actions with grace, R. J. Rushdoony (1916–2001) rejected the covenant of works as 'deadly wrong,' claiming that the disparity between God and creatures entails that all God's covenants with us can be only grace with the required response of faith and obedience. For Rushdoony, Adam's sin as a breach of God's *grace* grounds every covenant. God's covenant, therefore, 'always is a covenant of law' requiring works which seemingly govern blessings and curses in principally the same way before and after the fall.[148] A trajectory seemingly growing mostly out of the continental tradition brought widespread modern skepticism to the covenant of works.[149]

---

146. Klaas Schilder, 'The Covenant of Works and the Covenant of Grace,' in George Harinck, Marinus de Jong, and Richard Mouw (eds.), *The Klaas Schilder Reader* (Bellingham, WA: Lexham Press, 2022) 35-61; also Klass Schilder, *Heidelbergsche Catechismus*, 4 vol. (Goes: Oosterban & Le Cointre, 1947–51), 1:296-98, 319, 402-5, 489; 2:23-26.

147. Herman Hoeksema, 'The Covenant Concept (1),' *The Standard Bearer* 80 no 5 (Dec 2003): 105-7; Herman Hoeksema, 'The Covenant Concept (2),' *The Standard Bearer* 80 no 6 (Dec 2003): 129-32.

148. Rousas John Rushdoony, *Systematic Theology*, 2 vol. (Vallecito, CA: Ross House Books, 1994), 373-79. Thanks to Jim Cassidy for alerting me to Rushdoony's rejection of the covenant of works.

149. For more detailed survey and analysis of some criticisms of the covenant of works, see J. V. Fesko, *The Covenant of Works: The Origins, Development, and Reception of the Doctrine* (Oxford Studies in Historical Theology; New York, NY: Oxford University Press, 2020), 187-212; Cornelis Venema, *Christ and Covenant Theology: Essays on Election, Republication, and the Covenants* (Phillipsburg, NJ: P&R, 2017), 6-23;

Arguably, G. C. Berkouwer (1903–96) was the strongest example of attempting to appropriate appreciatively Barthian arguments within the confessional tradition.[150] Following Schilder, Berkouwer argued that human nature was a precondition for, but not itself, the divine image, amounting to a version of pure nature.[151] Amidst a wider (dialectical) discussion about how the preaching of the law and the gospel must stand together, specifically concerning bringing to light the nature of sin and our need to repent, Berkouwer then likewise rejected the traditional Reformed doctrine of the covenant of works.[152] Seeking to avoid dualism between works and grace, he rejected any antithesis between the covenants of works and grace, mistakenly thinking that the covenant of works poses that Adam lacked God's favor entirely and needed to earn divine love. Nonetheless, he failed to distinguish why Paul would point *sinners* away from works as the way to God, from how works could function for Adam in the upright state to advance his experience of communion with God to the consummate state.[153] Although demurring from Barth's particular inversion of the law-gospel distinction, Berkouwer nevertheless denied that the law ever came to man outside the context of grace.[154]

The fallout of this rejection of the covenant of works and the resulting inversion of the law-gospel distinction is more pronounced in more recent writers. Although not formally holding to the Reformed confessions, albeit commenting on our tradition, Daniel Fuller criticized covenant theology for its law-gospel emphasis. Based on his interpretation of the relation of law and grace in Galatians 3:12, which

---

150. e.g. G. C. Berkouwer, *The Triumph of Grace in the Theology of Karl Barth* (Grand Rapids, MI: Eerdmans, 1956).

151. G. C. Berkouwer, *Man: The Image of God* (Studies in Dogmatics; Grand Rapids, MI: Eerdmans, 1962), 54-66, 114-15. For response to Schilder and Berkouwer, see Hoekema, *Created in God's Image*, 17-18, 58-65.

152. G. C. Berkouwer, *Sin* (Studies in Dogmatics; Grand Rapids, MI: Eerdmans, 1971), 206-10.

153. Berkouwer expressed sympathy with criticisms of the federalist view of the imputation of Adam's sin, marking one consequence of his rejection of the covenant of works; *Sin*, 449-65.

154. Following John Murray, Hoekema rejected the covenant of works in favor of emphasizing 'aspects of grace' in the 'adamic administration'; Hoekema, *Created in God's Image*, 117-21; John Murray, 'The Adamic Administration,' in *Collected Writings of John Murray*, 4 vol. (Carlisle, PA: The Banner of Truth, 1976–82), 2:47-59.

explicitly addressed the perceived 'difficulty with its antithesis between law and gospel,' Fuller argued, 'some substantial changes would have to be made in the theology which stresses *sola scriptura* along with *sola fide*.'[155] Targeting both covenant theology and dispensational hermeneutics, he alleged that both systems failed to understand the unity of the old and new covenants because of their antithesis of law and gospel as the basis of salvation.[156]

Fuller also attacked how the Reformed understand the fall to affect our need for grace. First, he brushed aside the fall's significance for how we can be right with God by criticizing covenant theology for accepting a premise of works for Adam before the fall.[157] In the next breath, he balked at the standard Reformed view of rejecting 'that a sinful Israelite's salvation, during the Mosaic and kingdom eras, *depended in part on his striving by his unaided efforts to keep the law*.'[158] In other words, Fuller had a problem with sinless Adam earning a reward on the premise of works but found it totally acceptable that works could play a key role for sinners obtaining salvation.

Fuller integrated these theological critiques into his response to Reformed exegetical underpinnings for the law-gospel distinction. Reflecting on his disagreement with Calvin's exegesis of Romans 10:5-8 and Galatians 3:10-12, Fuller critiqued Calvin's view of law and gospel by concluding that 'the antithesis is only apparent and not real' which he noted 'will make the enjoyment of grace dependent on faith and good works.'[159] He argued that, in Galatians, the phrase 'works of the law' means 'rebellion against God' – entailing that Paul had to *convince* the Judaizers (who were attempting to impose works) that sin itself could not make them righteous in God's sight. Fuller then concluded that 'the law is not of faith' means simply that 'legalistic misunderstandings' were contrary to true faith.[160] This interpretation 'would remove all need

---

155. Daniel P. Fuller, 'Paul and "the Works of the Law",' *Westminster Theological Journal* 38, no. 1 (Fall 1975): 29, 42.

156. Daniel P. Fuller, *Gospel and Law: Contrast or Continuum? The Hermeneutics of Dispensationalism and Covenant Theology* (Grand Rapids, MI: Eerdmans, 1980), 1-64.

157. Fuller, *Gospel and Law*, 34.

158. Fuller, *Gospel and Law*, 34 (emphasis added).

159. Fuller, *Gospel and Law*, 63, also 108.

160. Fuller, *Gospel and Law*, 88-105.

for making a contrast between gospel and faith on the one hand, and the *revelatory* [i.e., rightly understood] law of Moses on the other.'[161] Thus, he explicitly rejected Calvin's conclusions, affirming that 'the law and the gospel are one and the same.'[162] Although denying that works' contribution to salvation gives us place to boast, Fuller argues that the difference between legalism and the obedience of faith is internal motivation of grace rather than pride.[163]

Fuller brought these considerations to bear on his understanding of faith itself. While acknowledging that Christ's death forgives our sin, Fuller's understanding of faith more resembles Friedrich Schleiermacher's notion of a feeling of utter dependence upon God than the Reformation's instrument of union with Christ.[164] Fuller, eliding the pre- and post-fall situations by arguing that 'the obedience of faith is the only kind of obedience that is ever acceptable,' contended that Adam needed to have obedient faith (never distinguished from the sort of faith we have in Christ) during his probationary test to obtain reward, which would be 'a work of grace.'[165] Fuller noted that the upshot of his view that undifferentiated grace always grounds obedience unto reward is that 'good works are made the instrumental cause of justification.'[166] Other scholars have noted that Fuller's view was a denial of the Reformation, and our earlier analysis reveals Fuller's great structural similarity to the Roman tradition on grace and merit.[167] Even then, Fuller goes further

---

161. Fuller, *Gospel and Law*, 99 (italics original).

162. Fuller, *Gospel and Law*, 103.

163. Fuller, *Gospel and Law*, 63-64, 73, 105-20; also Daniel P. Fuller, 'A Response on the Subjects of Works and Grace,' (Spring-Fall 1983): 75-76, 78. With notable similarity to Fuller's caveat, Kallistos Ware, from an Eastern Orthodox perspective, denied that prevenient grace enables merit even though 'we must certainly work for' salvation. Ware's affirmation comes within an explicit openness to outright Pelagianism; Timothy Ware, *The Orthodox Church: An Introduction to Eastern Christianity*, new ed. (Milton Keynes, UK: Penguin Random House UK: 2015), 215-16.

164. Fuller, *Gospel and Law*, 112-13, 114; Robert Merrihew Adams, 'Faith and religious knowledge,' in Jacqueline Mariña (ed.), *The Cambridge Companion to Friedrich Schleiermacher* (Cambridge: Cambridge University Press, 2005), 35-51.

165. Fuller, 'Response on the Subjects of Works and Grace,' 76

166. Fuller, 'Response on the Subjects of Works and Grace,' 79.

167. O. Palmer Robertson, 'Daniel P. Fuller's *Gospel and Law: Contrast or Continuum?*: A Review Article,' *Presbyterion* 8 no 1 (Spring 1982): 84-91; Meredith G. Kline, 'Of Works and Grace,' *Presbyterion* 9 no 1 (Spring-Fall 1983): 85-92; W. Robert Godfrey, 'Back to

than most medievals, save perhaps Biel, ultimately commending us to save ourselves while feeling like God saved us.

Norman Shepherd, who caused much controversy in the Reformed world for his teaching about justification, has argued that Reformed theology should revise its understanding of the covenant of works in ways that undermine the law-gospel distinction.[168] He, rightly, described the covenant works and the covenant of grace as having opposing principles so that the first requires 'the meritorious performance of good works' and the second poses faith as an instrumental condition 'to avoid saying that it is a meritorious condition.' He further, wrongly, juxtaposed these conditions so that the premise of works excludes relational aspects of fellowship, love, communion, and faithfulness. Rather than accept works and faith as two mutually exclusive covenantal principles for justification, Shepherd suggested that the covenantal situation before and after the fall 'is not a structurally different kind of relationship with the first one based on works and the last one based on grace. The program of redemption does not destroy creation but recreates, restores, and renews what was there from the beginning.'[169] In sum, Shepherd denied any radical difference concerning how the fall must change our covenantal relationship with God.

Shepherd demurred from the traditional works-grace covenantal system by posing that grace must always facilitate obedience. Reflecting on his rejection of the covenant of works, he contended that, 'The Lord God did not and never does deal with his image bearers in terms of a principle of works and merit but ever and always in terms of a principle of faith and grace.'[170] This premise applied to Adam so that he had to have faith that was obedient: 'The method of justification for Adam before the fall is exactly what it is for Paul after the fall: "The righteous will live by faith" (Rom. 1:17).'[171] In Shepherd's construct, sin is not so

Basics: A Response to the Robertson-Fuller Dialogue,' *Presbyterion* 9 no 1 (Spring-Fall 1983): 80-84.

168. For background on Shepherd's controversy and the related rejection of the covenant of works, see Guy Prentiss Waters, *The Federal Vision and Covenant Theology: A Comparative Analysis* (Phillipsburg, NJ: P&R, 2006), 96-107, 30-58.

169. Norman Shepherd, 'Law and Gospel in Covenantal Perspective,' *Reformation and Revival* 14 no 1 (2005): 74-75.

170. Shepherd, 'Law and Gospel,' 76.

171. Shepherd, 'Law and Gospel,' 76.

problematic as to revise the way of obtaining eschatological glory. For him, sin is not the reason that justification must be by faith, but sinners are justified by faith simply because obedient faith was always the means of fulfilling God's covenant.[172] In this sense, Shepherd subtly redefined both faith and works, thereby denying a clear conceptual distinction between them.

Shepherd denied that the good works of obedient faith that obtain justification are meritorious because he saw grace as the necessary context for those works. Problematically for Shepherd's position in this regard, the entire Roman system of merit – apart from Biel's fully Pelagian formulations – presumes that grace is the enabling factor for works to merit eschatological reward. Respectively, Shepherd's position then differs from Rome's traditional views only semantically – we might even suggest in a nominalist fashion. Since Shepherd posed faith as the same necessary condition for the performance of works for Adam and for sinners after the fall, relegating its significance to unite sinners to Christ as our mediator, presumably faith is ultimately just the *habitus* of grace empowering obedience to obtain justification and glorification. Roman theologians would disagree with this position primarily in explicitly describing faith as having a greater role in uniting us to Christ. As Pope Emeritus Benedict XVI (1927–2022) preached: 'Faith is looking at Christ, entrusting oneself to Christ, being united to Christ, conformed to Christ, to his life.'[173] Even as he interpreted law-gospel contrasts within a similar grid as Shepherd's claim that the difference of law and gospel reduces to the redemptive-historical shift from the Mosaic covenant to the new, Benedict reached radically different points about works and grace:

> It is precisely because of this personal experience of relationship with Jesus Christ that Paul henceforth places at the center of his Gospel an irreducible opposition between the two alternative paths to righteousness: one built on the works of the Law, the other founded on the grace of faith in Christ.

---

172. Shepherd, 'Law and Gospel,' 77-87.

173. Benedict XVI, 'General Audience: Der Hl. Paulus (13): Die Rechtfertigungslehre – Von den Werken zum Glauben,' *The Holy See*; St. Peter's Square: November 19, 2008; accessed on May 12, 2023 at https://www.vatican.va/content/benedict-xvi/de/audiences/2008/documents/hf_ben-xvi_aud_20081119.html; Glaube heißt auf Christus schauen, sich Christus anvertrauen, sich an Christus festhalten, sich Christus und seinem Leben angleichen.

The alternative between righteousness by means of works of the Law and that by faith in Christ thus became one of the dominant themes that run through his Letters.[174]

Shepherd's denial that God's covenant with Adam was a covenant of works with a different basis than the covenant of grace for salvation in Christ then represents an interpretive strategy at odds with Reformation principles to which not even a former Pope objects.

This interpretive strategy has its clearest expression when theologians supposedly of Protestant perspective try to reintegrate grace and merit. For example, David DeSilva has argued that opposing grace and merit is a 'highly problematic' approach, advocating:

> Paul understands a grateful response to have merit, and to contribute to the ongoing nurturing of the grace relationship, just as ingratitude contributes to the dissolution of the relationship (as in Gal 5:2-4), but God's grace is still the initiating force, and the human recipient always remains in the position of the one indebted to God. 'Merit,' in other words, exists in Paul's framework, but does not earn by indebting God.[175]

This reworking of the relationship between grace and merit rests on a reinterpretation of the social understanding of 'grace' in the first century.[176] DeSilva argued 'contrary to the notion of "imputed righteousness,"' that 'God *brings into being* within us the righteousness that Christ exhibited, changing us to become more like him, indeed inviting us to become vessels through which Christ's righteousness continues to express itself in real, impactful ways in the communities and world around us.'[177] Since he was explaining the meaning of justification itself, DeSilva sided with the Council of Trent against Christ's *imputed* righteousness in favor of, albeit without the exact term,

---

174. Benedict XVI, 'Die Rechtfertigungslehre,' (Aufgrund dieser persönlichen Erfahrung der Beziehung zu Jesus Christus stellt Paulus nun den tiefen Gegensatz zwischen zwei alternativen Wegen zur Gerechtigkeit in den Mittelpunkt seines Evangeliums: Der eine baut auf die Werke des Gesetzes, der andere ist auf die Gnade des Glaubens an Christus gegründet. Die Alternative zwischen der Gerechtigkeit durch die Werke des Gesetzes und der Gerechtigkeit durch den Glauben an Christus wird somit zu einem der vorherrschenden Leitmotive, die seine Briefe durchziehen).

175. David A. DeSilva, *The Letter to the Galatians* (New International Commentary on the New Testament; Grand Rapids, MI: Eerdmans, 2018), 261-62.

176. DeSilva, *Galatians*, 254-62.

177. DeSilva, *Galatians*, 221n278 (italics original).

infused righteousness.[178] The reordering of the law and the gospel so that grace *always* precedes the law promotes an understanding where grace's main function in salvation initiates and furthers the believers' ability to perform works that are necessary to obtain final salvation. The problem is active among even Protestant biblical scholars not realizing that what they perceive as innovative exegetical investigation is truly a return to almost the exact categories that the Reformation rejected.[179]

Bradley Green is repeatedly critical of what he categorized the law-gospel 'antithesis.'[180] His misguided emphasis on antithesis rather than distinction produces imprecise conclusions about how to explain the necessity of Christian obedience. That imprecision is especially clear when his argument about the priority of grace over law in the garden of Eden, which lacks a firm statement of the consummation unto the new creation, entails that we will need to maintain our life with God by our obedience even after the final judgment.[181] Citing John Frame, he also 'suggests that the gospel really comes *first* in God's dealings with man.'[182] Since his point lacked qualification, Green seemingly suggested that humanity always needed the gospel, even from creation, since the Reformed use of the law-gospel distinction profoundly emphasizes the difference between creation and fall. Of course, sinners need grace before we can properly endeavor after God's standards of obedience. On the other hand, the assertion that we always needed the *gospel* either entails that God created us in need for salvation from sin or misunderstands that 'gospel' is not simply a synonym for 'goodness' but the announcement that Christ died and rose to save his people from sin.

---

178. Session 6, chapter 10, 16; Schaff, *Creeds of Christendom*, 2:99, 108.

179. On this point, see Nathan Eubank, 'Configurations of Grace and Merit in Paul and His Interpreters,' *International Journal of Systematic Theology* 22 no 1 (2013): 7-17; Timo Laato, 'The New Quest for Paul: A Critique of the New Perspective on Paul,' in Matthew Barrett (ed.), *The Doctrine on which the Church Stands or Falls: Justification in Biblical, Theological, Historical, and Pastoral Perspective* (Wheaton, IL: Crossway, 2019), 295-326.

180. Bradley G. Green, *Covenant and Commandment: Works, Obedience and Faithfulness in the Christian Life* (New Studies in Biblical Theology; Downers Grove, IL: IVP Academic, 2014), esp. 60-72; also Shepherd, 'Law and Gospel,' 86; Fuller, *Gospel and Law*, xi, 5, 103.

181. Green, *Covenant and Commandment*, 147-66.

182. Green, *Covenant and Commandment*, 61 (emphasis original).

Green's mistaken presentation of the law-gospel distinction as an absolute antithesis overlooks ways that the Reformed tradition has related these concepts respective to various applications. First, his unfortunate emphasis on *antithesis* rather than distinction unhelpfully skews the categories, since law and gospel are antithetical *not absolutely* but only relatively as principles of justification, even if they are categorically always distinct. This relative antithesis concerning justification simply reflects the differing principle bases of the covenant of works and the covenant of grace. Respecting the ground for acceptance with God, Calvin commented on Galatians 5:6: 'We, again, refuse to admit that, in any case, faith can be separated from the Spirit of regeneration; *but when the question comes to be in what manner we are justified, we then set aside all works.*'[183] Thus, the law and the gospel are *always* distinct, *sometimes* antithetical specifically in application to justification, and *other times* harmonious when the law is not being considered as a principle for our right standing with God.

Second, the law and the gospel as principles are *always* distinct and *sometimes* harmonious when the law is not being considered as a principle for our right standing with God. They are distinct in that the law always tells of God's commands even when it is not a condition for having a relationship with God, and the gospel always tells of how Christ has earned our salvation. We need not conflate them even when explaining the ways in which they are not antithetical. Westminster Confession 19.7 affirms 'Neither are the forementioned Uses of the Law contrary to the grace of the Gospel, but do sweetly comply with it.'[184] The pertinent question is: What are the law's *forementioned* uses that sweetly comply with the gospel?[185] Westminster Confession 19.6 outlines these uses, first qualifying that 'Although true Beleevers be not under the Law, as a Covenant of Works, to be thereby justified, or condemned,' crucially indicating that the law's uses that comply with the gospel do not pertain to our justification or final standing with God since the law

---

183. John Calvin, *Commentaries on the Epistles of Paul to the Galatians and Ephesians*, trans. William Pringle (Grand Rapids, MI: Baker, 2009), 153 (emphasis added).

184. Bower, *Confession of Faith*, 218 (emphasis added).

185. Michael Allen, 'The Law in the Reformed Tradition,' in Jonathan A. Linebaugh (ed.), *God's Two Words: Law and Gospel in the Lutheran and Reformed Traditions* (Grand Rapids, MI: Eerdmans, 2018), 56-58.

can no longer condemn us. The uses that do comply with the gospel for believers include 'informing them of the will of God and their duty' which well introduces the more specific uses that can be summed up as guiding our walk in godliness and our efforts to recognize sin so we can repent.[186] Specifically the third use of the law as a guide to the Christian life complies with the gospel. The law is not antithetical to the gospel when it informs us how to live the life of gratitude. It does, however, still remain distinct from the gospel message properly.

Third, sometimes the Reformed use the categories of law and gospel to refer to redemptive historical development. In this respect, Westminster Confession of Faith 7.5 states that the covenant of grace 'was differently administered in *the time of the Law*, and in *the time of the Gospel*.'[187] The time of the law delivered the same substance of Christ and his benefits under types and shadows. The time of the gospel simply conveys the change 'when Christ, the substance, was exhibited.'[188] Calvin held together the principle and redemptive historical views, stating that the law can refer to God's commands as the rule of righteousness and to the 'form of religion handed down by God through Moses.'[189] This application of the law-gospel distinction to redemptive-historical categories did not displace, replace, or subvert its use as a difference of principles. It supplemented and cohered with it.[190] The redemptive-historical use helped to explain how the principles of law and gospel could be present in both the Old and New Testaments.[191] Green's discussion exemplifies how both ignorance of and ignoring these differing ways in which the Reformed applied the law-gospel distinction can create much confusion in theological discussions that does not help us keep clear distinctions in our understanding of the *ordo salutis* or the *historia salutis*.[192]

---

186. Bower, *Confession of Faith*, 217.

187. Bower, *Confession of Faith*, 205 (emphasis added).

188. Westminster Confession 7.6; Bower, *Confession of Faith*, 205.

189. Calvin, *Institutes*, 2.7.1.

190. Calvin, *Institutes*, 2.7.1-9

191. Calvin, *Institutes*, 2.10.23.

192. For excellent historical treatment of these wider applications of the law-gospel distinction, see Ryan McGraw, 'The Threats of the Gospel: John Owen on What the Law/Gospel Distinction is Not,' *Calvin Theological Journal* 51 (2016): 79-111.

Although without explicitly disparaging the pre-fall human nature or directly attacking justification by faith alone, Robert Letham argued that God always relates to us by grace that must be supplemented by obedience – a structure that begins to resemble some versions of medieval thought.[193] Letham claimed that the Reformed 'have viewed law and gospel as complementary .... Grace constitutes, law regulates.'[194] Admittedly, the truth of this statement depends on what Letham meant by 'complementary.' Regardless, the notion that grace constitutes our relationship with God and law regulates it in *all* contexts indeed looks more like medieval categories than Reformed exegesis.[195]

Letham's view has an intellectual background that must be considered. Letham stated his desire to uphold Reformed orthodoxy, so he did not mean to resemble medieval ideas.[196] Nevertheless, his dependence upon J. B. Torrance and T. F. Torrance in regard to covenant theology brought him closer to a Barthian interpretation of the law-gospel distinction than to the traditional Reformed view.[197] Although Letham rightly affirmed a distinct covenant of works, he still seems to have accepted Barth's basic structure by arguing that God always relates to us by 'grace regulated by law,' which he claimed 'in some undifferentiated sense, operates both before and after the fall,' so that law is not 'relegated to a minor role.'[198] He concluded, 'If there were no grace in the covenant of life [i.e. works], God would have related to humanity differently in creation than he does in all subsequent stages of human history.'[199] Letham argued that his is the Reformed view, but neither the primary nor secondary sources which he cited sustain the connection between the Reformed views of condescension and grace that he asserted.[200] In that respect, Letham interpreted Galatians 3

---

193. Letham, *Systematic Theology*, 349-65.

194. Letham, *Systematic Theology*, 360.

195. Oberman, *Harvest of Medieval Theology*, 120-84.

196. Letham, *Systematic Theology*, 383-84, 397.

197. Fesko, *Adam and the Covenant of Works*, xviii–xxv, 408-16; e.g. Torrance, 'Covenant or Contract?' 51-69; Torrance, *Scottish Theology*, 125-53; Rolston, *John Calvin Versus the Westminster Confession*.

198. Letham, *Systematic Theology*, 365.

199. Letham, *Systematic Theology*, 364.

200. Perkins, *Catholicity and the Covenant of Works*, 113-14.

exactly opposite of traditional Reformed commentators such as John Calvin, Robert Rollock, and William Perkins.[201]

Although Christian charity demands that we read others on their own terms and sympathetically allow for a diversity of expression, Letham's way of flattening the distinction between God's dealings with humanity before and after the fall into a comparable relationship of grace before law makes his view substantially problematic. His use of signs risks skewing our understanding the realities. As Turretin explained, the covenant of works and the covenant of grace differ concerning 'the author, because although God is the author of both covenants, nevertheless he must be considered under different relations, in the first as Creator and Lord; in the second, as Redeemer and Father; for the former, he was motivated by love and good will toward the upright creature, for the latter, by mercy and special grace toward a miserable creature.'[202] Richard Belcher rightly noted what is at stake when theologians flatten the pre- and post-fall situations: 'Views that do not recognize the differences between the prefall and postfall condition

201. Letham, *Systematic Theology*, 361; John Calvin, *Opera quae superunt omnia*, ed. Edouard Cunitz, Johann-Wilhem Baum, and Eduard Wilhem Eugen Reuss, 58 vol. (Corpus Reformatorum; Brunsigae: C.A. Schwetschke, 1863), 50:208-9, 214-15; John Calvin, *Commentaries on the Epistles of Paul to the Galatians and Ephesians*, trans. William Pringle (Edinburgh: The Calvin Translation Society, 1854), 88-91, 98-99; Robert Rollock, *Analysis Logica in Epistolam Pauli Apostoli ad Galatas* (London: Felix Kyngston, 1602), 54; William Perkins, *The Works of William Perkins*, 10 vol. (Grand Rapids, MI: Reformation Heritage Books, 2014–2020), 2:169, 175, 193 (Commentary on Galatians 3:10, 12, 18); Perkins, *Works*, 4:47-72 (commentary on Jude 3); see also Perkins, *Catholicity and the Covenant of Works*, 85-125.

202. Turrettinus, *Institutio*, 12.4.2, 9.11.7 (*Authoris*, quamvis enim Deus sit utriusque foederis author, sub diversa tamen σχίσει spectandus est, in primo qua Creator & Dominus; In secundo qua Redemptor & Pater, ad primum impulsus fuit amore & benevolentia erga Creaturam integram, ad posterius misericordia & gratia speciali erga Creaturam miseram); Herman Witsius, *De Oeconomia Foederum Dei cum Hominibus*, 3rd ed. (Utrecht, 1694), 1.3.26; Bavinck, *Reformed Dogmatics*, 3:225-28; Herman Bavinck, *The Wonderful Works of God: Instruction in the Christian Religion according to the Reformed Confession*, trans. Henry Zylstra (Glenside, PA: Westminster Seminary Press, 2019), 252-55; Richard A. Muller, 'The Covenant of Works and the Stability of Divine Law in Seventeenth-Century Reformed Orthodoxy: A Study in the Theology of Herman Witsius and Wilhelmus à Brakel,' in *After Calvin: Studies in the Development of a Theological Tradition* (Oxford Studies in Historical Theology; New York, NY: Oxford University Press, 2003), 181-83; Ligon Duncan, 'Foreword,' in Guy Prentiss Waters, J. Nicholas Reid, and John R. Muether (eds.), *Covenant Theology: Biblical, Theological, and Historical Perspectives* (Wheaton, IL: Crossway, 2020), 27; Brakel, *Christian's Reasonable Service*, 1:375-80.

of mankind tend to confuse the relationship between faith and works in salvation.'[203] Letham's view unintentionally relates more to the Barthian interpretation of the Reformed tradition than to the tradition itself.

Other scholars have noticed this recent trend in Protestant theology. Grant Macaskill argued that, even though evangelicals have begun to adopt it, this structure of grace regulated by the law is *precisely* the structure that the New Perspective on Paul has used with the effect of undermining Protestant views of salvation.[204] Undoubtedly, most evangelicals who have adopted this approach are unaware of the theological implications that Macaskill highlighted, likely even trying to maximize grace. Rather than simply a variant way of expressing the traditional Reformed model, Letham's formulation positions his view structurally closer to the medieval paradigm of the *donum superadditum* and the New Perspective's revision of justification.[205]

By contrast, early modern Reformed theologians clearly affirmed the distinction between the law and the gospel as mutually exclusive principles for relating to God. William Twisse (1578–1646), the first prolocutor of the Westminster Assembly, began his catechism by asking, 'How many ways does the Word of GOD teach us to come to the Kingdome of Heaven?' answering, 'Two.' These two are 'The Law and the Gospel' with the law saying, 'Do this and thou shalt live.' In contrast, the gospel says, 'Believe in Jesus Christ, and thou shalt be saved.' Twisse was clear that sinners cannot 'come to the Kingdome of Heaven by way of Gods Law' namely 'Because we cannot do it.'[206] Yet, Twisse's view was not idiosyncratic. James Ussher preached from a London pulpit, 'In the first Covenant, If thou can do that the Law commands, thou shalt be justified by the Law. Rom. 10:5. Moses describes the Righteousness of the Law that the man who does these things, shall live thereby.'[207]

---

203. Richard P. Belcher Jr., 'The Covenant of Works in the Old Testament,' in Waters et al, *Covenant Theology*, 78n71.

204. Grant Macaskill, *Living in Union with Christ: Paul's Gospel and Christian Moral Identity* (Grand Rapids, MI: Baker Academic, 2019), 15-38.

205. The same holds true of John Frame, *The Doctrine of the Christian Life* (A Theology of Lordship; Phillipsburg, NJ: P&R, 2008), 182-92.

206. William Twisse, *A Briefe Catechetical Exposition of Christian Doctrine* (1633), 3-4.

207. Cambridge University Library Manuscript Mm.6.55, fol. 21v (sermon on Gen. 3:1 dated July 3, 1642).

Reformed theologians have then traditionally maintained the distinction between law and grace as ways to be right with God.[208]

Conclusion

The diversity of the Reformed tradition reveals its developing nature as it solidified in the seventeenth century and through ongoing debates. Theologians retained an eclecticism about the earlier figures and ideas that they drew from and appropriated. Our consideration has not at all meant to suggest patterns of appropriation outside the narrow doctrinal issues in our focus. On these matters, there seemed to be a leaning preference for Thomas' theology of grace over and against Franciscan thinkers – exceptions are undoubtedly available. The point is also not truly about aligning the Reformed tradition with any one preceding thinker but to weave a tapestry about the nexus of doctrinal discussions, differences, and debates within which the Reformed tradition grew, expanded, and emerged as it received, refined, and *reformed* the trajectories of our preexisting Christian heritage.

The scope of our historical investigations has shown a long prevailing problem that rises from a wrong relation of grace and works. The medieval paradigm consistently placed grace before the law as the force that shored up the proportionality problem, posing grace as the measure to help overcome the inherent inadequacy in our works – both before and after the fall. That problem has preserved a strong foothold in modern scholarship, especially after Barth and affecting confessional Reformed theology directly to varying degrees.

With the considerations from chapters two to five in place, we stand on clearly surveyed historical ground better situated to formulate good answers to the issue of nature, grace, and supernature. Our next steps are to pose dogmatic articulations of the relationship between the image of God, original righteousness, covenant, and merit. The doctrine of covenantal merit in the covenant of works – but emphatically not in the covenant of grace – helps maintain our traditional Reformed concerns for the law-gospel distinction.

---

208. Charles Hodge, *Systematic Theology*, 3 vol. (Peabody, MA: Hendrickson, 2008), 2:117.

CHAPTER SIX

Covenant, God's Image, and the Nature/Grace Question

We need to reckon now with how we should articulate the relationship between how God created us as his image-bearing creatures and our eschatological destiny to enjoy God in the beatific vision. Our historical investigation set the backdrop of the medieval and later Roman doctrinal system wherein grace superadded supernatural ends and capacities to human nature. In the most thoroughgoing cases, humanity has entirely natural existence and purpose, being oriented to God only by something extrinsically conjoined to our nature. This formulation of the natural and supernatural orders entailed that grace was prevenient to and enabled merit. Even for Adam before the fall, grace elevated human nature to perform works that warranted heavenly reward. This chapter addresses nature's relationship to supernature, looking at how to correlate creation and covenant. The next chapter takes up the issue of covenantal merit in conjunction with the law-gospel distinction.

This chapter argues that God created us with an eschatological destiny woven into our nature. We should recognize the validity of certain *subordinate* ends pertaining to life in the natural realm, affirming our remaining responsibility to our penultimate endeavors for this age.[1]

---

1. Louis Berkhof, *Systematic Theology*, expanded ed. (Edinburgh: The Banner of Truth, 2021), 2:247; St. Thomas Aquinas, *Summa Theologica*, trans. by Fathers of the English Dominican Province, 5 vol. (New York, NY: Benziger Bros., 1948; repr. Notre Dame, IN: Christian Classics, 1981), 1a2ae.109.2.

Nonetheless, Westminster Shorter Catechism 1 best captures how we ought to conceive our fundamental reason for existing: 'Man's chief end is to glorify God, and to enjoy him forever.'[2] Our *chief* end, our *ultimate* purpose, is the blessed enjoyment of God in glory. Man's chief *end* as everlastingly glorifying and enjoying God suggests a Reformed telic statement about nature oriented toward the supernatural, at least in an eschatological sense. As Michael Horton has put it: 'There is one end, and it is naturally supernatural: to glorify God and enjoy God forever.'[3] The created order was built oriented toward the eschatological order. Both orders interface with the truly supernatural by – apart from sin's entry – facilitating our natural communion with God, albeit offering it to different degrees of enjoyment in the protological and consummate states.

Because our nature itself was created as ordered to communion with God protologically and with the prospect of eschatological destiny, the covenant of works must be a relationship of love.[4] Adam was, after all, God's creaturely Son (Luke 3:38).[5] Westminster Confession 6.2 explains that our first parents, by sinning, 'fell from their original righteousness and communion with God,' entailing that the original covenantal situation included humanity's *fellowship* with our Maker.[6] Reformed theology does have a (valid) forensic outlook, driven by our focus on covenants. Nonetheless, we cannot validate the criticisms about an overly juridical theology by reducing our covenant theology to its legal dimensions and evacuating its relational aspects. Reformed theology as much as any other ought to delight in the apostle John's affirmation that 'God is love' (1 John 4:7). His covenants with us are the matrix to experience, enjoy, and reciprocate his love, which is true of the covenant

---

2. Philip Schaff (ed.), *The Creeds of Christendom*, 3 vol. (New York, NY: Harper and Brothers, 1877), 3:676.

3. Michael Horton, *Justification*, 2 vol. (New Studies in Dogmatics; Grand Rapids, MI: Zondervan, 2018), 1:243.

4. J. V. Fesko, *Adam and the Covenant of Works* (Fearn: Mentor, 2021), 377-79, 391-96; David VanDrunen, *Divine Covenants and Moral Order: A Biblical Theology of Natural Law* (Grand Rapids, MI: Eerdmans, 2014), 58-61, 91-93.

5. Meredith G. Kline, *Kingdom Prologue: Genesis Foundations for a Covenantal Worldview* (Eugene, OR: Wipf and Stock, 2006), 45-46.

6. John R. Bower, *The Confession of Faith: A Critical Text and Introduction* (Principal Documents of the Westminster Assembly; Grand Rapids, MI: Reformation Heritage Books, 2020), 203.

of works as much as the covenant of grace. The covenant of works must include love, even happiness of communion, because it involves God's image.[7] God cannot but love his own character. He also cannot but hate when the reflection of his character is damaged. This connection explains why sin is so heinous both objectively as an infraction of God's law in respect to the covenant and subjectively as rebellion against him at the relational level. Because we bear God's image, the covenant of works is intrinsically relational and intrinsically focuses on God's love for us and our love for him, which we needed to express properly.[8]

This chapter then tackles three related aspects of our argument. We first reflect upon the relationship of creation and covenant, contending that they are interdependent categories that are distinct but inseparable. The payoff is to show that covenant is not a purely extrinsic imposition of religious life upon the bare creaturely state. In other words, our view of covenant rejects the notion of pure nature. Then, we reflect upon the connection between the image of God and eschatology, articulating how our image-bearing status in the created order intrinsically orients us toward the eschatological order. Finally, we consider the issue of grace in the covenant of works, arguing that our theological system is clearest if we restrict the application of grace to the redemptive order. The created order has its imbedded relation to supernature and to the eschatological order so that we need not speak of grace as extrinsically imposing that orientation.[9] In this outline, we do not collapse or discard nature or supernature but properly relate them according to a clearer presentation of the created and eschatological orders.

Creation, Covenant, and Condescension

The first issue to tackle is formulating our understanding of created nature as it relates to the covenant of works. This section argues that the confessional view of the covenant of works does not require the addition of grace to human nature as originally created in order to equip us to fulfill the conditions for entering eschatological life. We take our lead from Westminster Confession 7.1:

---

7. Franciscus Turrettinus, *Institutio Theologiae Elencticae*, 3 vol. (Geneva, 1679–85), 8.1.2.

8. Kline, *Kingdom Prologue*, 63-66.

9. Charles Hodge, *Systematic Theology*, 3 vol. (Peabody, MA: Hendrickson, 2008), 2:104-5.

> The distance between God and the Creature is so great, that although reasonable Creatures do owe obedience unto him as their Creator, yet they could never have any fruition of him as their Blessednesse and Reward, but by some voluntary condescension on God's part, which he has been pleased to expresse *by way of covenant*.[10]

The distance between God and the creature marks Reformed theology's concern to address the disproportion between Adam's creaturely obedience and an infinitely great supernatural reward.[11] This confessional statement shows that the Reformed overcome this disproportion by appealing to God's covenant rather than to an elevation of pure human nature through infused grace.[12] Multiple aspects of this description of covenant help us relate creation and covenant properly.

First, the principle in Westminster Confession 7.1 pertains both to the covenant of works and to the covenant of grace, which calibrates how it applies to the works condition in God's covenant with Adam. Concerning God's relationship to humanity, covenant is a concrete manifestation of his condescension to meet us for fellowship and provide a method for us to obtain his blessedness as our eschatological reward.[13] Given that the Westminster Assembly debated 'condescension' during deliberations about this chapter on the covenant, we should be hesitant about pinning down its meaning too specifically. We should instead tie it to the period's basic consensus understanding.[14] As Richard Muller highlighted, the notion of condescension closely relates to God's accommodation in revealing himself

---

10. Bower, *Confession of Faith*, 204 (emphasis added).

11. Bryan D. Estelle, Benjamin W. Swinburnson, Lane G. Tipton, A. Craig Troxel, and Chad V. Van Dixhoorn, 'Report to the 83rd (2016) General Assembly of the Committee to Study Republication' (Willow Grove, PA: The Committee on Christian Education of the Orthodox Presbyterian Church, 2016), 25-28.

12. N. Gray Sutanto, 'Consummation Anyway: A Reformed Proposal,' *Journal of Analytic Philosophy* 9 (Summer 2021): 228-29.

13. Geerhardus Vos, *Reformed Dogmatics*, 5 vol. (Bellingham, WA: Lexham Press, 2012–14), 2:31-32, 35-36.

14. Chad Van Dixhoorn (ed.), *The Minutes and Papers of the Westminster Assembly 1643–1652*, 5 vol. (Oxford: Oxford University Press, 2012), 3:658. Robert Letham appeals to spurious links that 'condescension' is closely related to God's grace; *The Westminster Assembly: Reading Its Theology in Historical Context* (Phillipsburg, NJ: P&R, 2009), 225-26. The specificity of his proposed interpretation contravenes its debated status even at the Westminster Assembly; Harrison Perkins, *Catholicity and the Covenant of Works: James Ussher and the Reformed Tradition* (Oxford Studies in Historical Theology; New York, NY: Oxford University Press, 2020), 111-14.

to his creatures, most especially in making himself known in creaturely language and concepts so that we can understand him. This principle 'for the communication of the law and the gospel' refers most basically to 'the manner or mode of revelation.'[15] In other words, God's condescension to commune with his image-bearing creatures is not limited to one principle but applies to both the covenant of works and the covenant of grace.

This notion of accommodation bears upon God's two words of law and gospel by informing how we must understand the relation between condescension and covenant. Accommodation as a principle of revelation must encompass a wide remit since revelation itself comprises general and special revelation – both of which are required for creatures to know God adequately. The principle of condescension by covenant applies to 'The first Covenant' as the covenant of works and 'a Second commonly called the Covenant of Grace' in that God reveals himself in the law and the gospel, facilitating a method to obtain eschatological life in both.[16]

Second, this covenantal principle is markedly different from, if not opposite of, the medieval paradigm of grace elevating nature to enable us to merit. Inasmuch as covenantal condescension relates to accommodation and revelation, it is not an ad hoc, extrinsic imposition upon the created order. In fact, the covenant is how God met the created order so that we would be ordered to our prospect of eschatological advancement. The stakes in this interpretation concern how thoroughly the Reformed calibrated our covenant theology in light of medieval problems. For example, Lee Irons argued that the principle of divine condescension in Westminster Confession 7.1 relies upon the reasoning of Scotist voluntarism.[17] His argument is problematic in presuming that God's covenantal condescension in 7.1 entirely respects the works principle of the covenant of works, exclusively addressing the problem of proportionality concerning works and reward. The problem in his presumption becomes clear in that it remains equally true after the fall that creatures still owe

---

15. Richard A. Muller, *Dictionary of Latin and Greek Theological Terms Drawn Principally from Protestant Scholastic Theology*, 2nd ed. (Grand Rapids: Baker Academic, 2017), 4-5.

16. Westminster Confession of Faith 7.2-3; Bower, *Confession of Faith*, 204; VanDrunen, *Divine Covenants and Moral Order*, 15, 90-91.

17. Lee Irons, 'Redefining Merit: An Examination of Medieval Presuppositions in Covenant Theology,' in Howard Griffith and John R. Muether (eds.), *Creator, Redeemer, Consummator: A Festschrift for Meredith G. Kline* (Greenville, SC: Reformed Academic Press, 2000; repr. Eugene, OR: Wipf and Stock, 2007), 259-62.

our obedience unto God but cannot experience him as our blessedness and reward apart from his covenantal condescension. In our case, that condescension comes via the covenant of grace forged upon a radically different principle than the covenant of works.[18] Although the next chapter appreciatively interacts with Irons' concerns in formulating divine justice, covenant, and merit, our more thorough historical understanding of the Westminster Confession's explanation of covenant shows that we should not set it in conflict with those concerns.[19] The confessional idea of covenantal condescension need not suggest a purely voluntarist concept of covenant or the place of works insofar as it includes God's revelation of himself and the means to everlasting life in both the law and the gospel.[20]

As should be obvious, then, accommodation should not be considered equivalent to grace in any meaningful sense. It is certainly not grace in the medieval sense of elevating nature as such. Neither is it grace in the Reformed sense of the renewal of our fallen nature. Even when Reformed theologians have applied the notion of grace to Adam before the fall, they typically qualify it as a different sort of grace than we experience after the fall. Augustine himself emphasized this distinction:

> Did Adam not have God's grace? On the contrary, he had it greatly but of a different kind. He was among blessings which he received by the Creator's goodness …. But the saints in this life to whom pertains that grace of deliverance are among evils from which they cry to God, 'Free us from evil' (Matt. 6:13).[21]

Thus, all things considered, to call prelapsarian accommodation 'grace' seems to play a fast and loose semantic game of equivocation.[22]

---

18. James Ussher, *A Body of Divinitie* (London, 1645), 159; Petrus Van Mastricht, *Theoretical-Practical Theology*, trans. Todd M. Rester, ed. Joel R. Beeke, 7 vol. (Grand Rapids, MI: Reformation Heritage Books, 2017–), 1.3.12.36.

19. Irons comes just short of recognizing this compatibility himself by seeing *only* Westminster Confession 7.1 as in conflict with his view; 'Redefining Merit,' 266-67.

20. William Perkins, *A Golden Chain*, in *The Works of William Perkins*, 10 vol. (Grand Rapids, MI: Reformation Heritage Books, 2014–20), 6:65-66, 151-55.

21. Augustine, *On Rebuke and Grace*, §29, in Jacques Paul Migne (ed.), *Patrologia Cursus Completus: Series Latina*, 221 vol. (Paris, 1844–64), 44:933 (Quid ergo? Adam non habuit Dei gratiam? Imo vero habuit magnam, sed disparem. Ille in bonis erat, quae de bonitate sui Conditoris acceperat: neque enim ea bona et ille suis meritis comparaverat, in quibus prorsus nullum patiebatur malum. Sancti vero in hac vita, ad quos pertinent liberationis haec gratia, in malis sunt, ex quibus elamant ad Deum, *Libera nos a malo* {Matth. 6:13}).

22. Hodge, *Systematic Theology*, 2:357.

This present argument, nevertheless, concerns establishing the *most* felicitous language. Remembering that we ought to focus on realities more than mere signs, some might define 'grace' in a more encompassing sense that includes all divine action. This meaning coheres with how this book implements the term 'supernature.' While emphasizing this potential agreement in concept so that we do not too quickly criticize, this wider use of grace still seems to require a more specific definition in application to soteriology. It then includes an inbuilt potential for confusion, driven by its attempt at terminological breadth.

This potential for confusion suggests that a more precise use of terms is more felicitous. The confessional language may be broad enough to permit that reading of accommodation as connected to grace if so desired – hence the Assembly's debate over the terminology. We should not, however, narrow its meaning further than it demands as to read in structures that we find problematic.[23] This accommodation is about God revealing himself to us as his creatures via a covenant (legal or gospel) to facilitate our way to him as blessedness and reward.[24]

This principle frees us to consider covenantal condescension as more closely related to creation itself, rather than an extrinsic imposition upon the created order. That closer relation helps us avoid Roman theology's bifurcation of the natural and supernatural orders. J. V. Fesko has well pointed out that creation itself is another voluntary condescension that provides the gift of knowing God.[25] This rationale suggests a greater unity between creation and covenant than some have suggested. In the Dutch Reformed tradition, Klaas Schilder denied that nature contributed to the covenant.[26] In Baptist theology, Samuel Renihan posed that all covenants are entirely supernatural and 'not

---

23. R. Scott Clark, 'Do This and Live: Christ's Active Obedience as the Ground of Justification,' in R. Scott Clark (ed.), *Covenant, Justification, and Pastoral Ministry: Essays by the Faculty of Westminster Seminary California* (Phillipsburg, NJ: P&R, 2007), 257-58n95; Fesko, *Adam and the Covenant of Works*, 98-100, 398-400; Perkins, *Catholicity and the Covenant of Works*, 59-66, 103-16.

24. Sutanto, 'Consummation Anyway,' 228-33.

25. Fesko, *Adam and the Covenant of Works*, 389.

26. Klaas Schilder, 'The Covenant of Works and the Covenant of Grace,' in George Harinck, Marinus de Jong, and Richard Mouw (eds.), *The Klaas Schilder Reader* (Bellingham, WA: Lexham Press, 2022), 49-50.

part of the natural created order.' Respectively, since covenants are not natural arrangement, they are entirely positive, making it impossible to assume that any one covenant can inform the structure of another.[27] Aligning with Renihan, Richard Barcellos contended that, 'there were two pre-fall states in which Adam existed – as a reasonable creature of God, owing obedience to his Creator, and as a reasonable creature of God in covenant with Him, owing obedience to his covenantal Lord.'[28] The covenant thus becomes fully ad hoc to human nature rather than a fitting accompaniment for it, veering near to a pure nature view of human constitution. Our covenant fellowship with God becomes an extrinsic addition to nature, divorcing the conditions and reward of the covenant of works from the created order. Barcellos applied the same point about the distance between our created and covenantal status to our eschatological orientation: 'The "voluntary condescension" of God was an act of His kind providence, not formally included in the initial act of man's creation. The promise of "the reward of life" is in addition to man's created status.'[29] That divorce leaves the created order as a version of pure nature in need of a superadded structure to establish the full bounds of religious fellowship with God. The suggestion that the covenant of works was not forged upon Adam's nature but later supplemented Adam's call introduces a version of pure nature – including the temporal gap of the full Franciscan-contra-Thomas variety – wherein we were not constitutionally a religious creature made in covenant with God for spiritual communion with the possibility of heightened experience of it. The covenant of works becomes a Protestant version of the *donum superadditum*. We set a better trajectory by understanding a closer link among our image-bearing status, the law, and our eschatological destiny, harmonizing creation and covenant more closely.

---

27. Samuel Renihan, *The Mystery of Christ: His Covenant and His Kingdom* (Cape Coral, Fl: Founders Press, 2020), 13-19.

28. Richard C. Barcellos, *Getting the Garden Right: Adam's Work and God's Rest in Light of Christ* (Cape Coral, FL: Founders Press, 2017), 43-44.

29. Barcellos, *Getting the Garden Right*, 48. Sometimes Barcellos seems to suggest otherwise when he claims, for example, that 'the eschatological is embedded in the protological' (*Getting the Garden Right*, 72). The two themes seem to run in tension throughout his arguments. Many of those arguments favoring the closer relation of creation and covenant are outstanding.

The Eschatology of Bearing God's Image

We avoid the problem of extrinsicism concerning creation and covenant by considering the fuller theological import of humanity's constitution in God's image. This section argues that the divine image, which is intrinsically part of human nature, demands a certain relationship among the created order, the moral law, and the eschatological order. Adam's original righteousness, which was natural to him as God's image bearer, contains an intrinsic relation to the conditions of the covenant of works and an inherent relation to the prospect of glorified life. The payoff, as Meredith Kline (1922–2007) argued, is that a non-covenantal created order unrelated to our eschatological destiny never existed.[30]

Creation and covenant then stand in significant continuity. The relationship is not as if covenant was divinely bolted onto creation, as if it were adding a more extravagant spoiler onto a sportscar.[31] Rather, creation and covenant relate more like a shoe and its laces: the shoe and laces are not identical with one another as if they can be conflated, but shoes and laces exist for one another. A shoe is not fully formed and functional unless its laces are threaded into the holes, which were crafted into the shoe's design precisely so that laces would fit it. In like manner, the covenant laces up humanity's created order, not as an extrinsic addition but as that which pulls together the features of creation to make them functional toward the ends for which they were designed. Geerhardus Vos stated in crisp form what this section substantiates more exegetically: 'By assuming the positive character of the covenant of works in this sense, we in no way intend to assert that Adam existed even for a single moment outside of the covenant of works … The distinction between natural relationship and the covenant of works is logical and judicial, not temporal.'[32] David VanDrunen, while still managing not to file the concepts of creation and covenant entirely into one another, has stated the relation even more finely in arguing that God created and covenanted with Adam in the same event.[33] Adam's created and

---

30. Kline, *Kingdom Prologue*, 92-93.

31. I feel compelled to note that these spoilers are always tacky.

32. Vos, *Reformed Dogmatics*, 2:32; Herman Witsius, *De Oeconomia Foederum Dei cum Hominibus*, 3rd ed. (1694), 1.2.1.

33. VanDrunen, *Divine Covenants and Moral Order*, 83-86.

covenantal features are mutually informing. They stand entirely together so that his natural endowments meant he was created in and for the covenant without dichotomy.[34]

In this respect, Vos and VanDrunen help us to offer a more refined description of how God's creating Adam relates to his covenanting with him as we consider the language of the Westminster Standards. Westminster Shorter Catechism 9–12 outlines God's *work* of creation, his creation of man, his general *works* of providence, and his 'special *act* of providence' in covenanting with Adam.[35] The language is important because elsewhere in the catechism, the terms 'work' and 'act' distinguish God's transformative and forensic acts. For example, effectual calling and sanctification are both 'works' in applying Christ's benefits to us, but justification and adoption are both 'acts' unto that same end.[36] These distinct terms establish the difference between what God does to change us in a real way and what he does concerning our judicial standing. Bringing that consideration to bear upon Adam's original condition, God performed the *work* of special creation in making the first man Adam from the dust, and performed the *act* of special providence in making a covenant with him. The intent to distinguish these terms seems even clearer as Westminster Shorter Catechism 11 refers generally to 'God's *works* of providence,' and then question 12 immediately switches to the singular 'special *act* of providence' that was the enactment of the covenant of works.

The distinction in confessional language leads us to consider the relation of this creative work and this providential act. Given the defined use of terms, the point of distinguishing the special work of Adam's creation and the special act of providence is not necessarily to indicate that they are separate events. We might think of a judge rapping his gavel. The work of swinging the gavel is distinguishable from the act of finalizing his judicial verdict. Judges can perform the motion of swinging their gavels as even in the courtroom setting they often – or so television dramas tell us – do pound their gavels to regain order in the

---

34. Wilhelmus à Brakel, *The Christian's Reasonable Service*, trans. Bartel Elshout, ed. Joel R. Beeke, 4 vol. (Grand Rapids, MI: Reformation Heritage Books, 1992), 1:384; Fesko, *Adam and the Covenant of Works*, 325-26.

35. Schaff, *Creeds of Christendom*, 3:677-78 (emphasis added).

36. Schaff, *Creeds of Christendom*, 3:682-83.

court, without it being the finalization of a verdict. Certainly, a judge can execute judicial verdicts in other capacities without use of his gavel. In a unique instance, however, the judge performs that work and that act simultaneously in one event. God created many creatures, but only one work of creation was bound to a special act of providence that forged a covenant with the creature being made. Thus, God's work of bringing about real change in the work of creating Adam by fashioning the dust of the earth into the living, breathing divine image bearer is truly distinct from his judicial act of covenanting with Adam.

Precisely because this act of covenant making was intwined within this work of creation and because it forged judicial realities upon natural strata, this *special act* of providence differs from God's other *general works* of providence by being unique in its relation to the work of creation and by being specifically a forensic act. Hence, that distinction of the work of creation from the special act of providence does not require that the work and the act are separate events. As VanDrunen contended, we should 'see the creation of human beings in God's image *as itself* an act of covenant establishment.'[37] From the external perspective, the creative work included the judicial act of special providence. As we saw in Vos, God simultaneously performed the creative work of specially creating Adam and the judicial act of covenanting with him in strict synchronicity.[38] In this way, following Vos, the covenant of works as a special act of providence is judicially and logically but not temporally distinct from the work of creation.[39]

The features of our created order have view to the covenant that supports this interpretation. Stephen Wellum helpfully articulates that God's covenant with Adam must be explained 'in less contractual terms and in more continuity with creation itself.' Drawing attention to the creational features of Adam's sonship, marriage, priest-king mandate, and demand for obedience, all which factor into the covenant between God and Adam, Wellum concluded that the initial covenantal relationship resulted from God creating humanity in his image. He concluded, 'The command, then, given to Adam in Genesis 2:16-17 did not create a

---

37. VanDrunen, *Divine Covenants and Moral Order*, 84-85.

38. Thanks to Lane Tipton, especially in personal correspondence and conversation, for helping me shape this point in a clearer direction.

39. See also Fesko, *Adam and the Covenant of Works*, 184-85, 325-37, 385-88.

"covenant of works" relationship subsequent to creation; instead, Adam, by virtue of his creation as God's image-son, was already in filial relation with his Creator-covenant Lord.[40] Wellum's contention aligns with the present argument that the covenant of works codified creational features so that the covenant did not rise *de novo* from the probationary command about the tree of knowledge of good and evil. Although Wellum previously distanced his view from the Reformed doctrine of the covenant of works, perceiving that it required a broader gap between creation and covenant, some Reformed theologians have formulated the covenant of works in much the same way, as has the version argued in this book.[41] The import of Wellum's argument for the covenant of works becomes obvious in how Michael Horton implemented the themes of sonship, kingship, and image as constitutive for how we should conceive of ourselves as God's covenant servants, summoned by nature to respond properly to our Maker.[42]

The biblical testimony displays the contours of the covenant of works as belonging to creation. Our orientation to the eschatological order is manifest in God's self-deliberation about the creation of humanity. In Genesis 1:26-30, God speaks humanity into existence:

> Then God said, 'Let us make man in our image, after our likeness. And let them have dominion over the fish of the sea and over the birds of the heavens and over the livestock and over all the earth and over every creeping thing that creeps on the earth.'

40. Peter J. Gentry and Stephen J. Wellum, *Kingdom Through Covenant: A Biblical-Theological Understanding of the Covenants*, 2nd ed. (Wheaton, IL: Crossway, 2018), 676; also VanDrunen, *Divine Covenants and Moral Order*, 85-86; cf. Barcellos, *Getting the Garden Right*, 60.

41. Gentry and Wellum, *Kingdom Through Covenant*, 675-77; cf. Stephen J. Wellum, 'Reflections on *Covenant Theology* from a Progressive Covenantal View,' *The Southern Baptist Journal of Theology* 26 no 1 (2022): 171, 175-76, which manifests a much greater reproachment between progressive covenantalism's formulation of God's covenant with Adam and the traditional Reformed doctrine of the covenant of works. For more reflections on the prospect of reproachment between Reformed covenant theology and progressive covenantalism – as well as more extensive argumentation about what differentiates both views from 1689 federalism as hinted above through the interaction with Renihan – see Harrison Perkins, 'Peering over the Fence: Presbyterian Reflections on Baptist Neighbors Doing Covenant Theology,' *The Southern Baptist Journal of Theology* (forthcoming).

42. Michael S. Horton, *Lord and Servant: A Covenant Christology* (Louisville, KY: Westminster John Knox Press, 2005), 104-12.

So God created man in his own image,
in the image of God he created him;
male and female he created them.

And God blessed them. And God said to them, 'Be fruitful and multiply and fill the earth and subdue it, and have dominion over the fish of the sea and over the birds of the heavens and over every living thing that moves on the earth.' And God said, 'Behold, I have given you every plant yielding seed that is on the face of all the earth, and every tree with seed in its fruit. You shall have them for food. And to every beast of the earth and to every bird of the heavens and to everything that creeps on the earth, everything that has the breath of life, I have given every green plant for food.'

Throughout the creation narrative, God's spoken fiats are loaded with oath-related freight. His declarations concerning humanity's creation invested us with the divine image.[43]

God's declaration over his creation of man as his image bearers carried purposive force. An innate connection binds creation in God's image and the task to have dominion. The grammatical link between 'let us make' and 'let them have dominion' expresses the idea that the task to exercise dominion flows from being made in God's image:

וַיֹּאמֶר אֱלֹהִים נַעֲשֶׂה אָדָם בְּצַלְמֵנוּ כִּדְמוּתֵנוּ וְיִרְדּוּ

Then God said, 'Let us make man in our image, according to our likeness *so that* they would have dominion …'

As Peter Gentry summarized the work of Hebraists Paul Joüon and Thomas Lamdin, the verb construction of a cohortative followed by an imperfect marks purpose or result.[44] The two prepositional phrases בְּצַלְמֵנוּ (in our image) and כִּדְמוּתֵנוּ (according to our likeness) then indicate that God created humanity to correspond to himself in some way. This correspondence again pertains to the doctrine of analogy wherein God made us to represent him and his goodness at the creaturely level. Hence, our analogical status as image bearers entails that God's purpose for our existence includes representing the divine king by ruling creation at the creaturely level.[45]

---

43. Kline, *Kingdom Prologue*, 15-18.

44. Gentry and Wellum, *Kingdom through Covenant*, 223.

45. Michael A. Wilkinson, *Crowned with Glory and Honor: A Chalcedonian Anthropology* (Studies in Historical and Systematic Theology: Bellingham, WA: Lexham Press, 2024), 58-61; Gentry and Wellum, *Kingdom through Covenant*, 222-38; VanDrunen, *Divine Covenants and Moral Order*, 61-67.

This connection marks our orientation to the eschatological order as God executed his creative intent for us and tied it with his pronouncement of blessing and commissioning. Within the same creative fiat by which God spoke humanity into existence, he worded our constitution to be angled toward something greater than what we first had, namely, to fill the earth and have dominion over every creature. Theologians throughout the ages have recognized that the divine image has structural features in certain human capacities (e.g. our intellect, our soul, our ethical sense), but it also has functional aspects.[46] For one, Adam's kingly remit was tied to our image bearing function, as Psalm 8:5-6 explicitly connects God's having 'crowned him' to how he had 'given him dominion.'[47] Moreover, the dominion mandate was not static since, although the garden was initially limited to a defined area in Eden, Adam was meant to expand his garden-kingdom to fill the whole earth.

The commission toward expansion has the obvious implication of eschatological advancement. The garden was God's first temple. To expand it meant to build the space of divine presence.[48] This aspiration was in-created in the human heart as one thread of the tapestry of being God's image. Since the garden imagery, especially the tree of life, returns in Revelation 21 to characterize the new creation after Christ returns, the garden's encompassing of the world encapsulates the consummate state.[49] God's work of speaking Adam into being as his image bearer wove eschatological prospects into

---

46. Turrettinus, *Institutio*, 5.10.15, 22; Fesko, *Adam and the Covenant of Works*, 322-23; VanDrunen, *Divine Covenants and Moral Order*, 40, 68; Anthony A. Hoekema, *Created in God's Image* (Grand Rapids, MI: Eerdmans, 1986), 68-73.

47. David VanDrunen, 'Natural Law and the Works Principle under Adam and Moses,' in Bryan D. Estelle, J. V. Fesko, and David VanDrunen (eds.), *The Law is Not of Faith: Essays on Works and Grace in the Mosaic Covenant* (Phillipsburg, NJ: P&R, 2009), 294-95; Gentry and Wellum, *Kingdom Through Covenant*, 230-32, 668-69; Hodge, *Systematic Theology*, 2:102-3; VanDrunen, *Divine Covenants and Moral Order*, 41-53; Kline, *Kingdom Prologue*, 42-51; Hoekema, *Created in God's Image*, 78-80.

48. G. K. Beale, *The Temple and the Church's Mission: A Biblical Theology of the Dwelling Place of God* (New Studies in Biblical Theology; Downers Grove, IL: IVP, 2004), 66-121; Kline, *Kingdom Prologue*, 47-49.

49. Beale, *Temple and the Church's Mission*, 313-34; for more specific links of the garden and the tree's connection to the covenant of works, see Harrison Perkins, *Reformed Covenant Theology: A Systematic Introduction* (Bellingham, WA: Lexham Press, 2024), 81-87.

human constitution, as Paul explained, 'If there is a natural body, there is also a spiritual body' (1 Cor. 15:44). As he cited Adam's first condition from Genesis 2:7 to ground this progression, Paul took it as a given of the created order that our created state in the natural body had the prospect to advance to eschatological state in the spiritual body, namely glorification.[50] In this respect, God's *work* of creation supplied our natural orientation to that eschatological prospect while his simultaneous judicial *act* of special providence to covenant with Adam supplied how we are ordered to that end.[51]

Humanity's natural orientation to the eschatological order appears further in our prospect of entering rest with God, established even at creation. G. K. Beale explained that, in ancient Near Eastern thought, temples were places of divine rest. They were the location where the divine being reposed after conquering opposing forces.[52] In Psalm 132:13-14, God announced that he made the Jerusalem temple his resting place as he reigned over his people through the Davidic throne:

> For the LORD has chosen Zion;
> he has desired it for his dwelling place:
> '*This is my resting place forever*;
> here I will dwell, for I have desired it.'

The connection also applies to the creation events. When God finished the work of creation, having subdued chaos and disorder and having completed his cosmic temple, he rested: 'Thus the heavens and the earth were finished, and all the host of them. And on the seventh day God finished his work that he had done, *and he rested* on the seventh day from all his work that he had done' (Gen. 2:1-2).[53] God's work resulted in his rest, not as if God were tired or ceased acting altogether, but in that he completed the task which he had set for himself, declaring it good.

---

50. 1 Corinthians 15:42-46 is one of the richest passages connecting the created order and our eschatological destiny, but I have treated it at length elsewhere and will not repeat those arguments here; Perkins, *Reformed Covenant Theology*, 69-73.

51. Thanks again to Lane Tipton for helping me wordsmith a more refined statement of this specific relation.

52. Beale, *Temple and the Church's Mission*, 60-66.

53. Kline, *Kingdom Prologue*, 26-30.

God's act of temple building followed by rest pertains to the eschatological orientation of the divine image. As we have seen, Adam's task to expand the garden was also an act of temple building. God worded him into existence tying the commission to fill the earth with the holy space of the garden-temple to the functional aspect of bearing God's image. Inasmuch as Adam's temple-building task mirrored God's own cosmic-level temple construction, it should likewise have a mirroring result of rest upon completion. Hence, God not only himself rested on the seventh day of creation but consecrated it for observance at the creaturely level as well to mark our prospect for eschatological rest upon fulfillment of the covenant of works: 'So God blessed the seventh day and made it holy, because on it God rested from all his work that he had done in creation.' (Gen. 2:3) Disobedience prevents us from obtaining that rest: 'And to whom did he swear that they would not enter his rest, but to those who were disobedient?' (Heb. 3:18) All the same, the same prospect of eschatological rest that was imbedded in our constitution as God's image bearers still awaits those for whom Christ fulfills the covenant of works as the second Adam. The result is that those in Christ by faith will join God in consummate rest: 'So then, there remains a Sabbath rest for the people of God, for whoever has entered God's rest has also rested from his works as God did from his' (Heb. 4:9-10). The eschatological dimension of our image-bearing constitution means that, just as we are meant to follow God in the pattern of his works, we are meant to follow him into his rest.[54] In other words, Adam's covenant had eschatological rest as its goal.[55] Christ completed his works after completing his mission of redemption as the second Adam. Christ's entry into this eschatological rest grounds our rest from being under the law and is why we strive forward to enter the rest that Christ has won for us.

This discussion's main contribution to our overall argument is that the eschatological order was not bolted onto the created order. It was

---

54. Geerhardus Vos, *Biblical Theology: Old and New Testaments* (Grand Rapids, MI: Eerdmans, 1948; repr. East Peoria, IL: The Banner of Truth Trust, 2020), 138-43; Kline, *Kingdom Prologue*, 33-40, 74-90; Horton, *Lord and Servant*, 128-30; VanDrunen, 'Natural Law and the Works Principle under Adam and Moses,' 295-96; VanDrunen, *Divine Covenants and Moral Order*, 69-74.

55. Gentry and Wellum, *Kingdom Through Covenant*, 244-53.

not a superadded afterthought but was hardwired into our natural constitution as God's image bearers. Eschatology is one intersection of creation and covenant.[56] Adam's created order was oriented toward the eschatological order by the very form in which God worded him into existence. The eschatological order's direct connection to the covenant of works as its proffered reward is well-known and non-controversial.[57] The additional aspect to incorporate into this eschatology is its connection to Adam's image-bearing status. Johannes Cocceius helpfully captured the upshot: 'Man, therefore, by the very fact that he was made according to God's image, has been constituted as in a covenant with God.'[58] Although the present argument refines Cocceius' point to avoid equating the image of God and the covenant, the eschatological order, which was the prospective reward in the covenant of works, was woven into the functional aspects of Adam's image-bearer constitution. In other words, the covenant of works provides rationale for why our supernatural destiny is not added to the natural order by grace but is baked into the created order.[59] The eschatological order is supernatural in the sense of exceeding our present state of affairs. It was not, however, extrinsically added to as a destiny foreign to our original constitution. God's work of creation endowed human nature with the prospect of eschatological advancement while his simultaneous act of special providence in covenanting with Adam judicially furnished the promise for how to reach that prospect.

Judicial Aspects of Eschatological Image Bearing

The prospect of joining God in his rest after mirroring his work raises the question about the nature of that work and its connection to the divine image. This section argues that the *imago Dei* and original righteousness stand in specific connection. Although the eschatologically oriented task of expanding the garden-temple displays the forward-looking aspect of our task as the divine-image bearers to reflect God at the creaturely level,

---

56. Hodge, *Systematic Theology*, 2:92.

57. For more detailed explanation and defense of this point, see Perkins, *Reformed Covenant Theology*, 47-76.

58. Johannes Cocceius, *Commentarius in Pentateuchum, Josuam, et Librum Judicum* (Amsterdam, 1669), 38 (Homo igitur eo ipso, quod fuit factus ad imaginem Dei, fuit constitutus quasi in foedere Dei).

59. VanDrunen, *Divine Covenants and Moral Order*, 74-77.

the deeper ethical dimension of our task is to reflect God's character at the creaturely level by conducting ourselves in holiness.[60]

The need to follow God in his work signals the connection between the image of God and Adam's original righteousness. In Genesis 1:27, God's declaration concerning humanity's creation, 'image,' and 'likeness' form a parallelism in the Hebrew text. John Calvin rightly interpreted these terms as two ways of expressing the same basic reality rather than two distinct aspects of what it means to be human in relation to God.[61] Bearing God's image means to represent him on the creaturely horizon. We have the purpose to project his character (in analogous fashion) into creation through our constitution and conduct. Reflecting God necessarily includes the obligation to manifest his righteousness.

The Reformed confessional tradition has recognized that our created order included natural righteousness as part of what it meant to be God's image bearers. The Canons of Dort 3/4.1 say, 'Man from the beginning was created in God's image, adorned with true and salutary knowledge in his mind of his Creator and spiritual realities, and righteousness in his will and heart, purity in every affection, and therefore was entirely holy.'[62] Westminster Larger Catechism 17 describes how God created man, stating that he 'made them after his own image, in knowledge, righteousnesse, and holinesse, having the Law of God written in their hearts, and power to fulfill it, with dominion over the creatures.'[63] The idea contains some self-evident biblical points as Paul wrote that our new creation means that we are 'being renewed in knowledge *after the image of its creator*' (Col. 3:10) and 'created *after the likeness of God* in true righteousness and holiness' (Eph. 4:24).[64] A deeper connection still

---

60. Rightly, Barcellos, *Getting the Garden Right*, 137-44; Hoekema, *Created in God's Image*, 66-68.

61. John Calvin, *Institutes of the Christian Religion*, trans. Ford Lewis Battles, ed. John T. McNeill, 2 vol. (The Library of Christian Classics; Louisville, KY: Westminster John Knox, 1960), 1.15.3; Hodge, *Systematic Theology*, 2:96-97; Hoekema, *Created in God's Image*, 13-14.

62. Schaff, *Creeds of Christendom*, 3:564 (Homo ab initio ad imaginem Dei conditus vera et salutari sui Creatoris et rerum spiritualium notitia in mente, et justitia in voluntate et corde, puritate in omnibus affectibus exornatus, adeoque totus sanctus fuit).

63. John R. Bower, *The Larger Catechism: A Critical Text and Introduction* (Principal Documents of the Westminster Assembly; Grand Rapids, MI: Reformation Heritage Books, 2010), 69.

64. See also Hodge, *Systematic Theology*, 2:99-102; Calvin, *Institutes*, 1.15.4 (emphasis added).

links this original righteousness and human nature as such, pertaining especially to our image-bearing constitution.[65]

Inasmuch as human nature is intrinsically stamped with the divine image, we have knowledge of the moral law written on our hearts. The relation stands because the moral law is simply a summary of God's holy character. The link of the image and the moral law fuses our created order with a legal dimension in addition to our orientation to the eschatological order.[66] Paul wrote in Romans 2:13-16:

> For it is not the hearers of the law who are righteous before God, but the doers of the law who will be justified. For when Gentiles, who do not have the law, by nature do what the law requires, they are a law to themselves, even though they do not have the law. They show that the work of the law is written on their hearts, while their conscience also bears witness, and their conflicting thoughts accuse or even excuse them on that day when, according to my gospel, God judges the secrets of men by Christ Jesus.

Justification, a legal declaration that obedience has satisfied the demands of righteousness, requires doing – fulfilling and completing – the law.[67] Insofar as justification pronounces *the completion* of the law's demand for obedience, it is eschatological in nature. That nature is clear from Paul's point that it concerns the day of judgment at Christ's return. Because our justification is grounded in Christ's fulfillment of the law for us, received by faith, it is a present *and permanent* benefit. Since Christ achieved perfect righteousness and imputes it to us, our present justification is the eschatological verdict applied now by faith. Thus, our orientation to the eschatological order, which we saw above is tied to our natural constitution as God's image bearers, is intrinsically legal in shape.[68]

Further, this legal shape of our eschatological end is itself branded into our very nature as God's image bearers. Anthony Hoekema

---

65. Vos, *Reformed Dogmatics*, 2:12; VanDrunen, 'Natural Law and the Works Principle under Adam and Moses,' 292-94.

66. For further exposition of the connection of image of God and original righteousness, see Perkins, *Reformed Covenant Theology*, 20-24.

67. For exegetical defense of this interpretation of Romans 2:13, see Perkins, *Reformed Covenant Theology*, 449-58.

68. VanDrunen, *Divine Covenants and Moral Order*, 231-51; VanDrunen, 'Natural Law and the Works Principle under Adam and Moses,' 296-301; Fesko, *Adam and the Covenant of Works*, 161-81, 323-25.

(1913–88) noted the significant and explicit biblical evidence that we still bear the divine image after the fall, meaning that sin has damaged but not removed God's likeness.[69] Paul highlighted that even Gentiles who had not heard any special revelation of God's law still knew its basic standards because it is, even after the fall, written on our hearts giving function to our conscience. Zacharius Ursinus connected the dots concerning our wider discussion about the relation of the created and eschatological orders, informing how we should think about the issue of nature and supernature: 'The law contains the natural covenant, which God began with men in creation, that is, it is known by men by nature and requires from us perfect obedience toward God and promises everlasting life to those who keep it but threatens everlasting death to those who do not keep it.'[70] John Owen argued much the same, affirming that, 'Man *in his creation*, with respect to the ends of God therein, was *constituted under a covenant*' and 'this covenant belonged unto the law of creation' so that 'it belongs unto and is inseparable from the law thereof.'[71] The law as the legal criteria for obtaining the eschatological order was imbedded in our created order, drawing tight lines between our nature and our relation to supernatural realities and ends.[72]

Our ontological condition of bearing God's image entails that original righteousness is part and parcel of our created order, also binding us to the criteria for eschatological advancement. Although the next chapter takes up the relation between creation, law, and covenantal conditions in relation to that heavenly reward, we see now that the legal conditions for that reward are none other than the perfect observance of the law that is *naturally* hardwired into our original constitution. In other words, original righteousness is natural to us, bound into our awareness of

---

69. Hoekema, *Created in God's Image*, 15-32.

70. Zacharius Ursinus, *Catechesis, Summa Theologiae*, in *Opera Theologica*, 3 vol. (Heidelberg, 1612), 1:14 (Lex continet foedus naturale, in creatione a Deo cum hominibus initum, hoc est, natura hominibus nota est, & requirit a nobis perfectam obedientiam erga Deum, & praestantibus eam, promittit vitam aeternam, non praestantibus minatur aeternas poenas).

71. John Owen, *Exercitations concerning the Name, Original, Nature, Use, and Continuance of a Day of Sacred Rest*, 3.10, in *The Works of John Owen, D.D.*, ed. William H. Goold, 20 vol. (Edinburgh: T&T Clark, 1862), 19:337 (first emphasis added; second italics original).

72. Horton, *Lord and Servant*, 100-3.

God's character which necessarily accompanies our constitution as his image bearers, not superadded to our nature by supernatural grace. Our investigation of even God's specially revealed stipulations will clarify and confirm this point.

Creation and Covenant

Despite these intimate connections, creation and covenant cannot be collapsed into an identical or exactly co-terminus concept. The divine image means that our created order is oriented toward the eschatological order in a covenantal way that is not in every way equivalent to nature. So, Vos noted that 'The Sabbath brings this principle of the eschatological structure of history to bear upon the mind of man after a symbolical and a typical fashion ..... The so-called "Covenant of Works" was nothing but an embodiment of the Sabbatical principle.'[73] Kline further explained that God's *appointment* of the seventh day, a creation fixture, as the sabbath ordinance marking our trajectory toward the eschatological order 'highlighted aspects of the creation order that were *distinctly covenantal*.'[74] The distinction is fine-toothed but needed.

The sabbath provides a helpful entryway into this discussion as it highlights the distinction and the unity of the natural and positive aspects of the covenant of works. Owen drew the connection in remarking concerning the image of God that 'it was not possible that such a creature should be produced, and not lie under an obligation unto all those duties *which the nature of God and his own, and the relation of the one to the other*, made necessary.'[75] Our relation to God as his image bearers entailed certain obligations imbedded in having that status as his creaturely analogue. Owen continued, 'Under this consideration alone, it was required, by the *law of man's creation*, that some time be separated unto the solemn *expression of his obedience*, and due performance of the worship that God required of him.'[76] Image bearers then have a *natural*

---

73. Vos, *Biblical Theology*, 140.

74. Kline, *Kingdom Prologue*, 19 (emphasis added); Ussher, *Body of Divinitie*, 124; Mastricht, *Theoretical-Practical Theology*, 1.3.12.18; Perkins, *Reformed Covenant Theology*, 78-81.

75. Owen, *Exercitations concerning ... a Day of Sacred Rest*, 3.10, in *Works*, 19:19:336-37 (emphasis added).

76. Owen, *Exercitations concerning ... a Day of Sacred Rest*, 3.10, in *Works*, 19:337 (first italics original; second emphasis added).

duty to set aside appropriate time for divine worship. That natural duty, however, requires some sort of positive prescription to establish when that time is.[77] In this instance, the necessity of that positive prescription of its time is true even if it has a certain theological fittingness as is the case for the seventh-day sabbath before Christ's coming pointing to the prospect of earning eschatological rest, and is the case for the Lord's Day on the first day of the week as the Christian sabbath, showing that we begin our work already enjoying the guarantee of eschatological rest in Christ.[78]

The sabbath then shows that positive commands do not conflict with natural obligations and even often clarify and focus them. Accordingly, Owen explained, 'although it should be true ... that moral and natural duties depend on and have their formal reason from the nature of God and man, yet it doth not follow that we do, or may, by the sole light of nature, know what doth so arise, with the due bound and just consequences of it.'[79] Just because a law is naturally binding or a relation naturally stands does not mean that we always know about it, its full extent, or its most fitting application naturally. In some cases, special revelation or positive command may address, clarify, and focus rather than supplement what is natural. With this consideration in mind, we turn to those features of the created order that were *distinctly* covenantal, or that are specially revelatory or positive while still remaining bound to the natural aspects of the covenant of works.[80]

---

77. Vos, *Reformed Dogmatics*, 2:44, 47.

78. Owen, *Exercitations concerning ... a Day of Sacred Rest*, 3.19-20, in *Works*, 19:345-46.

79. Owen, *Exercitations concerning ... a Day of Sacred Rest*, 3.14, in *Works*, 19:342.

80. In hindsight, I wish I had included this coordinate in my previous argument for the abiding validity of the moral law in relation to the fourth commandment; Perkins, *Reformed Covenant Theology*, 34-40. When I described the 'sabbath principle,' my contention was precisely Owen's position that our natural constitution as bearers of the divine image includes the obligation to set aside due time for worship of the Creator. Perhaps more pointedly than the other nine, the fourth commandment has both elements of natural obligation combined with a positive prescription. Respectively, many theologians in the past have seen it as a 'mixed' command composed of both natural and ceremonial aspects. Owen helpfully identified the natural obligation to set aside appropriate time for worship and God's positive prescription of the day. My view of the sabbath principle is that this natural obligation for set-aside time to worship abides but the positive prescription of day has changed from the seventh day to the first day of the week, when Christ rose from the grave, meaning that the Lord's Day is to be observed until Christ's return 'as the Christian Sabbath.' Westminster Confession of Faith 21.7; Bower, *Confession of Faith*, 221. I hope this clarification might contribute to the ongoing

The first reason against complete conflation of creation and covenant is that Adam did not stand for himself alone in the covenant of works but represented all his posterity as well.[81] In Romans 5:18-19, Paul explained this connection: 'Thus, therefore, in the same way that one trespass resulted in condemnation for all men, so also one act of righteousness results in justification unto life for all men because just as by the one man's disobedience the many were constituted as sinners, so by the one man's obedience the many will be constituted as righteous' (my translation). Although Adam had a plainly natural link to his posterity as the first father of every human person, the covenant circumscribed this natural role to include his function to represent them legally to obtain eschatological reward for them as well.[82] The created order of Adam's parentage covenantally related to the eschatological order.[83] Thus, the positive aspect of Adam's federal headship did not, strictly speaking, supplement his relationship to his posterity but *focused* his natural obligation to father and to be a good father by ordering it to the natural orientation toward eschatological advancement for the entire race.

The second reason that creation and covenant cannot be entirely conflated relates to the probationary command against eating from the tree of knowledge of good and evil. Westminster Confession 4.2 conjoins the natural aspects of the covenant with this special mandate, outlining how God created us 'indued with knowledge, righteousnesse and true holinesse, after his own Image; having the Law of God written in their hearts, and power to fulfill it' and still, 'Beside this Law written in their hearts, they received a command, not to eat of the tree of the Knowledge of good and evil, which whiles they kept, they were happy in

---

conversation with progressive covenantalism about what it means to set the sabbath command in its appropriate covenantal setting. Thanks to my friends Steve Wellum and Richard Lucas for our correspondence via email and in person about this topic.

81. Westminster Confession 7.2; Bower, *Confession of Faith*, 204; Westminster Larger Catechism 22; Bower, *Larger Catechism*, 70; Westminster Shorter Catechism 16; Schaff, *Creeds of Christendom*, 3:679; Ussher, *Body of Divinitie*, 142-43; Mastricht, *Theoretical-Practical Theology*, 1.3.9.34; Vos, *Reformed Dogmatics*, 2:31; Fesko, *Adam and the Covenant of Works*, 326-27.

82. Westminster Confession 6.3; Bower, *Confession of Faith*, 203; Vos, *Reformed Dogmatics*, 2:32-33, 42-43.

83. Kline, *Kingdom Prologue*, 73.

their Communion with God, and had Dominion over the Creatures.'[84] In Genesis 2:15-17, God declared this tree's role in Adam's covenantal life:

> The Lord God took the man and put him in the garden of Eden to work it and keep it. And the Lord God commanded the man, saying, 'You may surely eat of every tree of the garden, but of the tree of the knowledge of good and evil you shall not eat, for in the day that you eat of it you shall surely die.'

Lest we think that this command goes purely beyond Adam's natural remit, we should remember that God spoke Adam's constitution into being, conjoining it to his relationship to the plants of the garden. Adam's status as the divine image bearer then already correlated to his relationship to the covenant in his creational commission to have dominion over and expand the garden kingdom itself.

Furthermore, this tree command is not at all disconnected from Adam's requirement to fulfill the moral law as the condition of the covenant of works. God appointed the tree, covenantally, to represent Adam's *natural* obligation, showing why the covenant of works is both built on nature and has *ex pacto* features. The tree's function to focus Adam's natural obligations is perhaps clearest in the covenant's penalty. In Romans 1:20, Paul explained why Gentiles are accountable to God: 'For his invisible attributes, namely, his eternal power and divine nature, have been clearly perceived, ever since the creation of the world, in the things that have been made. So they are without excuse.' Every human being is without excuse because of what we know according to general revelation. Paul's discussion of how we all stand condemned by what we know as it is revealed 'in the things that have been made' culminates in how even those who violate general revelation most heinously 'know God's righteous decree that those who practice such things deserve to die' (Rom. 1:32). According to general revelation, which of course concerns our natural obligations, death is the penalty for sin. In the special revelation of the covenant of works about the tree, God warned that 'in the day that you eat of it you shall surely *die*' (Gen. 2:17). Thus, nature and the covenant agree and align that the penalty for sin is death. The tree command merely focused Adam's natural obligations even regarding the penalty for transgression.

---

84. Bower, *Confession of Faith*, 201.

The tree functioned to focus, not supplement, Adam's natural obligations concerning his need to fulfill his positive duties as well. In the ancient church, Tertullian (*c.* 155–220) argued that the command concerning the tree encapsulated all of Adam's responsibilities concerning the natural law:

> For at the world's beginning, God gave a law to Adam himself and to Eve, that they should not eat of the fruit from the tree planted in the middle of the garden; that if they did otherwise, they would certainly die (Gen. 2:7). This law would have been sufficient for them had it been kept. For *in this law* given to Adam, we recognize *the foundation of every command that was later set forth given through Moses*, that is: 'Love the Lord your God from your whole heart and by your whole soul' (Deut. 6:5), and, 'Love your neighbor as yourself' (Lev. 19:18), and, 'Do not murder, do not commit adultery, do not steal, do not bear false witness. Honor your father and mother' (Exod. 20:12-17), and 'do not covet what belongs to another' (Deut. 5:16-21). For the primordial law was given to Adam and Eve in paradise *as the womb of all God's commands*. In sum, if they had loved the Lord their God, they would not have acted against his command; if they had loved their neighbor, that is they would not have murdered themselves by cutting themselves off from immortality by acting against God's command. They would likewise have abstained from theft if they had not secretly tasted from the tree's fruit (Gen. 3:6), nor had they longed to hide themselves under the tree from the Lord God's sight (Gen. 3:8), nor would they have become partakers of the devil's false assertion by believing him that they would become like God (Gen. 3:8), and thus they would not have offended God, as Father, who formed them from the dust of the earth as if from the womb of a mother, if they had not lusted after another, they would not have tasted of the forbidden fruit. Therefore, in this general and primordial law of God, which God sanctioned to be observed in the tree's fruit, every command of the law, which was later specially imposed, was put forth.[85]

---

85. Tertullian, *Adversus Judeos*, §2, in Jacques Paul Migne (ed.), *Patrologia Cursus Completus: Series Latina*, 221 vol. (Paris, 1844–64), 2:599-600 (emphasis added; Namque in principio mundi, ipsi Adae et Evae legem dedit, ne de fructu arboris plantatae in medio paradisi ederent; quod si contra fecissent, morte morerentur (Gen. II. 7): quae lex eis sufficeret si esset custodita. In hac enim lege Adae data, omnia praecepti condita recognoscimus quae postea pullulaverunt data per Moysen, id est, *Diliges Dominum Deum tuum de toto corde tuo, et ex tota anima tua* (Deut., VI. 5); et. *Diliges proximum tibi tanquam te* (Levit. XIX. 18): et, *Non occides, non moechaberis, non furaberis, falsam testimonium non dices. Honora patrem tuum et matrem* (Exod., XX, 12 17): et,

By showing how God's prohibition against the tree of knowledge summed up Adam's every obligation to the natural law, Tertullian demonstrated that covenant and creation do not compete but cohere in God's decreed providence.[86] Nonetheless, this tree prohibition was a positive rather than entirely natural command. It functioned to set temporal limits upon Adam's probationary period to bring his covenantal obedience to consummation.[87] God appointed this positive law, which had no inherent reason besides divine ordination, to apply and test Adam's obedience to the moral law.[88]

Before progressing too quickly, we need to round out Tertullian's point. His glaring omission was not connecting the second and fourth commandments to the tree precept. At a basic level, Reformed theology confesses that the first four commandments pertain to the worship of God, making Adam's refusal to worship God by keeping his ordinances a violation of the whole first table.[89] We can be more specific in attaching significance from each command to Adam's transgression of the tree prohibition. For both, we must consider how Satan tempted Adam and Eve, contending – contrary to God's revelation – that 'You will not surely die. For God knows that when you eat of it your eyes will be

---

Alienum non concupisces (Deut., V. 16-21). Primordialis lex est enim data Adae et Evae in paradiso, quasi matrix omnium praeceptorum Dei. Denique, si Dominum Deum suum dilexissent, contra praeceptum ejus non fecissent: si proximum diligerent, id est semetipsos homocidum non commisissent, excidendo de immortalitate, faciendo contra Dei praeceptum; a furto quoque abstinuissent, si de fructu arboris clam non degustassent (Gen. III. 6), nec a conspectus Domini Dei sui sub arbore delitescere gestissent (ibid. 8): nec falsam asseveranti diabolo participes efficerentur, credendo ei quod similes Dei essent futuri (ibid. 8): atque ita nec Deum offendissent, ut patrem, qui eos de limo terrae quasi ex utero matris figuraverat: si alienum non concupissent, de fructu illicito non gustassent. Igitur in hac generali et primordiali Dei lege, quam in arboris fructu observari Deus sanxerat, omnia praecepti legis posterioris specialiter indita germinaverunt).

86. Reformed theologians have made the same connection between the tree and the moral law: Johannes Polyander, 'On the Fall of Adam,' in Dolf te Velde (ed.), *Synopsis Purioris Theologiae Volume 1/Disputations 1–23* (Leiden: Brill, 2015), 341; Hodge, *Systematic Theology*, 2:119-20; Mastricht, *Theoretical-Practical Theology*, 1.3.11.5; Turrettinus, *Institutio*, 8.4.3-5; Bavinck, *Reformed Dogmatics*, 2:572; John Murray, 'The Adamic Administration,' in *Collected Writings of John Murray*, 4 vol. (Edinburgh: The Banner of Truth Trust, 1976–82), 2:57.

87. Mastricht, *Theoretical-Practical Theology*, 1.3.9.37-38; 1.3.11.9; 1.3.12.2.C.2r, 11, 29-30; Kline, *Kingdom Prologue*, 103-7.

88. Vos, *Reformed Dogmatics*, 2:48-49.

89. Westminster Larger Catechism 102; Bower, *Larger Catechism*, 86.

opened, and you will be like God, knowing good and evil' (Gen. 3:4-5). The lure that, upon eating, Adam would 'be like God' is critical. Adam's violation of the tree command broke the second commandment in that his action was express idolatry – the heart of the prohibition against images. Rather than imaging God as God made him to do, he spiraled into self-worship, hoping to replace God on the ultimate throne of this garden-temple, so broke the law written on our hearts against making idols.[90] Adam's violation of the tree command broke the fourth commandment by attempting to circumvent the pattern of following God in his work only then to obtain eschatological rest. As above, the sabbath crowned the creation week as the mark of having completed the temple-building task, so achieving rest. Satan's temptation that 'you will be like God' drove Adam and Eve's eating of the forbidden fruit, showing how Adam attempted to obtain the glorified state, the eschatological order, by discarding the prerequisite of preceding work.

The tree culminated Adam's responsibility not to an arbitrary positive law but to the whole natural law by encapsulating the natural conditions of the covenant of works in one symbolic precept.[91] This positive law, as all good positive laws should, participated with a certain – in this case sacramental – fashion in God's moral law of nature.[92] As VanDrunen has summarized, 'The commands of [Gen.] 2:15–17 are best understood … not as *supplementing* Adam's natural moral obligation but as *focusing* it.'[93] James Ussher tied this point crisply to covenantal categories by arguing that 'The two trees' in Eden had the purpose to serve as 'outward seales' added to the law's covenantal premise of 'Doe this, and thou shalt live,' so that Adam 'might by the sight of them be put in mind of those things whereof they were signs and seales.'[94] Rather than adding some totally new responsibility, the tree of knowledge then

---

90. Horton, *Lord and Servant*, 122; Hoekema, *Created in God's Image*, 67, 84.

91. Franciscus Turrettinus, *Institutio Theologiae Elencticae*, 3 vol. (Geneva, 1679–85), 8.3.11; Mastricht, *Theoretical-Practical Theology*, 1.3.12.18, 29; Fesko, *Adam and the Covenant of Works*, 329-30, 334-35; VanDrunen, *Divine Covenants and Moral Order*, 62-66, 85-86. For fuller discussion of the probationary command within the covenant of works, see Perkins, *Reformed Covenant Theology*, 41-45.

92. Andrew Davison, *Participation in God: A Study in Christian Doctrine and Metaphysics* (Cambridge: Cambridge University Press, 2019), 362-65.

93. VanDrunen, *Divine Covenants and Moral Order*, 85 (italics original).

94. Ussher, *Body of Divinitie*, 125.

covenantally encapsulated Adam's natural obligations so that he would be visibly reminded of his duties by this probationary seal.[95] The tree command pinpointed Adam's broad obligation to the natural law in a narrow and concrete positive command. The tree of knowledge was a sign of those natural obligations under probation.[96]

Grace in the Covenant of Works?

The preceding discussion mounted a biblical defense that humanity was created with the intrinsic constitution of bearing God's image, irremovably plaiting our nature with original righteousness and relating it to the eschatological order. The point is that the created order, our nature, orients us toward even supernatural realities. Our nature is truly damaged and not entirely intact if original righteousness is marred. The image of God remains part of our constitution in a wider sense (Gen. 9:5-7) but is distorted in a narrower, moral sense. That distortion of the image means that the unrighteous use of our faculties is unnatural, since original righteousness was concreated and natural to us.[97] Rather than landing in some state of pure nature with adequately functioning capacities for our natural ends that do not pertain to supernatural destiny, our created nature becomes sub-natural on account of sin. Original righteousness was so intrinsic to our constitution after God's likeness that the loss of that moral excellence corrupts humanity's constitution as God's image.[98] God had ordered our very created state toward the covenantal realities of obedience and our eschatological destiny. The loss of our natural means for obtaining eschatological reward entails a fatal wound to the natural order.[99] This section unpacks how these principles of Reformed theology motivate us to reject the notion that the covenant of works required the imposition of extrinsic grace.

Inasmuch as Reformed theology sees that nature is supernaturally charged by God's design for his image bearers, we best formulate the covenant of works by stating this relation of the created order and the eschatological order while limiting the application of grace to the

---

95. Fesko, *Adam and the Covenant of Works*, 184-85.

96. For more on the probationary aspect, see Perkins, *Reformed Covenant Theology*, 41-45.

97. Thomas, *Summa Theologica*, 1a2ae.85.1–2.

98. Bavinck, *Reformed Dogmatics*, 2:551. Thanks to Carlton Wynne for this reference.

99. Vos, *Reformed Dogmatics*, 2:13-15.

redemptive order. Hans Boersma rightly lamented the theological outlook that desacralizes nature.[100] Boersma's main point that nature cannot be truly and rightly understood apart from its relation to God as a real rather than extrinsic or nominal connection is extremely salient.[101] With Boersma, unless nature has some participation in God, namely in analogous fashion as contingent upon divine ideas, then nature would not itself be truly revelatory of supernatural truths about God.

This metaphysical grounding for our supernatural orientation has further support in the specific shape of the Creator-creature distinction. Andrew Davison has made a helpful and complementary point to Boersma's in two steps. First, he argued that our metaphysically *analogous* participation in God's being as a creaturely fitting manner of imitating God's perfections protects the Creator-creature distinction.[102] After all, the alternative to analogously participating in God's being in a creaturely fitting way – which denies that participation can ever mean that God is the *material* cause of creatures – is to have our own standalone being, which amounts to creaturely autonomy at the ontological level. The result of that autonomy would be that God and creatures have their being in a univocal way, which destroys the transcendent view of God that participation aims to protect.[103] This understanding of participation, then, simply means that creatures have no aseity, and that God alone is *a se*; we have no original being but have only that being which God gives to us. Second, that we as creatures have contingent and dependent being rather than self-contained and self-derived being marks how we must bear God's likeness.[104] God made humanity to manifest his likeness by analogously imitating his ethical perfections in a specific way as his

---

100. Hans Boersma, *Heavenly Participation: The Weaving of a Sacramental Tapestry* (Grand Rapids, MI: Eerdmans, 2011), 19-99.

101. Boersma, *Heavenly Participation*, 103-90. Boersma's terminology of 'sacramental ontology' is not ideal from a Reformed perspective. His point is that creation points beyond itself, functioning as a sign, to sacred realities. The terminology is unideal because sacramental language is best used in a narrower sense in reference to appointed features of the covenant, signifying *specific* divine realities. For similar concern about Boersma's terminology, see Michael Allen, *Grounded in Heaven: Recentering Christian Hope and Life on God* (Grand Rapids, MI: Eerdmans, 2018), 45n18. This quibbling over signs should not detract from the fundamental agreement about realities.

102. Davison, *Participation in God*, 135-97.

103. Davison, *Participation in God*, 1-83.

104. Davison, *Participation in God*, 84-112.

image bearers. This purpose imbeds in us the final cause of God's glory, which means that God himself is likewise our final end.[105] Thus, our nature as those made to imitate God in a special way according to our manner of creaturely-fitting participation entails that our nature has its ultimate end beyond itself in supernatural communion with God, which is simply glorification in the eschatological order. In this way, we return to our claim that our Reformed view of the covenant of works truly has a stronger ontology than the Roman doctrine of pure nature with its need for the *donum superadditum*.

Nature then has God as the archetypal cause of all the perfections we experience in ectypal fashion. This relation of dependence is why we can know God through his effects in creation: his perfections are the archetypal template for the analogous reflections of his perfections. We as his image bearers are included in those effects, entailing that knowledge of God as our cause is innately woven into our being. The next chapter takes issue with Boersma's and Davison's criticisms of the forensic aspects of Reformed soteriology concerning how they apply participation to justification and merit. This chapter, however, furthers their more basic point about the needed real connection between nature and supernature. It shows that the best way to articulate the covenant of works is with a close connection of the creational and covenantal realities rather than by the Roman method of attaching supernatural ends to nature via superadded grace. Nature's revelatory capacity has been critical in Reformed theology.[106] In the Roman pure nature school, the ontological cast of grace strips nature of its own Godward valence by asserting that its supernatural orientation must be superadded.[107]

The significance of Adam's natural integrity forms the heart of our argument. Our above exploration of the image of God contended that God's law was written naturally on our hearts, also as the standard of the covenant of works. Our earlier historical investigations showed that the premise of the Roman view is that Adam's nature needed to

---

105. Davison, *Participation in God*, 113-31.

106. Geerhardus Vos, *Natural Theology*, trans. Albert Gootjes (Grand Rapids, MI: Reformation Heritage Books, 2022), 3-17; Bavinck, *Reformed Dogmatics*, 1:283-322, 356-59.

107. e.g. Andrew Dean Swafford, *Nature and Grace: A New Approach to Thomistic Ressourcement* (Eugene, OR: Pickwick, 2014), 17.

be elevated by infused grace for him to have supernatural communion with God, meaning that God would have to strengthen Adam's natural ability to equip him with the 'infused virtue' to perform the 'surpassing good' required to obtain the beatific vision.[108] By contrast, Westminster Larger Catechism 17 affirms that God 'created man, male and female' so 'made them after his own image, in knowledge, righteousness, and holiness, having *the Law of God* written in their hearts, and *power to fulfill it*.'[109] Inasmuch as the Reformed saw this natural law as the basic condition of the covenant of works, the affirmation of natural ability to fulfill that law forges disagreement with the claim that God had to elevate Adam's nature to make him able to perform works of 'surpassing good' meritorious of our supernatural end.

The point is that Reformed theology ties the performance of *natural* good to the obtaining of our eschatological end. Although the next chapter addresses how we ought to connect that natural good to heavenly reward, our present point is that God equipped us *by nature* to do that which he required of us to enter the eschatological order. Thomas Aquinas affirmed Adam's natural fitness for communion with God along with the potential for heightened communion by works.[110] Although Thomas had a logical distinction between nature and infused grace, his view had the practical outcome that Adam could perform the surpassing good to obtain his supernatural end from the beginning because God built this superadded gift into his constitution by creation.[111] Nonetheless, the Reformed more resemble Henry of Ghent's view that Adam's strength to fulfill the law unto his supernatural end was purely *concreatum* rather than *superadditum*.[112] Heidelberg Catechism 9 asks, 'Does not God,

---

108. Thomas, *Summa Theologica*, 1.12.5, 1a2ae.109.2.

109. Bower, *Larger Catechism*, 69 (emphasis added).

110. Thomas, *Summa Theologica*, 1a2ae.109.3.

111. Christopher M. Cullen, SJ, 'Bonaventure on nature Before Grace: A Historical Moment Reconsidered,' *American Catholic Philosophical Quarterly* 85 no 1 (2011): 163.

112. John Calvin, *Institutes of the Christian Religion*, trans. Ford Lewis Battles, ed. John T. McNeill, 2 vol. (The Library of Christian Classics; Louisville, KY: Westminster John Knox, 1960), 1.15.2; 2.12.6; Zacharias Ursinus, *The Commentary of Dr. Zacharias Ursinus on the Heidelberg Catechism*, trans. G.W. Williard, 4th American ed. (Cincinnati, OH: Elm Street Printing, 1888), 30-31; Robert Rollock, *Tractatus De Vocatione Efficaci* (Edinburgh, 1597), 8-10; Witsius, *De Oeconomia*, 1.2.11-14; Mastricht, *Theoretical-Practical Theology*, 1.3.12.17; Bavinck, *Reformed Dogmatics*, 2:571-72; Brakel, *Christian's Reasonable Service*, 1:323-26; Turrettinus, *Institutio*, 5.10.6-9.

then, wrong man by requiring of him in his law that which he can not perform?' answering, 'No; for God so made man that he could perform it; but man, through the instigation of the devil, by willful disobedience deprived himself and all his posterity of this power.'[113] The Irish Articles (1615), article 21, states:

> Man being at the beginning created according to the image of God (which consisted especially in the Wisedom of his minde, & the true Holynesse of his free will) had the covenant of the law ingrafted in his heart: whereby God did promise unto him everlasting life, upon condition that he performed entire and perfect obedience unto his Commaundements, *according to that measure of strength wherewith he was endued in his creation*, and threatned death unto him if he did not performe the same.[114]

Even if individual theologians might argue to the contrary, our *confessional* statements affirm that we were *naturally* able, according to natural original righteousness, to fulfill the law that was the standard of obtaining eschatological reward in the covenant of works.

One necessary coordinate is that only someone possessing original righteousness can perform works that are adequate to please God. Despite Reformed theology's closer alignment to Thomas' Augustinianism, we strongly reject his teaching that a restored sinner can again perform *meritorious* works. Our reason is that sinners – regenerate or not – cannot earn blessings from God by our works.[115] This disagreement loads nature with supernatural value in wild disagreement with nominalists, such as Gabriel Biel, who argued a view of merit even for salvation wherein God accepts whatever best but imperfect works a sinner performs as meritorious for grace and justification.[116] In this respect, at least Martin

---

113. Schaff, *Creeds of Christendom*, 3:310.

114. *Articles of Religion Agreed upon the Archbishops and Bishops, and the Rest of the Clergie of Ireland, in the Convocation Holden at Dublin in the yeare of 1615 for the avoiding of diviersities of opinions: And the establishing of consent touching true Religion* (Dublin: John Franckton, 1615), sig. B2v (emphasis added).

115. Westminster Confession 16.5; in Bower, *Confession of Faith*, 214; Rollock, *Tractatus De Vocatione Efficaci*, 14-15, 54-55; William Perkins, *A Reformed Catholike* (Cambridge, 1598), 104-5; John Brown, *The life of justification opened* (Utrecht, 1695), 481; Thomas, *Summa Theologica*, 1a2ae.109.2; Paul Helm, *Calvin at the Centre* (New York, NY: Oxford University Press, 2010), 309-22.

116. Heiko A. Oberman, *The Harvest of Medieval Theology: Gabriel Biel and Late Medieval Nominalism*, 3rd ed. (Grand Rapids, MI: Baker Academic, 2000), 120-84; Horton, *Justification*, 1:131-62.

Bucer sided with Thomas as one of the 'sounder scholastics' against the Franciscans 'when they [the Augustinian scholastics] deny that one can merit "first grace" and that the Holy Spirit is required for prevenient and cooperating grace, and that "we [the Reformed] do not disagree with the scholastics, who are somewhat more sound."'[117] The Reformed perceived the Augustinian heritage as more faithful in the closer alignment of our original, unfallen ability with the works that are sufficient for reward.[118]

Reformed theologians have historically recognized that certain configurations of grace and works make the covenant of grace too much like the covenant of works. This problem was true especially when the pre- and post-fall situations are not sufficiently differentiated. The construction that most exemplifies this issue is that man, before and after the fall, could work himself from pure nature into a graced state whereby further cooperation with grace in works result in justification and eventual obtaining heaven. This danger, transposed into Protestant language, is that regeneration effects the graced state of a renewed nature enabling a believer by grace to perform works that warrant their entry into everlasting life. In other words, making grace necessary for nature as such to enable us to fulfill the law adequately for eschatological reward inverts the law-gospel relationship in a way that makes everlasting life always dependent upon the merit of grace-enabled works.

The distinction between natural and superadded righteousness highlights Reformed theology's disagreement with Roman Catholicism concerning how extensively the fall damaged human nature.[119] For the Reformed, when Adam fell into sin, the loss of that original righteousness corrupted something essential to human nature. That corruption inherently disabled our ability to perform the works required for eschatological life.[120] Some early modern writers, such as

---

117. David S. Sytsma, 'Sixteenth-Century Reformed Reception of Aquinas,' in Matthew Levering and Marcus Plested (eds.), *The Oxford Handbook of the Reception of Aquinas* (Oxford: Oxford University Press, 2021), 130.

118. Sytsma, 'Sixteenth-Century Reformed Reception of Aquinas,' 121-38.

119. Karim Schelkens and Marcel Gielis, 'From Driedo to Bellarmine: The Concept of Pure Nature in the 16th Century,' *Augustiniana* 57 no 3/4 (2007): 435, 438-40.

120. Turrettinus, *Institutio*, 5.9.1-11, 5.11.1-17; 8.6.10; 9.7.14-17; 9.11.7; Vos, *Reformed Dogmatics*, 2:12-15; Bavinck, *Reformed Dogmatics*, 2:539-53, 571-72; 3:516-17, 573-79; Steven J. Duby, *God in Himself: Scripture, Metaphysics, and the Task of Christian Theology*

Herman Witsius and Pierre du Moulin (1568–1658), criticized Jacob Arminius' view of the covenant of grace on these terms, arguing that he had not adequately reckoned with sin's thorough damage to our nature.[121] Thus, the Reformed emphasized a radical difference between how Adam's works before the fall and how our works after the fall relate to everlasting blessing.

The Reformed affirmation that Adam by his natural strength could fulfill the covenant of works sidelines any notion that Adam had to advance from pure nature to the state of superadded righteousness before he could perform works pertaining to higher communion with God. Adam's nature was sufficient by creation for performing the righteousness required to fulfill the covenant of works, meaning God's grace did not need to supplement his ability. God, with no obligation, kindly promised to reward Adam with a higher reward for his works but did not supplement Adam's abilities to help him perform the duties required in the covenant.

Reformed authors from the early modern period until today attest this point. Robert Rollock (1555–99) argued that Adam's natural ability to fulfill the law was in fact the basis of the covenant of works:

> The covenant of works, which can be called both legal or natural, is founded in nature, which was in creation pure and holy, and in God's law, which was engraved in man's heart. For inasmuch as God created human nature pure and holy after his own image, and having engraved his law in his mind, he made a covenant with man in which he promised everlasting life to him under the condition of holy and good works, which should evidently accord with the holiness and goodness of his created nature,

---

(Studies in Christian Doctrine and Scripture; Downers Grove, IL: IVP Academic, 2019), 112-13, 123-25; Robert Letham, *Systematic Theology* (Wheaton, IL: Crossway, 2019), 329-32, 383-84, 397; Carl R. Trueman, 'Atonement and the Covenant of Redemption: John Owen on the Nature of Christ's Satisfaction,' in David Gibson and Jonathan Gibson (eds.), *From Heaven He Came and Sought Her: Definite Atonement in Historical, Biblical, Theological, and Pastoral Perspective* (Wheaton, IL: Crossway, 2013), 215-17; Paul Helm, 'Nature and Grace,' in Manfred Svensson and David VanDrunen (eds.), *Aquinas Among the Protestants* (Hoboken, NJ: Wiley Blackwell, 2018), 238-39; Fesko, *Adam and the Covenant of Works*, 385-88; Perkins, *Catholicity and the Covenant of Works*, 50-73, 89-90, 103-16.

121. J. V. Fesko, *The Covenant of Works: The Origins, Development, and Reception of the Doctrine* (Oxford Studies in Historical Theology; New York, NY: Oxford University Press, 2020), 52-53.

and should be conformed to his law. Moreover, that nature shaped by holiness, righteousness, and knowledge of the law, was the beginning of the covenant of works or ordered by it because it could not stand with God's righteousness to make a covenant under the condition of good works and perfect obedience to the law, except for the cardinal premise that he created his nature good and holy, and engraved his law upon him, from which these good works must proceed.[122]

Following Ursinus and anticipating the Irish Articles and Cocceius, Rollock grounded God's act of making of the covenant of works in God's work of creating humanity with our particular nature of bearing God's image, entailing knowledge of, obligation to, and ability to keep God's law.[123] Francis Roberts even argued that this natural ability is the precise reason why we are without excuse before God's judgment seat: 'Adam was fully able to keep covenant. Therefore Adam is left without all apology for his breach of covenant. He must needs justify God, and condemn himself under severest penalties for breach of covenant, for God gave him power completely to keep it.'[124] The natural ability to perform the law that is the standard of the covenant of works is a critical feature of Reformed understanding.

The integrity of Adam's original nature shows how our created order was compatible with supernatural realities and fit to obtain the eschatological order. In his infinite kindness and goodness, God covenanted with Adam to offer reward on the basis of works, underscoring God's rich and deep generosity. Still, God premised that covenant on human nature as he created it, without any need to supplement Adam's

---

122. Rollock, *Tractatus De Vocatione Efficaci*, 9 (Foedus operum, quod & legale sive naturale vocari postest, fundamentum est in natura quae fuit in creatione pura sanctaque, & in lege Dei, quae in prima creatione insculpta fuit hominis cordi. Postquam enim Deus naturam hominis creavit ad imaginem suam puram & sanctam, legemque suam insculpsit menti ipsius, percussit cum homine foedus, in quo promiset ei vitam aeternam sub conditione operum sanctorum & bonorum, quae nimirum responderent naturae creatae sanctitati & bonitati, legique ipsius essent conformia. Quod autem natura informata sanctitate, justitia, & legis notitia, sit fundamentum foederis operum vel ex eo apparet, quo non stetisset cum justitia Dei percutere foedus sub condtione bonorum operum & obedientiae legis perfectae, nisi ipse naturam prius creasset bonam sanctamq[ue], eiq[ue] legem suam insculpsisset, ex qua bona illa opera proficisci oporteret).

123. *Articles*, sig. B2v (article 21); Cocceius, *Commentarius in Pentateuchum*, 38; VanDrunen, *Divine Covenants and Moral Order*, 83-86.

124. Francis Roberts, *Mysterium & Medulla Bibliorum: The Mysterie and Marrow of the Bible, viz. God's Covenants with Man* (London, 1657), 35.

nature with grace to fulfill the covenant's demands.[125] Francis Turretin draws this connection, explaining that God's covenant with Adam 'as his creature in integrity concerning the giving of happiness and everlasting life under the condition of perfect and personal obedience,' was called the natural covenant 'because it was founded in human nature as first created, and on his integrity or strength.'[126] To our point about nature and grace, he asserted that the covenant 'added nothing above nature and the condition which man had from creation' and 'depended upon natural strength and obedience, which in accordance with that strength he owed to perform.'[127] Adding a promise is, after all, not the same as adding something to the constitution of our nature. The covenant of works then cohered with rather than supplemented our created order.

In Defense of the Redemptive Order

The theological upshot of drawing this tight connection between nature and the covenant of works is to protect the integrity of grace itself, specifically concerning the nature of salvation. In his analysis of grace in Thomas Aquinas' doctrine of predestination, even while remaining cautiously appreciative, Carl Trueman well contended that we best avoid confusion on critical issues by limiting our use of grace to the post-fall situation.[128] Ligon Duncan well summarized the stakes in this limited application of grace to the redemptive order: 'Grace in its fullness is God's saving blessing to us despite our demerit. Thus there can be no grace (in the fullest sense of the word) without sin, since

---

125. Roberts, *Mysterium & Medulla Bibliorum*, 33-35; Michael Horton, *Justification*, 2 vol. (Grand Rapids: Zondervan, 2018), 2:61-62.

126. Turrettinus, *Institutio*, 8.3.5 (Foedus naturae est, quod Deus Creator cum homine integro, tanquam sua creatura pactus est, de illo felicitate, & vita aeterna donando sub conditione perfectae & personalis obedientiae: Vocatur *naturale*, non ab obligatione naturali, quae nulla est Dei erga hominem; sed quia in natura hominis, prout primitus a Deo condita est, & in illius integritate, seu viribus fundatur).

127. Turrettinus, *Institutio*, 8.6.9b [This Latin edition misnumbered this section as a second 8.6.9, which should be 8.6.10] (Foedus naturale non ideo dicitur, quod nihil conferat supra naturam, & conditionem, quam homo habuerat a Creatione, sed quia nitebatur naturae viribus, & obediential, quam juxta illas praestare debuit). James Cassidy noted how Turretin reserved the specific term 'grace' for the covenant of grace rather than applying it in an improper sense to the covenant of works; James J. Cassidy, 'Francis Turretin and Barthianism,' *Confessional Presbyterian* 5 (2009): 202.

128. Carl R. Trueman, *Grace Alone: Salvation as a Gift of God* (The Five Solas Series; Grand Rapids, MI: Zondervan, 2017), 98-102.

grace is the love and goodness of God to his people in spite of their sin and their deserving of curse, judgment, and disfavor.'[129] Duncan concluded, 'rightly understood, the covenant of works protects the grace of the covenant of grace. So, grace is opposed to sin rather than human nature.'[130] In other words, the proper relation of nature and grace is necessary for the proper relation of grace and salvation.

This entailment rises clearly from how Reformed soteriology should differ from at least one aspect of Roman Catholic views on nature and grace. In the Roman paradigm, drawing heavily upon Aristotelian ideas, their concept of nature means that God owes whatever is strictly needed according to the intrinsic principles of a given nature. As considered in chapter four, Rome formally condemned the teaching of Michael Baius precisely because he espoused a strong version of Adam's prelapsarian integrity, lacking a need for elevating grace, and that the fall's effects extensively damaged human nature itself. The controversy around Baius' and Cornelius Jansen's views, which Rome found too accommodating in resemblance to Protestant theology, helped further the development of the pure nature tradition because their views entailed that grace was *strictly* necessary after the fall, therefore not itself gratuitous.[131]

This historical issue highlights why Protestant soteriology is stronger when we limit the need for, and application of, grace to only the redemptive order. The Roman response to Baius is incorrect to pose that grace is *strictly*, that is absolutely, necessary for nature after the fall. Rather, grace is *contingently* necessary, given God's decision to save sinners. The true alternative to our concreated supernatural end of the eschatological beatific vision is *damnation*, not a fulfillment of some penultimate natural end. God does not *unalterably* owe the beatific vision even to creatures who have it as our ultimate, natural end. God can justly deprive us of that end *as the penalty* for sin. All humanity will encounter God's direct presence for eternity, distinguished by whether we experience his everlasting wrath or everlasting blessing (2 Thess. 1:5-10). God does not owe grace to sinners, since we need grace

---

129. Ligon Duncan, 'Foreword,' in Guy Prentiss Waters, J. Nicholas Reid, and John R. Muether (eds.), *Covenant Theology: Biblical, Theological, and Historical Perspectives* (Wheaton, IL: Crossway, 2020), 29.

130. Duncan, 'Foreword,' 29; Bavinck, *Reformed Dogmatics*, 3:516-17, 573-79.

131. Swafford, *Nature and Grace*, 41-49.

only because we wrecked our nature as God created it by corrupting it through sin. On Protestant principles, God freely bestows grace to redeem us from the penalty and power of our sin. Hence grace is never a strictly necessary aspect of human nature.[132] We sinners need grace to obtain our supernatural end because of the problem we introduced through sin, not because of the limitations belonging to the proportions of our created nature.

Despite a recurring emphasis in the Reformed tradition that God built the conditions of the covenant of works on Adam's natural ability, not all agreed about whether the covenant included grace. In this respect, Fesko's carefully calibrated discussion about the use of the nature-grace distinction in early modern debates about the covenant of works recounted that there were (at least) two different ways of explaining this issue.[133] On the one hand, Arminius argued that Adam needed grace to perform the duties required of him, meaning that Adam needed grace concerning *his ability* in the covenant of works. This application of grace seemingly resembled medieval views that Adam needed grace to elevate his nature, prompting Witsius and du Moulin's criticism that Arminius was too close to Franciscan views of works and grace.[134] Arminius had employed the same terms (*naturalia, supernaturalia, gratiam superinfusam*) that Bonaventure implemented in this discussion.[135] They levied pushback against Arminius on account of their understanding that a right view of the covenant of works protects a proper understanding of the covenant of grace, which Arminius did not protect.[136]

On the other hand, some Reformed theologians, even in responding to Arminius, maintained a Thomistic understanding of the natural and supernatural orders, positing that God's grace superadded supernatural

---

132. Swafford, *Nature and Grace*, 42-43.

133. Fesko, *Covenant of Works*, 52-57.

134. See also, Wilhelmus à Brakel, *The Christian's Reasonable Service*, trans. Bartel Elshout, ed. Joel R. Beeke, 4 vol. (Grand Rapids, MI: Reformation Heritage Books, 1992), 1:355.

135. Bonaventure, *Commentary on the Sentences*, bk.2, dist. 29, art. 2. q. 2; in A.C. Peltier (ed.), *S.R.E Cardinalis S. Bonaventure ... Opera Omnia*, 15 vol. (Paris: Ludovicus Vivès, 1864–71), 3:316-17.

136. J. V. Fesko, *Arminius and the Reformed Tradition: Grace and the Doctrine of Salvation* (Reformed Historical Theological Studies; Grand Rapids, MI: Reformation Heritage Books, 2022), 13-29.

faculties or strength to fulfill the covenant of works. The previous chapter analyzed Francis Junius' interaction with Arminius wherein he argued that the supernatural was superadded to the natural order. Outside the continent, Samuel Rutherford (1600–61) also responded to Arminius by implementing grace as a way to explain Adam's path to blessed reward. Some of Rutherford's argument simply reflected the Augustinian doctrine of *auxilium*, noting that God did not owe Adam 'acts of the Lord's free predetermination to cause him to stand' so that 'the first command did engage Adam to rely upon God for strength and divine influence, as promised by any covenant.'[137] Although perhaps hued by his broader outlook on nature and grace, his core point aligned with the fundamentals of Augustinian and Reformed thought about our creaturely state of contingency.[138]

Rutherford also aligned with much early-modern Thomistic thought concerning ends necessarily being proportionately owed to nature. He thought that 'obeying God, was to Adam so created a connaturall end' so that every covenant must have 'some acts and outgoings of grace.'[139] Rutherford took issue with Arminius' contention that Adam's obedience could lead only to a natural end precisely because Adam could be eligible for a supernatural reward by the free promise of God over and above anything directly connected to nature.[140] Still, because he affirmed that God created Adam in supernatural grace, Rutherford had no place to consider Adam in pure nature. Rutherford's differing from Arminius comes to greater clarity in the object of elevating grace: whereas Arminius thought that infused grace elevated Adam's *person*, Rutherford thought that grace elevated Adam's *acts*.[141]

This difference concerning person and acts as the focus of grace in the covenant of works marks their paradigmatic variance. Arminius' view aligned with the Franciscan trajectory in Scotus' notion of *acceptatio personarum* as the premise of merit, which is exactly why Fesko detected the presence of the Franciscan Pactum in Arminius' theology. Rutherford's

---

137. Samuel Rutherford, *Influences of the Life of Grace* (London, 1658), 3.

138. Rutherford, *Influences*, 4-10, 15-17, 20.

139. Samuel Rutherford, *The Covenant of Life Opened; or, A Treatise on the Covenant of Grace* (Edinburgh, 1655), 22.

140. Rutherford, *Covenant of Life Opened*, 22-23.

141. Fesko, *Covenant of Works*, 56.

view resembled Thomas' doctrine of *ordinatio* that God predestines the elect to render meritorious obedience unto the beatific vision.[142] In Reformed fashion, Rutherford upheld the integrity of Adam's created nature since that grace in the covenant of works did not concern Adam's ability to perform the law's requirements. Rutherford's application of grace to the covenant of works regarded its reward.[143] Rutherford's point was that Adam naturally owed God obedience to the law – and had the ability to render that obedience – so God was not intrinsically obligated to reward Adam for it. In this sense, the covenant of works contained grace, not regarding Adam's ability, but addressing the disproportion between Adam's works and his potential reward.[144] The Reformed did not roundly reject Rutherford's view of grace in the covenant of works, and most who did speak of pre-fall grace seemingly intended this sense.[145]

Junius and Rutherford as exemplars of a Reformed appropriation of the Thomistic distinction of natural and supernatural ends were both supralapsarian. Rutherford's supralapsarianism has been well documented.[146] Junius' supralapsarianism played directly into his correspondence with Arminius. His initial complaint about Arminius' objection to the idea that God's act of election considered man as not yet made was that an eternal operation of God must precede the creature's existence. Otherwise, we introduce contingency into God's being, raising the exact issues tied into the *auxilium* debate.[147] Furthermore, Junius argued that no cause in the creature can determine God's decree, else again contingency be introduced. This point relativizes the factor of whether God considered man as fallen or unfallen in his act of election and reprobation.[148] Specifying his position further than the

---

142. Fesko, *Arminius and the Reformed Tradition*, 13-29.

143. Fesko, *Covenant of Works*, 53-57, 95-99.

144. Rutherford, *Covenant of Life Opened*, 40-47.

145. e.g. John Ball, *A Treatise on the Covenant of Grace* (London, 1645), 3, 7-11; Anthony Burgess, *Vindiciae Legis* (London, 1646), 113-14.

146. Guy M. Richard, 'Samuel Rutherford's Supralapsarianism Revealed: A Key to the Lapsarian Position of the Westminster Confession?' *Scottish Journal of Theology* 59 no 1 (2006): 27-44; Guy M. Richard, *The Supremacy of God in the Theology of Samuel Rutherford* (Studies in Christian History and Thought; Eugene, OR: Wipf and Stock, 2009), 116-31.

147. Jacob Arminius, *Amica cum Francisco Iunio de praedestinatione per literas habita collatio* (Leiden: 1613), 43-48.

148. Arminius, *de praedestinatione*, 48-51.

previous chapter, Junius noted that *in puris naturalibus* 'does not exclude supernatural aspects, which God joined with Adam, but is opposed to sin, which arrived later, and to the corruption of natural aspects.'[149] In other words, although Junius accepted the distinction of natural and supernatural orders, he saw them as coming together in opposition to the fallen condition. His view of pure nature then seriously differed from the Franciscan tradition that saw pure nature as fully intact even respecting sin's effects. The further upshot is that, in Junius' thought, nature in its own principles is not entirely closed off to supernature. His appropriation of the natural and supernatural orders therefore differs also from the later pure nature tradition as promulgated by Cajetan and Bellarmine. In contrast to Arminius, Junius saw the object of predestination as man in pure nature without respect to sin as a factor within God's decree of election and reprobation.[150] The coordination of supralapsarianism and an appropriation of the distinction of natural and supernatural orders is potentially a fruitful avenue for future research to explore.

Although the historical data is not uniform, the trajectory of Reformed theologians who denied grace in the covenant of works altogether best serves our theological construction. In their context, these theologians had greatest cause to resist Roman theology, at least on these issues pertaining to nature and grace. In contending against Robert Bellarmine, as the previous chapter explored, David Paraeus acknowledged that Adam depended on God and argued against any grace in the covenant of works.[151] James Ussher, the primary author of the Irish Articles, drew upon this exact point to distinguish the covenant of works and the covenant of grace, writing, 'Which of them was first? The Law, for it was given to Adam in his integrity, when the promise of *grace was hidden* in God.'[152] He noted agreement between the covenant of works and the covenant of grace in 'that they be both of God, and

---

149. Arminius, *de praedestinatione*, 91 (*In puris naturalibus*, si qui dicunt, non excludunt supernaturalia, which cum Adamo communicavit Deus, sed pecato (quod supervenit postea) & naturalibus corruptis opponitur).

150. Arminius, *de praedestinatione*, 92-95.

151. David Paraeus, *De Gratia Primi Hominis Explicatus and Castigatus* (Heidelberg, 1612), 36-67.

152. Ussher, *Body of Divinitie*, 124 (emphasis added); quoting Thomas Cartwright, *Christian Religion* (London 1611), 68.

declare one kind of righteousnesse, though they differ in offering it unto us.' The covenants differ in that:

> the Law was grounded on mans own righteousnesse, requiring of every man in his own person perfect obedience; *Deut. 26:26* and in default for satisfaction everlasting punishment, *Ezek. 18:14*; *Gal. 3:10, 12.* but the Gospell is grounded on the righteousnesse of Christ, admitting payment and performance by another in behalfe of so many as receive it, *Gal. 3:13, 14.*[153]

As Ussher stated in covenantal categories, the inclusion of grace before the fall endangers the principles of law and gospel as distinct premises for relating to God for righteousness and life. Grace is God's freely given favor *to sinners* and not part of the pre-fall situation.

This denial of grace before the fall does not entail the Franciscan position of 'pure nature' prior to grace since the paradigm is completely different. The Franciscans denied that Adam was created with infused grace but affirmed that he needed to obtain grace as that which orders humanity to an end beyond our nature and enables us to perform works that are meritorious of such supernatural reward. In contrast, the Reformed theologians who deny that grace was needed before the fall intend to short-circuit the entire premise of the Franciscan argument. Witsius underscored Adam's natural ability to obtain everlasting reward without further infusion of grace:

> God entrusted his own image to man to be kept as the all-surpassing deposit of heaven, and, if kept pure and holy, the down payment of the greater good. To that end, he built him with sufficient strength from his very composition, to such degree so that he had no need of habitual grace in addition.[154]

In contrast to the Franciscan view that Adam needed to obtain infused grace in order to have power to perform meritorious works worthy of supernatural life, Witsius posited that God built Adam with 'sufficient strength from his very composition' for the purpose of obtaining heaven even that 'he had *no need of habitual grace* in addition.'[155] The Franciscan

---

153. Ussher, *Body of Divinitie*, 159.

154. Witsius, *De Oeconomia*, 1.2.13 (Imaginem hanc sui, ceu praestantissimum coeli depositum, &, si caste sancteque servaretur, majoris boni arrham, custodiendam homini Deus commiserat: quem eum in finem ab ipso conditu sufficientibus viribus instruxerat, adeo ut nulla gratia habituali praeterea opus haberet).

155. Witsius, *De Oeconomia*, 1.2.13 (emphasis added).

denial of pre-fall grace was *provisional* as Adam had to obtain the grace he needed to fulfill the law. In contrast, the Reformed denial of pre-fall grace was *categorical* because God accommodated the terms of the covenant of works precisely to Adam's nature so that he could fulfill the conditions by his natural strength.

God was *good and kind* to Adam in the covenant of works to promise a reward on the condition of the works that Adam would have been obligated to render anyway. God's promise to reward Adam surely flows 'from the very nature of the divine goodness, that God gives himself to be enjoyed by a holy creature, proportionable to its state.'[156] At the same time, in light of an increased understanding of medieval theology combined with recent debates within Reformed circles concerning various movements that have undermined the doctrine of justification, it seems clearer and easier to distinguish God's pre-fall goodness from his grace to fallen sinners.[157] Herman Bavinck (1854–1921), in his characteristic concern for creation's goodness and order, explained the covenant of works:

> It was called a 'covenant of nature,' not because it was deemed to flow automatically and naturally from the nature of God or the nature of man, but because the foundation on which the covenant rested, that is, the moral law, was known to man by nature, and because it was made with man in his original state and could be kept by man with the powers bestowed on him in the creation, *without the assistance of supernatural grace*.[158]

He further clarified: 'In its real sense, it [grace] was not necessary in the case of Adam before the fall but has only become necessary as a result

---

156. Witsius, *De Oeconomia*, 1.4.19; also 1.4.19-22; see also Vos, *Reformed Dogmatics*, 2:32.

157. Concerning those recent debates, see Guy Prentiss Waters, *Justification and the New Perspective on Paul: A Review and Response* (Phillipsburg, NJ: P&R, 2004); Guy Prentiss Waters, *The Federal Vision and Covenant Theology: A Comparative Analysis* (Phillipsburg, NJ: P&R, 2006); Cornelis Venema, *The Gospel of Free Acceptance in Christ: An Assessment of the Reformation and New Perspectives on Paul* (Edinburgh: Banner of Truth Trust, 2006); R. Scott Clark, 'Do This and Live: Christ's Active Obedience as the Ground of Justification,' in R. Scott Clark (ed.), *Covenant, Justification, and Pastoral Ministry: Essays by the Faculty of Westminster Seminary California* (Phillipsburg, NJ: P&R, 2007), 241-43, 254-58; Michael Horton, 'Which Covenant Theology?' in *Covenant, Justification, and Pastoral Ministry*, 197-228; Michael S. Horton, *Covenant and Salvation: Union with Christ* (Louisville, KY: Westminster John Knox Press, 2007); Cornelis P. Venema, *Christ and Covenant Theology: Essays on Election, Republication, and the Covenants* (Phillipsburg, NJ: P&R, 2017), 285-364; Estelle et al, 'Report ... to Study Republication,' 5-6.

158. Bavinck, *Reformed Dogmatics*, 2:567 (emphasis added).

of sin.'[159] In other words, grace comes to its fullest and best meaning when we restrict its application to the redemptive order to uphold both the goodness and integrity of the created order as well as to block the introduction of legalism into salvation.[160]

Conclusion

This chapter addressed the problem of extrinsicism. The notion of pure nature with a supernatural end *post hoc* superadded to human existence makes our orientation toward eschatological, consummate communion with God extraneous to God's more basic, natural purposes for creating us. On the front end, we should not discard the distinction of the natural and supernatural orders but should apply it precisely and correctly. Concerning the issues of revelation, we know that some truths are beyond our natural capacity to learn without special revelation. In this respect, we ought to accept that the natural and supernatural orders shape the way we do theology. Johann Heinrich Alsted helps us on this point: 'Though not everything that is true can be demonstrated by reason, since truth is more extensive than the ends of reason (for some truths are of greater magnitude than reason, if we look to the kingdom of grace), nevertheless no war exists between reason and faith, nature and grace.'[161] For this reason, 'we believe in the supernatural order in order to understand.'[162] This need for faith in what special revelation reveals has ground in nature because 'natural knowledge of the creator God is twofold, implanted and acquired.'[163] God is by definition *supernatural*, and so is the way that we know many things about God and our relationship with him. Thus, we have to be receptive to supernatural realities that must be delivered to us within the realm of nature.[164]

---

159. Bavinck, *Reformed Dogmatics*, 3:577.

160. Bavinck, *Reformed Dogmatics*, 3:516-17, 573-79.

161. Johann Heinrich Alsted, *Theologia Naturalis* (Frankfurt, 1615), 4 (Etsi non omne, quidquid verum est, ratione demonstrari potest, cum multo latius pateant Veritatis, quam rationis fines (est enim veritatas maioris amplitudinis quam ratio, si spectemus regnum Gratiae.) nullum tamen bellum est inter rationem ac fidem, naturam ac gratiam).

162. Alsted, *Theologia Naturalis*, 6 (*supernaturalia credimus, ut intelligamus, non intelligimus ut credamus*).

163. Alsted, *Theologia Naturalis*, 14 (cognitio naturalis Dei creatoris est duplex, insita et acquisita); Calvin, *Institutes*, 1.3.1; 1.5.1.

164. J. V. Fesko, 'The Scholastic Epistemology of Geerhardus Vos,' *Reformed Faith and Practice* 3 no 3 (2018): 25-36.

The question is whether God had to superadd anything to our created nature to orient us to those supernatural realities. Our claim is that God fashioned humanity with the natural structure to be ordered toward the supernatural. In other words, God made human nature so that our inherent faculties were oriented to the reception of the supernatural order. That the capacity to know God and related supernatural truths is natural to human constitution, on account of being made in God's image, is required by the doctrine that at least Adam, before the fall, had *innate* knowledge of God.[165] The *faculties* in which the virtues of faith, hope, and love reside are, therefore, aspects of our natural structure. God fashioned them as features of human nature so that we were built for knowing, receiving, and cherishing supernatural realities.[166] Sin did not remove supernatural faculties for knowing and loving God but broke natural faculties that were given to us by nature. Because God designed humanity as his image bearers for the chief end to glorify and enjoy him, he fit our nature with the proper faculties to orient us to the supernatural order.

These considerations directly raise the need for the categories of the created, eschatological, and redemptive orders. In the older scheme of nature and grace, grace orients nature to the supernatural order as our destiny. The problem with that scheme is that it restricts our supernatural end to an ontological dimension rather than emphasizing the eschatological dimension of human destiny. In other words, this paradigm uses grace to relate us ontologically to the supernatural order.

In our proposed scheme of the created, eschatological, and redemptive orders, we always have a relation to the supernatural order, although it is not bolted onto our natural constitution by grace. The impetus for the distinction of natural and supernatural orders has always been to protect God's freeness in offering that supernatural end to us. Hence, the Roman view remains that God must give whatever is due to a particular kind of nature, including the means to fulfill its end. We can easily maintain God's freeness, however, by the simple doctrine that God did

---

165. Abraham Kuyper, 'The Natural Knowledge of God,' trans. Harry van Dyke, *Bavinck Review* 6 (2015): 75-79, 84-93, 108-11; Turrettinus, *Institutio*, 1.3.1, 4, 6, 13. Thanks to J. V. Fesko for alerting me to the Kuyper source.

166. See especially, Turrettinus, *Institutio*, 8.2.1-10; VanDrunen, *Divine Covenants and Moral Order*, 34.

not have to create a creature that was naturally ordered toward the beatific vision as its appointed end.[167] By free decision, God ordered humanity by nature toward a supernatural end. He is the one who crafted us for an eschatological destiny.

Accordingly, there is good use for the dictum 'grace perfects nature' when rightly interpreted. In respect to our eschatological destiny, we considered above that God created us with that supernatural end in view. The covenant of works supplements the premise of God's freedom regarding creation of a creature ordered to a supernatural end. It alleviates the traditional concern about a creature being entitled to that heavenly reward. Specifically, it poses that God fashioned us in covenant not *as entitled* to our supernatural end but as *able to obtain entitlement* to it according to the covenant – an issue explored at length in the next chapter. The covenant of works also helps resolve the confusion of orders because it ordered the created order to the eschatological order. Room remains for the supernatural to have its relation to both. Anthony Tuckey (1599–1670), a Westminster divine, in his refutation of the *donum superadditum*, ties the point to original righteousness: 'We, on the contrary, though we would not quarrel about the terms *natural* and *supernatural*, if it stood only for the reality itself, nevertheless we say in the sound sense that this *righteousness* was *natural to our first parents*, not (as they would have it) a completely natural gift.'[168] Even an annotator on Tuckney's text questioned if this sentence's end should be 'not a completely *supernatural* gift,' but the point stands the same either way because Tuckney's argument was that righteousness was natural to Adam as created but had a supernatural orientation. The fundamental constitution of bearing God's image has a supernatural edge.

The right application of the dictum 'grace perfects nature' then properly regards the redemptive order. We might even tweak the dictum to 'grace consummates fallen nature' to show its eschatological thrust in reference to our sinful condition. Although Adam forfeited

---

167. Turrettinus, *Institutio*, 5.9.9.

168. Anthony Tuckney, *Praelectiones Theologicae* (Amsterdam, 1679), 3:145 (quaet. 18) (Nos contra, quamvis de vocibus *Naturalis* & *Supernaturalis* non litigaremus, si modo de re ipsa constiterit, dicimus tamen sano sensu *Rectitudinem* istam *primi parentis naturalem* fuisse, non (ut illi volunt) *donum omnino naturale*). Note this source's pagination restarts multiple times, hence the first number before the colon and the question number in parentheses. See also Mastricht, *Theoretical-Practical Theology*, 1.4.2.26 (emphasis original).

the new creation as offered in the created order, God's covenant of grace has re-opened that door via the redemptive order. Reflecting on Ecclesiastes 7:29, Tuckney noted that some 'concede this place in Ecclesiastes to signify "righteous," and that Adam was created righteous, but they deny that it follows from it that this righteousness was natural to him and assert that it was supernaturally added to him extraneously for curbing and restraining the flesh's natural impulses.'[169] Some Reformed writers applied the maxim to nature as such in true Thomistic fashion, or concerning disproportion.[170] Nevertheless, many of our theologians apply it to the sinful condition, or in our terms to the redemptive order, even if some of the same writers might use it more broadly in other instances too.[171] The historical point is that the Reformed tradition contains precedent for limiting the maxim to the redemptive order. The theological point is that grace did not need to perfect nature as God created it but is needed for sinners in need of redemption.[172]

The extrinsicist problem must pertain specifically to nature in its integrity, meaning intrinsicist principles of communion with God and of eschatological advancement work only in regard to our upright nature. God must act in special grace upon fallen nature to restore it and to provide all that we need for salvation. Some sort of extrinsicism must then apply to soteriology, even if we are able to construe that in a way that does not undermine the intrinsic connection between our relation to both the natural and supernatural orders, as the next chapter explores.

---

169. Tuckney, *Praelectiones Theologicae*, 3:147 (quast. 18) (At Pontificii Rectum in hoc loco Ecclesiastis justum significare, & *Adamum justum creatum fuisse* concedent; at justitiam hanc ei naturalem fuisse, ex hoc sequi negant, quam ab extra supernaturaliter ei additam fuisse ad naturales carnis impetus refroenandos et cohibendos contendunt).

170. e.g. Anthony Burgess, *Spiritual Refining: or, a Treatise of Grace and Assurance* (London, 1652), 93-94; John Norton, *The Orthodox Evangelist* (London, 1654), 340.

171. e.g. Franciscus Junius, *De Politiae Mosis Observatione* (Leiden, 1593), 12; Johannes Scharpius, *Cursus Theologicus* (Geneva, 1620), 601; Edmund Calamy, *The Monster of Sinful Self-Seeking* (London, 1655), 6; Francis Roberts, *Mysterium & Medulla Bibliorum, the Mysterie and Marrow of the Bible, viz. God's Covenants with Man* (London, 1657), 1134-35; Samuel Clarke, *Medulla Theologiae: or the Marrow of Divinity* (London, 1659), 27; William Pemble, *The Works of that Late Learned Minister of God's Holy Word, Mr William Pemble*, 4th ed. (Oxford, 1659), 90; Tuckney, *Praelectiones Theologicae*, 2:6; Samuel Annesley, *A Continuation of Morning Exercise Questions and Cases of Conscience* (London, 1683), 121.

172. VanDrunen, *Divine Covenants and Moral Order*, 31-36.

CHAPTER SEVEN

Merit in the Covenant of Works

From our creation's outset, we have lived with God in a covenantal order. God has made himself known to us by way of covenant and shown us the path to consummate life with him upon covenantal principles. In the covenant of works, its principle was obedience to the law. In the covenant of grace, its principle is the free offer of the gospel of Jesus Christ. In both, the covenant was the means by which we know God to pursue him for everlasting blessedness. These covenants also represent concrete manifestations of the law and the gospel as distinct covenantal principles.

These covenantal principles must affect how we think about the issues under discussion throughout this book. The previous chapter dealt with the issue of the natural and supernatural orders, arguing that the created order was oriented by God's design to the eschatological order. Contrary to extrinsic paradigms of human nature and destiny, God did not need to bolt the ultimate destiny of eschatological blessedness onto human nature by any superaddition or grace. The reason is that he designed us for that end in our nature in the way that he fashioned us. Our orientation to the eschatological order was included in his work of creation as he tailored Adam according to the divine image. This chapter now deals with one ramification of that argument for the integrity of our natural constitution as related to and ordered toward supernatural realities, thinking more specifically about the internal dynamics of that special act of providence wherein God covenanted with Adam. Again, in respect to Adam, God's work of creation and his act of covenanting were strictly simultaneous so that they occurred in the same event. This chapter then addresses the specific premise of the covenant of works and its meritorious condition to expand our defense of the law-gospel distinction.

Our restriction of the application of grace to the redemptive order entails a clearer formulation of God's goodness to us in the created order. As chapter five showed, the medieval and Roman construction of grace's priority, especially as it relates specifically to nature, affected the modern Reformed discussion by inverting the traditional law-gospel distinction in a fashion that undermined the integrity of justification by grace alone. Even the most modest formulations imply that grace enables and regulates works in basically the same way in the pre- and post-fall contexts. The result is that we sinners are supposedly able by grace to render the faithfulness needed to enter heavenly, glorified life. The further implication is that the pre- and post-fall situations differ primarily in that we would need more grace in the estate of sin, grace that now comes from Christ.[1] From a Reformed perspective concerned to uphold a thorough understanding of the creation-fall-redemption-consummation pattern of redemptive history, this paradigm is significantly lacking.

Drawing eclectically from the preceding tradition to codify a Reformed statement of merit, this chapter argues that the covenant of works defines the terms of merit. As chapter two contended, much of the Reformed tradition pressed against the Roman paradigm of condign and congruent merit by arguing for *meritum ex pacto*. Lee Irons helpfully grasped the implication of the Reformed covenantal outlook, summarizing 'There is no such thing as non-covenantal, condign merit because merit is *by definition* constituted by fulfilling what is stipulated in the covenant.'[2] This chapter's basic idea is that God covenanted with Adam according to his natural ability as the divine image bearer, forging

---

1. See the helpful overview of this concern in Lee Irons, 'Redefining Merit: An Examination of Medieval Presuppositions in Covenant Theology,' in Howard Griffith and John R. Muether (eds.), *Creator, Redeemer, Consummator: A Festschrift for Meredith G. Kline* (Greenville, SC: Reformed Academic Press, 2000; repr. Eugene, OR: Wipf and Stock, 2007), 253-55; Meredith G. Kline, 'Of Works and Grace,' *Presbyterion* 9 (1983): 85-92; Meredith G. Kline, 'Covenant Theology under Attack' *New Horizons* 15 no 2 (Feb 1994): 3-5; Meredith G. Kline, *Kingdom Prologue: Genesis Foundations for a Covenantal Worldview* (Eugene, OR: Wipf and Stock, 2006), 107-9.

2. Irons, 'Redefining Merit,' 268 (italics original).

the premise of merit to reward him with eschatological blessedness. The fundamental contention is that Reformed theology best addresses the relation of the natural and supernatural orders, better the created and eschatological orders, by recognizing that God's covenant defined the proportion of creaturely works in relation to heavenly reward.

Although the point could come across as arcane, the basic premise is obvious in the fundamentals of life. Parents have the right to demand that their children, if still living at home, clean their room. They also have the right to attach the offer of going for ice cream upon completion of cleaning their room. Although this promise annexed to the child's natural obligation is free, we would hardly call it grace. After all, parents should facilitate rich communion with their children. The impulse in godly parents to build such communion with their kids reflects how God treated us from the outset. Still, the other upshot of that offer of ice cream upon completion of the non-negotiable condition is that, once offered, the parent better come through on the reward. A breach of justice would occur if the child completely cleaned his or her room only to be turned away from the offer of ice cream with 'I was just kidding.' The point is that once a covenant has been made, fulfillment of the required condition merits its reward on the premise of justice, not grace, even if that justice is familial, caring, and warm-hearted.

This argument for covenantal merit has the wider payoff of defending the law-gospel distinction. Covenantal merit, as articulated here, forms the principle difference concerning the differing conditions between the covenant of works and the covenant of grace. Since this chapter argues that the standard for merit according to the covenant of works is the perfect fulfillment of our *natural* obligations as God's image bearers, any works that we perform after the fall when our nature is distorted by sin cannot meet that standard. James Ussher helps us articulate both sides of this point. Covenantal merit as belonging to the covenant of works is no longer a condition that we can viably meet 'Because we not onely cannot doe it, but through the perversenesse of our nature (and not by the fault of the Law) it maketh our old man of sin elder, and we more hasting to destruction.'[3] This inadequacy in our fallen condition lays bare the principal difference between the covenant of works and the covenant of

---

3. James Ussher, *A Body of Divinitie* (London, 1645), 157-58.

grace, displaying the law-gospel distinction. Hence, Ussher asked how the covenant of grace differed from the covenant of works, answering:

> Much in every way; for, first, in many points the Law may be conceived by reason; but the Gospell in all points is farre above the reach of mans reason. Secondly, the Law commandeth to doe good, and giveth no strength, but the Gospell enableth us to doe good, the Holy Ghost writing the Law in our hearts; Jer. 31.33. and assuring us of the promise that revealeth this gift. Thirdly, the Law promised life onely; the Gospell righteousnesse also. Fourthly, the Law required perfect obedience, the Gospell the righteousnesse of Faith. Rom. 3.21. Fifthly, the Law revealeth sin, rebuketh us for it, and leaveth us in it: but the Gospell doth reveal unto us the remission of sins, and freeth us from the punishment belonging thereunto. Sixthly, the Law is the ministery of wrath, condemnation, and death: the Gospell is the ministery of grace, Justification and life. Seventhly, the Law was grounded on mans own righteousnesse, requiring of every man in his own person perfect obedience; *Deut. 26:26* and in default for satisfaction everlasting punishment, *Ezek. 18:14*; *Gal. 3:10, 12.* but the Gospell is grounded on the righteousnesse of Christ, admitting payment and performance by another in behalfe of so many as receive it, *Gal. 3:13, 14.* And this covenant abolisheth not, but is the accomplishment and establishment of the former, Rom. 3.31. 10.4.[4]

Accordingly, the covenant of works and the covenant of grace both 'declare one kind of righteousnesse' but offer it to us differently. The former demands our performance of it and the latter gives it freely to believers 'forasmuch as they have in Christ all that the Law doth aske.'[5] Only two covenantal principles stand between God and man for everlasting life: the demand of perfect obedience or the demand of faith, which our defense of covenantal merit demonstrates.[6]

---

4. Ussher, *Body of Divinitie*, 159; similarly Geerhardus Vos, *Reformed Dogmatics*, 5 vol. (Bellingham, WA: Lexham Press, 2012–14), 2:93-94; Bryan D. Estelle, Benjamin W. Swinburnson, Lane G. Tipton, A. Craig Troxel, and Chad V. Van Dixhoorn, 'Report to the 83rd (2016) General Assembly of the Committee to Study Republication,' (Willow Grove, PA: The Committee on Christian Education of the Orthodox Presbyterian Church, 2016), 9.

5. Ussher, *Body of Divinitie*, 159; Petrus Van Mastricht, *Theoretical-Practical Theology*, trans. Todd M. Rester, ed. Joel R. Beeke, 7 vol. (Grand Rapids, MI: Reformation Heritage Books, 2017–), 1.3.12.17; Vos, *Reformed Dogmatics*, 2:33.

6. Charles Hodge, *Systematic Theology*, 3 vol. (Peabody, MA: Hendrickson, 2008), 2:117.

Original Righteousness Redux

In the Reformed view, original righteousness was natural to man. This view ran contrary to Roman theology's assertion of supernatural righteousness and contrary to Pelagians, who said Adam was created innocent but not positively righteous.[7] As the previous chapter argued, the moral law, which reflects God's own character, is the ethical ripple of the divine image hardwired into human nature. Our original righteousness, therefore, brands us with our intimate relation to our Maker.[8] So, our constitution as God's image bearers with original righteousness orders us by nature to supernatural reality.[9] Due at least to original righteousness as at least partly constitutive of our status as God's image bearers, our created nature contains native principles that intrinsically relate us to God.

This section explains the connection between original righteousness and the condition of the covenant of works. The deeper payoff is that original righteousness is that which was needed to obtain eschatological reward. This role for original righteousness is why the pure-nature view – both Franciscan and non-covenantal creation – posits that Adam's original righteousness was supernatural. In contrast, we argue that the covenant of works has nature as its foundation, siding with those Reformed voices that argue that God's creating and covenanting with Adam as the same event. For example, Herman Witsius said the labels 'covenant of works,' 'covenant of the law,' and 'covenant of nature' are interchangeable because it was 'prescribed by the law, demanded works as the condition, and is founded upon and also coeval with nature.'[10] Ussher contended that

---

7. Mastricht, *Theoretical-Practical Theology*, 1.3.9.40.2-3; 1.3.9.42.3; 1.4.2.26.

8. David VanDrunen, *Divine Covenants and Moral Order: A Biblical Theology of Natural Law* (Grand Rapids, MI: Eerdmans, 2014), 23-24; Mastricht, *Theoretical-Practical Theology*, 1.3.10.25; 1.3.11.5.

9. I am here using 'supernatural reality' in a broader sense and not as synonymous with the eschatological order. In other words, by saying original righteousness *orders* by nature to supernatural reality, I have not contravened my argument that our created nature *orients* us to eschatological advancement but the covenant *orders* us to it. The present point is that our specific nature as God's image bearers created with original righteousness intrinsically relates us to God – who himself is a supernatural reality.

10. Herman Witsius, *De Oeconomia Foederum Dei cum Hominibus*, 3rd ed. (1694), 1.2.1 (Quia *Lege* praescribitur, *Opera* ut conditionem exigit, et *Naturae* superstructum ac

'the special order of government which God useth towards mankind in this world' is that 'he ordereth them according to the tenor of a twofold covenant ...'[11] Ussher's phrase that God *orders* our life by the covenants of works and grace gets precisely to the nub of our point that the covenant is the intersection of the created and eschatological orders. In the first covenant, Adam's full term of obedience would have merited entry into the new creation.

Although not often emphasized in research about historic Reformed theology, many Reformed theologians have articulated this view of covenantal merit. Johannes Cocceius commented on Genesis 1: 'In this pact, heavenly life is considered as the reward that must be reckoned according to what is owed, which is usually called merit.'[12] Witsius described how Adam, 'upon joining the covenant and performing the condition, having fulfilled it, acquired some right to demand what God has promised.' This right is because God 'by his promises, freely made himself a debtor to man. Or, so speaking in a more divinely fitting way, he willed to owe to his own self, to his goodness, to his righteousness, and to his truth that he perform what is promised.'[13] John Colquhoun also wrote, 'Since it requires perfect obedience, as the condition of eternal life, it makes the reward to be of debt' and later that this is a 'meritorious or at least a pactional, title to the reward promised by the other.'[14] Charles Hodge explained,

> The word 'condition,' however, is used in two senses. Sometimes it means the meritorious consideration on the ground of which certain benefits are bestowed. In this sense perfect obedience was the condition of the covenant originally made with Adam. Had he retained his integrity he would have

coaevum est); Vos, *Reformed Dogmatics*, 2:32; VanDrunen, *Divine Covenants and Moral Order*, 83-86.

11. Ussher, *Body of Divinitie*, 123.

12. Johannes Cocceius, *Commentarius in Pentateuchum, Josuam, et Librum Judicum* (Amsterdam, 1669), 38 (In hoc pacto consideratur vita coelestis ut merces reputanda κατ' ὀφείλημα. Hoc meritum dici solet).

13. Witsius, *De Oeconomia*, 1.1.14 (Homo autem foederis astipulans, & conditionem praestans, ea praestita, jus aliquod acquirit ad exigendum a Deo promissum. Deus enim se promissis suis liberaliter homini debitorem fecit. Aut, ut magis θεοπρεπῶς loquar, sibi ipsi, Bonitati, Justitiae ac Veracitati suae hoc debere voluit, ut promissa praestet).

14. John Colquhoun, *A Treatise on the Covenant of Works* (Edinburgh: Thomsons, Brothers, 1821), 12, 44.

merited the promised blessing. For to him that worketh the reward is not of grace but of debt.[15]

And Herman Bavinck argued, 'There was a merit *ex pacto* (arising from a covenant), not *ex condigno*.'[16] Summarizing his historical analysis, Carl Trueman concluded that the Reformed have typically found covenant 'helps explain the federal headship of Adam and the *nature of human merit* in relation to an infinite God who, in himself, is no one's debtor.'[17] As chapter two gestured, Trueman's point applies to the host of Reformed authors who implemented this category.[18]

The reason why we can posit Adam's potential to merit rewards before the fall but deny any possibility for sinners to do so after is premised on the Reformed understanding of Adam's upright nature by creation. Robert Rollock explained, 'the ground of the covenant of works was not Christ, nor in God's grace in Christ, but man's nature shaped in the first creation with holiness, integrity, and knowledge of the law.'[19] Even as God designed us so that 'man's natural end must suppose

---

15. Hodge, *Systematic Theology*, 2:364.

16. Herman Bavinck, *Reformed Dogmatics*, ed. John Bolt, trans. John Vriend, 4 vol. (Grand Rapids, MI: Baker Academic, 2003–2008), 2:544.

17. Carl. R Trueman, *John Owen: Reformed Catholic, Renaissance Man* (Aldershot: Ashgate, 2007), 99 (emphasis added). Thanks to Peter Bell and Nick Fullwiler for drawing my attention to this passage.

18. e.g. John Calvin, *Opera quae superunt omnia*, ed. Edouard Cunitz, Johann-Wilhem Baum, and Eduard Wilhem Eugen Reuss, 58 vol. (Corpus Reformatorum; Brunsigae: C.A. Schwetschke, 1863), 49:56; John Owen, 'Exercitation XXVIII,' in *An Exposition of the Epistle to the Hebrews*, 4 vol. (London: Thomas Tegg, 1840), 2:473-74; John Owen, Θεολογουμενα Παντοδαπα, sive De Natura, Ortu, Progressu, et Studio, Verae Theologiae, ed. by William Goold (New York, NY: Robert Carter and Brothers, 1854), 39-43; Brown, *life of justification opened* , 481; Franciscus Turrettinus, *Institutio Theologiae Elencticae*, 3 vol. (Geneva, 1679–85), 8.3.5, 14, 16-17; 8.6.10-11; Colquhoun, *Covenant of Works*, 12-13, 17-18, 41, 43-44, 79-85; Vos, *Reformed Dogmatics*, 2:32; Scott R. Swain, 'The Gospel in the Reformed Tradition,' in Jonathan A. Linebaugh (ed.), *God's Two Words: Law and Gospel in the Lutheran and Reformed Traditions* (Grand Rapids, MI: Eerdmans, 2018), 95-96; Richard P. Belcher Jr., *The Fulfillment of the Promises of God: An Explanation of Covenant Theology* (Fearn, UK: Mentor, 2020), 31-33; Richard P. Belcher Jr., 'The Covenant of Works in the Old Testament,' in Waters et al, *Covenant Theology*, 69n311; Cornelis P. Venema, *Christ and Covenant Theology: Essays on Election, Republication, and the Covenants* (Phillipsburg, NJ: P&R, 2017), 32-35, 88-89, 136n86.

19. Rollock, *Tractatus De Vocatione Efficaci*, 9–10 (Ergo fundame[n]tum foederis operum erat, non quidem Christus, non gratia Dei in Christo, sed natura hominis in prima creatione sancta integra & legis notitia informata).

natural means unto obtaining it, but blessedness had been man's natural end,' Francis Turretin connected those dots that 'he must have natural means, which could be none other than original righteousness.'[20] Our original righteousness can both include the strength we need to fulfill the covenant of works and be the standard of righteousness leading to eschatological blessing because it is the creaturely analog of conformity to God's own righteous character (Job 3:12).[21] In this way, Reformed theologians have bound God's work of creation in closest connection to his special act of providence in covenanting with Adam.

God's law, which is the condition of the covenant of works, is then hardwired into our human constitution as God's image bearers. Unless we accept that God superadded the divine image to human nature by grace, then the law *must* precede grace in the created order because the law is simply the ethical thread in the tapestry of bearing God's likeness. This law comes melded into our image-bearing constitution and still itself served as the covenant of works, merely summed up in sacramental fashion by the tree of knowledge. Thus, Westminster Confession 4.2 says that God made us 'indued with knowledge, righteousnesse and true holinesse, after his own Image; having the Law of God written in their hearts, and power to fulfill it.'[22] Westminster Confession 19.1 even repeats that when God gave the law to Adam as a covenant of works, he 'indued him with power and ability to keep it,' leaving this view doubly enshrined within the same confession. In the created order, God gave that law which was branded on our nature to Adam 'as a Covenant of Works, by which he bound him, and all his posterity to personall, entire, exact, and perpetuall obedience; promised life upon the fulfilling, and threatned death upon the breach of it.'[23] The law that was the covenant of works was naturally grafted onto Adam's nature. He also had power

---

20. Turrettinus, *Institutio*, 5.11.10 (Finis naturalis hominis, supponere debet media naturalia ad illius consecutionem, sed beatitude fuit finis naturalis hominis. Ergo media debuit habere naturalia, quae non alia potuerunt esse, quam justitia originalis).

21. Witsius, *De Oeconomia*, 1.3.7; Mastricht, *Theoretical-Practical Theology*, 1.3.10.25; Johannes Polyander, 'Concerning the Law of God,' in Dolf te Velde (ed.), *Synopsis Purioris Theologiae Volume 1/Disputations 1–23* (Leiden: Brill, 2015), 437-47.

22. John R. Bower, *The Confession of Faith: A Critical Text and Introduction* (Principal Documents of the Westminster Assembly; Grand Rapids, MI: Reformation Heritage Books, 2020), 201.

23. Bower, *Confession of Faith*, 217.

to fulfill this law that was the covenant of works. Thus, Petrus van Mastricht synthesized Colossians 3:10 and Ephesians 4:24 about Adam: 'intrinsically, he was equipped with a perfect principle of obeying, namely, original righteousness.'[24] Further, in the confessional terms of Westminster Confession 4.2 and 19.1, inasmuch as God gave the law to Adam as a covenant of works by creating him with it engrafted on his heart, the distinct work of creation and the act of special covenanting providence occurred simultaneously in the event. In this respect, our view follows the interpretation of the Confession that 'the implantation of the moral law in the human conscience is coincident with creation,' while 'the creation of a covenant falls under the realm of providence' so that 'this law on their hearts was not naked; it was clothed from … the beginning in a covenantal arrangement.'[25] The punch of human nature with original righteousness was the covenantal formula, made such at the time of Adam's creation with the moral law naturally ingrafted by God's simultaneous act of providence.[26]

Scripture patently marks these connections when reflecting on nature and God's image. In Genesis 9:5-7, God's instruction in the establishment of the Noahic covenant linked the image of God with humanity's judicial responsibility.

> And for your lifeblood I will require a reckoning: from every beast I will require it and from man. From his fellow man I will require a reckoning for the life of man.

---

24. Mastricht, *Theoretical-Practical Theology*, 1.3.12.19.

25. Estelle et al, 'Report … to Study Republication,' 19.

26. Keeping in mind the previous chapter's distinction and relation of the work of creation and the special act of providence, as Estelle, Swinburnson, Tipton, Troxel, and Van Dixhoorn have contended, 'the law of God was implanted in us at creation, and yet we cannot flourish without covenant, and so God brought our first parents into a covenantal relationship with himself through a "special act of providence" (SC 12). This means, among other things, that creation does not seem to be synonymous with covenant.' Estelle *et al*, 'Report … to Study Republication,' 19. Although covenant and creation were not synonymous, they were, according to our argument, following Vos, simultaneous. The concreated law given to Adam by engrafting it on his heart via creation (Westminster Confession 4.2) becomes the base terms of the covenant of works by God's special act of providence, which occurs distinctly but simultaneously in the same event. As the authors of this report acknowledge, the Westminster Confession does not *require* our interpretation. Our lines of argument, however, fit well within the report's parameters for understanding the confession's categories for relating creation, law, and covenant; Estelle *et al*, 'Report … to Study Republication,' 18-20.

'Whoever sheds the blood of man,
by man shall his blood be shed,
for God made man in his own image.

And you, be fruitful and multiply, increase greatly on the earth and multiply in it.'

Interpreters vary on how to explain the connection in this passage of the *imago Dei* to shedding a murderer's blood. The clear point, however, is that our image-bearing role entails some sort of principle of reciprocity concerning justice.[27] Although this Genesis mandate is judicially negative, we also know that 'whoever would draw near to God must believe that he exists and that he rewards those who seek him' (Heb. 11:6). Some principle of reciprocity then stands in our relationship with God.

Although we cannot cover it in exhaustive detail, perhaps the clearest demonstration of these interconnecting links appears in Romans 1:18–2:16. This passage's overall contribution grounds Paul's argument in Romans 1:18–3:20 that all sinners stand condemned before God. We are accountable because 'what can be known about God is plain to them, because God has shown it to them. For his invisible attributes, namely, his eternal power and divine nature, have been clearly perceived, ever since the creation of the world, in the things that have been made. So they are without excuse' (1:19-20). The principles of natural revelation then leave us with inescapable knowledge of God, his nature, and our moral obligations. We cannot dilute the connection that his divine nature, including the standards of righteousness, is manifest in created realities, particularly concerning our existence as God's image bearers. Hence, we all 'know God's righteous decree that those who practice such things deserve to die' (Rom. 1:32). The judicial repercussions for breaking the natural law are hardwired into our covenantally shaped image-bearing existence.

The flipside of this natural knowledge is also true, namely, that the principle of reward is known to us as well. In Romans 2, Paul pressed home that Jews, even though having divine special revelation, were equally condemned along with Gentile sinners. Following the principle of 'God's righteous judgment,' which resonates of his righteous decree that we know by nature the consequence of sin, 'He will render to

---

27. VanDrunen, *Divine Covenants and Moral Order*, 53-58.

each one according to his works' (vv. 5-6). The universal reckoning includes that 'to those who by patience in well-doing seek for glory and honor and immortality, he will give eternal life' (v. 7), granting 'glory and honor and peace for everyone who does good' (v. 10). According to the standards of nature as we are created in God's image, which sinners cannot successfully meet, the works principle includes not only punishment for law breakers but also glorious reward for law keepers.[28]

The intersection of nature, law, and reciprocity ought to be clear, but we do not want to lose sight of this section's intended argument. Drawing the wider connection to the covenant of works altogether, Mastricht explained: 'God expressly prescribed obedience, to be given first to the natural laws inscribed on his heart (Rom. 2:15), and then to the positive law to abstain from the tree of the knowledge of good and evil. God urged this obedience at that time as the condition of the covenant of works, to merit by its aid eternal life.'[29] The covenant of works runs on the principle of merit so that the rendering of expected obedience obtains the proffered reward.

The standard of that obedience was what is expected of us according to our original righteousness. By nature, we have the strength we need to merit because the covenant of works is bound to our created order. The works which Adam should have performed to merit entry into the eschatological order were simply his natural obligations according to his original righteousness, covenantally encapsulated in the probationary command about the tree of knowledge. Put negatively, Adam as created did not need to be elevated to the supernatural order of grace by a *donum superadditum* to perform meritorious deeds. The expectation for living as God's image bearers and the condition to merit within the covenant of works are identical: act properly according to our nature as endued with original righteousness (Eccles. 7:29).[30]

Navigating the Straits of Proportionality

This section tackles that problem of proportionality that has been the mist hanging over this whole book's major discussion points. Put another

---

28. VanDrunen, *Divine Covenants and Moral Order*, 209-57.

29. Mastricht, *Theoretical-Practical Theology*, 1.3.9.38.1.

30. Witsius, *De Oeconomia*, 1.3.12.

way, now we aim to formulate our doctrine of covenantal merit by stating its principles and by avoiding the shortcomings of medieval and Roman paradigms. Those paradigms resort to ontological explanations, regardless of whether those are intellectualist or voluntarist versions of sanctifying grace needed to merit. One key factor sharply distinguishes the view argued here from those medieval and Roman positions: whereas sanctifying grace *supplements* the value of our works to make them meritorious, the covenant *defines* their value to make them meritorious.

This section argues that the covenant defines the proportion of works and reward, so defining the terms of merit. Irons provides us with some guiding principles for the relationship of covenant and merit. Limiting the sphere of merit ideology, he premised, first, that 'Rather than an ontological state intellectually registered in the divine mind, merit is *constituted* only by fulfillment of a divinely-sanctioned covenant' and, second, 'The *measure* of merit is defined by the terms of the covenant, which itself is the only possible revelation and definition of divine justice.' The implication is that, 'There is no such thing as non-covenantal, condign merit because merit is *by definition* constituted by fulfilling what is stipulated in the covenant.'[31] Adam's natural ability to render obedience to the law without the help of additional grace, as defended in the previous chapter and above, inevitably raises questions about the value of Adam's works. Although God was not intrinsically obligated to reward Adam for his obedience, when he founded the terms of the covenant of works upon Adam's natural ability to keep the law, he forged a type of covenantal merit. In other words, by making a covenant, God established just terms by which Adam could merit his reward if he fulfilled them. Again, merit simply concerns whether someone has a right to claim a reward justly.

In this regard, the description of a covenant in Westminster Confession 7.1 is again significant, in that creatures can 'never have any fruition of him as their Blessednesse and Reward but *by some voluntary condescension* on God's part, which he has been pleased to expresse by way of Covenant.'[32] By his voluntary condescension, which was certainly a loving act of kindness, God promised to reward his creatures for the

---

31. Irons, 'Redefining Merit,' 268.
32. Bower, *Confession of Faith*, 204 (emphasis added).

works that we owe anyway with higher blessedness in communion with God. This relationship was a covenant.

This covenantal merit is emphatically because of God's covenant arrangement with Adam and not some supposed demand that a creature could make from God simply for rendering obedience if there were no covenant.[33] Reflecting Geerhardus Vos' insight defended in the previous chapter, J. V. Fesko rightly explained: 'Pure nature versus Adam's state in covenant is merely a theological distinction so that one might understand how nature and covenant relate to one another. Nature and covenant are ultimately concreated realities and thus inseparable, though distinguishable.'[34] The previous chapter's discussion of Westminster Shorter Catechism 9–12 about the relation of God's work of creating Adam to God's covenanting act of special providence has already made clear how this unity within the distinction should be understood. Now, note well that Fesko's reference to pure nature was only in a judicial sense in conjunction with the covenant, not to nature as self-contained without reference to the eschatological order or the supernatural order. In this covenantal sense, God accommodated the condition of the covenant of works to human nature, fashioned in his image with original righteousness. In sum, God decided to create his image bearers in this particular covenant relationship.

This covenantal merit secures the works principle of the covenant of works but also avoids suggesting that a creature could outright demand blessings from God in exchange for obedience. John Halsey Wood explained, 'The reward Adam would have presumably received had he fulfilled his covenant obligations was based on the strict justice established in God's covenant. "Do this, and you will live." God covenanted with Adam, and that covenant had the strict stipulations for both Adam and God. The covenant enjoined Adam to obedience, and it enjoined God to reward Adam for his obedience .... All this obtains because God *ordained* that this be so.'[35] One necessary feature

---

33. Estelle et al, 'Report ... to Study Republication,' 19.

34. J. V. Fesko, *Adam and the Covenant of Works* (Fearn: Mentor, 2021), 325; Vos, *Reformed Dogmatics*, 2:32; Turrettinus, *Institutio*, 8.3.11.

35. John Halsey Wood Jr., 'Merit in the Midst of Grace: The Covenant with Adam Reconsidered in View of the Two Powers of God,' *International Journal of Systematic Theology* 10 no 2 (April 2008):145 (italics original). I prefer 'goodness' to 'grace' for all the

of the covenant of works is that it rests upon the demand for strict obedience to God's natural law, which was a requirement imbedded in our image-bearing constitution in original righteousness. Because God created Adam in this covenant that had the condition of fulfilling his natural obligations, Adam was genuinely capable of obtaining the offered reward by his works according to the terms of the agreement that God gave to him.

This formulation brings together several key biblical concerns. The Creator-creature distinction means that we cannot get around the unassailable basis that we can never have *ontological* demand against our Creator to place him in our debt. In Luke 17:10, Jesus laid out this clear principle: 'So you also, when you have done all that you were commanded, say, "We are unworthy servants; we have only done what was our duty."' Adam's works could warrant heavenly reward, despite his creaturely inferiority, because of God's covenant with him. On the one hand, the covenant established the terms of justice, qualifying this principle's prelapsarian significance. On the other hand, this principle applies to us after the fall as bare and unqualified, so that our perfect obedience (if we could somehow perform it) cannot be meritorious. Adam broke the covenant of works, nullifying its works principle's validity for merit. As Westminster Shorter Catechism 16 affirms, given that the covenant was made *with Adam* for himself and his posterity, all who descend from him by ordinary generation are under the *broken* covenant of works.[36] The merit principle belongs only to the covenant founded upon Adam's upright nature and not to some ontological correspondence between God and his creaturely image. Consequently, even a hypothetical perfect obedience rendered by anyone who descended ordinarily from Adam cannot merit because no covenant relates that creaturely work to the eschatological reward. The unworthy-servant principle does not leave the creation covenant susceptible to some voluntaristic annulment upon Adam's fulfillment of its terms, because God committed to this covenant on the principles

---

reasons detailed across the scope of this book, but – in the spirit of dealing with realities rather than merely signs – Wood's point is structurally the same as mine; Wood, 'Merit,' 133-48; Fesko, *Adam and the Covenant of Works*, 377-79, 391-97.

36. Philip Schaff (ed.), *The Creeds of Christendom*, 3 vol. (New York, NY: Harper and Brothers, 1877), 3:679.

of nature. When Adam broke the covenant, he destroyed its principle of merit and closed it off to any of his posterity.[37]

Moreover, this unworthy-servant principle rests on the wider premise that we owe everything, including our very existence and any standing we have, to the Lord who created us and gave us every gift we possess. As Paul wrote in his grand doxology in Romans 11:34-36:

> 'For who has known the mind of the Lord,
>   or who has been his counselor?'
> 'Or who has given a gift to him
>   that he might be repaid?'

> For from him and through him and to him are all things. To him be glory forever. Amen.

Turretin reflected on this passage to draw the conclusion of covenantal merit, arguing:

> since our first parents themselves could by no means merit anything for themselves except from the pure and unadulterated pact of a promise, that they could neither have merited for their posterity, except from the same pure and unadulterated pact, because the creature cannot merit anything from condignity from the Creator, for who has first given to him, that it should be recompensed to him? From him and through him are all things (Rom. 11:35-36).[38]

God's own inherent freedom from being a debtor to a creature is clear, but we must then ask: what supports the notion of Adam's merit?

God's covenant defined the proportion of Adam's works so that, on the premise of perfect obedience according to original righteousness, Adam would have earned entry to the eschatological order. The concreated law given to Adam by engrafting it on his heart via creation (Westminster Confession 4.2) becomes the base terms of the covenant of works by God's special act of providence (Westminster Confession 19.1), which occurs distinctly but simultaneously in the same event. Above, we already considered the reciprocity principle in connection to the image of God, natural law, and original righteousness. We also see the straightforward statements of the works principle. Paul wrote in Romans 4:4-5: 'Now to the one who works, his wages are not counted

---

37. R. Michael Allen, *Reformed Theology* (London: T&T Clark, 2010), 42.

38. Mastricht, *Theoretical-Practical Theology*, 1.3.12.27.

as a gift but as his due. And to the one who does not work but believes in him who justifies the ungodly, his faith is counted as righteousness.' There is a premise that a worker, presuming he renders adequate works, earns his wages as due, as deserved, as merited. This premise explains our natural instincts that undergird our earlier illustration about how parents would be unjust to renege on their offer of ice cream as a reward if their child cleans his or her room.

This basis of the works principle, not God's divine freedom concerning how to create creatures in covenant or not, determines the law-gospel distinction. God established this principle with us by his decree concerning how he made us and related us to our obligation to obey him. Grace does not enable meritorious works: 'But if it is by grace, it is no longer on the basis of works; otherwise grace would no longer be grace' (Rom. 11:6). In Galatians 3:10-12, Paul explained: 'For all who rely on works of the law are under a curse; for it is written, "Cursed be everyone who does not abide by all things written in the Book of the Law, and do them."' The reason is, as Paul applied Leviticus 18:5, that 'the law is not of faith, rather "The one who does them shall live by them."' Once grace is in place as the basis of being right with God and obtaining the beatific vision, the works principle is off the table entirely. The covenant of grace does not send us back to the covenant of works, as Turretin said: 'For the covenant of works promises life only to the perfectly just and meriting man. But the covenant of grace promises not only life but also salvation to the completely demeriting and unworthy man, namely to a sinner.'[39] The exclusivity of the principles of works and grace means that the works principle in the covenant of works cannot be based on grace, though it must relate to God's freedom.

Again, God's first covenant defined the proportion of works and reward. This premise appears in Christ's parable of the laborers in the vineyard, found in Matthew 20:1-16. This parable compares the kingdom of heaven to the master of a house hiring workers to tend his vineyard. The master hired some laborers in the morning, 'agreeing with the laborers for a denarius a day' (Matt. 20:2). As the day progresses,

---

39. Turrettinus, *Institutio*, 8.6.12 (Nam foedus operum vitam tantum homini perfecte justo et meranti promittit. Sed foedus gratiae non vitam tantum, sed etiam salutem homini plane immerenti et indigno, puta peccatori pollicetur) The English translation numbers this section 8.6.13.

the master continued to hire more laborers. At the end of the workday, he paid each worker the full day's wage, no matter how many hours they had worked. The workers hired at the start of the day thought this recompense unfair, since they labored much longer. The master replied that he can assign whatever reward he pleases to acceptable work.[40]

This principle of defined work and reward according to roles predominates the parable. Its clear point is that all believers enter equally into everlasting life no matter how long they had walked with God, rebuking the disciples who asked for more prestigious roles in the consummate kingdom of heaven (Matt. 19:23-30).[41] Still, the workers had to do the work given to them to obtain their wages. Even as the passage concerns God's fair treatment of all his servants, it cannot be used to justify the Roman doctrine of congruent merit. Because it tells of the master assigning an abundant reward to *proper* work performed, it rules out especially Biel's sense wherein God would accept even a sinner's works as meritorious of life in heaven. The master does not agree to accept deficient or corrupted work, even if its extent is circumscribed, but to provide an abundant reward assigned as the proportion to a proper job completed. The fall made it so that humanity cannot render any sort of proper work before God.

All the same, the parable states the principle that the master, certainly representing the Lord, can generously define the proportion of a great reward to whatever work was supposed to be fulfilled.[42] Although the everlasting reward offered to Adam in the covenant of works was significantly or even infinitely disproportionate to the intrinsic value of the creaturely work, the parable suggests that God is able to overcome this disproportion by defining the proportion. God's agreement with Adam could not have included bargaining since Adam was a creature with no platform for haggling with the Lord. At the same time, God made Adam an offer that he could not refuse – both because it came from the sovereign Lord whose decree he could not reject as he was created into this covenant and because

---

40. Donald A. Hagner, *Matthew 14–28* (Word Biblical Commentary; Dallas, TX: Word Books, 1995), 571-72.

41. Hagner, *Matthew 14–28*, 569.

42. R. T. France, *The Gospel of Matthew* (New International Commentary on the New Testament; Grand Rapids, MI: Eerdmans, 2007), 748-52.

it was an infinitely good and appealing offer. By this 'agreement,' God sovereignly proportioned a reward to Adam's works by way of the covenant of works. This covenantal merit established the fixed relationship between *this* particular work that Adam was obligated to perform and *this* particular reward of incorruptible life. Adam's nature was then covenantally related to obtaining his heightened condition.

Disproportion is a true problem only if we hope to downplay the familial dimension of God's covenant with Adam to make it *only* legal, devoid of God's love and kindness in how he treated Adam. That problematic approach would rob that covenant of its biblical texture and in some ways dilute the heinousness of Adam's sin.[43] Our solution leaves room for God's warm-hearted action in how he crafted Adam in this particular covenantal life. Even set within a firm assertion of the necessity of God's *auxilium* for Adam to persevere, Turretin affirmed God's goodness in the covenant of works: 'Certainly, God by his own right was able to prescribe obedience to man created by him without any promise of reward, but, in order to temper that supreme dominion with his goodness, he attached a covenant that consisted in the promise of reward and in the stipulation of obedience.'[44] God accommodated the covenant to our natural capacities as the creatures bearing his image, rather than superadding any additional supernatural faculties. Some of our natural faculties do bear more direct relation to supernatural realities. That does not mean God added something to our nature to supplement the value of our works to make them ontologically meritorious. Rather, he defined the merit of our works covenantally.

The point is that God molded us with those capacities according to our natural constitution as his image bearers. We must, therefore, be naturally oriented above the raw created plain because of our purpose to glorify and enjoy God. It should not unsettle us that we are dependent upon God's decision to create us as his covenantal creatures rather than have a deeper ontological ground about what is 'owed' to nature regardless of how he decreed to create us. Whereas Rome saw the solution to the disproportion

---

43. Rightly, Fesko, *Adam and the Covenant of Works*, 384-85.

44. Turrettinus, *Institutio*, 8.3.2 (Poterat quidem Deus pro jure suo obedientam homini a se condito praescribere sine ulla praemii pollicitatione; sed ut supremum illud dominium bonitate sua temperaret, foedus addidit, quod promissione praemii, et obedientiae stipulatione constat); Fesko, *Adam and the Covenant of Works*, 101-02.

between works and reward as the ontological elevation of nature to superadd strength to make our efforts supernaturally meritorious, the Reformed should see the covenant of works as established in the integrity of our original nature. Merit is then covenantal rather than ontological and pertained only to our first condition.

That conclusion naturally raises the question about how our formulation of merit relates to the various medieval views. As is the case across our historical trajectory, applying to the whole field of theological study, the Reformed were eclectic in their appropriation of the preceding tradition. Specific historical coordinates, depending on the analytical lens used, might suggest tighter links to a Thomistic or voluntarist background in the development of Reformed covenant theology. Variety, especially on such complicated matters, must be expected as inevitable. In our constructive work here, however, we argue that neither Thomas Aquinas' intellectualist premise nor John Duns Scotus' voluntarist idea of *acceptatio* is an exact fit to our argued formulation. Rather, eclectic elements from both need to come together.

On the one hand, our view is not Scotus' voluntarist idea of *acceptatio*. Richard Muller has suggested how the *ex pacto* category in some ways has links to the medieval Scotist doctrine of God's ordained power, which taught that God appointed specific means to acquire grace. Muller also contended that the Reformed developed this notion in quite different directions from the Scotists.[45] After all, theologians like Rutherford denied that the covenant which connected obedience to reward was written in Adam's heart, instead affirming the idea of a 'created right' as he interpreted Matthew's vineyard parable.[46] Nevertheless, chapter two showed that many Reformed theologians implemented the *ex pacto* category precisely as a polemic against Roman Catholic paradigms of merit that were perhaps more closely related to the Scotist/Franciscan notions of merit.

Contra Scotus and the voluntarist tradition, true merit, which is covenantal, is not that God arbitrarily accepts *some sort* of work as deserving. True, covenantal merit is that God swore to honor as

---

45. Richard A. Muller, *Dictionary of Latin and Greek Theological Terms Drawn Principally from Protestant Scholastic Theology*, 2nd ed. (Grand Rapids: Baker Academic, 2017), 114.

46. Samuel Rutherford, *The Covenant of Life Opened; or, A Treatise on the Covenant of Grace* (Edinburgh, 1655), 22, 41-43.

meritorious what Adam truly ought to have perfectly done. Moreover, Scotus' view involved the *acceptatio personarum* – the acceptation of persons – meaning that God's *acceptio* of a work for merit depended upon a prior acceptation of the person performing the work via sanctifying grace. For *merit*, the Reformed emphasize God's impartiality, noting that the *work* must be perfect (Rom. 2:11). We need to agree with Thomas that merit must be real, that is, it must have a true integrity that coheres with the righteousness of God's character, which is the basis of all moral laws. Johannes Braun demonstrates the real premise of merit, even while denying Thomas' premise of pre-fall grace: 'Because there was no grace in the case of Adam, the one building favor, when everything he would have was from God. Merit, therefore, was to its extent by the covenant, following the stipulation of the covenant, by the mere good pleasure of God.'[47] Our premise follows Thomas' intellectualist principles by insisting God *cannot* will a standard for our obedience as the basis of the works principle other than the perfect fulfillment of his law. This standard must apply because the moral law expresses at the creaturely level God's own eternal, holy character.[48] Thus, the Reformed version of *acceptation*, if we must call it such, lacks Scotus' voluntarist hue, denying that the standard of covenantal merit can change. Johannes Cocceius related the *imago Dei*, original righteousness, and covenant:

> The covenant of works is immutable and indispensable because it depends upon God's image, and thus upon God's nature, that is upon eternal uprightness and justice, which is established by him, who is God, and has all divinity; and for that reason the covenant cannot be changed, unless the principal reality is changed.[49]

---

47. Johannis Braunii, *Doctrina Foederum sive Systema Theologiae*, 2 vol. (Amsterdam, 1691), 3.2.13 (citations formatted as part.chapter.section) (quia in Adama nulla fuit gratia gratum faciens, cum Omnia a Deo habuerit. Ergo meritus ex pacto tantum, secundum stipulationem foederis, ex mero beneplacito Dei).

48. St. Thomas Aquinas, *Summa Theologica*, trans. by Fathers of the English Dominican Province, 5 vol. (New York, NY: Benziger Bros., 1948; repr. Notre Dame, IN: Christian Classics, 1981), 1a2ae.91.1-2, 93.1-6, 94.1-6.

49. Cocceius, *Commentarius in Pentateuchum*, 38-39 (§128. XV. Foedus operum est immutabile & indispensabile. Quia nititur imagine Dei, & sic natura Dei, h[oc].e[st]. aeterna veritate & justitia, quae fundatur in eo, quod Deus est, & omnem divinitatem habet; atque ideo foedus mutari non potest, nisi prima veritas mutetur).

With Thomas, then, righteousness is a reality that must be truly achieved if we are to merit eschatological blessedness. In contrast to Scotus, the standard for merit is grounded fully in nature and cannot be altered.

Against Thomas, we should reject any ontological basis for merit's warrant of reward. More emphatically, we must affirm against Thomas that not even God's predestination can direct *sinners* to obtain this (or any) sort of merit by their own deeds. Instead of an ontological premise, God founded the covenant of works on our very nature as he created us constituted with original righteousness and integrity. He accommodated the conditions to the rendering of perfect obedience, which we could fulfill in our original integrity. In a sense, respecting our eclecticism, divine accommodation has a formal similarity to Scotus' doctrine of *acceptatio* because God freely, albeit not distinctly from creation, fixed the reward to the obedience which we would be obligated to render as creatures bearing God's image. In contrast to Thomas, the link between the performance of real righteousness and reward is not ontological.

Covenantal merit for Adam as voluntary condescension distinguishes the Reformed view from medieval views. It differs from Thomas' view that human works are intrinsically meritorious based on infused grace. It also differs from especially the later Franciscan view that God arbitrarily assigns merit to even sin-stained human works done from 'pure nature.' Rather, God's covenant with Adam defined the proportionate relationship that Adam's *absolutely perfect* works were the condition that would earn everlasting blessing. Adam had to render perfect obedience by the strength of his nature rather than by grace-enabled or imperfect best efforts. Still, these realistically perfect works were meritorious because God had covenanted to reward them with the appropriate blessings.

Our Reformed eclectic appropriation of the prior tradition for our view of Adam's merit highlights two aspects of our position. First, it is latent with a certain ecumenicity built upon appreciative but critical engagement with our prior tradition. Second, it marks why we ought to see Adam's merit as covenantal. Our resolution to this issue of disproportion already appeared in the parable of the laborers in the vineyard, presenting God's act of assigning the value of a work that may appear disproportionate to its reward. Ussher explained the issue at length, unsurprisingly (by now) appealing to Thomas to support his view:

Originally therefore and in itself, we hold that this reward proceeds merely from God's free bounty and mercy: but accidentally, in regard that God hath tied himself by his word and promise to confer such a reward, we grant that it now proves in a sort to be *an act of justice* .... For promise, we see, amongst honest men is *counted as due debt*, but the thing promised being free, and on our part altogether undeserved, if the promiser did not perform, and proved not to be so good as his word; he could not properly be said to doe me wrong, but rather to wrong himself, by impairing his own credit. And therefore Aquinas himself confesses, 'that God is not hereby simply made a debtor to us, but to himself; inasmuch as it is requisite that his own ordinance should be fulfilled.'[50]

Ussher implemented traditional themes, even concerning merit, to further Protestant doctrine by reconciling it with Augustine.[51] Moreover, his citation of Thomas is striking because, although significant differences stood between them, Ussher read Thomas as being very close to his own Reformed covenantal merit premise: 'Hence man's merit with God, exists only on the presupposition of the Divine *ordination*.'[52] Although Thomas at times meant that God had predestined some to everlasting life, ordaining also that they would achieve the necessary merit, he also meant that God ordained (*ordinatio*) the value of a meritorious work: 'if we speak of man in the first state, there is only one reason why man cannot merit eternal life without grace, by his purely natural endowments, viz., because man's merit depends on the Divine pre-ordination.'[53] For the Reformed, God made a pact that the *perfect* works which he created us to do were the condition to merit everlasting communion with him.[54]

---

50. James Ussher, *An Answer to a Challenge Made by a Jesuite in Ireland* (Dublin, 1624), 494-95 (emphasis added); citing Thomas, *Summa Theologica*, 1a2ae.114.1-3; McGrath, *Iustitia Dei*, 156-57; Wawrykow, *God's Grace and Human Action*, 161-64.

51. Alistair E. McGrath, *Iustitia Dei: A History of the Christian Doctrine of Justification*, 4th ed. (Cambridge: Cambridge University Press, 2020), 160-63.

52. Thomas, *Summa Theologica*, 1a2ae.114.1 (emphasis added); Joseph P. Wawrykow, *God's Grace and Human Action: Merit in the Theology of Thomas Aquinas* (Notre Dame, IN: University of Notre Dame Press, 2016), 9-12, 77-83, 179-89.

53. Thomas, *Summa Theologica*, 1a2ae.114.2.

54. R. Scott Clark, 'Do This and Live: Christ's Active Obedience as the Ground of Justification,' in R. Scott Clark (ed.), *Covenant, Justification, and Pastoral Ministry: Essays by the Faculty of Westminster Seminary California* (Phillipsburg, NJ: P&R, 2007), 258-59.

In this sense, covenantal merit upholds the integrity of human nature and Adam's natural ability as God created him, as well as God's free goodness in offering Adam an eschatological reward. This view pushes directly against Cajetan's and the Franciscans' separation of so-called pure nature from our supernatural destiny in heightened communion with God.[55] It rejects a dichotomy of natural and supernatural ends by affirming that God ordered humanity naturally to supernatural ends *by the covenant* so that Adam's nature without any addition had a trajectory for eschatological advancement. God's covenant did not require any supplement to our nature but constituted Adam's natural obligations, which he could fulfill, as the means to supernatural communion with the Lord. God's covenant defined the proportion of Adam's natural works to give them their meritorious value. Even with his strong connection between the *imago Dei* and the covenant of works, Cocceius contended that the resolution to the problem of proportionality concerning a work's merit resides in the judicial aspect of the covenant: 'They [works] certainly do not begin to be proportionate and equal, therefore, it is because God has fixed, has prepared, and has promised an eternal reward to them,' thus 'the merit belonging to works comes into being by the covenant.'[56] The eclectic nature of the Reformed appropriation of the preceding tradition is apparent here by combining a stress on human nature as *concreated* with the gift of original righteousness, rejecting the Franciscan trajectory, with the necessity that God decreed to assign our works their value in the covenant.[57]

In reference to the creation-covenant relationship, the covenant ordered Adam's natural obligations by defining their value as meritorious and focusing them in the probationary command so to make them the terms for eschatological reward. Put the other way

---

55. Rupert Johannes Mayer, 'Man is Inclined to His Last End by Nature, though He cannot Reach It by Nature but Only by Grace: The Principle of the Debate about Nature and Grace in Thomas Aquinas, Thomism and Henri de Lubac. A Response to Lawrence Feingold,' *Angelicum* 88 (2011): 923-26.

56. Cocceius, *Commentarius in Pentateuchum*, 76 (Non enim incipiunt esse proportionate & aequalia, ideo quia Deus illis destinavit, praeparavit & promisit praemium aeternum. 2. Verum est, quod meritum operum proveniat ex pacto).

57. McGrath, *Iustitia Dei*, 114-15, 163-68; Richard Cross, 'Duns Scotus and William of Ockham,' in Matthew Levering and Marcus Plested (eds.), *The Oxford Handbook of the Reception of Aquinas* (Oxford: Oxford University Press, 2021), 61-62, 65.

round, the terms of the covenant are concreated with human nature *inasmuch as* their obligations, strictly speaking, were engrafted on Adam's heart by creation in the moral law, but they become terms *as such* only on account of God's covenanting act. As chapter six showed was the case with many features of creation, such as the sabbath principle and Adam's role as the biological and federal head of the entire race, the natural becomes covenantal by virtue of God's positive act.[58] Upon this very premise, Fesko helpfully explained God's work of creation of Adam in relation to his special act of providence toward Adam in clear scholastic terms: 'we can designate Adam's image-bearing nature as the material cause of the covenant of works and the administration of the divine commands as its formal cause. That is, there is no covenant of works apart from Adam's natural endowments, but likewise there is no covenant with Adam apart from God's special act of providence.'[59] God's work of creating Adam and his act of covenanting with him are conceptually distinct but nonetheless stand together in one event precisely on account of this covenant's encompassing relation to Adam's natural condition as a bearer of God's image with original righteousness.

This relation of concreated obligations assumed as the covenantal terms is essential to maintain our bulwark against extrinsicism. Any arrangement wherein supplemental obligations that are foreign to our created nature are imposed as the covenant's terms takes us right back into an extrinsicism. In the above formulation, Adam's natural obligations were taken up into the covenant by voluntary condescension. That is, God accommodated the covenant to our very nature so that our owed obedience became the covenant's conditions. By contrast, if the obligations that were the terms of the covenant are superadded to Adam's natural condition, then his nature had to be supplemented to be ordered to an eschatological destiny. On the premise that the covenant's obligations were something additional to natural, not just focused by the positive features, then we have left the sphere of divine accommodation and reverted to the idea of ontological elevation. Inasmuch as the medieval and Roman doctrine of sanctifying grace in all its versions

---

58. Westminster Confession 6.3; Bower, *Confession of Faith*, 203.
59. Fesko, *Adam and the Covenant of Works*, 325.

was about a quality added to our nature to enable our merit, we must avoid extrinsic impositions to Adam's nature and insist upon divine accommodation to it. Rather than adding anything to his nature, God's voluntary condescension brought Adam's person, along with his natural obligations, into covenant.

Critically, this construal says nothing more than that the two premises of Westminster Confession 7.1 should be brought together in application to formulation of the covenant of works. On the one hand, we have natural obligations to God since 'reasonable Creatures do owe obedience unto [God] as their Creator.'[60] This obedience to the moral law is inextricably related to our status as God's image bearers, since Westminster Confession 4.2 links our status as reasonable creatures with natural obligation to obey God to the law written on our hearts according to the *imago Dei*: 'he created man, male and female, *with reasonable and immortall souls*, indued with knowledge, righteousnesse and true holinesse, after his own Image; *having the Law of God written in their hearts*, and power to fulfill it.'[61] Our existence as reasonable creatures then includes natural obligation to the law which is a concreated reality in us by virtue of the divine image and original righteousness. On the other hand, from Westminster Confession 7.1, the covenant of works expresses the 'voluntary condescension on Gods part' that orders our natural obligations to God as our blessedness and reward in eschatological communion.[62] This voluntary condescension focused Adam's natural obligations via positive aspects, which themselves encapsulated the natural duties, to give them probationary application and terminus. The voluntary condescension that is the covenant of works is that special act of providence that encompasses our natural obligations to the concreated reality of original righteousness related to bearing God's image, which we have argued occurred concurrently with Adam's creation as a creature owing natural obedience to God. Thus, the natural and covenantal remain conceptually distinct even when they are truly inseparable due to simultaneous occurrence, as was the case with God's moral law in the covenant of works.

---

60. Bower, *Confession of Faith*, 204.

61. Bower, *Confession of Faith*, 201.

62. Bower, *Confession of Faith*, 204.

Let us be clear, as the beginning of the previous paragraph gestured, this construction for bringing together the two premises of Westminster Confession 7.1 in this way can operate rightly *only* in application to the covenant of works. Chapter six contended that Westminster 7.1 is rightly understood as a rubric for understanding how both the covenant of works, as well as the covenant of grace, function. On the one hand, in the covenant of works, God's voluntary condescension tied those two premises together precisely by binding his covenant to the obedience that reasonable creatures owe to him *de facto* as the condition to grant himself as the fruition of our blessedness and reward – that is the beatific vision. On the other hand, in the covenant of grace, those premises must be kept functionally distinct, first, because we still owe God obedience as his reasonable creatures, but sinners cannot render that obedience in fulfillment of the terms for reward, and second, because God's voluntary condescension in the covenant of grace sets faith in Jesus Christ as the condition to obtain fruition of God in the beatific vision. That faith is not conditional as if it is a work that God voluntaristically accepts faith as if it is meritorious. That faith is conditional in that, despite how we sinners are reasonable creatures who owe but cannot render true obedience, God expresses his voluntary condescension in the covenant of grace by accepting Christ's perfect obedience and sacrifice as having fulfilled that obedience *for* all who are united to him by true faith. Faith is then that bond of union whereby we receive and rest upon Christ for what he alone has achieved to provide us with everlasting life. Both covenants then rest upon God's voluntary condescension, but only the covenant of works stipulates our naturally owed obedience as the meritorious condition for obtaining eschatological reward.

Theological Clarifications of Covenantal Merit

Thus far, we have argued for the premise of covenantal merit. We contended from Scripture and the Reformed tradition that, had Adam fulfilled the terms of the covenant of works by faithfully executing his natural duties according to his natural strength, he would have earned entry into the eschatological order. We further argued that the proper way to frame the principle of this merit was that the covenant itself defined the proportion of how Adam's works related to his potential reward. No ontological necessity undergirded this arrangement, but only God's decision to fashion Adam as his image bearer in such a way that he was created into this covenant. Two issues linger, rising from sources upon which we have appreciatively relied, that need some resolution: First, how does the covenant relate to God's nature? Second, does covenantal merit reintroduce an extrinsicism when it comes to the doctrine of imputed righteousness?

The first issue rises from Irons' case for covenantal merit. In the previous chapter, although demurring from his criticism of Westminster Confession 7.1, our own argument against grace in the covenant of works fully aligned with his. Earlier in this chapter, his formulation of the relationship of the covenant to merit well guided our own argument. Now, we argue that, although correct about the relationship between merit and the covenant, Irons posed an unhelpful relationship between the covenant and the divine nature. Irons was rightly concerned to avoid versions of late-medieval hard voluntarism that could render God untrustworthy. Nevertheless, his over-reliance on only one secondary source for his understanding of medieval theology stymied his ability to give a nuanced response to this issue.

As some background, one predominant theme in medieval theology was the distinction between God's *absolute* and *ordained* power.[63] Under the nominalist paradigm, as we saw in chapter three concerning William of Ockham and Gabriel Biel, no safeguards put any stopgaps on God's absolute power, allowing him to break laws of contradiction and command a creature to hate him, upending the whole moral law. In an acceptable construction of this distinction, which avoids the extremes of that hard voluntarism, God is able according to absolute power to do anything *that accords with his nature*.[64] For example, although God cannot lie, since he is truth according to his nature, he could decree anything for creation that does not violate his character. For instance, according to his absolute power, he *could have* justly left sinners to die in their sins. On the other hand, in his ordained power, God has decreed what *will* come to pass in history. For instance, God decreed not to leave

---

63. Heiko A. Oberman, *The Harvest of Medieval Theology: Gabriel Biel and Late Medieval Nominalism*, 3rd ed. (Grand Rapids, MI: Baker Academic, 2000), 30-56; Muller, *Dictionary*, 271-72.

64. Toni C. Saad, 'Francis Turretin's Thomistic Theology of Natural Law,' *Journal of Reformed Theology* 16 (2022): 27-47.

all sinners to die justly for their sins but to save some through Christ the mediator. Although God cannot renege on any promise, he did not have to make every promise that he has. God did not have to promise not to destroy the world with a flood again, but now that he has, he would be unjust to break that promise. This distinction provides explanatory power for things that God *appointed* to be as they are but that could be otherwise.

In terms of the covenant of works, God hypothetically did not have to provide a covenant for Adam to obtain a higher reward. God's nature does constrain him to love what is holy, so obligating him to care for and be good to Adam, whom he made after the divine likeness with knowledge, righteousness, and holiness. In this sense, Witsius explained 'God is not able to work from his goodness without bestowing communion with himself upon the holy creature.'[65] Still, God *ordained* to offer Adam the reward of even better than his natural communion with God, even if this appointment most fittingly flows from that same character aspect of God's goodness. Witsius again helps distinguish the conceptual difference between abstract nature and God's covenant with Adam:

> that this communion with God of which we are speaking, which the goodness of the Supreme God demands be granted to the holy creature, is not yet the covenant's promise, which must finally be given when the condition is fulfilled .... This covenant's promises, therefore, encompass a greater kind of communion with and fruition of God than the kind that Adam enjoyed while he was still in the state of examination.[66]

Although God's nature compelled him to love his holy creature, his making his creature as his eschatologically oriented image bearer was above and beyond that obligation. Still, this abundant kindness flows from that same divine goodness, as Witsius again highlighted: 'For, on the one hand, it appears to me difficult and rightly audacious to say,

---

65. Witsius, *De Oeconomia*, 1.4.19 (Unde colligitur, non posse Deum a bonitate sua impetrare, quin communionem sui creaturae sanctae indulgeat).

66. Witsius, *De Oeconomia*, 1.4.20 (Id autem rursus hic inculcandam ... quod haec, qua de loquimur communio Dei, quam Supremi Numinis Bonitas exigit ut creaturae sanctae largiatur, nondum sit promissum foederis: quod demum dandum est, conditione impleta ... Pollicitationes ergo foederis majora complectuntur hac qualicunque communione & fruitione Dei, qua Adamus, quum etiamnum in statu explorationis esset, jam tum gaudebat).

if someone alleged abruptly that it would have been unworthy of God and his virtues to covenant with men in this way.'[67] So, God appointed in his ordained power to create Adam fit for an eschatological reward, which he could obtain according to the covenant.

That Adam's merit is covenantal, rather than simplistically natural, is obvious from the fact that Adam's success depended most pointedly or most concretely upon passing his probation concerning the tree of knowledge of good and evil. Even though that probationary command circumscribes and encompasses Adam's natural obligations by focusing them into a concrete expression, no explanation reasonably accounts for the tree of knowledge as the probationary fulcrum apart from a positive command that cannot be reduced to the sheer natural relation between God and his image-bearing creature. Adam's merit cannot be entirely natural, as if God's absolute power was limited on this point, because its culminating test was the symbolic law not to eat from this probation tree. The natural law did not intrinsically forbid eating from the tree of knowledge of good and evil. Rather, as Peter Lombard explained, God gave the command about this tree to establish the nature of Adam's merit in connection with his eschatological reward:

> On the transfer of humankind to a better state and on the two goods: the one given here, and the other promised. Such was man's establishment before sin according to the condition of his body. But from this state, he was to be transferred with his entire posterity to a better and worthier state, where he would enjoy the heavenly and eternal good which had been prepared for him in the heavens. — For just as man is composed of a double nature, so the Creator prepared for him two goods from the beginning: one temporal, the other eternal; one visible, the other invisible; one for the flesh, the other for the spirit. And because *that which is animal is first, and afterwards that which is spiritual* [1 Cor. 15:46], he gave the temporal and visible good first; but he promised the invisible and eternal one, and made it known that it was to be sought by merits.
>
> That God gave to man natural reason and a command so that he might preserve the good which he had received and become worthy of that which he had been promised. To preserve what he had given and for the deserving of what he had promised, God added the command of obedience to the

---

67. Witsius, *De Oeconomia*, 1.4.21 (Etenim ab una parte arduum dictu & justo audacious mihi videtur, si quis praefracte afferat, Deo & virtutibus suis indignum fuisse futurum, hoc modo cum hominibus pacifici:).

natural reason that had been placed in the soul of man at creation, by which he was able to discern between good and evil. By observing this command, man would not lose what he had been given and would obtain what had been promised, so that he might come to his reward through merit.[68]

Although this command links sacramentally to the moral law of nature, God added it as a symbolic probationary feature – a kindness because it would have facilitated the terminus of Adam's tenure under testing.[69]

Reformed theology employed the doctrine of God's ordained power as a key factor in the relationship between works and rewards to refine our formulation of Adam's covenantal arrangement. On the one hand, this doctrinal construction protected God's freedom according to his absolute power, so that God was never placed in subjection to his creatures. On the other, it also clarified how Adam was able to earn eschatological communion with God. As John of Damascus interpreted Adam's test with the tree of knowledge: 'And so it was necessary first for man to be tested, since one who is untried and untested deserves no credit. Then, when trial had made him perfect through his keeping of the commandment, he should thus win incorruptibility, the reward of virtue.'[70] This command sharpens Adam's probation into a climactic test, showing – since it was symbolic of but not co-extensively synonymous with the obedience Adam naturally owed to God – that Adam's merit was fundamentally covenantal.

We can further that point by noting that Adam's merit could not reasonably be non-covenantal because of this representative principle. Adam's potential to merit concerned himself and his posterity since he acted federally as a public person. Nothing in the revelation of divine justice as such could guarantee that the personal fulfillment of the works

68. Peter Lombard, *The Sentences Book 2: On Creation*, trans. Giulio Silano (Ontario: Pontifical Institute of Medieval Studies, 2008), 20.6.1-2 (italics original).

69. Tertullian, *Adversus Judeos*, §2 in Jacques Paul Migne (ed.), *Patrologia Cursus Completus: Series Latina*, 221 vol. (Paris, 1844–64), 2:599; Calvin, *Opera*, 23:44; John Calvin, *Commentaries on the First Book of Moses Called Genesis*, trans. John King, 2 vol. (Edinburgh: Calvin Translation Society, 1847), 1:125-26; Johann Heinrich Heidegger, *The Concise Marrow of Theology*, trans. Casey Carmichael (Grand Rapids, MI: Reformation Heritage Books, 2019), 63.

70. John of Damascus, *An Exact Exposition of the Orthodox Faith*, 2.30; in *The Fathers of the Church: St. John of Damascus: Writings*, trans. Frederic H. Chase, Jr. (Washington, D.C.: The Catholic University of America Press, 1958), 265-66.

principle would warrant eschatological reward for oneself *and others* whom that one represents. This principle governs even the covenant of redemption. Christ's mediatorial obedience was intrinsically perfect, yet only the covenantal dimension of his merit determined the remit to whom his earned reward applied – unless we embrace hypothetical universalism wherein, put over crassly, Christ impetrated truly in a sense for all humanity but applies that impetration only to the elect by virtue of the decree.

Irons rightly wanted to keep realist checks on this issue to avoid reshaping Reformed covenant theology with pure voluntarist overtones, but went too far. By suggesting that God had no freedom in how to create Adam as his image bearer, Irons bound God too necessarily to the creature's debt and reintroduced the very ontological categories that he sought to refute. Irons concluded that 'once God freely determined to create a rational being endowed with the divine image in terms of his God-like ethical consciousness and dominion over the creation, then he was no longer free not to enter into a covenant with this creature.' He then forged his unbreakable premise between the divine nature and the covenant's necessity in that 'by making man in his own image he constituted him a covenant being whose very nature longed to attain to the higher status of an eternal and nonforfeitable enjoyment of God. And how could a good and just God implant such a desire within a man without also making available the means by which man could achieve that higher status?'[71] Irons' other premise was that the covenant defined merit, entailing here that truly the analogous relation between God himself and his image-bearing creature necessitated this creature's ability to merit from God.

The trouble is that Irons' conclusion resembles Roman Catholic reasoning behind ontological notions of merit, which was precisely what he aimed to refute. The Roman argument is that God must give what is due to any given nature, inspiring them to distinguish the natural order from the supernatural and to introduce the *donum superadditum* in order to protect the gratuity of man's eschatological destiny. By suggesting that the God-image relation as such *necessarily* involves the relation of the covenant of works and its principle of merit, Irons has posed that Adam's

---

71. Irons, 'Redefining Merit,' 267.

ontic status in God's likeness entitles him to the opportunity to merit. In other words, the principle of merit concerns what God necessarily owes to Adam on account of Adam's nature. Despite his intent, Irons failed to 'eliminate all ontological and modal considerations from the outset.'[72] He instead implemented the exact ontology of nature and merit that drives Roman conclusions about superadded grace. He differed in rejecting that God had freedom to forge that principle of merit, rather making it a necessarily corollary of the Creator-creature relationship. Respectively, he has adopted Thomas' premise that a specific ontological category creates the ability to merit but went further than Thomas in arguing that this category is none other than being our sort of creature in relation to God.

The culminating problem is that to equate fully the image of God and the covenant of works seems to entail that the Christian's renewal after God's image would include a renewal of the covenant of works.[73] This confusion undermines Irons' own concerns to protect the doctrine of justification by faith alone on account of Christ's imputed righteousness. Irons' necessary link between the image of God and the works principle, however, suggests the imputation of Christ's righteousness for justification with our accompanying renewal after God's image reopens the works principle in some fashion.

Irons missed several key points that might have rescued this half of his otherwise helpful premise. First, he too strictly limited God's freedom in creation itself. God could have created an image-bearing creature that was made in the confirmed state of glory. Even given that our image-bearing role includes original righteousness, thereby knowledge of and strength to keep the law, nothing necessitated that God made us in the sub-eschatological state with the need to merit entry into the eschatological order. God chose to create us naturally oriented to advance to the glorified, spiritual state, to which he ordered us by way of covenant to have by covenantal merit. God *ordained* that Adam could obtain eschatological existence if he fulfilled the law of nature, setting the covenantal bond between *this* natural condition and *this* reward of eschatological destiny. God had already given communion to

---

72. Irons, 'Redefining Merit,' 267.

73. Thanks to Ryan McGraw for this point.

Adam in the garden, making it a grave mistake to strip this covenant of all familial and intimate facets in favor of a basely legal arrangement. If someone believes that we cannot trust God to be good to us, to keep his promises, and to shower his children with blessings unless we can find something ontologically deeper in his nature than his truthfulness and faithfulness, as revealed in Scripture's overarching narrative, that necessitates his commitment to us besides what he has eternally decreed, it raises serious pastoral concerns.[74] We should not be skeptical of the explanatory power of God's love.

Second, Meredith Kline helps us to see how God choosing to create man in covenant provides a sounder biblical rationale. Concerning the divine fiats of creation, Kline wrote: 'Nothing could more plainly show that this covenant was a sovereign administration of God's lordship. The vassal had had nothing to say about the terms of the covenant; he did not previously exist. Whatever he was or had, everything was a gift of creation. And how lavishly the Creator's goodness had been expressed.'[75] That God exercised rule, rather than acted by necessity, in developing the covenantal world and man as his covenantal creature shows God's goodness. On the one hand, Kline argues that 'God's covenant word' is 'the definer of justice' meaning that God has established the relationship of work to reward by stipulating the standard of merit.[76] By contrast, Irons defaults to an ontological premise that the prescription of the merit-reward relationship is built intrinsically into our image-bearing constitution. His premise is the same as we saw throughout the medieval and Roman tradition that God must give whatever is proper to a particular nature. He posited that the *imago Dei* is the ontological aspect of human nature that demands our natural merit-reward relation to the eschatological order.

---

74. If Irons follows Kline's interpretation of Genesis 1:26 that the plural deliberation 'Let us make man in our image' addressed the heavenly council of angels who also seemingly bear the divine image, then the angels' seeming lack of prospect for eschatological advancement – since best we know the elect angels seem simply confirmed in their original condition – undermines Irons' contention that God's relation to the divine image as such has the merit-reward potential intrinsically inbuilt; Meredith G. Kline, *Images of the Spirit* (Eugene, OR: Wipf and Stock, 1999), 20-23; see Vos, *Reformed Dogmatics*, 2:40-41.

75. Kline, *Kingdom Prologue*, 59.

76. Kline, *Kingdom Prologue*, 114-16.

Although Irons was exactly right in how he defined the relationship of merit and covenant, his misstep concerned the relationship between the covenant and God's nature. Kline helpfully delimited the divine justice that defined the proportion of works and reward in terms of meritorious conditions to God's *acts*, which 'is expressed in the covenant he institutes.'[77] Irons pressed beyond God's acts to the divine nature itself as restricting God's freedom in relation to how he could define the covenantal terms of merit, so inevitably contending that creaturely works are in fact *ontologically* proportionate to the divine nature for heavenly reward.[78]

David VanDrunen advances Kline's trajectory in a more balanced way. He too noted that God was not intrinsically obligated but made creatures in his image so that the works principle was inscribed in their nature.[79] Human beings were not:

> on some kind of ontologically level ground with God so as to enable them to earn something from him, but that God as a free gift created human beings in his image, in a covenant relationship (the covenant of creation). As an image-bearer in covenant with God, Adam was naturally enabled to follow God's archetypal pattern of ruling well in this world and then attaining rest in an eschatological new creation as a just reward.[80]

In other words, as we have argued, Adam has the potential to merit eschatological life because God chose to create him of a specific sort, covenanting with him as the particular manner of freely revealing himself for the protological situation when he created him.[81] Jacob Wood connected God's design to our end: 'In every state, humanity desires that end which God has assigned to us; but since God has called us *in the present, historical state* to the beatific vision, human nature has a natural desire for its supernatural end.'[82] Vos gave us the helpful insight that God's

---

77. Kline, *Kingdom Prologue*, 115.

78. Irons, 'Redefining Merit,' 265-68.

79. David VanDrunen, 'Natural Law and the Works Principle under Adam and Moses,' in Bryan D. Estelle, J. V. Fesko, and David VanDrunen (eds.), *The Law is Not of Faith: Essays on Works and Grace in the Mosaic Covenant* (Phillipsburg, NJ: P&R, 2009), 291.

80. VanDrunen, *Divine Covenants and Moral Order*, 33.

81. VanDrunen, *Divine Covenants and Moral Order*, 90-91.

82. Jacob W. Wood, *To Stir a Restless Heart: Thomas Aquinas and Henri de Lubac on Nature, Grace, and the Desire for God* (Thomistic Ressourcement Series; Washington, DC: Catholic University of America Press, 2019), 403 (italics original).

inclination for 'unremitting kindness' to humanity may ground why God would create man in this sort of covenant, but does not impose an *intrinsic* human right to expect and demand reward, making the covenant of works positive as ordained by God.[83] Hence we can discard Irons' claim that the relation itself of divine essence to image bearer defines merit, and resort back to the Reformed tradition's paradigm that God proportioned Adam's works to his potential reward by covenant. As Turretin concluded after asserting Adam's natural strength to perform his due obedience: 'If a proportion is not conferred between the prescribed duty and the benefit of heavenly life, it does not follow that so excellent a promise cannot have a place because it is supposed to no purpose and falsely that the proportion of our merit regulates God's promises, when on the contrary, they depend upon God's will and goodness.'[84] God is a kind and loving Father and created us in covenant to be how he wanted us to be, not how he had to make us. God as Creator treats us in a manner consistent with the orientation and ordering which he committed himself to give us.[85]

The other theological clarification concerns whether our view of covenantal merit reintroduces an aspect of extrinsicism. The underlying issue in this point is that the covenant of works included not only the principle of merit for personal, perfect, and perpetual obedience but also the principle of imputation. Since Adam represented all humanity in the covenant, the record of his triumphing or transgressing in the covenant would be credited to all his posterity. Because he broke the covenant, his sin was imputed to all who descended from him by ordinary generation.[86] The parallel holds in the covenant of grace that

---

83. Vos, *Reformed Dogmatics*, 2:32, 41.

84. Turrettinus, *Institutio*, 8.6.9b [This Latin edition misnumbered this section as a second 8.6.9, which should be 8.6.10] (Foedus naturale non ideo dicitur, quod nihil conferat supra naturam, & conditionem, quam homo habuerat a Creatione, sed quia nitebatur naturae viribus, & obediential, quam juxta illas praestare debuit. Nec si proportio non datur inter officium praescriptum, & coelestis vitae beneficium; sequitur locum habere non posse talem promissionem, quia gratis & falso supponitur promissiones Deo regulate secundum proportionem meriti nostril, cum contra pendeant a voluntate & bonitate Dei).

85. Andrew Davison, *Participation in God: A Study in Christian Doctrine and Metaphysics* (Cambridge: Cambridge University Press, 2019), 355-61.

86. J. V. Fesko, *Death in Adam, Life in Christ: The Doctrine of Imputation* (Reformed Exegetical and Doctrinal Studies; Fearn, UK: Mentor, 2016); John Murray, *Imputation of Adam's Sin* (Phillipsburg, NJ: P&R, 2012).

Christ represented his people, so his merit is imputed to us as the ground of our justification by faith. There is then an active principle for both covenants wherein we receive the imputation of a status that someone else attained – for ill or for good.

We need to provide some integration of our metaphysical position that God created humanity for the supernatural/eschatological end with our covenantal outlook about how we are ordered to that end. This integrative work is warranted because some of the theologians who have furnished us with our fruitful reflection about nature's relationship to God have been critical or unclear when applying the principle of analogical participation to the doctrine of justification. On one hand, Hans Boersma has critiqued the Reformation doctrine of justification by faith alone for its teaching about Christ's imputed righteousness.[87] He claimed that the aspect concerning judicial status harks to nominalism and that the aspect concerning imputation itself is a reintroduction of extrinsicist religion. On the other hand, Andrew Davison has tried to press analogical participation, which is highly useful concerning the Creator-creature distinction, into service for explaining the doctrine of justification and merit.[88] The strength of their metaphysical arguments warrants response to them on this soteriological issue.

We should be clear that this response is aimed at clarifying and refining the principles of this discussion to demonstrate how classical Christian metaphysics stand coherently with Reformed soteriology.[89]

---

87. Hans Boersma, *Heavenly Participation: The Weaving of a Sacramental Tapestry* (Grand Rapids, MI: Eerdmans, 2011), 92-94; Hans Boersma, *Scripture as Real Presence: Sacramental Exegesis in the Early Church* (Grand Rapids, MI: Baker Academic, 2017), 259-63.

88. Davison, *Participation in God*, 260-300.

89. I should note that I find much of Boersma's argument throughout *Scripture as Real Presence* for Christ's real presence in Scripture and the historical events recorded in the Old Testament persuasive and outstanding. More pertinently, his basic point is a foundational consideration for the Reformed doctrine of the covenant of grace, namely that the Son *incarnandus* was active as the only mediator between God and man even before he came historically in the incarnation. Boersma's historical case for this view among the patristic writers highlights the traditional nature of the Reformed tradition's understanding of the continuity of Old and New Testaments with Christ as the scope (and substance) of both. I believe that the arguments which I have made elsewhere concerning Christ as the one way of salvation across the scope of redemptive history to be received through the means of grace (including Scripture) appointed in each covenant administration fundamentally coheres with the main contours of Boersma's case; Harrison Perkins, *Reformed Covenant Theology: A Systematic Introduction* (Bellingham, WA: Lexham Press, 2024), 187-216, 273-99.

After all, this book sees the doctrines of Reformation soteriology as completely compatible, if not the entailment of, a robust metaphysic about the Creator-creature relationship. Our aim is more on this clarifying and advancing effort than on attacking their holistic points. The posture of great appreciation is maintained, as the previous chapter expressed, for Boersma's efforts to reintegrate the natural and supernatural orders to overturn notions of pure nature and a true extrinsicism and for Davison's contributions to how nature can be truly revelatory of God without collapsing the Creator-creature distinction. Regarding Boersma, he seemed to make mistaken assumptions in his argument about how the legal categories for the imputation of Christ's righteousness can relate to a more basic ontological realism. Regarding Davison, he attempted to incorporate his creational categories for how we as God's image bearers have an analogical participation in God's righteousness into his soteriological categories for forensic justification.

Our response depends upon re-highlighting the connection of covenant and nature. Boersma himself contended that our relationship to God must be covenantal alongside the metaphysical, rejecting that creation can relate to God with '*just* an external, or nominal, connection.'[90] Davison allowed for the forensic to sit alongside the participatory so long as the forensic does not mean that Christ's substitutionary work 'rests only on the choice of God, and not on a grounding in the incarnate life, death, and Resurrection of Christ.'[91] Further, he suggested that forensic and substitutionary models are non-participatory 'only once no ontological change is thought to proceed from the work of Christ to the redeemed person.'[92] As this and the previous chapter have contended, our covenantal relation to God is not some merely extrinsic imposition. Thus, it is not some merely nominalist construction lacking realist grounds.[93] It is the judicial connection between our created order and the eschatological order.

---

90. Boersma, *Heavenly Participation*, 24-25 (emphasis added); also Boersma, *Scripture as Real Presence*, 260-62.

91. Davison, *Participation in God*, 264.

92. Davison, *Participation in God*, 264-65.

93. The explanation of this point should distance our view from those Davison criticized as being substitutionary to the exclusion of the participatory; Davison, *Participation in God*, 263-65, esp. 264n17.

Without suggesting that Boersma and Davison have necessarily made this mistake, we should not presume that legal facets of our lives are utter fabrications. Judicial realities are still true realities.

The covenant was not an afterthought to creation since God created and covenanted with Adam in the same event. Westminster Larger Catechism keeps room for this interpretation by asserting that God created man 'having the Law of God written in their hearts, and power to fulfill it.'[94] Westminster Confession 19.1 comments on this aspect of our creation that 'God gave to Adam a Law, *as a Covenant of Works*,' which same law – according to Westminster Confession 19.2 – was the same moral law delivered in summary form through the decalogue at Sinai.[95] Westminster Larger Catechism 20 then discusses God's special providence toward man which includes putting him in the garden, describing his responsibility, ordaining marriage, 'affording him communion with himself, instituting the Sabbath, and entering into a Covenant of life with him, upon condition of personall, perfect, and perpetuall obedience, of which the Tree of Life was a pledge, and forbidding to eat of the Tree of the Knowledge of good and evil, upon pain of death.'[96] Some of these features of special providence cannot be divorced from the creation itself. For example, marriage, although not constitutive of our human identity, obviously flows from our created order that desires communion and has anatomical capability to reproduce.[97] As already argued in the previous chapter, God's institution of the Sabbath simply declared the created reality's covenantal function. So too with God's special revelation about the trees, since these commands encapsulated the condition and reward imprinted onto our nature.[98] As God created and covenanted with Adam in the same

---

94. Question 17; John R. Bower, *The Larger Catechism: A Critical Text and Introduction* (Principal Documents of the Westminster Assembly; Grand Rapids, MI: Reformation Heritage Books, 2010), 69.

95. Bower, *Confession of Faith*, 217.

96. Bower, *Larger Catechism*, 69-70.

97. cf. Richard C. Barcellos, *Getting the Garden Right: Adam's Work and God's Rest in Light of Christ* (Cape Coral, FL: Founders Press, 2017), 43-46.

98. This point is another reason to reject the strictly positivist view of covenants outlined in Samuel Renihan, *The Mystery of Christ: His Covenant and His Kingdom* (Cape Coral, Fl: Founders Press, 2020), 13-19. Primarily, if the first covenant is not conjoined to nature, then our eschatological destiny is not naturally part of our human constitution, then we

event, the covenanting aspect is conceptually distinguishable in that it established Adam's natural obligations according to his natural strength as the covenantal condition. Our use of covenant, therefore, already mitigates Boersma's concern about the judicial aspects of our relation to God being extrinsic.

Moreover, the structures of imputation are also not part of a nominalist extrinsicism. As argued above, the condition for covenantal merit was perfect obedience according to the standards *written upon our nature* as God's image bearers. Adam had to fulfill his natural potential, performing obedience in one special test, which God set as the terminus of his probation. This point integrates readily into Davison's participatory metaphysic. According to the premises of analogical participation, Adam's natural call as God's image bearer was to imitate God's ethical perfections in a manner fitting to the creature. The notion that humanity has a nature deriving its ethical orientation from a certain relationship to God easily fits both the metaphysical and the covenantal/judicial registers. Davison has framed this point from the metaphysical angle of participation, which we can affirm. The covenantal or judicial framing of the same point would be that Adam was obligated to fulfill the moral law which is imbedded in human nature. The covenantal declaration of justification would then be simply that Adam had adequately performed this natural duty of analogical participation, specifically concerning original righteousness, to fulfill the covenant's terms so to gain its reward.[99] Alternatively stated,

---

have a true acceptance of the Roman view of the supernatural order as superadded to pure nature. On the contrary, God designed our nature with inbuilt eschatological capacity (1 Cor. 15:42-49). Secondarily, Renihan's view is fully susceptible to all the criticisms of extrinsic religion since he sees every covenant as purely positivist rather than natural.

99. The omission of this connection of the participatory and the covenantal dimensions to the forensic declaration of justification explains why some have thought that the imputation of Christ's active obedience is unnecessary on grounds of a dichotomy between merit and relational categories, e.g. Michael F. Bird, 'Progressive Reformed View,' in James K. Beilby and Paul Rhodes Eddy (eds.), *Justification: Five Views* (Spectrum Multiview Books; Downers Grove, IL: IVP Academic, 2011), 148-52; Michael F. Bird, 'Progressive Reformed Response,' in *Justification: Five Views*, 115-16. The covenantal contours to Adam's original obligation to reflect his participatory relationship to God unite merit and relational participation together so that we cannot set our demerit/lack of merit against a broken relationship as opposing explanations of the problem of sin. They belong together. This point should also clarify that not every debt can be reduced to monetary terms. In other words, the forensic aspects of Reformed covenant theology do not cast personal righteousness as if it is money to be accrued for use as capital with

once Adam fulfilled his duties to the moral law of nature to the end of his probation, he would have fulfilled the covenant of works and merited its reward. As we saw in chapter two, Benedict Pictet argued along the same lines, setting clear precedent in the Reformed tradition:

> If the first man would have endured in innocence, then he would have been justified by fulfilling the natural law, which God had imprinted upon his heart .... The way by which God would have justified the innocent person would have been a declaration of the person's holiness and righteousness, and that justification, therefore, can be defined as God's act as judge, by which he grants everlasting life and glory to the perfectly holy person.[100]

Davison's case for justification as God causing us to participate increasingly in his righteousness so that we become meritoriously righteous seemingly omits the premise of needing a legal assessment of that righteousness that grounds our justification.[101] The legal declaration of justification concerns how well we have fulfilled our participatory purpose of reflecting God's righteousness at the creaturely level.

This framing for justification as a covenantal and legal declaration concerning the recognition of a realist need for God's image bearers to render obedience to God as part of our creaturely imitation of his righteousness ought to defuse any suspicions of nominalism for our paradigm of covenant theology. Regarding his accusation of nominalism, Boersma was then mistaken concerning the Reformed doctrine of Christ's imputed righteousness in a twofold way. First, he was incorrect to see any sort of nominalism in the doctrine of imputation because the status of 'justified' crowns only works that have truly met the real standard of righteousness, namely those works cohering with our original righteousness inbuilt by virtue of our image-bearing constitution. In this respect, the standard undergirding the judicial status accords with

---

God. Rather, we ontologically owe the debt of performing righteousness because we were created intrinsically ordered to reflect God's character. The debt is then real while God's assessment and declarative verdict would be forensic.

100. Benedict Pictet, *Theologia Christiana* (Geneva, 1716), 704-5 (Dicimus autem quod primus homo, si in innocentia permansisset, justificatus fuisset adimplendo legem naturalem, quam ipsius cordi impresserat Deus, & alia praecepta, quae Deus ipsi praescribere poterat, diligendo perfecte Deum suum & proximum .... Modus quo Deus justificasset hominem innocentem, fuisset declaratio sanctitatis & justitiae hominis; unde justification illa definiri potuisset; Actio Dei judicis, qua hominem perfectè sanctum vita donat aterna & gloria).

101. Davison, *Participation in God*, 287-95.

our analogical connection to God in the Creator-creature distinction. This point aligns with the major concerns of Boersma's (and Davison's) participatory metaphysics.[102]

Second, Boersma incorrectly suggested an extrinsic component to the doctrine of imputation. The demands of the law are written upon every human heart. We stand under the requirement of the covenant of works by nature, meaning the obligation to attain the status of righteousness that is justification is an intrinsic aspect of how God created us in covenant. We intrinsically need to obtain that judicial status to enter the eschatological order, which is also natural in that God built our nature with an eschatological capacity (1 Cor. 15:42-49).[103] The redemptive order includes Christ's fulfillment of the law's demands that intrinsically bound us by nature, joining us to himself so that we are made righteous by his perfect righteousness and made new by participating in his resurrection life.[104] Christ did achieve an alien righteousness for us that remains the grounds of our justification, and has joined us to himself by faith so that we share in his benefits.

In truth, the voluntarist notion of merit, wherein God accepts our best efforts, introduces the extrinsicism into the doctrine of justification. On the premise of the Franciscan Pactum, God imposes an external assessment upon a work by calling it 'righteous' when that status is not intrinsic to the work itself. In the paradigm of covenantal merit, God does not accept a deficient work as righteous. Rather, he recognizes an intrinsically righteous work for what it is, and honors it with the reward that is determined by the covenant's terms. The work itself must be truly righteous, cohering with Thomas' realist notion of merit, even if its corresponding reward surpasses its intrinsic value. The Protestant doctrine of justification on the basis of imputed righteousness maintains an intrinsicism in that the works that ground our justification must be truly righteous without any imperfection and must be the sort of righteous

---

102. Michael S. Horton, 'Participation and Covenant,' in James K. A. Smith and James H. Olthuis (eds.), *Radical Orthodoxy and the Reformed Tradition: Creation, Covenant, and Participation* (Grand Rapids, MI: Baker Academic, 2005), 107-32; Justin S. Holcomb, 'Being Bound to God: Participation and Covenant Revisited,' in *Radical Orthodoxy and the Reformed Tradition*, 243-62.

103. Perkins, *Reformed Covenant Theology*, 47-76.

104. Michael S. Horton, *Lord and Servant: A Covenant Christology* (Louisville, KY: Westminster John Knox Press, 2005), 133.

works that our nature demanded that we perform. The declaration of justification then demands a true realist premise of righteousness that accords with our calling as God's image bearers to imitate God's righteousness, so to reflect his character, at the creaturely level.

It just so happens that Jesus Christ has attained that righteousness in our place and credits it to those who are joined to him by faith alone. Jesus has merited justification for us by his record of intrinsic righteousness – the reward promised to him was in fact that his merits would justify those given to him in the covenant of redemption. Justification must be by faith alone because we, as those who have broken our original righteousness, cannot attain true merit. We cannot imitate God as his likeness to show forth his righteousness as we were made and meant to do. Justification does come to us on the basis of true merit, however, because Christ's real merit is credited to us in union with him (Rom. 5:18-21).[105]

This covenantal doctrine of justification has several strengths in the wake of our full study. It coheres with wider concerns from classical metaphysics by presuming a premise of realism respecting the righteousness required for justification. It aligns with a strong view of the Creator-creature distinction by acknowledging that we, as God's image bearers, were commissioned to reflect God at the creaturely level, so doing justice to our participatory doctrine of analogy. This alignment helps us to see how our nature must have an intrinsic supernatural valence, which God fashioned to be oriented to the eschatological order.

Nonetheless, our paradigm of covenantal merit refuses to load ontological transformation into the doctrine of justification itself. Its strength is also in being able to incorporate judicial and ontological categories without having to jettison one to give due place to the other. Our formulation of the judicial and metaphysical concerns holds them together. The contrast with Davison's position is that we want to locate the transformative aspect of Christ's work in the correct benefits of salvation.[106] In justification's wake comes the benefits of advancement to eschatological blessings, which have their transformative and even

---

105. Perkins, *Reformed Covenant Theology*, 217-70.

106. Davison himself acknowledged that this distinction coheres with his larger argument; *Participation in God*, 264-65, 281-85.

ontological entailments.[107] Our doctrine of covenantal merit for justification most honors our metaphysical obligation to imitate God's righteousness by asserting that God will apply the status of 'righteous' only to the record that has truly and fully reflected his own righteousness in a way that can be performed by creatures. For justification, the obedience rendered must be truly and intrinsically righteous because as 'God will render to each one according to his works,' he 'shows *no* partiality' (Rom. 2:6-11). Christ came in human nature so that he could render that true expression of divine righteousness on the creaturely horizon. Since he was God the Son, he could perform perfectly in alignment with God's own righteousness.[108] Since the Son assumed our nature, he could render that righteousness as obedience to law to fulfill the requirements for justification *for us* and so earn our entry into the eschatological order.[109]

Conclusion

God fashioned us for communion with himself, making us in such a way that our communion with him was covenantal in nature. Apart from any ontological demands for how he might create us, God chose to create us in covenant. In this way, he blessed us with initial fellowship with himself and offered to advance us to the eschatological order to know even deeper communion with him in the beatific vision. God pledged himself to us and offered us more of himself. Cornelis Venema well summarized the shape of this communion in that God 'bound himself by the promises as well as the demands of that covenant' entailing that:

> Adam's obedience to the stipulated obedience, though it were an outworking and development within the covenant communion in which he was placed by God's prevenient favor, would nonetheless 'merit' or 'deserve' the reward of righteousness God himself had promised. In the covenant itself God bound himself to grant, as in some sense a reward

---

107. Perkins, *Reformed Covenant Theology*, 243-70.

108. Westminster Larger Catechism 38; Bower, *Larger Catechism*, 72-73.

109. Westminster Larger Catechism 39; Bower, *Larger Catechism*, 73. The Son had to assume human nature if his righteous acts were going to be *obedience*. The Son *as God* is fully equal to the Father, having one common will among the Trinity, so cannot as such obey. His *obedience* was rendered to the law in our nature because humanity is obligated to obey God; Perkins, *Reformed Covenant Theology*, 101-23.

well-deserved, the fullness of covenant fellowship into which Adam was called.[110]

Covenantal merit is then a traditional Reformed idea that upholds the fundamental concerns of God's goodness in creating Adam upright and good as well as God's justice in making a covenant to reward Adam's works with higher blessings.

Our closing engagement with Boersma fittingly concludes this book's main contours because it recenters us directly in our main idea: a defense of the law-gospel distinction through the lens of the image of God. The principle of covenantal merit as we have articulated it removes any extrinsicism from our religious anthropology because it grounds the covenant in nature as God made us to bear his image, suffused with original righteousness as constitutive of our image-bearing capacity. This judicial aspect of our identity is hardwired into how God created us to be ordered to supernatural realities and oriented, as well as covenantally ordered, toward our eschatological destiny. Our sin, by lacking conformity unto and transgressing God's law, shattered our personal pathway to our supernatural end. In the gospel, however, Jesus Christ has *merited* our citizenship in the new creation where, upon being raised on the last day, we will behold our triune God in everlasting communion.

---

110. Venema, *Christ and Covenant Theology*, 33.

Pastoral Reflections on Covenant Theology for Communion with God

This book has explored what it means to have been made for fellowship with God. We sought to think down to the bottom about the implications of being created after God's image and in his likeness. The ethical implications have resounded throughout because we have contended that the image of God and original righteousness are bound together if not nearly the same.[1] The corollary of man's image-bearing constitution then 'means above all that he is disposed for communion with God, that all the capacities of his soul can act in a way that corresponds to their destiny only if they rest in God.'[2] In Augustine's incomparable prayer about God's design for man: 'You stimulate him to take pleasure in praising you, because you have made us for yourself, and our hearts are restless until they find peace in you.'[3] Our ultimate end is God, that we might know him in everlasting, incorruptible life (John 17:3).

The argument has been that a proper understanding of our original righteousness structures our eschatology and undergirds the Protestant

---

1. Geerhardus Vos, *Reformed Dogmatics*, 5 vol. (Bellingham, WA: Lexham Press, 2012–14), 2:12.

2. Vos, *Reformed Dogmatics*, 2:13.

3. Saint Augustine, *The Confessions of Saint Augustine*, trans. Rex Warner (New York, NY: Signet Classics, 1963), 1.1.

law-gospel distinction. The original righteousness with which Adam was naturally endowed was the shape of the communion with God for which we were made. As God's image bearers, we were meant to reflect him by shining his righteousness into creation at the creaturely level. This purpose included the ethical execution of mirroring the exercise of his kingship. Had Adam fulfilled this task to the other side of his encounter with the serpent at the tree of knowledge of good and evil, he would have placed us beyond probation and earned entry to join God in his rest. Our original righteousness then had an eschatological ordering.

The covenant of works was God's accommodation to how he created us in original righteousness. It bound our created order to the prospective eschatological order even according to our natural constitution. God did not have to change or supplement our nature to fit us for our covenantal duties or to orient us toward supernatural realties. The covenant was the judicial bridge that defined the proportion between our works and the eschatological reward for which God made us.

We have traversed a lot of historical and theological ground, unearthing several complicated but intertwined concepts that have driven this discussion across the breadth of the Christian tradition. This conclusion reflects upon some basic takeaways from the scope of both our historical and theological argumentation. Theology in its proper use cannot be a raw academic exercise because it is for God's people. It facilitates our contemplation of the divine. It is the engine of our communion with God in this age. The following reflections, therefore, aim to show how I, as a pastor, hope this book will help us to feed Christ's sheep.

Historical

This book's historical-theological account was winding and yet should help us reckon with some aspects of the Christian life. The church's reflection upon Scripture and our shaping of sacred doctrine developed over time one step at a time. The process of theological refinement was slow, as theologians usually recognized the deficiency of isolated premises one at a time. Theological development worked somewhat like replacing one cog in the machine at a time as a more efficient sort of cog became available. As we considered Reformed interactions with medieval thought, it was clear that our theologians, historically speaking, continued the same process of working with existing paradigms and exchanging cogs in the theological machinery still in isolated fashion. Some of those cogs were much larger and more pivotal than had been swapped in previous eras of theological development. The Reformers nonetheless saw themselves working upon the same machine that had always been there, even though they perceived that it had become dilapidated by the eve of the Reformation.

A wide-angle upshot from this perspective on historical theology is that the process of theological development has never worked as the competition of truly hermetically sealed systems wherein one system is wholesale swapped out for another. Although Reformed and Roman theology now represent two independent models for doing and describing theology, at the historical level, our Reformed system was not a brand-new machine set in place of the previous one. The Reformation intended to *reform* the existing theological machinery, not build a new one from scratch. Although we may have, over time, realized that more components needed to be replaced or upgraded than we first recognized, we have never thought that our Reformed system was entirely disconnected from the premises and trajectories of our preceding catholic tradition. The quest to present, from an historical angle, Reformed theology as a programmatic system that is entirely self-contained and airtightly disconnected from the ideas, discussions, and formulations of the full Christian tradition is grounded far more in idealist philosophy, which obscures historical consciousness in favor of timelessly rationalistic truths, than in responsible assessment of the historical data. That quest is like searching for a unicorn on the seafloor: we would be looking in the wrong place for something that does not even exist.

For Christians, moral implications of some degree pertain to all our endeavors, historiography included. The strategy of reducing the Reformed tradition down to a self-contained set of ideas without at least an initial porous interaction with the preceding tradition facilitates pride and lazy sloppiness. If we pretend that we have a perfect, self-contained doctrinal system that has always been comprehensively distinct from all other theological traditions, all we have left to do is criticize any disagreement with what we already confess. This prideful posture precludes genuine interaction with challenging and even opposing ideas that might help us strengthen and develop our doctrinal system. That posture certainly feels intellectually safer, which may be a comfort to those who feel that the system can be correct only if every detail is properly interpreted. I am not convinced that the comfort of intellectual safety is our calling as theologians. Growth means facing challenges. The only way to avoid complication and difficulty in contending for what we believe prescriptively is to generalize alternative doctrinal systems so much that they contain no challenge worthy of consideration even for the sake of refining our beliefs. That stance manifests an inadequate and self-satisfied academic mindset that refuses to grapple with the nuances of history and the prospect for future refinement of our own understanding of theology.

The pastoral upshot from these historiographical observations is that the complicated version of historical theology demonstrates Christ's faithfulness to his promise that he would never abandon his church. Jesus swore: 'I will build my church, and the gates of hell shall not prevail against it' (Matt. 16:18). The outcome, since gates are defensive, is that Christ would always, overall, advance the church in truth and spiritual victory. God promised to the church as he promised to Joshua as the leader after Moses, 'I will never leave you nor forsake you' (Heb. 13:5; Josh. 1:5), grounding our ability to advance in the Christian responsibilities described in the surrounding context. In his upper room discourse, outlining his forthcoming post-ascension commitment to his people, Jesus promised, 'I will not leave you as orphans; I will come to you' (John 14:18). Filling out what this promise entailed, he explained, 'the Helper, the Holy Spirit, whom the Father will send in my name, he will teach you all things and bring to your remembrance all that I have said to you' (John 14:26). The church has never – including now in our Reformed circles – had perfect and comprehensive understanding of the truth, at times having significantly less than pure articulations of some doctrines. Nonetheless, we ought to believe Jesus that he was always teaching his church by the Spirit.

We should, therefore, not posit that the Reformed tradition is some holistic swap of an entire system as if complete consistency has ever been possible or necessary to have a grasp of divine truth. Brute facts may not exist, but God has and does often preserve us in useful understanding of himself and our relationship to him regardless of how *we* do not perfectly interpret every fact even in relation to our own other beliefs.

Even as we might find the clearest or our most preferred expressions in more recent Reformed writers, we cannot assert that their views *exhaust* the Reformed tradition as if those prior Reformed theologians who had not reached their same conclusions should be wholesale shut out of the tradition. Historical-theological development is a testimony to God's grace as we Reformed people stand in providential continuity with the church of ages past as the legacy of Christ's promises to teach and preserve us despite our shortcomings, even in doctrinal formulation.

Theological

The main payoff from this book is to help us take better account of what we were meant to be, what we are, and what Christ does for us. The integration of our orientation to supernatural realities into our natural constitution suffuses human existence with an all-pervasive relationship to God. We cannot exist outside relation to our Maker since our very constitution reveals him to us and orients us to him and life with him. How are we to think about living in light of our original position, where we are now, and the gospel? Or more simply put, what is the life of grace?

The real difference between Rome and the Reformation concerning this point focuses our attention on the deepest aspects of life before the Lord. In the Roman outlook, God made humanity but still had to apply *gratia gratum faciens* – that is, sanctifying grace or grace that makes pleasing. That grace is a quality which we are said to need even in our created order, according to our nature, to set us in relation to supernatural realities.[4] All the more, some explanations among the Franciscans pose that we must first earn that *gratia gratum faciens* before we enter that state of sanctifying grace, suggesting that even God's base favor for us in the created state must be earned.[5] In the Reformed paradigm, at least as this book has argued it given the tradition's eclectic diversity, God had no need to elevate our nature from how it stood in the created order. He could and did create us exactly how he wanted us to be for fellowship with him. No discrepancy stood between our nature and blessed fellowship with God, including the possibility of advancing to even deeper fellowship in the glorified state. In our view, God made us so

---

4. Herman Bavinck, *Reformed Dogmatics*, ed. John Bolt, trans. John Vriend, 4 vol. (Grand Rapids, MI: Baker Academic, 2003–2008), 2:539-42; 3:574-77.

5. Bavinck, *Reformed Dogmatics*, 2:540-41.

that we were pleasing to him, rather than needing to add grace to make us pleasing. In the view argued here, grace is, therefore, accidental to nature on account of sin rather than its absolutely necessary completion.[6] Grace belongs only to the redemptive order.

This paradigm does fuller justice to the rupture caused by sin. One of the concerns that undergirds the pure nature doctrine in Roman thought regards the state of nature now. They are concerned to affirm that our present existence is natural in that we are not less than what it means to be human. We can sympathize with Roman theology's desire to explain the present state of affairs to help people navigate how to live in this age. We should still offer a more satisfactory answer for why this age includes the tension of knowing that the world is meant to be good but presently manifests a tragic state of affairs.

In our paradigm, we affirm that the problems caused by sin run far deeper. The rupture caused by sin truly has damaged nature as such. We are not what we were meant to be. Inasmuch as we lost our original righteousness, so damaging our image-bearing capacities, we function at the sub-natural level. We are sustained in our quotidian affairs only by God's general providence in common grace. Our view's explanatory force is certainly less affirming than the Roman notion of pure nature as undamaged in what it needs to be. Nevertheless, it provides more consolation because it helps people reckon with what is truly wrong with the world. We should not pretend that sin's effects are mere glitches in the operating system. In truth, the hard drive is cracked but still running by divine preservation. The book of Ecclesiastes is in the inspired canon for a reason.

The damaging of that natural condition that had its inbuilt orientation to the supernatural and eschatological totally undermines the notions of pure nature particularly as they appear in Gabriel Biel and Robert Barron. In this nominalist paradigm, grace is so all-encompassing that essentially all grace is common grace that can work even to a saving extent, if it even be ultimately necessary. In reality, sin left our nature broken, original righteousness shattered, and our ordering to supernatural realities distorted so that we now operate sub-naturally.[7]

---

6. Bavinck, *Reformed Dogmatics*, 3:577-79.

7. Vos, *Reformed Dogmatics*, 2:14-15; Bavinck, *Reformed Dogmatics*, 2:542-48; Jan Veenhof, 'Nature and Grace in Bavinck,' *Pro Rege* 34 no 4 (2006): 16-18.

Our position is that we had an end of supernatural destiny woven into our nature. We have a God-shaped hole so much that we are not fulfilled without it. This concern drove Rome's paradigm of pure nature because they assume that something was wrong with our constitution as such if we did not attain that end. The real problem, however, is that by sin we wrecked our natural course to that end. The fall has truly ruined our nature, leaving us incomplete and malformed in comparison to God's original design for us in original righteousness. It is a problem that sin prevents us from reaching our eschatological end, which is the exact nature of condemnation. Everlasting torment includes being blocked off from that rich, unending communion that we were fashioned to attain.

Thus, our view of creation and the fall paves the way for our proclamation of the gospel. The world under sin has real need. We are not fine as we stand on our own. We are broken, and we are liable for our brokenness because it belongs to us on account of our sin. Although every deed has its wage, 'the wages of sin is death' (Rom. 6:23). This bad news situation arose from Adam's broken covenant.

Thankfully, God made another covenant, the covenant of grace. Although we owe a debt to render obedience that is beyond our damaged capacity to perform and deserve to die on account of breaking God's holy law, the second Adam came to pay our debts. The gospel is that Christ succeeded where Adam failed and earned what he forfeited, granting it to all who believe in him.

The principle of Adam's covenantal merit informs the gospel as well. God the Son owed no obedience since he is God by nature. Even coming in our nature would not determine any specific reward for his complete accordance with divine righteousness because he by nature owns all things and possesses the divine character that was the archetype for creaturely original righteousness. The covenant of redemption defined his work and its reward, namely, to become the surety for the elect and to earn his own self-re-exaltation and his justified people.[8] On the grounds of the triune God's decreed arrangement, Christ merited everlasting life specifically for those whom the Father gave to him to redeem.

Whereas the premise of Adam's covenantal merit set forth the procurement of blessings if he met the law's demand, the gospel is that

---

8. Harrison Perkins, *Reformed Covenant Theology: A Systematic Introduction* (Bellingham, WA: Lexham Press, 2024), 101-23, 163-82.

Christ has procured all those blessings by his merit to give to his people. Christ places us beyond probation. The notion of surety includes that he took upon himself all that needed to be fulfilled and nothing on our end can endanger those procured blessings. The apostle Peter explains how Christ is guarding every benefit of grace to give to those who believe in him:

> According to his great mercy, he has caused us to be born again to a living hope through the resurrection of Jesus Christ from the dead, to an inheritance that is imperishable, undefiled, and unfading, kept in heaven for you, who by God's power are being guarded through faith for a salvation ready to be revealed in the last time (1 Pet. 1:3-5).

Christ guarantees our entry into the eschatological order (Phil. 3:20; Rev. 2:7; 22:1-3, 14). He came in our nature to render the meritorious works that we owed 'that he might advance our nature' which happens because he did 'perform obedience to the Law, suffer and make intercession for us in our nature.'[9] He attained the eschatological order for us and will bestow that advanced state of glory upon his people in full at the resurrection.

In countless instances running throughout the medieval period into modern Roman theology and within Protestant theology, the impulse to prioritize grace in an absolute sense regarding nature, not just to address sin, resulted in the undermining of true grace. Placing grace before works, in a derivative sense gospel before law, for the created order produces a back door to reintroduce the condition of merit within the post-fall situation of grace. Even with the qualification that grace differs in kind before and after the fall, the paradigm for the covenant of works is still a system of grace where works are *consequently* necessary to earn blessings from God. Nothing in principle then prevents the same system from applying to the covenant of grace. The difference would be that grace now comes from Christ. Perhaps this grace is of a different kind, or perhaps we just need more of it. Regardless, the premise is readily at hand to make the covenant of grace like the grace-laden covenant of works, wherein a system with an initial bestowal of grace then consequently

---

9. Westminster Larger Catechism 39; John R. Bower, *The Larger Catechism: A Critical Text and Introduction* (Principal Documents of the Westminster Assembly; Grand Rapids, MI: Reformation Heritage Books, 2010), 73.

necessitates works *to earn blessings from God*. In the covenant of grace, good works *of sanctification* do flow from the logically prior grace of justification, but these works are fruits and evidences of the status that Jesus Christ merited for us, not tokens of congruent merit sustaining or finally securing our entry into the eschatological order.[10] We must then keep the proper order in the law-gospel distinction, emphasizing that the law connected to our original righteousness could be kept by our natural strength. Grace became necessary in the redemptive order to address our sin.[11]

Jesus Christ has merited our everlasting life and grants it by grace. Because of his work for us, 'the covenant of grace is the implementation of the covenant of works in the surety for us.'[12] Christ's obedience is why the law-gospel distinction must be kept intact.[13] Entry into the eschatological order must be *earned*. Adam was supposed to do that as our first representative. If he had needed grace to do so, then we would be in the same place as Adam but with a damaged nature unable to fulfill what must be done. Grace is that someone else has done what we were supposed to do: 'All the benefits of the covenant that Christ acquired and the Holy Spirit applies can be summed up in the word "grace."'[14] Grace is the full bestowment of blessing upon us because someone else fulfilled the terms of earning it.

The covenant of works points to God's love. By a covenant, God promised to reward creaturely obedience with supernatural reward, so binding a supernatural end directly into our nature. In this respect, Herman Bavinck reflected upon how Rome's doctrine of the *donum superadditum* rightly considered how God was not intrinsically obligated to reward his creatures with heavenly blessings for their works, but wrongly tries to solve this problem by positing an ontological elevation of human nature to have supernatural ability 'because Rome does not

---

10. Westminster Confession of Faith 16.2; Bower, *Confession of Faith*, 213.

11. Westminster Confession of Faith 4.2; Bower, *Confession of Faith*, 201; Irish Articles 21; *Articles of Religion Agreed upon the Archbishops and Bishops, and the Rest of the Clergie of Ireland, in the Convocation Holden at Dublin in the yeare of 1615 for the avoiding of diviersities of opinions: And the establishing of consent touching true Religion* (Dublin, 1615), sig. B2v.

12. Vos, *Reformed Dogmatics*, 2:36.

13. Vos, *Reformed Dogmatics*, 5:85-87.

14. Bavinck, *Reformed Dogmatics*, 3:571.

know the doctrine of the covenant of works.' Positing a covenantal rather than Rome's ontological solution, he concluded that Reformed theology should maintain that God's image and the ability to keep the law were natural to humanity, as well as that God attached an infinitely blessed reward to obedience by the covenant of works.[15] In this sense, Reformed theology's covenant of works properly replaced the *donum superadditum* but should not be considered a Reformed version of it.[16] So, with a properly applied Creator-creature distinction, Adam strove to obtain a reward, not by cooperating with ontological elevation, but by fulfilling the covenant.

God's love is manifest as he created us into this sort of covenant. God wanted us to have eschatological life. Otherwise, he would not have created us with the constitution or covenantal capacity for it. As Geerhardus Vos put it, this covenant had 'an element of reward, *ex pacto*. By the free ordination of God, Adam received the right to eternal life if he fulfilled the conditions of the covenant of works.'[17] We should not be leery of God's decision to make the covenant of works, trying to restrict its entire premise to his nature without a willed component. The covenant of works was a covenant of love, composed of loving communion and offering even more of it.

The covenant of works and its principle of covenantal merit also points to God's love by opening the way to enjoy our sanctification. James Ussher rejected merit in *our* good works and denied them any place in justification, explaining why we are motivated to them in light of justification.[18] The principle of merit is closed to sinners entirely because the covenant of works required perfect obedience to our capacity in original righteousness. We are fallen and depraved, which eliminates the possibility of our works contributing to our justification or final salvation. After all, Jesus has merited those blessings for us.

In this respect, Bonaventure and John Duns Scotus might have one closing salvo for us that does help: Their doctrine of God's *acceptatio personarum*, wherein God accepted someone's work as meritorious

---

15. Bavinck, *Reformed Dogmatics*, 2:571-72.

16. Fesko, *Adam and the Covenant of Works*, 325-26.

17. Vos, *Reformed Dogmatics*, 2:32.

18. James Ussher, *A Body of Divinitie* (London, 1645), 338-41.

because he already accepted their person on account of sanctifying grace. We just posed that Christ merited justification for us, entailing everlasting life. The principle of merit has, therefore, been fulfilled. Bonaventure and Scotus' doctrine of *acceptatio* provides no help in understanding justification or our right to everlasting life, which depends entirely on Christ's already finished merits.

Sanctification is also something that Christ merited for us as our present experience of the spiritual life that we receive by faith in him. Because sanctification is something already merited for us, our works of sanctification can hardly contribute to earning anything else or making extra sure that we finally receive something Christ already earned for us. We then apply Bonaventure and Scotus' doctrine of *acceptatio* to the reason why we can find delight in progressing in our sanctification: God is pleased with our sanctified works precisely because he views them through what Christ has already merited for us. God is not assessing our works to see if they are worthy to obtain anything else. Following on the denial in the preceding paragraph of our merit as sinners for anything from God, Westminster Confession 16.6 says,

> Yet notwithstanding, the persons of Beleevers being accepted through Christ, their good workes also are accepted in him, not as though they were in this life wholly unblameable and unreproveable in God's sight; but that, he looking upon them in his Son, is pleased to accept, and reward that which is sincere, although accompanied with many weaknesses and imperfections.[19]

In *sanctification*, our justified persons are already accepted by God, making our works acceptable but not meritorious. Jesus is the sole meritor of all blessings in the eschatological order. His merit, applied to us by grace alone received by faith alone, is sufficient that all those who trust in him are 'received into the highest heavens, where they behold the face of God in light and glory.'[20] Although in justification God can show no partiality in assessing the obedience rendered, in sanctification God has already accepted our persons and so showers abundant partiality

---

19. John R. Bower, *The Confession of Faith: A Critical Text and Introduction* (Principal Documents of the Westminster Assembly; Grand Rapids, MI: Reformation Heritage Books, 2020), 214.

20. Westminster Larger Catechism 86; Bower, *Larger Catechism*, 82.

upon us to delight in fatherly fashion over the ways we seek to serve him. Praise be to Christ that his obedience has made God partial to us so that our imperfect works can be pleasing in his sight. Praise be to Christ that he has kept the law so that he can give us grace. Praise be to Christ from whom all saving blessings flow.

When we recognize how the legal category of covenant coheres with a broader metaphysical outlook concerning the created, eschatological, and redemptive orders, we can also see how Reformed covenant theology makes space for an exciting and invigorating understanding of sanctification. While expressing his sympathy with some critiques of the Reformation doctrine of justification by faith alone, Hans Boersma asked, 'But doesn't the grace of God change believers internally? Don't we actually *become* virtuous or righteous when we put on Christ?' and 'While both Luther and Calvin no doubt recognized the importance of union with Christ, the question remains: Did they see this as implying that we come to participate in a *real* way in the righteousness of Christ?'[21] Our answer to these questions should be unequivocally: Yes! The confusion is that Boersma at times seemed to suggest that the only way to include this infusion of grace and the role of real virtue in our understanding of salvation is if it is part of our doctrine of justification.

The distinction of justification and sanctification as two different but also essential benefits that Christ grants to believers helps to preserve a full-orbed soteriology. From a Reformed perspective, the mistake that seems widespread in Roman Catholic and wider evangelical theology is to suppose that every necessary facet of salvation must belong to justification. Rome includes transformation within justification so that it is indispensable. Sometimes, evangelicals dispense with the necessity of personal transformation for our growth in godliness because they recognize that justification is exclusively legal rather than also renovative. In contrast to both versions of this mistake, the Reformed affirm that justification is exclusively legal but is not the only necessary facet of salvation. God transforms those whom he justifies.

Because God reconciles us to himself in our justification on account of Christ's righteousness imputed to us, he also renews and renovates us in our sanctification by infusing righteousness into us by the power

---

21. Hans Boersma, *Scripture as Real Presence: Sacramental Exegesis in the Early Church* (Grand Rapids, MI: Baker Academic, 2017), 261, 262.

of the indwelling Spirit. We should affirm imputed and imparted righteousness and should apply them in terms of distinct benefits of salvation.[22] On the one hand, 'to the one who does not work but believes in him who justifies the ungodly, his faith is counted as righteousness' (Rom. 4:5). In justification, God imputes the true merits of Christ to us by faith to give us a new legal standing before him. On the other hand, in light of the ministry of reconciliation, 'if anyone is in Christ, he is a new creation. The old has passed away; behold, the new has come. All this is from God, who through Christ reconciled us to himself and gave us the ministry of reconciliation' (2 Cor. 5:17-18). In sanctification, God works upon those who are reconciled to him in Christ to grow us in holiness and our ability to walk faithfully with him. In salvation, God's act of legally declaring us righteous in Christ despite our sin and his work of renewing us in true righteousness are distinct but inseparable blessings that he bestows upon his people. Recognizing that God saves us from sin's penalty and sin's power in distinct aspects of our salvation in no way dispenses or relegates either blessing but properly orders them within the redemptive economy.

This application of Reformed covenant theology provides a full-orbed soteriology by giving robust expression to judicial and transformative facets of salvation, albeit coordinated to distinct benefits of Christ. Westminster Larger Catechism 77 emphasizes salvation's legal and renovative aspect by affirming both but relating them precisely.

Wherein do Justification and Sanctification differ?

Although Sanctification be inseparably joined with Justification; yet they differ, in that God in Justification imputeth the righteousnesse of Christ, in Sanctification his Spirit infuseth grace, and enableth the exercise thereof; in the former sin is pardoned, in the other it is subdued; the one doth equally free all beleevers from the revenging wrath of God, and that perfectly in this life, that they never fall into condemnation; the other is neither equall in all, nor in this life perfect in any, but growing up to perfection.[23]

---

22. J. V. Fesko, 'Aquinas's Doctrine of Justification and Infused Habits in Reformed Soteriology,' in Manfred Svensson and David VanDrunen (eds.), *Aquinas Among the Protestants* (Hoboken, NJ: Wiley Blackwell, 2018), 249-63.

23. Bower, *Larger Catechism*, 80.

As inseparable benefits, joined in special relation coming from Christ who has earned both for us, justification and sanctification stress the importance both of God declaring us to have Christ's perfectly righteous record and of God re-making us to be increasingly like Christ in his righteousness.[24] Christ imputes *and* imparts his righteousness to us but in application to distinct benefits of salvation.

Reformed Christians should see sanctification as exciting because it is a blessing that comes to us from Christ.[25] We should not be shy about how blessed it is to know increasing freedom from sin's enslaving hold upon us, even as we recognize that we do not experience perfect freedom from it in this life. After all, 'For this is the will of God, your sanctification: that you abstain from' the whole host of sins that Paul listed here and undoubtedly every other aspect of ungodliness too (1 Thess. 4:3-8). We should then clarify Boersma's claim that, in the Protestant doctrine of justification, 'the righteousness of Christ is related to the believer *only* through the rule of law' namely in an exclusively external way.[26] Christ's righteousness is truly related to the believer in this solely legal way *in justification*. Justification, however, is not the only benefit of salvation. *For sanctification*, on the other hand, we whole-heartedly affirm with Boersma that salvation 'is a process of growing in virtue, and so a growing in perfection and in the life of God. Salvation [in reference to sanctification] is a process of changing ever more to become like God. Salvation [concerning sanctification] ... is the process in which our real or participatory relationship with God gets worked out.'[27] In addition to imputing Christ's righteousness to the believer for justification, God does give us a real experience of Christ's righteousness by infusing it into us through the indwelling Holy Spirit for sanctification.

The Reformed contribution in this area is that our sanctification is not a condition that we must achieve to secure final salvation but is a blessing that Christ by the Spirit works in us because he has already granted us the right to everlasting life. We emphasize that Christ's

---

24. For considerations in how justification and sanctification are distinct but connected in a specifically ordered relation, see Perkins, *Reformed Covenant Theology*, 243-70.

25. Perkins, *Reformed Covenant Theology*, 233-40.

26. Boersma, *Scripture as Real Presence*, 261 (emphasis added).

27. Boersma, *Scripture as Real Presence*, 263.

perfect merit credited to us as the certain and irrevocable ground of our right to everlasting life is the motive and incitation for increasing obedience. Westminster Confession of Faith 18.3 explains, the 'infallible assurance' that we can have in Christ means for every believer 'thereby his heart may be inlarged in peace and joy in the holy Ghost, in love and thankfulnesse to God, and in strength and chearfullnesse in the duties of obedience, the proper fruits of this assurance.'[28] The infallible assurance that is available because of the sure certainty of justification on account of Christ's imputed righteousness gives way to the 'proper fruits' of a transformed life and even delight in obeying God. The life of sanctification is a joyful experience of renewal wherein God increasingly strengthens us to die unto sin and live unto righteousness so that we continually grow in virtue and godliness.[29] Praise be to Christ that his obedience has merited our acceptance as citizens of heaven so that even in this life we can freely and joyfully taste more and more of his character as he works it within us by the Spirit.[30]

Adam's potential for merit underscores one of our fundamental points that the covenant of works was about God's love for his image-bearing creature. Adam was *righteous by design*, having inbuilt knowledge of God's character and readiness to reflect him. God loved Adam, for that matter all humanity, as his creaturely analog, the reflection of his image in creation. God loved Adam so much that he offered him an even deeper experience of communion with our Maker, which would have belonged to us all had Adam passed the covenant of works. In that vein, believer, God loves you so much that he sent the second Adam, Jesus Christ, to obtain your entry into the eschatological order so that we might know him in the everlasting communion of beholding our God face-to-face.

---

28. Bower, *Confession of Faith*, 216.

29. Westminster Shorter Catechism 35; Philip Schaff (ed.), *The Creeds of Christendom*, 3 vol. (New York, NY: Harper and Brothers, 1877), 3:683.

30. For more extensive exploration of virtue ethics, see Perkins, *Reformed Covenant Theology*, 416-34.

Bibliography

Manuscripts

Cambridge University Library Manuscript Mm. 6.55 (James Ussher's Sermons)

Print Sources

à Brakel, Wilhelmus. *The Christian's Reasonable Service*. Trans. Bartel Elshout, ed. Joel R. Beeke, 4 vol. Grand Rapids, MI: Reformation Heritage Books, 1992.

Adams, Marilyn McCord. *William Ockham*. Combined edition. South Bend, IN: University of Notre Dame Press, 1989.

Adams, Robert Merrihew. 'Faith and religious knowledge,' in Jacqueline Mariña (ed.), *The Cambridge Companion to Friedrich Schleiermacher*. Cambridge: Cambridge University Press, 2005. 35-51.

Adams, Thomas. *A commentary or, exposition vpon the diuine second epistle generall, written by the blessed apostle St. Peter*. London, 1633.

Adedara, Francis 'Kunle. 'The Possibility of Merit Before God According to Thomas Aquinas,' *Bodija Journal* 9. Oct. 2015. 39-59.

Alexander of Hales. *Summa Theologiae, Pars Secunda*. Venice: Franciscum Franciscium, 1575.

Allen, Michael. *Grounded in Heaven: Recentering Christian Hope and Life on God*. Grand Rapids, MI: Eerdmans, 2018.

Allen, Michael and Scott R. Swain (eds.). *The Oxford Handbook of Reformed Theology*. Oxford: Oxford University Press, 2020.

Allison, Gregg R. *Roman Catholic Theology and Practice: An Evangelical Assessment.* Wheaton, IL: Crossway, 2014.

Alsted, Johann Heinrich. *Theologia Naturalis.* Frankfurt, 1615.

Annesley, Samuel. *A Continuation of Morning Exercise Questions and Cases of Conscience.* London, 1683.

Aquinas, Thomas. *Compendium of Theology*, trans. Richard J. Regan. New York, NY: Oxford University Press, 2009.

———. *Opera Omnia*, 34 vol. ed. Stanislai Eduardi Fretté and Pauli Maré. Paris, 1871–80.

———. *Quodlibetal Questions*, trans. Turner Nevitt and Brian Davies. New York, NY: Oxford University Press, 2020.

———. *Summa Contra Gentiles*, 4 vol. Notre Dame, IN: University of Notre Dame Press, 2009.

———. *Summa Theologica*, trans. by Fathers of the English Dominican Province, 5 vol.New York, NY: Benziger Bros., 1948; repr. Notre Dame, IN: Christian Classics, 1981.

Baius, Michael. *Opera*, 2 vol. Cologne, 1696.

Ball, John. *A Treatise on the Covenant of Grace.* London, 1645.

Ballor, Jordan J. *Covenant, Causality, and Law: A Study in the Theology of Wolfgang Musculus.* Refo500 Academic Studies; Göttingen: Vandenhoeck & Ruprecht, 2012.

Ballor, Jordan J., Matthew T. Gaetano, and David S. Sytsma (eds.). *Beyond Dordt and* De Auxiliis*: The Dynamics of Protestant and Catholic Soteriology in the Sixteenth and Seventeenth Centuries.* Leiden: Brill, 2019.

Barcellos, Richard C. *Getting the Garden Right: Adam's Work and God's Rest in Light of Christ.* Cape Coral, FL: Founders Press, 2017.

Barrett, Matthew, (ed.). *The Doctrine on which the Church Stands or Falls: Justification in Biblical, Theological, Historical, and Pastoral Perspective.* Wheaton, IL: Crossway, 2019.

———. *The Reformation as Renewal: Retrieving the One, Holy, Catholic, and Apostolic Church.* Grand Rapids, MI: Zondervan Academic, 2023.

———. *Simply Trinity: The Unmanipulated Father, Son, and Spirit.* Grand Rapids, MI: Baker, 2021.

Barth, Karl. *Church Dogmatics*, ed. G. W. Bromiley and T. F. Torrance, trans. G. W. Bromiley, 14 vol. Peabody, MA: Hendrickson, 1936–77.

Barth, Timotheus A. 'Die Stellung der univocatio im Verlauf der Gotteserkenntnis nach Lehre des Duns Skotus,' *Wissenschaft und Weishei* 5. 1938. 235-54.

———. 'De univocationis entis Scotisticae intent principali necnon valore critico,' *Antonianum* 28. 1953. 72-110.

Bavinck, Herman. 'Foreword to the First Edition (Volume 1) of the *Gereformeerde Dogmatiek*,' trans. John Bolt, *Calvin Theological Journal* 45. 2010. 9-10.

———. *Reformed Dogmatics*, ed. John Bolt, trans. John Vriend, 4 vol. Grand Rapids, MI: Baker Academic, 2003–2008.

———. *The Wonderful Works of God: Instruction in the Christian Religion according to the Reformed Confession*, trans. Henry Zylstra. Glenside, PA: Westminster Seminary Press, 2019.

Baxter, Richard. *Richard Baxter's Admonition to William Eyre of Salisbury concerning his Miscarriages in a Booke lately Written for the Justification of Infidels.* London, 1654.

Beach, J. Mark. *Christ and the Covenant: Francis Turretin's Federal Theology as a Defense of the Doctrine of Grace.* Göttingen: Vandenhoeck & Ruprecht, 2007.

Becanus, Martin. *Summa Theologiae Scholasticae.* Rouen, 1652.

Belcher Jr., Richard P. *The Fulfillment of the Promises of God: An Explanation of Covenant Theology.* Fearn, UK: Mentor, 2020.

Bellarmine, Robert. *De Controversiis Christianae Fidei, tomus quartus.* Satorius, 1601.

Bellucci, Dino, S. J. *Fede e Giustificazione in Lutero: Un Esame Teologico Dei 'Dictata Super Psalterium' e Del Commentario Sull' Epistola Al Romani (1513–1516).* Rome: Libreria Editrice Dell Universita Gregoriana, 1963.

Berkouwer, G. C. *Man: The Image of God* (Studies in Dogmatics). Grand Rapids, MI: Eerdmans, 1962.

———. *Sin* (Studies in Dogmatics). Grand Rapids, MI: Eerdmans, 1971).

———. *The Triumph of Grace in the Theology of Karl Barth*. Grand Rapids, MI: Eerdmans, 1956.

Biel, Gabriel. 'The Circumcision of the Lord,' in Heiko A. Oberman, *Forerunners of the Reformation: The Shape of Late Medieval Thought*. London: Lutterworth Press, 1967; repr. Cambridge: James Clarke & Co., 2002. 165-74.

———. *Collectorium circa quattuor libros Sententiarum*, ed. Wilfridus Werbeck and Udo Hofman, 6 vol. Tübingen: Mohr Siebeck, 1973–92.

———. *Sacri Canonis Missae Lucidisse Expositio*. Brescia: Thomas Bozzolam, 1576.

———. *Sermones dominicales Gabrielis biel Spirensis Hyemales Estiuales De Tempore*. Hagenua, 1510.

Boersma, Hans. 'Accommodation to What? Univocity of Being, Pure Nature, and the Anthropology of St Irenaeus,' *International Journal of Systematic Theology* 8 no. 3. July 2006. 266-93.

———. *Heavenly Participation: The Weaving of a Sacramental Tapestry*. Grand Rapids, MI: Eerdmans, 2011.

———. 'Nature and Supernature in *la nouvelle théologie*: The Recovery of a Sacramental Mindset,' *New Blackfriars* 93 no. 1043. Jan 2012. 34-46.

———. *Nouvelle Théologie and Sacramental Ontology: A Return to Mystery*. Oxford: Oxford University Press, 2009.

———. *Scripture as Real Presence: Sacramental Exegesis in the Early Church*. Grand Rapids, MI: Baker Academic, 2017.

———. *Seeing God: The Beatific Vision in Christian Tradition*. Grand Rapids, MI: Eerdmans, 2018.

———. 'Theology as Queen of Hospitality,' *Evangelical Quarterly* 79 no. 4. 2007. 291-310.

Bonaventure. *S.R.E Cardinalis S. Bonaventure … Opera Omnia*, ed. A. C. Peltier, 15 vol. Paris: Ludovicus Vivès, 1864–71.

Bonino, OP, Serge-Thomas (ed.). *Surnaturel: A Controversy at the Heart of Twentieth-Century Thomistic Thought*, trans. Robert Williams. Faith and Reason: Studies in Catholic Theology and Philosophy. Ave Maria, FL: Sapientia Press, 2009.

Bower, John R. *The Confession of Faith: A Critical Text and Introduction*. Principal Documents of the Westminster Assembly. Grand Rapids, MI: Reformation Heritage Books, 2020.

————. *The Larger Catechism: A Critical Text and Introduction*. Principal Documents of the Westminster Assembly. Grand Rapids, MI: Reformation Heritage Books, 2010.

Braunius, Johannis. *Doctrina Foederum sive Systema Theologiae*, 2 vol. Amsterdam, 1691.

Brown, John. *The life of justification opened*. Utrecht, 1695.

Bucey, Camden M. *Karl Rahner*. Great Thinkers; Phillipsburg, NJ: P&R, 2019.

Burgess, Anthony. *Vindiciae Legis*. London, 1646.

————. *Spiritual Refining: or, a Treatise of Grace and Assurance*. London, 1652.

Burman, Frans. *Synopsis theologiae et speciatim oeconomiae Foederum Dei, ab initio saeculorum usque ad consummationem eorum*, 2 vol. Utrecht, 1671–72.

Bushlack, Thomas J. 'The Return of Neo-Scholasticism? Recent Criticisms of Henri de Lubac on Nature and Grace and their Significance for Moral Theology, Politics, and Law,' *Journal of the Society of Christian Ethics* 35 no. 2. Fall/Winter 2015. 83-100.

Cajetan, Thomas. *Summa Sacrae Theologiae … Commentariis*, 3 vol. Bergamo: Comini Venturae, 1590.

Calamy, Edmund. *The Monster of Sinful Self-Seeking*. London, 1655.

Calvin, John. *Commentaries on the First Book of Moses Called Genesis*, trans. John King, 2 vol. Edinburgh: Calvin Translation Society, 1847.

————. *Institutes of the Christian Religion*, trans. Ford Lewis Battles, ed. John T. McNeill, 2 vol. The Library of Christian Classics; Louisville, KY: Westminster John Knox, 1960.

————. *Opera quae superunt omnia*, ed. Edouard Cunitz, Johann-Wilhem Baum, and Eduard Wilhem Eugen Reuss, 58 vol. Corpus Reformatorum; Brunsigae: C.A. Schwetschke, 1863–1900.

Cartwright, Thomas. *Christian Religion*. London 1611.

Chamier, Daniel. *Corpus Theologicum Seu Loci Communes Theologici*. Geneva, 1653.

————. *Panstratiae Catholicae*, 4 vol. Geneva, 1626.

Clark, R. Scott. 'Christ and Covenant: Federal Theology in Orthodoxy,' in Herman J. Selderhuis (ed.), *A Companion to Reformed Orthodoxy*. Leiden: Brill, 2013. 403-28.

————. (ed.). *Covenant, Justification, and Pastoral Ministry: Essays by the Faculty of Westminster Seminary California*. Phillipsburg, NJ: P&R, 2007.

Clarke, Samuel. *Medulla Theologiae: or the Marrow of Divinity*. London, 1659.

Cocceius, Johannes. *Commentarius in Pentateuchum, Josuam, et Librum Judicum*. Amsterdam, 1669.

————. *Summa Doctrinae de Foedere et Testamento Dei*. Leiden, 1654.

Colquhoun, John. *A Treatise on the Covenant of Works*. Edinburgh: Thomsons, Brothers, 1821.

Combs, Jeffrey. 'The Possibility of Created Entities in Seventeenth-Century Scotism,' *Philosophical Quarterly* 43 no. 173. Oct. 1993. 447-59.

Cortez, Marc. *Resourcing Theological Anthropology: A Constructive Account of Humanity in Light of Christ*. Grand Rapids, MI: Zondervan, 2017.

Courternay, William J. 'The King and the Leaden Coin: The Economic Background of "Sine Qua Non" Causality,' *Traditio* 28. 1972. 185-209.

————. 'Nominalism and Late Medieval Thought: A Bibliographical Essay,' *Theological Studies* 33 no. 4. 1972. 716-34.

Crakanthorpe, Richard. *Defensio Ecclesiae Anglicanae*. London, 1625.

Cross, Richard. *Duns Scotus*. Great Medieval Thinkers; New York, NY: Oxford University Press, 1999.

Cullen, Christopher M. *Bonaventure*. Great Medieval Thinkers; Oxford: Oxford University Press, 2007.

————. 'Bonaventure on nature before Grace: A Historical Moment Reconsidered,' *American Catholic Philosophical Quarterly* 85 no. 1. 2011. 161-76.

————. 'The Natural Desire for God and Pure Nature: A Debate Renewed,' *American Catholic Philosophical Quarterly* 86 no. 4. 2012. 705-30.

de Lubac, Henri. *Augustinianism and Modern Theology*, trans. Lancelot Sheppard. Milestones in Catholic Theology; New York, NY: Crossroad Publishing, 2000.

————. *A Brief Catechesis on Nature and Grace*, trans. Richard Arnandez. San Francisco, CA: Ignatius Press, 1984.

————. *Catholicism: Christ and the Common Destiny of Man*, trans. Lancelot C. Sheppard and Sister Elizabeth Englund, OCD. San Francisco, CA: Ignatius Press, 1988.

————. 'Duplex hominis beatitude. Saint Thomas, 1a2ae, 1.62, a.1.' *Recherches de Science Religieuse* 35. 1948. 200-99.

————. *The Mystery of the Supernatural*, trans. Rosemary Sheed. Milestones in Catholic Theology; New York, NY: Crossroad Publishing, 1998.

————. *Surnaturel: études historiques*. Théologie; Paris: Aubier-Montaigne, 1946.

Denlinger, Aaron C. *Omnes in Adam ex Pacto Dei: Ambrogio Catarino's Doctrine of Covenantal Solidarity and Its Influence on Post-Reformation Reformed Theologians*. Reformed Historical Theology; Göttingen: Vandenhoeck and Ruprecht, 2010.

Dennison, Jr., James T. (ed.). *Reformed Confessions of the 16th and 17th Centuries in English Translation*, 4 vol. Grand Rapids, MI: Reformation Heritage Books, 2008–14.

DeSilva, David A. *The Letter to the Galatians*. New International Commentary on the New Testament. Grand Rapids, MI: Eerdmans, 2018.

Dezza, Ernesto. 'John Duns Scotus on Human Beings in the State of Innocence,' *Traditio* 75. 2020. 289-310.

Donnelly, J. P. 'Calvinist Thomism,' *Viator* 7. 1976. 441-55.

––––––. 'Discussions on the Supernatural Order,' *Theological Studies* 9 no. 2. 1948. 213-49.

––––––. 'The Gratuity of the Beatific Vision and the Possibility of a Natural Destiny,' *Theological Studies* 11 no. 3. 1950. 374-404.

––––––. 'The Supernatural: Father de Lubac's Book,' *The Review of Politics* 10 no. 2. April 1948. 226-32.

––––––. 'The *Surnaturel* of P. Henri de Lubac, S.J.,' *Catholic Theological Society of America Proceedings* 3. 1948. 108-21.

Duby, Steven J. *God in Himself: Scripture, Metaphysics, and the Task of Christian Theology*. Studies in Christian Doctrine and Scripture; Downers Grove, IL: IVP Academic, 2019.

Eglinton, James. *Bavinck: A Critical Biography*. Grand Rapids, MI: Baker Academic, 2020.

Eglinton, James, and George Harinck (eds.). *Neo-Calvinism and the French Revolution*. London: T&T Clark, 2014.

Estelle, Bryan D., Benjamin W. Swinburnson, Lane G. Tipton, A. Craig Troxel, and Chad V. Van Dixhoorn. 'Report to the 83rd (2016) General Assembly of the Committee to Study Republication.' Willow Grove, PA: The Committee on Christian Education of the Orthodox Presbyterian Church, 2016.

Estelle, Bryan D., J. V. Fesko, and David VanDrunen (eds.). *The Law is Not of Faith: Essays on Works and Grace in the Mosaic Covenant*. Phillipsburg, NJ: P&R, 2009.

Eubank, Nathan. 'Configurations of Grace and Merit in Paul and His Interpreters,' *International Journal of Systematic Theology* 22 no. 1. 2013. 7-17.

Farthing, John L. *Thomas Aquinas and Gabriel Biel: Interpretations of St. Thomas Aquinas in German Nominalism on the Eve of the Reformation.* Duke Monographs in Medieval and Renaissance Studies; Durham, NC: Duke University Press, 1988.

Feingold, Lawrence. *The Natural Desire to See God according to St. Thomas Aquinas and his Interpreters*, 2nd ed. Faith and Reason: Studies in Catholic Theology and Philosophy. Naples, FL: Sapientia Press, 2001.

Fesko, J. V. *Adam and the Covenant of Works.* Fearn: Mentor, 2021.

————. *Arminius and the Reformed Tradition: Grace and the Doctrine of Salvation.* Reformed Historical Theological Studies; Grand Rapids, MI: Reformation Heritage Books, 2022).

————. *The Covenant of Works: The Origins, Development, and Reception of the Doctrine.* Oxford Studies in Historical Theology. New York, NY: Oxford University Press, 2020.

————. *Death in Adam, Life in Christ: The Doctrine of Imputation.* Reformed Exegetical and Doctrinal Studies. Fearn, UK: Mentor, 2016.

————. *The Need for Creeds Today: Confessional Faith in a Faithless Age.* Grand Rapids, MI: Baker Academic, 2020.

————. 'The Scholastic Epistemology of Geerhardus Vos,' *Reformed Faith and Practice* 3 no. 3. 2018. 21-45.

Fiorenza, Francis Schüssler, and John P. Galvin (eds.). *Systematic Theology: Roman Catholic Perspectives*, 2nd ed. Minneapolis, MN: Fortress Press, 2011.

Flynn, Gabriel, and Paul D. Murray (eds.). *Ressourcement: A Movement for Renewal in Twentieth-Century Catholic Theology.* New York, NY: Oxford University Press, 2012.

Frame, John. *The Doctrine of the Christian Life.* A Theology of Lordship. Phillipsburg, NJ: P&R, 2008.

France, R. T. *The Gospel of Matthew.* New International Commentary on the New Testament. Grand Rapids, MI: Eerdmans, 2007.

Fuller, Daniel P. 'A Response on the Subjects of Works and Grace.' Spring-Fall 1983. 72-79.

―――. *Gospel and Law: Contrast or Continuum? The Hermeneutics of Dispensationalism and Covenant Theology*. Grand Rapids, MI: Eerdmans, 1980.

―――. 'Paul and "The Works of the Law",' *Westminster Theological Journal* 38 no. 1. Fall 1975. 28-42.

―――. *The Unity of the Bible: Unfolding God's Plan for Humanity*. Grand Rapids, MI: Zondervan, 1992.

Garrigou-Lagrange, Reginald. *Grace: Commentary on the Summa Theologica of St. Thomas 1a2ae q.109–14*, trans. the Dominican Nuns. St. Louis: B. Herder Book Co. 1952.

―――. 'La possibilité de la vision béatifique peut-elle se démonstrer?' *Revue Thomiste* 38 no. 80. 1933. 669-88.

―――. 'Utrum gratia sanctificans fuerit in Adamo dos naturae an donum personae tantum,' *Angelicum* 2. 1925. 133-44.

Gentry, Peter J., and Stephen J. Wellum. *Kingdom through Covenant: A Biblical-Theological Understanding of the Covenants*, 2nd ed. Wheaton, IL: Crossway, 2018.

Gibson, David, and Jonathan Gibson (eds.). *From Heaven He Came and Sought Her: Definite Atonement in Historical, Biblical, Theological, and Pastoral Perspective*. Wheaton, IL: Crossway, 2013.

Gilson, Etienne. 'Avicenne et le point de depart de Duns Scot,' *Archives d'histoire doctrinale et littéraire du moyen âge* 2. 1927. 89-149.

Godfrey, W. Robert. 'Back to Basics: A Response to the Robertson-Fuller Dialogue,' *Presbyterion* 9 no. 1. Spring-Fall 1983. 80-84.

Gomarus, Franciscus. *Opera Theologica Omnia*. Amsterdam, 1664.

Green, Bradley G. *Covenant and Commandment: Works, Obedience and Faithfulness in the Christian Life*. New Studies in Biblical Theology. Downers Grove, IL: IVP Academic, 2014.

Gregory, Brad S. *The Unintended Reformation: How a Religious Revolution Secularized Society*. Cambridge, MA: The Belknap Press of Harvard University Press, 2013.

Grummett, David. 'De Lubac, Grace, and the Pure Nature Debate,' *Modern Theology* 31 no. 1. Jan 2015. 123-46.

———. 'Eucharist, Matter and the Supernatural: Why de Lubac Needs Teilhard,' *International Journal of Systematic Theology* 10 no. 2. April 2008. 165-78.

Hagner, Donald A. *Matthew 14–28*. Word Biblical Commentary. Dallas, TX: Word Books, 1995.

Hahn, Scott W. *Covenant and Communion: The Biblical Theology of Pope Benedict XVI*. Grand Rapids, MI: Brazos Press, 2009.

———. *Kinship by Covenant: A Canonical Approach to the Fulfillment of God's Saving Promises*. New Haven, CT: Yale University Press, 2009.

Hamm, Berndt. *Promissio, Pactum, Ordinatio*. Tübingen: J.C.B. Mohr (Paul Siebeck).

Hart, David Bentley. *You Are Gods: On Nature and Supernature*. Notre Dame, IN: University of Notre Dame Press, 2022.

Healy, Nicholas J. 'Henri de Lubac on Nature and Grace: A Note on Some Recent Contributions to the Debate,' *Communio* 35. Winter 2008. 535-64.

Heidegger, Johann Heinrich. *The Concise Marrow of Theology*, trans. Casey Carmichael. Grand Rapids, MI: Reformation Heritage Books, 2019.

Helm, Paul. *Calvin at the Centre*. New York, NY: Oxford University Press, 2010.

Hemming, Laurence Paul. '*Analogia non Entis sed Entitatis*: The Ontological Consequences of the Doctrine of Analogy,' *International Journal of Systematic Theology* 6 no. 2. April 2004. 118-29.

Henry of Ghent. *Aurea Quodlibeta*, 2 vol. Venice, 1613.

Herbermann, Charles G., Edward A. Pace, Condé B Pallen, Thomas J. Shahan, John J. Wynne (eds.). *The Catholic Encyclopedia*, special ed., 15 vol. New York, NY: The Encyclopedia Press, 1913.

Herzer, Mark A. 'Adam's Reward: Heaven or Earth,' in Michael A. G. Haykin and Mark Jones (eds.), *Drawn into Controversie: Reformed Theological Diversity and Debates within Seventeenth-Century British Puritanism*. Göttingen: Vandenhoeck & Ruprecht, 2011. 162-82.

Hodge, Charles. *Systematic Theology*, 3 vol. Peabody, MA: Hendrickson, 2008.

Hoekema, Anthony A. *Created in God's Image*. Grand Rapids, MI: Eerdmans, 1986.

Hoeksema, Herman. 'The Covenant Concept (1),' *The Standard Bearer* 80 no. 5. Dec. 2003. 105-7.

————. 'The Covenant Concept (2),' *The Standard Bearer* 80 no. 6. Dec. 2003. 129-32.

Horan, OFM, Daniel P. *Postmodernity and Univocity: A Critical Account of Radical Orthodoxy and John Duns Scotus*. Minneapolis, MN: Fortress Press, 2014.

Horton, Michael. *Covenant and Salvation: Union with Christ*. Louisville, KY: Westminster John Knox Press, 2007.

————. *Justification*, 2 vol. New Studies in Dogmatics. Grand Rapids, MI: Zondervan, 2018.

————. *Lord and Servant: A Covenant Christology*. Louisville, KY: Westminster John Knox Press, 2005.

Houck, Daniel W. *Aquinas, Original Sin, and the Challenge of Evolution*. Cambridge: Cambridge University Press, 2020.

Irons, Lee. 'Redefining Merit: An Examination of Medieval Presuppositions in Covenant Theology,' in Howard Griffith and John R. Muether (eds.), *Creator, Redeemer, Consummator: A Festschrift for Meredith G. Kline*. Greenville, SC: Reformed Academic Press, 2000; repr. Eugene, OR: Wipf and Stock, 2007. 253-69.

Jansenius, Cornelius. *Augustinus, seu Doctrina Sancti Augustini de Humanae Naturae Sanitate*, 3 vol. Paris, 1641.

Janz, Denis. 'A Reinterpretation of Gabriel Biel on Nature and Grace,' *The Sixteenth Century Journal* 8 no. 1. April 1977. 104-8.

John of Damascus. *An Exact Exposition of the Orthodox Faith*, 2.12, in *The Fathers of the Church: St. John of Damascus: Writings*, trans. Frederic H. Chase, Jr. Washington, D.C.: The Catholic University of America Press, 1958.

Jones, Kevin E. 'Bonaventure on Habitual Grace in Adam: A Change of Heart on Nature and Grace?' *Franciscan Studies* 76. 2018. 45-52.

Junius, Francis. *De Politiae Mosis Observatione*. Leiden, 1593.

_____. Πρωτοκτισα. Heidelberg, 1589.

_____. *A Treatise on True Theology*, trans. David C. Noe. Reformation Heritage Books, 2014.

Kerr, Fergus. *After Aquinas: Versions of Thomism*. Oxford: Blackwell Publishing, 2002.

Kline, Meredith G. 'Covenant Theology under Attack' *New Horizons* 15 no. 2. Feb. 1994. 3-5.

_____. *Images of the Spirit*. Eugene, OR: Wipf and Stock, 1999.

_____. *Kingdom Prologue: Genesis Foundations for a Covenantal Worldview*. Eugene, OR: Wipf and Stock, 2006.

_____. 'Of Works and Grace,' *Presbyterion* 9. 1983. 95–92.

_____. 'Of Works and Grace,' *Presbyterion* 9 no. 1. Spring-Fall. 1983. 85-92.

Kretzmann, Norma and Eleonore Stump (eds.). *The Cambridge Companion to Aquinas*. New York: CUP, 1993.

Kuhner, Matthew. 'The Lesser Light is Not Dimmed: On the Significance of Thomas Aquinas's Treatise on the Incarnation for the Relationship between Nature and Grace,' *Angelicum* 93 no. 4. 2016. 751-84.

Küng, Hans. *Justification: The Doctrine of Karl Barth and a Catholic Reflection*, trans. Thomas Collins, Edmund E. Tolk, and David Grandskou. London: Burns & Oates, 1964.

Kuyper, Abraham. 'The Natural Knowledge of God,' trans. Harry Van Dyke, *Bavinck Review* 6. 2015. 73-112.

Lamb, Matthew L., and Matthew Levering (eds.). *The Reception of Vatican II*. Oxford: Oxford University Press, 2017.

Larsen, Sean. 'The Politics of Desire: Two Readings of Henri de Lubac on Nature and Grace,' *Modern Theology* 29 no. 3. July 2013. 279- 310.

Lee, Brian J. *Johannes Cocceius and the Exegetical Roots of Federal Theology: Reformation Developments in the Interpretation of Hebrews 7–10*. Göttingen: Vandenhoeck & Ruprecht, 2009.

Lehmann, Paul. 'Barth and Brunner: The Dilemma of the Protestant Mind,' *The Journal of Religion* 20 no. 2. April 1940. 124-40.

Letham, Robert. *Systematic Theology*. Wheaton, IL: Crossway, 2019.

———. *The Westminster Assembly: Reading Its Theology in Historical Context*. Phillipsburg, NJ: P&R, 2009.

Levering, Matthew and Marcus Plested (eds.). *The Oxford Handbook of the Reception of Aquinas*. Oxford: Oxford University Press, 2021.

Lindbeck, George. 'Nominalism and the Problem of Meaning as Illustrated by Pierre D'Ailly on Predestination and Justification,' *Harvard Theological Review* 52 no. 1. 1959. 43-60.

Linebaugh, Jonathan A. (ed.). *God's Two Words: Law and Gospel in the Lutheran and Reformed Traditions*. Grand Rapids, MI: Eerdmans, 2018.

Lombard, Peter. *The Sentences*, 4 vol. trans. Giulio Silano. Ontario: Pontifical Institute of Medieval Studies, 2007-10.

Long, Steven A. *Natura Pura: On the Recovery of Nature in the Doctrine of Grace*. New York, NY: Fordham University Press, 2010.

Macaskill, Grant. *Living in Union with Christ: Paul's Gospel and Christian Moral Identity*. Grand Rapids, MI: Baker Academic, 2019.

Mansini, Guy. 'Henri de Lubac, the Natural Desire to See God, and Pure Nature,' *Gregorianum* 83 no. 1. 2002. 89-109.

Marrone, Steven P. 'Henry of Ghent and Duns Scotus on the Knowledge of Being,' *Speculum*. Jan. 1988. 22-57.

Matava, R. J. 'A Sketch of the Controversy *de auxiliis*,' *Journal of Jesuit Studies* 7. 2020. 417-46.

Mayer, Rupert Johannes. 'Man is Inclined to His Last End by Nature, though He cannot Reach It by Nature but Only by Grace: The Principle of the Debate about Nature and Grace in Thomas Aquinas, Thomism and Henri de Lubac. A Response to Lawrence Feingold,' *Angelicum* 88. 2011. 887-939.

McAnnally-Linz, Ryan. 'Extrinsic Grace and Eccentric Existence,' *Modern Theology* 31 no. 1. Jan. 2015. 179-94.

McCosker, Philip, and Denys Turner (eds.). *The Cambridge Companion to the Summa Theologiae*. Cambridge: Cambridge University Press, 2016.

McFarland, Ian A. 'Rethinking Nature and Grace: The Logic of Creation's Consummation,' *International Journal of Systematic Theology* 24 no. 1. Jan. 2022. 56-79.

McGrath, Alister E. *Iustitia Dei: A History of the Christian Doctrine of Justification*, 4th ed. Cambridge: Cambridge University Press, 2020.

McInerny, Ralph. *Aquinas and Analogy*. Washington DC: Catholic University of America Press, 1996.

Meinert, John. 'St. Thomas Aquinas, Perseverance, and the Nature/Grace Debate,' *Angelicum* 93 no. 4. 2016. 823-42.

Mettepenningen, Jürgen. *Nouvelle Théologie – New Theology: Inheritor of Modernism, Precursor of Vatican II*. London: T&T Clark, 2010.

Meyendorff, John. *Byzantine Theology: Historical Trends and Doctrinal Themes*. New York, NY: Fordham University Press, 1979.

Michelson, Jared. 'Reformed and Radically Orthodox?: Participatory Metaphysics and Radical Orthodoxy's Critique of Modernity,' *International Journal of Systematic Theology* 20 no. 1. Jan. 2018. 104-28.

Migne, Jacques Paul (ed.). *Patrologia Cursus Completus: Series Latina*, 221 vol. Paris, 1844–64.

Milbank, John. *The Suspended Middle: Henri de Lubac and the Renewed Split in Modern Catholic Theology*, 2nd ed. Grand Rapids, MI: Eerdmans, 2014.

Moloney, SJ, Raymond. 'De Lubac and Lonergan on the Supernatural,' *Theological Studies* 69. 2008. 509-27.

Muller, Richard A. *After Calvin: Studies in the Development of a Theological Tradition*. Oxford Studies in Historical Theology. New York, NY: Oxford University Press, 2003.

———. *Calvin and the Reformed Tradition: On the Work of Christ and the Order of Salvation*. Grand Rapids, MI: Baker Academic, 2012.

———. *Dictionary of Latin and Greek Theological Terms: Drawn Principally from Protestant Scholastic Theology*, 2nd ed. Grand Rapids, MI: Baker Academic, 2017.

_____. *Divine Will and Human Choice: Freedom, Contingency, and Necessity in Early Modern Reformed Thought*. Grand Rapids, 2017.

_____. 'Not a Scotist: Understandings of Being, Univocity, and Analogy in Early-Modern Reformed Thought,' *Reformation and Renaissance Review* 14 no. 2. 2012. 127-50.

_____. 'Reflections on Persistent Whiggism and Its Antidotes in the Study of Sixteenth- and Seventeenth-century Intellectual History,' in Alister Chapman, John Coffey, and Brad S. Gregory (eds.). *Seeing Things Their Way: Intellectual History and the Return of Religion*. Notre Dame: University of Notre Dame Press, 2009. 134-53.

_____. 'Toward the Pactum Salutis: Locating the Origins of a Concept,' *Mid-America Journal of Theology* 18. 2007. 11-65.

Murray, John. *Collected Writings of John Murray*, 4 vol. Edinburgh: The Banner of Truth Trust, 1976–82.

_____. *Imputation of Adam's Sin*. Phillipsburg, NJ: P&R, 2012.

Musculus, Wolfgang. *Common Places of Christian Religion*. London, 1563.

Niebuhr, Reinhold. *The Nature and Destiny of Man: A Study of Human Nature from the Perspective of Christian Faith*, 2 vol. New York, NY: Charles Scribner's Sons, 1964.

Norton, John. *The Orthodox Evangelist*. London, 1654.

Oberman, Heiko A. 'Das tridentine Rechtfertigungsdekret im Lichte spätmittelalterlicher Theologie,' *Zeitschrift für Theologie und Kirche* 61 no. 3. 1964. 251-82.

_____. *The Harvest of Medieval Theology: Gabriel Biel and Late Medieval Nominalism*, 3rd ed. Grand Rapids, MI: Baker Academic, 2000.

ó Hual500acháin, Colmán. 'Duns Scotus and 13th Century Philosophy,' *University Review* 1 no. 10. Autumn 1956. 30-43.

O'Malley, John. *What Happened at Vatican II*. Cambridge, MA: Belknap Press of Harvard University Press, 2008.

Omerod, Neil. 'The Grace-Nature Distinction and the Construction of a Systematic Theology,' *Theological Studies* 75 no. 3. 2014. 515-36.

Owen, John. *An Exposition of the Epistle to the Hebrews*, 4 vol. London: Thomas Tegg, 1840.

_____. *Θεολογουμενα Παντοδαπα, sive De Natura, Ortu, Progressu, et Studio, Verae Theologiae*, ed. by William Goold. New York, NY: Robert Carter and Brothers, 1854.

Ozment, Stephen E. *The Age of Reform, 1250–1550: An Intellectual and Religious History of Late Medieval and Reformation Europe*. New Haven, CT: Yale University Press, 1980.

_____. *Homo Spiritualis: A Comparative Study of the Anthropology of Johannes Tauler, Jean Gerson and Martin Luther – 1509–1516 – In the Context of Their Theological Thought*. Leiden: Brill, 1963.

Paraeus, David. *De Gratia Primi Hominis Explicatus and Castigatus*. Heidelberg, 1612.

Pelikan, Jaroslav. *The Growth of Medieval Theology (600–1300)*. Chicago, IL: University of Chicago Press, 1978.

Perkins, Harrison. *Catholicity and the Covenant of Works: James Ussher and the Reformed Tradition*. Oxford Studies in Historical Theology. New York, NY: Oxford University Press, 2020.

_____. 'Meritum ex Pacto in the Reformed Tradition: Covenantal Merit in Theological Polemics,' *Mid-America Journal of Theology* 31. 2020. 57-87.

_____. 'Reconsidering the Development of the Covenant of Works: A Study in Doctrinal Trajectory,' *Calvin Theological Journal* 53 no. 2. 2018. 289-317.

_____. *Reformed Covenant Theology: A Systematic Introduction*. Bellingham, WA: Lexham Press, 2024.

Perkins, William. *A Reformed Catholike*. Cambridge, 1598.

_____. *Works of William Perkins*, 10 vol. Grand Rapids, MI: Reformation Heritage Books, 2014–20.

Pictet, Benedict. *Theologia Christiana*. Geneva, 1716.

Pidel, SJ, Aaron. 'Erich Przywara on Nature-Grace Extrinsicism: A Parallax View,' *Modern Theology* 37 no. 4. October 2021. 865-87.

Pini, Giorgio (ed.). *Interpreting Duns Scotus: Critical Essays.* Cambridge: Cambridge University Press, 2022.

Porro, Pasquale. 'Divine Predestination, Human Merit and Moral Responsibility: The Reception of Augustine's Doctrine of Irresistible Grace in Thomas Aquinas, Henry of Ghent and John Duns Scotus,' in Pieter d'Hoine and Gerd van Riel (eds.). *Fate, Providence and Moral Responsibility in Ancient, Medieval and Early Modern Thought: Essays in Honor of Carlos Steel.* Leuven: Leuven University Press, 2014. 553-70.

———. 'Henry of Ghent (before 1240–1293),' in Karla Pollmann and Willemien Otten (eds.). *The Oxford Guide to the Historical Reception of Augustine.* Oxford: Oxford University Press, 2013; online version 2014.

———. '"Rien de Personnel": Notes sur la question de l'*acceptio personarum* dans la théologie scolastique,' *Revue des Sciences philosophiques et théologiques* 94 no. 3. July–Sept 2010. 481-509.

Rahner, Karl. 'Concerning the Relationship between Nature and Grace,' in *Theological Investigations Volume 1.* New York, NY: Seabury Press, 1974. 297-317.

Ratzinger, Joseph (Pope Emeritus Benedict XVI). *The Theology of History in Saint Bonaventure*, trans. Zachary Hayes, OFM. Providence, RI: Cluny, 2020.

———. 'General Audience: Der Hl. Paulus (13): Die Rechtfertigungslehre - Von den Werken zum Glauben,' *The Holy See* (St. Peter's Square: November 19, 2008; accessed on May 12, 2023 at https://www.vatican.va/content/benedict-xvi/de/audiences/2008/documents/hf_ben-xvi_aud_20081119.html).

Richard, Guy M. 'Samuel Rutherford's Supralapsarianism Revealed: A Key to the Lapsarian Position of the Westminster Confession?' *Scottish Journal of Theology* 59 no. 1. 2006. 27-44.

———. *The Supremacy of God in the Theology of Samuel Rutherford.* Studies in Christian History and Thought. Eugene, OR: Wipf and Stock, 2009.

Roberts, Alexander, and James Donaldson (eds.). *Ante-Nicene Fathers*, 10 volumes. Buffalo: The Christian Literature Publishing Co., 1885.

Roberts, Francis. *Mysterium & Medulla Bibliorum: The Mysterie and Marrow of the Bible, viz. God's Covenants with Man.* London, 1657.

Robertson, O. Palmer. 'Daniel P. Fuller's *Gospel and Law: Contrast or Continuum?*: A Review Article,' *Presbyterion* 8 no. 1. Spring 1982. 84-91.

Rollock, Robert. *Tractatus De Vocatione Efficaci.* Edinburgh, 1597.

Rolston III, Holmes. *John Calvin Versus the Westminster Confession.* Richmond: Westminster John Knox Press, 1972.

Rosenberg, Randall S. *The Givenness of Desire: Human Subjectivity and the Natural Desire to See God.* Toronto, Buffalo, London: University of Toronto Press, 2017.

Rosenthal, Alexander S. 'The Problem of the *Desiderium Naturale* in the Thomistic Tradition,' *Verbum* 6 no. 2. 2004. 335-44.

Rushdoony, Rousas John. *Systematic Theology*, 2 vol. Vallecito, CA: Ross House Books, 1994.

Rutherford, Samuel. *The Covenant of Life Opened; or, A Treatise on the Covenant of Grace.* Edinburgh, 1655.

————. *Influences of the Life of Grace.* London, 1658.

Ryan, Peter F. 'How Can the Beatific Vision both Fulfill Human Nature and Be Utterly Gratuitous?' *Gregorium* 83 no. 4. 2002. 717-55.

Saad, Toni C. 'Francis Turretin's Thomistic Theology of Natural Law,' *Journal of Reformed Theology* 16. 2022. 27-47.

Salladin, James. 'Nature and Grace: Two Participations in the Thought of Jonathan Edwards,' *International Journal of Systematic Theology* 18 no. 3. July 2016. 291-303.

Sanz Sanchéz, Santiago, and John Watson. 'The Revival of Pure Nature in Recent Debates in English Speaking Theology,' *Annales Theologici* 31. 2017. 171-250.

Schaff, Philip (ed.). *The Creeds of Christendom*, 3 vol. New York, NY: Harper and Brothers, 1877.

Scharpius, Johannes. *Cursus Theologicus.* Geneva, 1620.

Schelkens, Karim and Marcel Gielis. 'From Driedo to Bellarmine: The Concept of Pure Nature in the 16th Century,' *Augustiniana* 57 no. 3/4. 2007. 425-48.

Schilder, Klass. *Heidelbergsche Catechismus*, 4 vol. Goes: Oosterban & Le Cointre, 1947–51.

Schumacher, Lydia. *Early Franciscan Theology: Between Authority and Innovation*. Cambridge: Cambridge University Press, 2019.

Scotus, John Duns. *Opera Omnia*, editio nova, 26 vol. Paris, 1891–95.

Shepherd, Norman. 'Law and Gospel in Covenantal Perspective,' *Reformation and Revival Journal* 14 no. 1. 2005. 73-88.

Shields, Christopher and Robert Pasnau. *The Philosophy of Aquinas*, 2nd ed. New York, NY: Oxford University Press, 2016.

Skinner, Quentin. *Visions of Politics: Volume 1: Regarding Method*. Cambridge: Cambridge University Press, 2002.

Smith, George D. (ed.). *The Teaching of the Roman Catholic Church: A Summary of Catholic Doctrine*, 2 vol. Waterloo, Ontario: Arouca Press, 2021.

Smith, James K. A., and James H. Olthuis (eds.). *Radical Orthodoxy and the Reformed Tradition: Creation, Covenant, and Participation*. Grand Rapids, MI: Baker Academic, 2005.

Stanley, Alan P. (ed.). *Four Views on the Role of Works at the Final Judgment*. Counterpoints; Grand Rapids, MI: Zondervan, 2013.

Steinmetz, David. 'Medieval Nominalism and the *Clerk's Tale*,' *The Chaucer Review* 12 no. 1. 1977. 38-54.

Stump, Eleonore, and Thomas Joseph White (eds.). *The New Cambridge Companion to Aquinas*. Cambridge: Cambridge University Press, 2022.

Sutanto, N. Gray. 'Consummation Anyway: A Reformed Proposal,' *Journal of Analytic Philosophy* 9. Summer 2021. 223-37.

———. '*Gevoel* and Illumination: Bavinck, Augustine, and Bonaventure on Awareness of God,' *Pro Ecclesia* 30 no. 3. 2021. 265-78.

———. 'Questioning Bonaventure's Augustinianism?: On the Noetic Effects of Sin,' *New Blackfriars* 102 no. 1099. May 2021. 401-17.

Svensson, Manfred, and David VanDrunen (eds.). *Aquinas Among the Protestants*. Hoboken, NJ: Wiley Blackwell, 2018.

Swafford, Andew Dean. *Nature and Grace: A New Approach to Thomistic Ressourcement*. Eugene, OR: Pickwick, 2014.

Sytsma, David S. 'Herman Bavinck's Thomistic Epistemology: The Argument and Sources of His *Principia* of Science,' in John Bolt (ed.), *Five Studies in the Thought of Herman Bavinck*. Lewiston, NY: Edwin Mellon, 2011. 1-56.

_____. 'Vermigli Replicating Aquinas: An Overlooked Continuity in the Doctrine of Predestination,' *Reformation & Renaissance Review* 20 no. 2. 2018. 155-67.

te Velde, Dolf (ed.). *Synopsis Purioris Theologiae Volume 1/Disputations 1–23*. Leiden: Brill, 2015.

Torrance, J. B. 'Covenant or Contract? A Study of the Theological Background of Worship in Seventeenth Century Scotland,' *Scottish Journal of Theology* 23. 1970. 51-69.

Torrance, T. F. *Scottish Theology: From John Knox to John McLeod Campbell*. Edinburgh: T&T Clark, 1996.

Trueman, Carl R. *Grace Alone: Salvation as a Gift of God*. The Five Solas Series. Grand Rapids, MI: Zondervan, 2017.

_____. *John Owen: Reformed Catholic, Renaissance Man*. Aldershot: Ashgate, 2007.

Tuckney, Anthony. *Praelectiones Theologicae*. Amsterdam, 1679.

Tuininga, Matthew J. *Calvin's Political Theology and the Public Engagement of the Church: Christ's Two Kingdoms*. Cambridge: Cambridge University Press, 2017.

Turner, Denys. *The Darkness of God: Negativity in Christian Mysticism*. Cambridge: Cambridge University Press, 1995.

Turrettinus, Franciscus. *Institutio Theologiae Elencticae*, 3 vol. Geneva, 1679–85.

Twisse, William. *A Briefe Catechetical Exposition of Christian Doctrine*. 1633.

United States Conference of Catholic Bishops. *Catechism of the Catholic Church*, 2nd ed. Washington, DC: Liberia Editrace Vaticana, 1997.

Ursinus, Zacharias. *The Commentary of Dr. Zacharias Ursinus on the Heidelberg Catechism*, trans. G. W. Williard, 4th American ed. Cincinnati, OH: Elm Street Printing, 1888.

Ussher, James. *A Body of Divinitie*. London, 1645.

_____. *An Answer to a Challenge Made by a Jesuite in Ireland*. Dublin, 1624.

van Asselt, Willem J. 'The Doctrine of Abrogations in the Federal Theology of Johannes Cocceius, 1603–69.' *Calvin Theological Journal* 29. 1994. 101-16.

_____. 'Expromissio or Fideiusso? A Seventeenth-Century Theological Debate between the Voetians and Coccians about the Nature of Christ's Suretyship in Salvation History,' *Mid-America Journal of Theology* 14. 2003. 37-57.

_____. *The Federal Theology of Johannes Cocceius (1603–1669)*, trans. Raymond A. Blacketer. Leiden: Brill, 2001.

van der Laan, H. 'Nature and Supernature according to Duns Scotus: An Analysis of the First Part of Duns Scotus' Prologue to his "Ordinatio",' *Philosophia Reformata* 38 no. 1. 1973. 62-76.

van Nieuwenhove, Rik. *An Introduction to Medieval Theology*. Cambridge: CUP, 2012.

van Nieuwenhove, Rik, and Jospeh Wawrykow (eds.). *The Theology of Thomas Aquinas*. Notre Dame, University of Notre Dame Press, 2005.

VanDrunen, David. *Divine Covenants and Moral Order: A Biblical Theology of Natural Law*. Grand Rapids, MI: Eerdmans, 2014.

Veenhof, Jan. 'Nature and Grace in Bavinck,' *Pro Rege* 34 no. 4. 2006. 10-31.

Venema, Cornelis. *Christ and Covenant Theology: Essays on Election, Republication, and the Covenants*. Phillipsburg, NJ: P&R, 2017.

_____. *The Gospel of Free Acceptance in Christ: An Assessment of the Reformation and New Perspectives on Paul*. Edinburgh: Banner of Truth Trust, 2006.

Vijgen, Jörgen. 'Biblical Thomism: Past, Present, and Future,' *Angelicum* 95 no. 3. 2018. 371-96.

von Balthasar, Hans Urs. *The Theology of Henri de Lubac*. San Francisco, CA: Ignatius Press, 1991.

Vos, Geerhardus. *Biblical Theology: Old and New Testaments*. Grand Rapids, MI: Eerdmans, 1948; repr. East Peoria, IL: The Banner of Truth Trust, 2020.

————. *Natural Theology*, trans. Albert Gootjes. Grand Rapids, MI: Reformation Heritage Books, 2022.

————. *The Pauline Eschatology*. Princeton, NJ: Princeton University Press, 1930; repr. Phillipsburg, NJ: P&R, 1994.

————. *Reformed Dogmatics*, 5 vol. Bellingham, WA: Lexham Press, 2012–14.

Washburn, Christian D. 'The Transformative Power of Grace and Condign Merit at the Council of Trent,' *The Thomist* 79. 2015. 173-212.

————. 'The Shaping of Modern Catholic Anthropology in the Context of the Counter-Reformation: St. Robert Bellarmine and the Transformative Power of Grace,' in Bertram Stubenrauch and Michael Seewald (eds.), *Das Menschenbild der Konfession – Achillesferse der Ökumene?* Freiburg: Herder, 2015. 217-48.

Waters, Guy Prentiss, J. Nicholas Reid, and John R. Muether (eds.). *Covenant Theology: Biblical, Theological, and Historical Perspectives*. Wheaton, IL: Crossway, 2020.

————. *The Federal Vision and Covenant Theology: A Comparative Analysis*. Phillipsburg, NJ: P&R, 2006.

————. *Justification and the New Perspective on Paul: A Review and Response*. Phillipsburg, NJ: P&R, 2004.

Wawrykow, Joseph P. *God's Grace and Human Action: Merit in the Theology of Thomas Aquinas*. Notre Dame, IN: University of Notre Dame Press, 2016.

————. 'On the Purpose of "Merit" in the Theology of Thomas Aquinas,' *Medieval Philosophy and Theology* 2. 1992. 97-116.

Wellum, Stephen J. 'Reflections on *Covenant Theology* from a Progressive Covenantal View,' *The Southern Baptist Journal of Theology* 26 no. 1. 2022. 164-87.

White, Thomas Joseph. 'How Barth Got Aquinas Wrong: A Reply to Archie J. Spencer on Causality and Christocentrism,' *Nova et Vetera* 7 no. 1. 2009. 241-70.

Wilkinson, Michael A. *Crowned with Glory and Honor: A Chalcedonian Anthropology*. Studies in Historical and Systematic Theology: Bellingham. WA: Lexham Press, 2024.

———. 'Review of Lawrence Feingold, *The Natural Desire to See God according to St. Thomas Aquinas and his Interpreters*, 2nd ed.,' *The Thomist* 74 no. 3. July 2010. 461-67.

William of Ockham. *Quodlibeta*. Leiden: Janon Carcain, 1488.

———. *Quodlibetal Questions*, trans. Alfred J. Freddoso and Francis E. Kelly, 2 vol. New Haven, CT: Yale University Press, 1991.

Williams, Thomas (ed.). *The Cambridge Companion to Duns Scotus*. Cambridge: Cambridge University Press, 2003.

Wilson, Gordon A. *A Companion to Henry of Ghent*. Brill's Companions to the Christian Tradition. Leiden: Brill, 2011.

Witsius, Herman. *De Oeconomia Foederum Dei cum Hominibus*, 3rd ed. Utrecht, 1694.

Wood, Jacob W. 'Henri de Lubac, *Humani Generis*, and the Natural Desire for a Supernatural End,' *Nova et Vetera* 15 no. 4. 2017. 1209-41.

———. *To Stir a Restless Heart: Thomas Aquinas and Henri de Lubac on Nature, Grace, and the Desire for God*. Thomistic Ressourcement Series. Washington, DC: The Catholic University of America Press, 2019.

Wood Jr., John Halsey. 'Merit in the Midst of Grace: The Covenant with Adam Reconsidered in View of the Two Powers of God,' *International Journal of Systematic Theology* 10 no. 2. April 2008. 133-48.

Woolsey, Andrew A. *Unity and Continuity in Covenantal Thought: A Study in the Reformed Tradition to the Westminster Assembly*. Grand Rapids, MI: Reformation Heritage Books, 2012.

Subject Index

A

Abrahamic covenant 63
acceptatio 101, 117, 299,
300, 334-335
acceptation 300
accommodation 237
Adam. *See also* covenant of works
beatific vision of.............. 97-98,
105, 138-139
civil goods and.....................138
communion with God
by................. 97-98, 109, 263,
312-313, 339
covenantal merit of 301,
331-332
covenant-keeping ability
of 188
created nature of 75
dependence on God by 272
elevated nature of.................. 84
eschatology and.............. 97-98,
295, 303
Essence of God and 93
everlasting blessing of 109
extranatural grace to 151-152
faith of 222
favor of God and 219
filial relation of.................... 244
fulfillment of duties
by..............................319-320
garden tasks of 248

as God's image
bearer............. 87, 92-93, 186,
246-247, 304, 319
God's ordination toward..... 308
God's promise to..................275
good works of 98, 107, 135
grace of 89-90, 238, 270
headship of...................254, 287
infused grace to...................109
justification of 107-108
kingship of.................. 246, 326
as knowing God........93-94, 187
law as created in.................. 288
Lombard on 85-88
merit of 71, 310-311
meritum ex pacto and..............72
natural ability of ... 99, 135, 138,
266-267
natural means of 287-288
natural obligation of 255
natural strength of 189
nature of.................35, 266, 267
need for grace by....................86
obedience of...... 45, 47, 76, 222,
271, 272, 292,
301, 323
obligation of................ 167, 291,
303, 304
as obtaining grace 90-91
order of nature of................ 187
as oriented to God 94

original righteousness
    of 48, 54, 87, 116,
        125, 164, 192, 287-288
potential eschatological
    communion with
    God of 44
pre-fall states of 240
probation of 309, 310
pure nature of 164, 293
rectitude of 94
reward of 22, 38, 70-71
righteousness of 19-20,
        30, 339
sanctifying grace (gratia
    gratum faciens) and 105,
        113, 162, 193
sin of 18, 45, 143, 166,
        194-195, 234, 265
as spiritually
    underdeveloped 116
strength of 274
superadded grace
    (donum superadditum)
    of 135, 143, 162
supernatural blessing of 107
supernatural communion
    with God by 88
supernatural endowment
    of grace to 95
supernatural grace on 271
Thomas Aquinas on 88-103
tree of the knowledge of
    good and evil
    and 254-258, 309-310
as turning to God 162
twofold end of 103-104
unworthy-servant
    principle and 294-295
virtues of 86-87
will of 111
works of 151-152, 292, 295
Adams, Thomas 65
adoption 174
aeterni patris 157
Alsted, Johann Heinrich 276

amor creaturate 152n63
analogia proportionalitatis 24
angels 71-72
antithesis 169n143, 225-226
Arianism 33
Aristotle 96
Arminius, Jacob 184-185,
        208-209, 266, 270, 271, 272
Augustine of Hippo 28-29, 33,
        51-52, 90, 107, 238, 325
auxilium 205-213, 271

B

Baius, Michael 145-146,
        181, 199, 269
Bàñez, Domingo 143
baptism 113
Barcellos, Richard 240
Barrett, Matthew 126, 202
Barron, Robert 175-176, 330
Barth, Karl 33, 216-217
Bavinck, Herman 275-276, 287
Baxter, Richard 57, 59
Beale, G. K. 247
beatific vision 92-93, 97-98,
        105, 135, 138-139, 147, 272
Belcher, Richard 229-230
Bellarmine, Robert 68, 69,
        153-157, 181, 184, 191,
        198-199, 209-210, 215
Benedict XVI (pope) (Joseph
    Ratzinger) 173-174, 223-224
Berkhof, Louis 197-198
Berkouwer, G. C. 219
Beza, Theodore 60-61, 194
Biel, Gabriel
    on auxilium 207-208
    on congruent merit 57
    on God's absolute power 307
    on grace 180
    on human condition 148
    Luther against 190
    on merit 180, 264
    nominalism of 123-131,
        142, 202

on original righteousness 180
Pelagian tendencies of 206
on pure nature 330
radical theology origin of.....203
scholasticism of 199
on works 297
blessings.................... 100, 287-288
Boersma, Hans 95, 96, 203, 261,
316, 317, 321, 336
Bonaventure of
Bagnoregio 103, 180,
191-192, 334-335
Bradwardine, Thomas...............130
Braun, Johnnes 70-71, 300
Breviloquium (Bonaventure
of Bagnoregio)............... 103-118
Bucer, Martin 264-265
Burman, Frans......................71-74

C

Cajetan, Thomas.. 98, 138-143, 181
Calvin, John 29-30, 62-64, 184,
215, 220-221, 227, 250
Calvinism 160-161
*Catechism of the Catholic
Church*...................................173
The Catholic Encyclopedia 163
Chamier, Daniel 60-63
circumcision 113
Cocceius, Johannes......... 66, 67-70,
249, 286, 300, 303
Colquhoun, John......................286
concursus, doctrine of 212
condescension 235-240
condign merit ...... 53, 161-162, 163.
See also covenantal merit; merit
congruent merit.. 59, 123, 163-164.
See also covenantal merit; merit
constitutus (constituted), 143
Council of Trent..........31, 143-145,
162, 181, 224-225
Counter-Reformation 153
covenant. *See also* covenant
of works
Abrahamic..............................63

Adamic............19-20, 22-23, 44,
47, 64-65, 67, 72, 79,
88, 282-283, 297-298
as bridge................................38
continuity of 241
creation and 241, 253-260,
281-282
defined 292
disproportionality and 76-77
function of............................19
God's revelation
through...........................281
of grace 73
with humanity 234-235
Mosaic....................................63
Noahic 289-290
overview of................... 235-240
in parenting 283
pure nature and 293
of redemption....................73-74
in Reformed theology 39
as reward............................. 44
covenantal merit
of Adam 301, 331-332
Christ's obedience and 55
conditions for......................319
covenant of works and 283
defined 20, 61
felicity of..........................46-48
function of...........................72
imago Dei and 67
integrity of human
nature and 303
of Jesus Christ............55, 61-62
law-gospel distinction and ...283
nature and.............................45
overview of..... 49, 299-300, 324
in parenting 283
perfect obedience and 46, 56
production of nature and.......69
proportionality and.......291-306
Reformed doctrine
of............................ 46, 51-82
sin and 48
tension regarding 56-60

theological clarifications
of 306-323
covenant of grace. *See* grace/
covenant of grace
covenant of works
Adam's created nature
and 75, 189
Adam's demand through 286
basis of 266-267
as belonging to creation 244
condescension from 238
covenantal merit and 283
covenant of grace as
compared to 229,
272-273, 284
elements of 235
eschatological life as
reward in 88
fulfillment of moral law in.... 255
as God's accommodation 326
God's goodness in 275, 298
God's nature and 314
God's order through 285-286
God's voluntary
condescension in..... 305, 306
grace in 260-268
human nature and 293
imago Dei (image of God)
and 300
as immutable 66, 67
law as condition of 288
love of God in 234-235,
333-334
merit and 48, 69
meritum ex pacto
and 55-56, 70-71
moral law and 49
natural obligations and 88
nature and 301
obedience to the law
in 281, 294, 301
original righteousness
and 285-291
overview of........ 55-56, 275-276
power to fulfill 288-289

principles of......................... 222
as Protestant version of
donum superaddium 240
redemptive history and 214
rejection of 218-220
as relational 235
reward from 291
sabbath and 187
superadded features of .. 187, 211
terms of 292
covenant theology 37
Crakanthorpe, Richard............. 64
created charity 119-120
creation
covenant and........ 241, 253-260,
281-282
eschatology in 18
as God's temple 247-248
orientation by 19
overview of 235-240
special 19
Creator-creature distinction 178,
200-201, 204-205, 294,
303-304, 312
Cromwell, Oliver 65
Cross, Richard 109

D

Davison, Andrew 261, 316,
317, 319, 320
death, as penalty for
sin 255, 331
DeSilva, David 224
disobedience 248
disproportionality 70, 76-77, 298
divine revelation 29
doctrine, social contexts
and 169n143
doctrine of antithesis 169n143
doctrine of concursus 212
Dominicans 89, 138
dualisms 34
Duncan, Ligon 268-269
Dutch Reformed
theology 169n143

E

Eastern Orthodoxy 176-178
Edict of Nantes.......................60-61
effectual calling 242
eschatology 18, 19, 20, 249, 281
eternal life.............77, 78, 144, 147,
                  161-162, 286-287
ex pacto category 299
extrincisicm 276, 279, 315

F

faith
    of Adam 222
    as condition for grace...........306
    defined 223
    demand for............................284
    justification through 215, 316
    obedience of 221
    Spirit of regeneration and.....226
    understanding of..................221
faithfulness 282
the fall
    Adam prior to 86-87
    damage from 99, 147, 195
    effects of....................... 161, 197
    human faculties following....198
    inclusion of grace prior to....274
    merit as impossible from......149
    need for grace and............... 220
Feingold, Lawrence.......35, 36, 150
Fesko, J. V. 25, 239,
                  270, 293, 304
filial adoption 174
forgiveness 122
Frame, John 225
Franciscan
    Pactum 89, 100, 149, 321
Franciscans 103-118
free will 130
French Revolution 168
Fuller, Daniel......................219-222
fundamentals of life 283

G

garden of Eden 225, 246,
            254-258, 309-310, 318

Garrigou-Lagrange,
    Reginald........160-163, 165, 200
gavel analogy 242-243
general revelation....................255
Gentiles 252, 255
Gentry, Peter 245
Gilson, Étienne.................. 167-168
God
    abilities of............................. 119
    absolute power of .. 121-122, 307
    acceptance of......................... 117
    accommodation of 237
    Adam's communion
        with 98-99, 109, 263,
                  312-313, 323
    adoption by........................... 174
    attributes of......................... 290
    beatific vision and 92-93
    as condescending 37
    covenants with us by.....234-235
    as Creator...................200, 242,
                  247-248, 312
    Creator-creature
        distinction and 178
    as debtor 302
    dependence on 262
    difference from
        humanity and...........200-201
    distance from humanity
        and 236
    election of 100, 133
    faithfulness of 76
    favor of.................................219
    fellowship with.............. 176-177
    as final end............................262
    as first mover.......................212
    five proofs of existence of..... 159
    forgiveness from 122
    freedom of............................312
    general works of....................243
    goodness of ...298, 308-309, 315
    help from 205-206, 211
    humanity's cooperation
        with 07-108
    humanity's owing to 295

image of 20
impartiality of 300
inequality with humanity
     and 174
as infinite 287
justification from 335,
                              336, 337
kindness of 310, 314-315
knowledge of 93-94, 108,
                        159-160, 191
love of 235, 333-334
natural revelation of 290
nature of 314
obedience to 21
ordained power of 57-58, 121,
                        129, 307-308, 310
perfections of 262
power of 119
predestination of 100-101,
                              207, 272, 301
presence of 269
pure nature influence of 125
in Reformed theology 38
relation to 20n7, 200
rest by 247-248
revelation of ... 29, 237, 239, 281
reward promise from 292-293
in Roman theology 38
sanctification from 337
sovereignty 100
special act of 243
as supernatural 276
supernatural order of 40
as ultimate end 96
voluntary condescension
     of 305, 306
will of 119, 167
good works
     of Adam 98, 107, 135
as condignly meritorious 156
eternal life and 77, 78, 147
of justified people 144
as merit 155
reward for 156
for salvation 120, 123

gospel 214-231, 237
See also law-gospel distinction
grace/covenant of grace
     of Adam 86, 89-90
as all-encompassing 330
benefits of 332
as bridge 36
clarification of 34-46
condescension from 238
cooperation and 175
covenant of 73
covenant of works and 32,
                        43-44, 229, 260-268,
                              272-273, 284
created charity and 119-120
defined 166, 268-269
as dependent on
     Christ 174-175
effects of 126-127
as elevating 36, 85, 233
as enabling merit 144
as exceeding 116
faith as condition for 306
following good works 98
in Franciscan Pactum 89
function of 126
general 216
as gift 126
God as dispensing 92, 100
God's obligation regarding 150
God's ordained power
     and 129
God's voluntary
     condescension in 306
gratefulness for 106
human nature and 127
infused 109
as initiating force 224
internal changes from 336
law as preceding 288
love and 122-123
meritorious work and 296
nature as needing 85
as necessity 145, 220,
                              265, 268-270

as opposing principle
to merit...........................151
as opposing sin.......................45
original righteousness
and 111-112
overview of..........................331
as perfecting nature 98, 278
as precondition for merit 86
preparation for 92
as principle of merit 144-145
principles of........................ 222
priority of...........................100
as producing sanctifying
grace 163
redemptive history and 214
Reformed uses of...................32
relationship with merit
and 224
as requirement for
merit 175
in Roman theology 36-37,
84, 179-182
as salvation..........................216
sanctification in 84, 333
for sin...........................47, 100
specific uses of 44
supernatural endowment
of 95
transformative.....................127
twofold perfection of 104
undermining
gratuitousness of..............170
as unfruitful........................106
as unnecessary for
merit 152n63
whole of human life in.........170
Green, Bradley.................. 225-226
Gregory, Brad 203
Gregory of Rimini... 125, 130, 206

H

Hamm, Berndt 58
happiness 96, 97, 140, 185
Hart, David Bentley.................177
Heidelberg Catechism 263-264

Helvetic Formula Consensus......79
Henry of Ghent.........131-134, 146,
151, 181, 194, 201, 215, 263
historical conscientiousness 99
Hodge, Charles................. 286-287
Hoekema, Anthony 251-252
Hoeksema, Herman 218
holiness....................................173
Holy Spirit................162, 186, 265
Horton, Michael......202, 234, 244
Hugh of St. Victor.....................84
humanity
as absolutely 140
adoption of........................... 174
after the fall 198
chief end of 234
cooperation with God
by...............................107-108
Creator-creature
distinction and 178
destiny of 20-21
distance from God and........236
eschatological destiny
of......................................233
eschatology in nature of........ 20
fallen state of.......................109
fellowship function of... 176-177
fundamental element
for existing by..................234
God as final end of 262
God's covenants
with 234-235
God's differences to 200-201
God-shaped hole in............. 331
God's special providence
toward 318
as Godward creatures........... 165
good of................................195
help from God to......... 205-206
as image of God.....................83
inequality with God and...... 174
kingship of........................... 244
as mortal 176
natural impulses of 195-196
natural righteousness of.......250

nature of.............................17-18
obedience of...........................21
obligation of.......................305
as ordained unto
    happiness........................140
as ordered toward the
    supernatural....................277
participation in divinity
    by............................. 177-178
as pleasing to God 329-330
purely natural state of.......... 185
purpose of............................ 17
qualities of 288
relation to God by 20n7, 200
sin's effects on 196
sonship of........................... 244
as subject to God 211-212
supernatural destiny of 41
supernatural gifts of.............109
surpassing good of.................96
as turning to God................213
twofold end of...............103-104
unfallen state of 109

I

imago Dei (image of God)
    in Adam.................... 87, 92-93,
        186, 246-247, 304, 319
    bearing.............................. 20
    capacities in.........................298
    covenantal merit and 67
    covenant of works and 300
    eschatology of
        bearing 241-249
    function and task in 176
    human constitution
        and 190-191
    humanity as 83
    in intellectual nature.............92
    judicial aspects of
        eschatological...........249-253
    justice reciprocity and 290
    knowing God in 191
    law through........................ 288
    likeness and.................. 191-192

natural and supernatural
    ends of...................... 185-186
natural duty from 253-254
natural obligation in 283
natural revelation and 290
obligation in.........................305
original righteousness
    and 94-95
principle of spiritual life
    in 186
purpose of.............................326
relationship with God and... 177
sin as irrational regarding.... 197
as supernatural grace............ 184
truth about God in 159-160
understanding of.................. 145
immaculate conception............. 111,
    113-114
immortality 164
    See also eternal life
imputation............................. 321
infused virtue 108
integrity, as preternatural gift...164
Irish Articles............................ 264
Irons, Lee..................237, 282, 307,
    311-312, 313-314, 315

J

James I.......................................65
Jansenius, Cornelius 147-153,
    181, 269
Jensenius, Cornelius................. 199
Jesus Christ
    covenantal merit of 55, 61-62
    effectual calling and.............242
    as empowerment of
        meriting........................... 167
    as enabling people to merit.. 155
    exaltation of 73-74
    faith and 223
    faithfulness of 328
    as fulfillment........................ 321
    grace as dependent on... 174-175
    grace benefits from...............332
    grace through.......................333

imputed righteousness
   of 224-225
as mediator................... 18, 308
merits of ...70, 78, 324, 335, 337
meritum ex pacto of 55
obedience of 45-46, 56,
   78, 333, 336
parable of the laborers
   of 296-297
presence of 328
principles from 294
redemption in 210
relationship with 155
as representation 315-316
as restorer...............................18
resurrection of.......................18
reward of................................78
as righteousness........... 322, 323
righteousness of....................338
salvation through 114, 175
sanctification and............... 242,
   335-336
sanctification of....................186
John of Damascus 132, 310
Joüon, Paul 245
judge analogy 242-243
Junius, Francis 184-186, 271,
   272-273
justice 173-174, 290
justification
   Augustine on 51-52
   defined 79, 251
   by faith............................ 69, 316
   free will and 130
   function of 335, 336, 337
   legal declaration of..............320
   obtaining..................... 107-108
   Protestant doctrine
     of 321-322
   righteousness and 254
   as salvation benefit...............338
   from sin...............................223
   strength through..................144
   through faith.......................215
   Turretin on.......................77-78

K

Kant, Immanuel 158-159
Kline, Meredith 241, 253,
   313, 314
knowledge of God 93-94, 108,
   159-160, 191
Küng, Hans 31, 217

L

laborers, parable of 296-297
Lamdin, Thomas 245
language, function of 28-29
Laud, William 65
law
   Christ as fulfillment
     of 321
   as coming to kingdom
     of heaven 230
   communication of...............237
   covenant of works and 288
   justification and 251
   obedience to 281, 294
   as preceding grace............... 288
   preserving...................... 214-231
   redemptive historical
     development and 227
   sabbath and......................... 187
   voluntarism and 129
law-gospel distinction 154,
   214-231, 283, 296
Leonine Thomism...... 157-167, 200
Leo XIII (pope) 157
Letham, Robert 228-229
likeness, *imago Dei* (image
   of God) and 191-192
Lombard, Peter.........29, 84, 85-88,
   179, 309-310
love 21, 120,
   122-123, 229
love of God 152n63, 234-235,
   333-334
Lubac, Henri de......... 168, 169-171
Lumen Gentium...................... 174
Luther, Martin...............58-59, 175,
   190, 194

M

Macaskill, Grant...................... 230
Machen, J. Gresham...................25
Magnus, Albert.........................193
marriage....................................318
Mary (mother of Jesus)............. 111,
113-114
McGrath, Alistair....... 58, 129-130
McGuckin, John Anthony........ 177
merit
    absolute.................................. 61
    after the fall...........................68
    blessing from........................ 117
    condign........... 53, 161-162, 163
    condition for 117
    congruent........59, 123, 163-164
    as convention 141
    covenantal..............................45
    defined 46, 53, 163, 282, 292
    divine convention and... 156-157
    divine ordination as
        principle of 161
    eternal life and.....................286
    ex pacto.................................287
    felicity of...........................46-48
    following sin 115
    as God's gift.........................101
    good works as 155
    grace as enabling..................144
    grace as principle of 144-145
    grace as requirement for....... 175
    grace as unnecessary
        for.............................. 152n63
    human action regarding....... 167
    as impossible from the
        fall 149
    of Jesus Christ......... 70, 78, 324,
335, 337
    justice and.................... 173-174
    measure of...........................292
    as opposing principle
        to grace..........................151
    perseverance and.................102
    predestination and 100-101,
133-134

premise of 167, 300
proportionality and....... 166-167
relationship with grace
    and 224
reward and 140
Roman views
    of.............. 179-182, 311-312
sanctifying grace (gratia
    gratum faciens) for............103
soteriological 152n63
supernatural 52-53
understanding.......................23
voluntarist basis for...... 118, 321
works as righteous
    obedience for...................146
meritum ex pacto........ 55-80, 81-82
metaphysics........ 201-202, 203-204
Meyendorff, John..................... 176
Miller, B. V.......................164, 166
modernity...........................157-167
Molina, Luis de 208, 209
moral law............... 118-119
See also law
moral proportion 24
Mosaic covenant.........................63
Moses.................................... 230
Moulin, Pierre du 266, 270
Muller, Richard............. 46, 57-58,
236-237, 299
mystery.................................27-28

N

natural acts.............................. 116
natural ends.............. 139, 185-186
natural law............................... 119
See also law
natural revelation..............290-291
natural righteousness........250, 265
natural theology 199-200
nature
See also pure nature
    clarification of.................34-46
    covenantal merit and 45
    damage to 260
    as defective...................103-104

eschatological destiny
and 42-43, 281
as fallen.................................98
good of................................196
grace as necessary for...........265
grace as perfecting 98, 278
natural end of 138
as needing grace....................85
sin as damaging to...............330
supernature *versus* 44
twofold perfection of 104
upright 95
nature-grace distinction........34-46,
47, 54, 138-157, 270
Neo-Scholasticism 171
neo-Thomism.............. 157-167, 182
Netherlands 168-169
Noahic covenant.............. 289-290
nominalism....60n23, 118-131, 204
Nostra Aetate...................... 174-175
nouvelle théologie..............167-176

O

obedience
of Adam................45, 47, 66-67,
76, 222, 271, 272, 301, 323
in covenant of works............281,
294, 301
demand for...........................284
as expression of love.............. 21
of faith 221
human strength for..............190
of Jesus Christ............45-46, 56,
78, 333, 336
to the law......................281, 294
as meritorious.........................46
obligation of........................305
perfect............................46, 56,
66-67, 211-212
standard of........................... 291
strength for 291
value of.................................24
Oberman, Heiko 57-58, 89, 207
Olevianus, Casper................... 209
ordinatio..............100, 272

original righteousness
as accidental to
nature 94-95
of Adam.............. 116, 125, 192
auxilium and 211-212
as *concreated* gift
(donum concreatum)............83
confessional consensus
of 194
covenant of works
and 285-291
created order and 188
defined 189
eschatological
advancement and......252-253
before the fall........................87
as gift 196
as given constitution 88-89
grace and......................111-112
image of God and........... 94-95
as intrinsic to human
nature 131
as natural 110
overview of...........................48
as part of created
order 252-253
as perfect tranquility
result............................... 110
pure nature disconnection
from..........................139-140
purpose of 192
redux 285-291
Roman views of 179-182
sanctifying grace
and 111, 114-115, 193
as superadded.........84, 154, 157,
162-163, 164
as supernatural.............153-154,
188-189
upright nature and................95
original sin.......... 109, 111-112, 114
See also sin
Owen, John 186-188,
252, 253-254
Ozment, Stephen..........58-59, 123

P

parable of the laborers 296-297
parenting 283
Pareus, David 192-193, 194,
                        209, 210, 272
Paul.............26, 219, 224, 247, 250,
                  252, 254, 255, 295, 338
Pelagianism...................... 122, 130
Pelagius........................... 122, 130
Perkins, William...................56-57,
                        63-64, 229
perseverance............................102
Peter.......................................332
Pictet, Benedict.............78-80, 320
Pius V (pope)..........................145
Pius XII (pope).......................171
Pohle, J. 163
Poirot, Hercule 27
Porro, Pasquale 133
practical reason........................159
preambula fidei.......................159
predestination........... 100, 133-134,
                        207, 272, 301
proportionality
    beatific vision and................150
    defined 36
    of merit and
        supernatural end.......166-167
    in nature-grace distinction.....54
    navigating 291-306
    as obstacle 37
    overview of............... 24-25, 141
    superadded grace and............ 96,
                        187-188
Protestantism............ 153, 154, 199
protology 19
pure nature
    See also nature
    acceptance of.......................124
    of Adam 164, 293
    as basic................................ 115
    Biel on................................124
    covenant and........................293
    defined 195-196
    forgiveness and....................122

Henry the Ghent on 131-132
humanity as in......................185
meritorious acts through......126
natural and supernatural
    order and.........................161
original righteousness
    disconnection from ...139-140
overview of.............................35
rejection of doctrine of... 147-148
righteousness as gift in..........132
sanctifying grace for
    merit in............................153
sin's damage to.....................148
state of 163
supernatural grace to 164-165
pure reason 159

R

Radical Orthodoxy...................203
Rahner, Karl...................... 171-172
Ratzinger, Joseph (Pope
    Benedict XVI).............. 173-174
reason, interpretations of..........159
reciprocity principle...........295-296
redemption 73-74, 331
redemptive order....... 268-276, 279
Reformed theology
    See specific aspects
regeneration 226, 265
Renault, Laurence.................... 118
Renihan, Samuel 239-240
rest.....................................247-248
reward....................... 24, 140, 283,
                        290-291, 295-296
righteousness
    Augustine on.....................51-52
    capabilities in 23
    as gift.............................83, 132
    human nature and 38
    as imputed.....................224-225
    as infused.....................336-337
    of Jesus Christ............. 322, 323
    justification and 254
    natural..................................84
    in Reformed theology 39

sin as damaging 150
    as supernatural gift 109, 164
Roberts, Francis 267
Rollock, Robert 229, 266, 267
Roman theology/Roman
    Catholicism. *See specific aspects*
Rushdoony, R. J. 218
Rutherford, Samuel 271-272

S

sabbath 187, 248, 253-254, 318
Sabellians 33
sacraments 113
salvation
    Christ's merits and 70
    function of 337
    good works for 120, 123
    as grace of God 216
    merit for 264
    need for 216
    sanctification and 338-339
    through Christ 114, 175
    working principles of 119
sanctification 186, 242, 333,
                335-336, 337, 338-339
sanctifying grace (*gratia
    gratum faciens*)
    as acceptable to God 104
    actual grace as producing 163
    for Adam 105, 113, 162
    defined 161, 166
    function of 104, 137, 162
    merit need of 105
    as not needing God 209-210
    original righteousness
        and 111, 114-115, 193
    original sin and 112-113
    overview of 103
    purpose of 213, 214
    resistance to evil and 105
    supernatural grace as
        distinct from 153
    as supernatural supplement .. 116
    for works 125
Sarez, Francisco 98

Schilder, Klass 218, 239
Schleiermacher, Friedrich 221
Scotus, John Duns
    accepatito personarum of 101,
        230, 271, 299, 334-335
    on the fall 198
    on grace 180
    Luther against 190
    on merit 59-60, 68, 147,
                180, 301
    on metaphysics 201-202,
                203-204
    on original
        righteousness 132, 180
    overview of 109-118
    on pure nature 194
secularism 204
The Sentences in Four Books
    (Lombard) 85-88
Shepherd, Norman ... 222-223, 224
sin
    of Adam 166, 265
    consequences of 194-195
    covenant of grace and 45-46
    damage from 145, 195
    death as penalty for 255, 331
    as disordering faculties 99
    effects of 150, 196, 199,
                215, 277, 330
    forgiveness for 122
    grace need for 47, 100,
                268-270
    as irrational in *imago Dei*
        (image of God) 197
    justification from 223
    merit following 115
    meritorious works from 264
    ordered appetites and 111
    original 109, 111-112, 114
    rectitude of 110
    as wrecking pure nature 148
sincerity 175
Smith, George D. 164-166
soteriological merit 152n63
See also merit

soteriology 19
Soto, Domingo de 146-147, 208
Spirit of regeneration 226
Steinmetz, David 57
strength, in justification 144
Suàrez, Francisco 143
Summa Theologica
(Aquinas) 88-103, 107, 143
superadded grace *(donum superadditum)*
acceptance of 124
to Adam 162
Adam as losing 143
beatific vision and 135
Beil on 126-127
as bridge 162
covenant-keeping ability and 188
as distinct from human nature 139
as gift of original righteousness 157
for Godward creatures 165
Henrician exception regarding 131-134
original righteousness as 84, 162-163
as preservation of human nature 166
proportionality and 96
proportionality and 187-188
Roman theology view of 84
supernatural acts, sanctifying grace *(gratia gratum faciens)* and 116
supernatural endowments 186-187
supernatural ends 139, 166-167, 185-186
supernatural gifts.....................184
supernatural grace 153
See also grace
supernatural merit 52-53
See also covenantal merit; merit
supernatural righteousness........285

supernature, nature *versus*.......... 44
supralapsarianism 272
surpassing good, as humanity's highest goal...........................96
Synod of Dort 209

T

temples, significance of.............247
Tertullian................................257
theology................................ 26-33
Thomas Aquinas
auxilio of 195, 205-213, 271
on connatural relation..........213
on Creator-creature distinction 204-205
as distanced from Calvinism 160-161
distortion of teaching of 167-168
on the fall 195
five proofs of existence of God by 159
on God...................... 26, 27-28
on grace.........107, 135, 179, 193
on *imago Dei* (image of God) 190-191, 197
intellectualist premise of 299
on merit 179, 214
on nature............................196
ordinatio of.................. 195, 272
on original righteousness 179
overview of....................88-103
predestinarianism of ... 206, 302
on pure nature 195-196
on righteousness...................301
on sanctifying grace............214
on sin 194-195, 196, 197-198
on supernatural endowment of grace..........................186
support for 190
on surpassing good 263
Ussher on 302
on virtue 196-197
Thomism 157-167

Torrance, J. B. 217, 228
Torrance, T. F. 217, 228
Towers, E. 165-166
Tree of Life 318
tree of the knowledge of
    good and evil 254-258,
        309-310, 318
Trinity....................................... 40
Trueman, Carl 268, 287
truth 159-160
Tuckey, Anthony.............. 278, 279
Tuininga, Matthew.....................63
Turretin, Francis.....74-77, 188-189,
        229, 268, 288, 295,
        296, 298, 315
Twisse, William 230

U

univocity.......................... 200, 204
unworthy-servant
    principle 294-295
Ursinus, Zacharius............252, 267
Ussher, James............................ 52,
        259, 272-273, 274, 283,
        284, 285-286, 301-302, 334

V

VanDrunen, David ... 241, 259, 314
van Mastricht, Petrus 189-190,
        211-212, 289, 291
Vatican II 167-176, 182
virtues.....................86-87, 196-197
voluntarism.......................... 60n23,
        118-119, 129
Vos, Geerhardus................ 18, 192,
        199-200, 218, 241, 243,
        253, 314-315, 334

W

wages 65
Ware, Kallistos................... 176-177
Washburn, Christian 156
Wawrykow, Joseph............100, 116,
        160, 206
Wellum, Stephen............... 243-244

Westminster Confession
    of Faith 37, 207, 226,
        235-236, 288, 292,
        305, 306, 335, 339
Westminster Larger
    Catechism 39-40, 250,
        263, 318, 337
Westminster Shorter
    Catechism ...234, 242, 293, 294
the will 110-111
William of Auxerre.....................84
William of Ockham 118-131,
        152n63, 180, 199,
        202, 203, 307
will of God 167
Witsius, Herman..........74, 78, 266,
        270, 274, 285,
        286, 308-309
Wood, Jacob 314
Wood, John Halsey...................293
works
    as *acceptatio*..........................142
    of Adam 107, 151-152,
        292, 295
    covenant of.....32, 38, 43-44, 47
    God's acceptance of 128,
        142, 156-157
    God's appointment of 129
    God's authority regarding.... 141
    imperfect..........................63-64
    as meritorious.............. 115, 116,
        117, 142
    perfect 64
    as performing which
        is within us......................149
    reward for......................295-296
    as righteous obedience 146
    sanctifying grace and...........125
    supernatural blessings
        from................................100
    to supernatural capacity.......165
Wuellner, Bernard.......................24

Z

Zanchi, Jerome 197, 210-211

Scripture Index

Old Testament

Genesis
1:26-30 244
1:27.............................. 17, 250
2:1-2.......................................247
2:3...248
2:7.................................. 247, 257
2:15-17 ....256, 259
2:16-17 243
2:17 256
3:4-5 259
3:6...257
3:8...257
9:5-7 .... 260, 289

Exodus
20:12-17 257

Leviticus
19:18 257

Deuteronomy
5:16-21 257
6:5...257
26:26 ....274, 284

Joshua
1:5...328

Job
3:12...288

Psalms
8:5-6 246

73:25, 28..................................17
132:13-14 247

Ecclesiastes
3:11 19
7:29.............................279, 291
7:30...94

Isaiah
53:10 78

Jeremiah
31:33 284

Lamentations
5:21...92

Ezekiel
18:14 ....274, 284

New Testament

Matthew
6:13...238
16:18 328
19:23-30 297
20:1-16 296
20:2...296

Luke
1:35...114
3:38...234
17:10 .... 67, 76

John
1:12 17

14:18 328
14:26 328
17:3 325

Acts
4:12 78
17:28 210
20:28 78

Romans
1:17 222
1:18-2:16 290
1:18-3:20 290
1:19-20 290
1:20 .... 42, 256
1:32 ....256, 290
2:5-6 290–291
2:6-11 323
2:7 291
2:10 291
2:11 300
2:13-16 251
2:15 291
3:1 76
3:21 284
3:31 284
4:4-5 295–296
5:18-21 322
8:16-21, 29-30 18
8:18 76
11:6 296
11:34-36 295
11:35-36 295
14:23 51
16:25-26 27

1 Corinthians
15:20-23, 35-49 18
15:35-49 41
15:42-46 .... 247n50
15:42-49 321
15:44 247

2 Corinthians
3:5 92
5:17-18 337

Galatians
3:10, 12 ....274, 284
3:10-12 .... 220, 296
3:12 219
3:13, 14 ....274, 284
5:2-4 224
5:6 226
5:22-23 27

Ephesians
4:24 ....250, 289

Philippians
2:13 212
3:20 332

Colossians
3:10 .... 92, 250, 289

1 Thessalonians
4:3-8 338

2 Thessalonians
1:5-10 269

2 Timothy
2:13 76

Titus
1:1 26

Hebrews
3:18 248
4:9-10 248
9:12 78
11:6 290
13:5 328

1 Peter
1:3-5 332

1 John
4:7 234

Revelation
2:7 332
21 246
22:1-3, 14 332

Christian Focus Publications

Our mission statement –

STAYING FAITHFUL

In dependence upon God we seek to impact the world through literature faithful to His infallible Word, the Bible. Our aim is to ensure that the Lord Jesus Christ is presented as the only hope to obtain forgiveness of sin, live a useful life and look forward to heaven with Him.

Our books are published in four imprints:

CHRISTIAN FOCUS

Popular works including biographies, commentaries, basic doctrine and Christian living.

CHRISTIAN HERITAGE

Books representing some of the best material from the rich heritage of the church.

MENTOR

Books written at a level suitable for Bible College and seminary students, pastors, and other serious readers. The imprint includes commentaries, doctrinal studies, examination of current issues and church history.

CF4•K

Children's books for quality Bible teaching and for all age groups: Sunday school curriculum, puzzle and activity books; personal and family devotional titles, biographies and inspirational stories – because you are never too young to know Jesus!

Christian Focus Publications Ltd,
Geanies House, Fearn, Ross-shire,
IV20 1TW, Scotland, United Kingdom.
www.christianfocus.com